What's Wrong with Democracy?

FROM ATHENIAN PRACTICE
TO AMERICAN WORSHIP

Loren J. Samons II

UNIVERSITY OF CALIFORNIA PRESS

BERKELEY   LOS ANGELES   LONDON

University of California Press
Berkeley and Los Angeles, California

University of California Press, Ltd.
London, England

© 2004 by the Regents of the University of California

Library of Congress Cataloging-in-Publication Data

Samons, Loren J.
    What's wrong with democracy? : from Athenian prac-
tice to American worship / Loren J. Samons II.
        p.   cm.
    Includes bibliographical references and index.
    ISBN 0-520-23660-2 (cloth : alk. paper).
        1. Democracy—History.   2. Direct democracy—
Greece—Athens.   3. Republicanism—United States—
History.   4. Representative government and representa-
tion—United States.   5. Political culture—United
States—History.   6. United States—Civilization—Greek
influences.   I. Title.
JC421.S32 2004 2007
    321.8—dc22   2004008500

Manufactured in the United States of America
13 12 11 10 09 08 07 06 05 04
10 9 8 7 6 5 4 3 2 1

The paper used in this publication is both acid-free and
totally chlorine-free (TCF). It meets the minimum
requirements of ANSI/NISO Z39.48–1992 (R 1997)
(Permanence of Paper).

To Jim and Brendan

*For it is not at all pleasant to rail at incurable practices and
errors that are far developed, though sometimes it is necessary.*

THE ATHENIAN
Plato, Laws 660c–d (trans. Thomas L. Pangle)

BOSWELL: *So, Sir, you laugh at schemes of political
improvement?*
JOHNSON: *Why, Sir, most schemes of political improvement
are very laughable things.*

S. JOHNSON
Boswell's Life of Johnson

. . . *democracy means simply the bludgeoning of the people by
the people for the people.*

O. WILDE
Soul of Man under Socialism

. . . *a state in which the mass of citizens is free to do whatever
it pleases or takes into its head is not a democracy [but rather
mob-rule]. But where it is both traditional and customary to
reverence the gods, to care for our parents, to respect our elders,
to obey the laws, and in such a community to ensure that the
will of the majority prevails——this situation it is proper to
describe as a democracy.*

POLYBIUS 6.4
(trans. Ian Scott-Kilvert)

SOCRATES: *What device could we find to make our rulers,
or at any rate the rest of the city, believe us if we told them a
noble lie, one of those necessary untruths of which we have
spoken? . . . Can you suggest any device which will make our
citizens believe this story?*
GLAUCON: *I cannot see any way to make them believe it
themselves, but the sons and later generations might, both
theirs and those of other men.*

PLATO
Republic 414b–c, 415c–d (trans. G. M. A. Grube, adapted)

MENE, MENE, TEKEL, UPHARSIN.   DANIEL 5:25

CONTENTS

LIST OF MAPS AND ILLUSTRATIONS   *xi*

PREFACE   *xiii*

ABBREVIATIONS   *xix*

Introduction   *1*

1 Athenian Society and Government   *19*
Athens and Polis Government   20
Athens after Solon's Reforms   26
Athenian History in the Classical Period   31

2 Democracy and Demagogues:
Election, Voting, and Qualifications for Citizenship   *41*
Qualifications for Citizenship   45
Did the Demos Rule Well?   49
Leaders versus Demagogues: The Case of Pericles   54
Modern Confusion about Election   68

3 Public Finance:
Democracy and the People's Purse   *72*
The Spoils of Battle and the Fruits of the Earth (483/2–431)   73
War, Taxes, Debt, and Revolution (431–399)   85
Digression: Democracy and the Athenian Self-Image   92
Epilogue: Paying the Public or Funding the Military? (399–322)   95

4 Foreign Policy I: Democracy Imperial   *100*
Early Athenian Ambitions in the Aegean (ca. 561–490)   101
The Persian Wars and the Creation of the Athenian Empire (ca. 490–463)   105
Reversed Alliances and Continuing Expansion (ca. 462/1–430s)   111

5   Foreign Policy II: The Peloponnesian War   *117*

The Effects of the Peloponnesian War   *117*

Digression: Historical Causation and the Aesthetics of History   *119*

Prelude to War   *124*

Pericles and the Causes of the Peloponnesian War   *127*

The Peloponnesian War (431–404)   *131*

6   National Defense: Democracy Defeated   *143*

A Fourth-Century Empire?   *143*

The Rise of Macedon and the End of Athenian Democracy   *147*

7   Democracy and Religion   *163*

Digression: Man's Desire for Society   *166*

Athens and the Integral Society   *168*

Modern America and the Religion of Democracy   *175*

Freedom, Choice, and Diversity   *181*

Conclusion: Socrates, Pericles, and the Citizen   *187*

Socrates and Pericles as Citizens and Leaders   *198*

NOTES   *203*

SELECT BIBLIOGRAPHY   *279*

INDEX   *297*

MAPS AND ILLUSTRATIONS

MAPS

1. Ancient Hellas   *21*

2. Peisistratid-Cimonid foreign policy interests   *103*

3. The Peloponnesian War   *126*

FIGURES

1. Athenian coin ("owl"), ca. 450–440 B.C.   *74*

2. Reconstructed Athenian trireme   *76*

3. First tribute stele   *81*

TABLE

1. Athenian and Spartan military action in the
mid fifth century   *136*

A couple of years ago my wife Jamie and I attended a dinner party in Boston
hosted by a close friend. At the party was an eminent sociologist, and as the
evening wore on, the conversation turned to sociological methods and statistical sampling as a way of gauging public attitudes. In response to the sociologist's description of the techniques used to ensure representative sam-
ples, I laid out several strange facts from my own background: born a
Southerner but having lived in the Southwest, the Northwest, and the
Northeast; reared among Baptists as a Presbyterian and trained first at a very
conservative Baptist college and then at a very liberal Ivy League university,
surrounded by a group of friends that were primarily Catholic, but with a significant admixture of agnostics and atheists; married to a Canadian-born,
Northeastern/Catholic-reared and Texas-schooled Episcopalian; and ultimately having developed an extremely odd set of beliefs that seem (even to
me) insusceptible of easy categorization. How, I wondered, could statistical
sampling compensate for the complexities and contradictions within individual members of a sampled population?

   I fully expected the sociologist to tell me that individuals' views and particular influences were not the issue; that, in fact, while such matters were interesting, and perhaps even important, they presented a subject outside the
field of the social sciences proper. But I was mistaken. "Given a large enough
sample," the sociologist said, "all the influences you mention could be reflected in the survey results." At that I balked: I did not see how even a hundred thousand interviews could result in anything but the reduction of idiosyncratic complexities to simplified collective categories that mask overlaps
and overemphasize distinctions between putatively identified "groups" holding particular views. At this point, my wife deftly interrupted what was in
danger of becoming a speech: "Well," she said, "you are just a statistical out-

lier," and the sociologist seemed to agree (although he had known me for only about three hours).

I relate this anecdote to emphasize my doubts about techniques designed to gauge what a complex entity like "the American (or Athenian) people" believe(d) at some given moment. I also seek indulgence for drawing conclusions about contemporary America based largely on my own observations. Where American democracy is concerned, what follows are the idiosyncratic views of an ancient historian (not a modern sociologist) and an admitted "statistical outlier" (although one who has lived in several parts of the United States and taught students from all over the country). I recognize that those who think differently might use statistics to show that my conclusions about America are unfounded, and to them I can only confess that I find myself less swayed by statistics than by my own experiences. I cite no statistical data to support my contention that, thanks to mass media (especially television and the Internet), an atomized and hypermobile population, and a federal government that reaches into so many corners of life, the "democratic" culture of the big American city—a culture that idealizes freedom, choice, and diversity—is fast engulfing the older community-oriented culture of the country town and urban neighborhood. I argue that this process exposes America to both the dangers of democratic practices (which the Athenians also faced) and the perils of democratic faith (which the Athenians largely avoided).

Reactions from individuals kind enough to have read all or part of it encourage me to state, at the outset, what this book is not. It is not a call for any particular political action in contemporary America: indeed, it is one of the book's theses that things generally associated with democratic political action—campaigning for particular candidates, organizing political parties, or working for amendments to the Constitution—are unlikely to bring about significant positive change in American society or government. If anything, I attempt to persuade the reader that looking to political action to make improvements in American society reflects a misplaced faith in the political process, a faith sometimes spawned by the modern idealization of democracy. Seeking to improve society through politics reinforces the view that the solutions to human problems are usually political and thus fosters a belief that politics should play a central role in our lives. It is this kind of thinking that I seek to address. So if this work is to be associated with a call for any particular action, that action must begin with changing individuals' minds.

Often after criticizing ancient or modern democracy I am asked to produce a workable alternative. To this reasonable demand I have a two-part response. First, I believe that the best qualities traditionally associated with modern democratic government stem from citizenship and the rule of law, both of which may be separated from democracy per se. A regime could require duties from and grant privileges to its citizens and rely on the rule of law without practicing "democracy" as it is usually conceived of today (government by officials chosen through relatively frequent elections by adults who need meet only very low qualifications for citizenship), or as it was usually conceived of in antiquity (government under direct popular control through an assembly of citizens meeting very low or no property qualifications, possessing a popular judicial system, and employing state payments for public service).

Second, I argue that the question of a practical alternative to the political form of democracy currently practiced in America is largely irrelevant, since the harmful "values" that democratic thinking has generated no longer rely directly on our political system for support. I suggest that democratic values have become the fundamental social and moral principles of American society and that they now threaten the constitutional and representative form of American government more than they reflect it. In short, America's problems today stem more from American values than from America's Constitution. Changing the form of American government, therefore, is not strictly desirable nor would it be likely to solve very many of the problems this volume describes.

Rather than laying out a theoretically superior regime for the United States, I would ask readers to examine their own beliefs about the value of things like the vote and government through elected officials who profess to be seeking "what the American people want." Readers, I presume, begin with a bias in favor of the vote and of politicians that claim to do (or actually do) what the majority of their constituents desire: I seek to reverse that bias. I hope to create some discomfort with the idea of government by officials chosen by popular vote and to instill a profound distrust of politicians who claim to know, or actually seek to implement, the will of "the American people." I also hope to identify dangers faced by a society or system that encourages thinking of the popular will as a moral good. To achieve these goals, I examine certain events in the history of ancient Athens, the society that created a government called *demokratia*.

Although some historians and classicists have now begun to hold up Athens as a model for contemporary democratic theory or practice, classical scholars in the past century have written few books that attempt to grasp the ancient world with one hand while pointing directly to the contemporary scene with the other. Important, but nevertheless very different, antecedents for this book would include Victor Hanson's *The Other Greeks,* Paul Rahe's

Republics Ancient and Modern, and, especially, M. I. Finley's classic *Democracy Ancient and Modern.* These works share a more or less explicit belief in the continuing relevance of ancient thought and experience for the modern world. More such works are needed: in particular, I believe we need works that look specifically at the actual events that make up Athenian (and other) history and that then attempt to relate these events to our own world. In short, we need more of what I call "practical history"—history that examines practices and events (as well as institutions and ideology) in a way intended to have practical effects in our own world.

Of course, one hopes that there will always be an exalted place in the academy for pure scholarship, such as technical works that establish the most probable readings of ancient texts or the likely dates of particular events, or that attempt to describe institutions such as the Athenian assembly or council. But surely we also need professional scholars to write books that attempt to present history as both the aesthetic and utilitarian genre the ancient Greeks created—that is, works that seek to provide material that is useful in the world today in a way that also satisfies man's desire for beauty. (Too often we humanities professors state that study of classic texts and ancient history is "useful" or that it can "help" modern readers confront moral and social problems without discussing precisely how these benefits are to be realized.)

Although mindful of the important differences between ancient and modern politics, I have occasionally employed terms like *democrat, conservative,* or *radical democracy* in my discussions of Athens. These are meant to serve as a kind of shorthand and should not be taken to imply direct analogies with modern political positions or the existence of anything like today's political parties (with members and platforms) in classical Athens. By *democrat* I mean to connote those who generally supported the liberalization of Athenian government through such measures as expanded public payments to the citizenry and the restriction on the Areopagus Council's powers, and who (in the fifth century) often favored an aggressive stance toward Sparta or its allies (e.g., Ephialtes, Pericles, Cleon). By *conservative* I mean to connote those individuals who resisted such liberalization, and who (in the fifth century) usually preferred peace with Sparta to a policy that might antagonize it (e.g., Cimon, Nicias). I do not mean to imply that there was not significant common ground, cooperation, and overlap between these groups—both, for example, apparently tended to approve of Athens's fifth-century empire, if they sometimes differed on how precisely it should be managed. *Radical democracy* is a term sometimes applied by modern historians to Athenian government after Ephialtes' reforms in 462/1; but it should be admitted that

Athens's government was hardly radical by modern standards, even if the poorer Athenian citizens enjoyed a level of political power probably unprecedented in the ancient world.

Many people have assisted me in the completion of this book, but all of them, I am sure, would wish to be distanced from much or most of what follows. Thus I would ask the reader not to lay any blame for the views expressed here at the feet of those to whom I offer my sincere gratitude for reading, criticizing, and discussing parts of this volume: Lucia Athanassaki, Peter Dreyer, Steven Esposito, Cindy Fulton, Victor Hanson, Jeffrey Henderson, Brian Jorgensen, Donald Kagan, Anna Kim, Mary Lamprech, Amanda Lynch, Kurt Raaflaub, Peter Rhodes, David Roochnik, Dan Samons, James Sickinger, Walter Stevenson, and Kate Toll. I must especially thank Amanda Lynch for her invaluable assistance in research and in preparing the manuscript for the press.

Two people in particular have deeply affected my thoughts on the subjects of democracy, American society, and Athenian history. The first taught me some years ago to examine history, culture, and ideas in novel ways, always demanding more from me than the ready-to-hand slogans and preconceived notions of the newspaper and the textbook. James Kennelly's influence on the way I approach any intellectual problem has been profound, and his ruthless critique provoked—when it did not inspire—many of the thoughts that ultimately found their way into this book.

The second individual has consistently tested my ideas against his own deep understanding of history and human nature. He has helped me develop an approach to history that attempts to see men and women and the societies they create as the complex, irrational, wonderful, and terrible creatures they really are. Brendan McConville is a scholar and a historian in the truest and best senses of those words, and he has lived this book with me as it took form in my mind and on the page.

Finally, I would thank my wife, Jamie, who has read, listened, criticized, and argued, and who has never stopped teaching me about things far more important than democracy.

ABBREVIATIONS

Ancient authors and their works are abbreviated after the fashion of the *Oxford Classical Dictionary*, 3d ed., S. Hornblower, A. Spawforth, eds. (Oxford: Oxford University Press, 1996), sometimes expanded or translated for clarity. Some key acronyms and abbreviations are listed below.

ATL B. D. Meritt, H. T. Wade–Gery, and M. F. McGregor, *The Athenian Tribute Lists,* 4 vols. (Cambridge, Mass. and Princeton, N.J.: American School of Classical Studies at Athens, 1939–53).

CAH III.3² *The Cambridge Ancient History,* 2d ed., vol. 3, pt. 3, *The Expansion of the Greek World, Eighth to Sixth Centuries* B.C., John Boardman and N. G. L. Hammond, eds. (Cambridge: Cambridge University Press, 1982).

CAH V² *The Cambridge Ancient History,* 2d ed., vol. 5, *The Fifth Century* B.C., D. M. Lewis, J. Boardman, J. K. Davies, and M. Ostwald, eds. (Cambridge: Cambridge University Press, 1992).

CAH VI² *The Cambridge Ancient History,* 2d ed., vol. 6, *The Fourth Century* B.C., D. M. Lewis, J. Boardman, S. Hornblower, and M. Ostwald, eds. (Cambridge: Cambridge University Press, 1994).

FGrHist F. Jacoby, et al., *Die Fragmente der griechischen Historiker* (Berlin and Leiden: Brill, 1923–).

Fornara C. W. Fornara, ed. and trans., *Archaic Times to the End of the Peloponnesian War,* Translated Documents of Greece and Rome, vol. 1, 2d ed. (Cambridge: Cambridge University Press, 1983). References are to item numbers.

Harding Phillip Harding, ed. and trans., *From the End of the Peloponnesian War to the Battle of Ipsus,* Translated Documents of Greece and Rome, vol. 2 (Cambridge: Cambridge University Press, 1985). References are to item numbers.

IG i³   *Inscriptiones Graecae,* 3d ed., vol. 1, fasc. 1, D. Lewis, ed. (Berlin: De Gruyter, 1981).

ML   Russell Meiggs and David Lewis, eds., *A Selection of Greek Historical Inscriptions to the End of the Fifth Century* B.C. (Oxford: Oxford University Press, 1969; rev. ed., 1988).

schol.   *scholia:* marginal notes, commentary, or explanations added to the manuscripts of ancient texts in antiquity and the middle ages.

SEG   *Supplementum Epigraphicum Graecum,* 1923–.

Tod   M. N. Tod, ed., *Greek Historical Inscriptions,* 2 vols. in 1 (reprint, Chicago: Ayer, 1985).

Introduction

IT IS THE PURPOSE OF THIS BOOK to present and foster criticism of modern democracy. I wish to emphasize that I mean criticism of, and not simply "debate about" or a "discourse concerning" democracy. This criticism will be aimed at the philosophical foundations of democracy, the popular conception of democracy, the practice of representative government through democratic elections, and the social and intellectual environment generated by democratic thought and practice in contemporary America.

Of course, every student of political science knows that the American system of government codified in the United States Constitution is not actually a "democracy" as that term was defined in the eighteenth century. In fact, most of the American Founders considered "pure" democracy like that practiced in ancient Athens—where the people ruled themselves directly through votes in a popular assembly—to be a particularly unstable and dangerous form of government. Commenting on the dangers of large assemblies, James Madison famously opined that "Had every Athenian citizen been a Socrates, every Athenian assembly would still have been a mob," and other Founders expressed similarly dubious views of the Athenian regime.[1] To the extent that they drew on classical governments for inspiration or illustration, the Founders much preferred republican Rome (or even timocratic Sparta) to Athenian democracy.[2] They used the terms *republic* and *democratic republic,* or sometimes *representative democracy,* to describe early American state governments and the new national system.[3]

The Constitution and the most influential strain of early American political thought reflected a profound distrust of submitting the state's control directly to the popular will. Nevertheless, despite this aversion to democracy and the absence of a popular assembly dictating policy by majority vote in the

United States, American government could be said to embody the principle of "popular sovereignty," under which the government exercised only those powers temporarily ceded to it by the sovereign people.[4] Over the course of the nineteenth century, Americans themselves and those who examined their regime increasingly applied the words *democracy* and *democratic* to America's government and society.[5] This development paralleled the rising popularity of ancient Athens and Hellenism in Europe, illustrated in England by George Grote's *History of Greece,* which praised Athenian democracy.[6] By the twentieth century, the term *democracy* had largely ceased to carry the stigma of mob rule that many had attached to it in early America.

Combined with an egalitarian and increasingly rights-oriented American society, all these factors ultimately brought about the complete victory of the adjective *democratic* and the noun *democracy* in popular descriptions of the United States' form of government. In essence, the term *democracy* was gradually redefined: having lost its association with direct popular rule, *democracy* became capable of describing the American form of government, in which a people express their sovereign power through elected representatives, under a Constitution that ensures individual rights.

Few Americans today understand the background and the changed meaning of the term *democracy,* but most nonetheless conceive of their government as a democracy and see themselves as the democratic people par excellence. Perhaps it is not surprising, therefore, that the word *democracy* has come to stand for whatever is good in government.[7] Our leaders praise regimes or statesmen America supports as "democratic" and label governments or leaders they wish to criticize as "undemocratic." Meanwhile, American politicians encourage the idea that the United States is something like an ancient democracy by frequently claiming to align themselves with what they maintain "the American people" want or believe at a given moment. By praising public opinion in this way and by basing actual policy decisions on polling data or focus groups, our leaders obscure the fact that American government was designed as a representative republic, in part, *in order to shield elected leaders from the sometimes volatile popular will.* Our politicians and the media therefore encourage us to think of our government as the very thing many Founders feared. Madison, for example, praised the difference between real democracy and American government, writing that the "true distinction between [the ancient democracies and republics] and the American governments lies *in the total exclusion of the people in their collective capacity,* from any share in the *latter,*" a distinction which "must be admitted to leave a most advantageous superiority in favor of the United States."[8]

Events of November and December 2000 underscored the very real gulf between America's democratic ideology and its representative republican government: many citizens awoke on the morning of November 8 to the rude fact that they did not actually live in a democracy and that the popular vote did not directly determine who would serve as their president. Far from using this as an opportunity to instruct their constituents about the reasons behind the distance between the people's voice and political action in American government, many politicians continued to speak of heeding the "popular will," as if it actually were a sovereign force under the Constitution.

Modern Americans' belief that our regime is a "democracy" (loosely defined as something like government through officials elected by the whole citizenry and bound to honor the popular will while protecting the people's rights) has encouraged the view that democracy is the only legitimate form of government, an opinion now shared by much of the Western world.[9] That this phenomenon is odd was noticed over thirty years ago by the ancient historian M. I. Finley in his classic treatise *Democracy Ancient and Modern.*

> From one point of view, this consensus [about the preferability of democracy] amounts to the debasement of the concept to the point of analytical uselessness, as we have seen. However, it would be a mistake to leave the matter at that. If such bitter opponents as the academic advocates of the elitist theory [i.e., that a workable democracy is made possible by minimal participation of the people and control by "elites"] and the student advocates of the demonstration and the continuous mass meeting both claim to be defending real or genuine democracy, we are witnessing a new phenomenon in human history, the novelty and significance of which deserve underscoring. We must consider not only why the classical theory of democracy appears to be in contradiction with the observed practice, but also why the many different responses to this observation, though mutually incompatible, all share the belief that democracy is the best form of political organization.
>
> The historical aspect of this situation is receiving less attention than it merits. It is not self-evident, I submit, that there should now be such near unanimity about the virtue of democracy when during most of history the reverse has been the case.[10]

Finley noted perceptively that the West had come to agree about the political and moral superiority of democracy at precisely the moment that the word had lost much of its original meaning. Modern democracy, Finley lamented, received support from political theorists in part through an "elitist theory" that touted the control of a largely (and in their view thankfully) apathetic populace by a small group of elites. Some theorists, Finley noted, even treated modern democracy as an end in itself, and thereby threatened to sever the connection between democratic government and *moral goals,* which lay beyond the system of government and which democracy (it could be argued) should foster. On the other hand, Finley argued that *real* democracy—with a high level of popular involvement and similar to that practiced in Athens in spirit, if not in structure—was not only defensible but preferable to the form championed by many contemporary political theorists.[11]

But even Finley might have been surprised that in the past decade some classical scholars and ancient historians have begun to turn to Athens and Athenian *demokratia* as a possible source for the study and practice of modern democracy. Josiah Ober and Charles Hedrick, for example, offer us "the historical Greek experience of democracy as a resource for building normative political theory."[12] In part responding to the 2,500-year anniversary of the Athenian reforms that resulted in *demokratia* and reacting to what they describe as the usurpation of the classical legacy by "conservatives," some scholars have suggested (among other things) that the Athenians' democratic form of government and their supposed endorsement of the ideals of "liberty and equality"—ideals often associated with modern democracy—make Athens a possible laboratory or even model for modern democratic theory or practice.[13]

Although often differing in approach and agenda, many recent works (implicitly or explicitly) share the view that whatever was "right" with ancient *demokratia* stems from its putative endorsement of liberty and equality or other ideals that the present generation holds dear. Current authorities also seem to agree with the popular opinion that, if democracy is not the ultimate form of government, it is at least the best form devised by and practicable for human beings.[14] Moreover, contemporary detractors of ancient *demokratia* often base their criticisms on the failures of the Athenian system to live up to the modern ideals of democracy. Thus these diverse voices—those who look to Athens for positive examples of "liberty and equality" and those who see Athenian government or society as the betrayal of these same modern values—seem to agree that, to the extent that Athens *failed,* it was because the Athenians *were not democratic enough.*[15] The (often unspoken) corollary to this conclusion is that America must learn how to be more democratic.[16]

Is this not a bizarre tale? Athenian democracy—the ancient form of a government that the United States does not possess and a form that the creators of the American regime thought problematic (at best)—has now been presented to contemporary Americans as a resource for improving, or at least an ideological sister of, modern representative constitutional government.[17] This situation surely reflects the overwhelmingly positive image democracy now has in the popular mind. Once *democracy* became a word of approbation rather than condemnation, the rehabilitation of Athenian *demokratia* as a political forebear of modern democracy followed naturally. To modern Americans, democracy equals "good government," and since Athens possessed a democracy (of whatever type), it must have enjoyed not only good government, but the best government available in antiquity. Moreover, in circular fashion, by maintaining that Athenian government and ideology were democratic and thus superior in antiquity, moderns are able to confirm the idea that democratic thought and practice are superior today.

Once we have reached the point where we not only call our government by a misleading name, but also look to the ancient creator of that name in order to justify or to better understand our misnamed government, the situation has become perverse. But it is also possible that the current situation presents dangers more threatening than merely the semantic cloud surrounding the word *democracy.* For although Americans now suffer from a kind of national delusion, in which we live in a constitutional representative republic but believe we live in a democracy, we also have come to act, and to expect our political leaders and system to act, as if our government *is* a democracy (as traditionally defined) and as if the popular will represents a moral "good" in society. Like any patient suffering from a psychosis, American society perhaps needs to be put on the analyst's couch and forced to confront the realities of its own nature and democracy's sordid past.

To help modern Americans break the grip of democratic thought, I intend to analyze the history of Athens during the period of its democratic government in the fifth and fourth centuries B.C. In so doing, I admittedly am responding and thus adding to the recent body of classical scholarship that looks to ancient Athens as a possible object lesson for modern government, society, and political thought.[18] However, many of these works present an arguably distorted picture of Athenian democracy and society, to a great degree because they look at Athens through the lens of the professed modern democratic values such as "freedom and equality."[19] By treating our modern values as preeminent, these works too often produce anachronistic pictures of Athens—pictures seemingly designed to reflect and reaffirm our own political and social values.

Of course, many Athenians, like most Greeks, did admire liberty *(eleutheria)* and equality *(isonomia),* but they did not conceive of them in the same way moderns do, and neither were these ideals the fundamental or distinctive features of Athens or even of Athenian democracy. So far as we can determine, *eleutheria* and *isonomia* were more or less universal Greek values, not special Athenian or democratic ideals. They apparently emerged with the independent, property-owning yeoman farmer and the polis ("city-state") form of regime that dominated Hellas after about 800 B.C.[20] *Demokratia* was a subspecies of the form of government found in most Greek city-states, a form that everywhere rested (but only in part) on the principles of "liberty" (of the polis from external control and the individual citizen from slavery) and rough "equality" (among the citizens, an already limited group). Spartans or Thebans would probably have attached these values to their own cities and laughed at any special Athenian claim on them. Finding the ideals of liberty and equality expressed in Athenian literature or art tells us little more than that the Athenians were Greeks.

Moreover, if modern scholars seek comparative models or lessons for modern political thought or government in Athens, they should not limit themselves to identifying those areas where the Athenians supposedly spoke or acted like today's democrats or where the Athenians betrayed or fell short of modern democratic ideals. Such a procedure, if somewhat comforting, betrays the intellectual and moral standards set for us by the ancient Greeks. No classical Greek poet, historian, or philosopher known to us began his work with the premise that democracy or even "liberty and equality" were the most important elements in human government or society.[21] Most, in fact, criticized democratic government or the principles behind it.

The modern desire to look to Athens for lessons or encouragement for modern thought, government, or society must confront this strange paradox: the people that gave rise to and practiced ancient democracy left us almost nothing but criticism of this form of regime (on a philosophical or theoretical level). And what is more, the actual history of Athens in the period of its democratic government is marked by numerous failures, mistakes, and misdeeds—most infamously, the execution of Socrates—that would seem to discredit the ubiquitous modern idea that democracy leads to good government. Anyone turning to Athens for political lessons must confront the facts that democratic Athens dominated and made war on the states most like itself, suffered two internal revolutions, exiled or executed many of its own leaders, squandered vast public resources, and preserved its autonomy for less than two centuries. Athenian democracy should not be separated from the larger picture presented by Athenian society and history.

Understandably, Athens's remarkable cultural and literary achievements have often overshadowed its problematic domestic politics and foreign policy. Like earlier generations, we admire the Athenians for producing writers and thinkers such as Sophocles, Thucydides, and Plato and aesthetic masterpieces such as the Parthenon and Erechtheion. One could argue compellingly that the classical Athenians of the fifth and fourth centuries B.C. produced as great a collection of literary and cultural masterpieces as any modern nation during an equivalent timespan. Moreover, they did so with a population of only 30,000 or so citizens, occupying an area roughly the size of Rhode Island. The Athenians need not have possessed a particularly praiseworthy form of government in order to evoke our admiration, and neither do they need to be reinterpreted as the purveyors of modern democracy's structural or ideological underpinnings to ensure their place in history. Indeed, neither they nor we need be self-consciously democratic in order to profit from the study of the classical Athenians.

HISTORY VERSUS THE "HISTORY OF IDEOLOGIES"

The current search for modern ideals and other putatively relevant forms of thought in ancient Athens has encouraged an approach sometimes called the "history of ideologies."[22] This history of ideologies seeks, in the words of Josiah Ober, to replace "an analysis of institutions and prosopography" with an "ideological [approach demanding] close study of political language, in order to show what it was that constituted the will of the demos ["the people"], and in order to trace how the popular will was translated into individual and collective action within the evolving framework of institutional political structure."[23] The Athenian regime, Ober argues, depended on the "ideological hegemony of the masses": political leaders were forced to speak and act in ways acceptable to the demos at large, which thereby controlled Athenian government.[24]

The suggestion that political leaders need to adapt their language to the views of the electorate may readily be conceded. But the special explanatory power of this idea for the study of Athenian history deserves to be questioned: for, just as in the case of *eleutheria* and *isonomia*, Athens cannot be singled out as the source of the idea of popular sovereignty, a concept present in Sparta long before the creation of Athenian *demokratia*.[25] Moreover, Greek statesmen living in city-states all over Hellas—like many statesmen throughout history, including wise monarchs with no conception of popular government—faced the need to tailor their rhetoric to public opinion.

Those employing the history of ideologies must also grapple with the fact that a people's political ideology may be extremely superficial or may be belied by its actions or social relations. The fact that American politicians believe they must say certain types of things in order to be elected—continually aligning themselves with what "the American people" supposedly want or feel, for example—does tell us something about what a large portion of the American populace likes to think about itself: "We are a nation that acts based on majority opinion, and the majority is usually right."[26] But this sentiment also represents merely one of the convenient (and perhaps necessary) lies on which a democratic political regime relies. It masks all kinds of special interest politics, religious views, economic factors, and irrational forces that move politicians and individual members of the electorate. Simply put, this "American ideology" cannot explain any particular event or the particular actions of any individual citizen or politician; it cannot explain the election of Jimmy Carter or Ronald Reagan; it cannot even explain the bombing of Serbia or the first Gulf War.

Obviously historians endeavoring to analyze any period must evaluate the thoughts and beliefs of those they study, first attempting to identify the beliefs or tendencies of individuals, then examining those of particular subgroups of the electorate, and finally attempting to test the way these "ideologies" *may* have affected those who held or manipulated them in specific instances. But this can form only a part of the historian's work, which must also allow for the manifold factors outside of ideology that motivate human beings.[27] Historians should also admit that any ideology held by so large a group as the majority of a nation's (or polis's) electorate may be so shallow as to have little explanatory power for particular events. The current application of the "history of ideologies" as a thing that can stand on its own or serve any great interpretive purpose represents an extremely unsubtle development in historiography. Surely it is time to move beyond any approach to history that promises a better explanation of man's past through narrowing—rather than broadening—the historian's perspective.

Ironically, those who practice the "history of ideologies" and others who have turned to Athens as a possible model for modern democratic thought have largely ignored, rejected, or virtually explained away the Athenians' own criticisms of their regime.[28] Modern scholars often discount the ancient critique of democracy by noting the aristocratic bias of the ancient authorities.[29] Yet some students of antiquity have recently begun to argue either that the ancient critics have been misunderstood or that seeming anti-democrats such as Plato, Thucydides, and Aristophanes were in fact closet (or unwitting) democrats.[30] There are great ironies inherent in these approaches. For is it not strange that while most scholars embrace Athens's art, literature, and form of government, they often dismiss or attempt to palliate the direct and pointed criticism leveled by Athenians at their own regime? The Athenians, it would seem, were brilliant artists, poets, and statesmen, but very poor political analysts.

PRACTICAL HISTORY

Another very influential school of political and philosophical analysis has rejected the modern tendency to treat Plato or Xenophon as either democratic sympathizers or politically hopeless aristocrats. Leo Strauss and his students and followers have held up these ancient authorities as intellectual giants capable of speaking to us across the centuries with real relevance and power. Rightly understood, they argue, the ancients speak eloquently to those addressing the problems of modern government and society.[31]

Of course, one may disagree with particular "Straussian" interpretations of individual passages or authors while still appreciating the attempt to take the ancients seriously. However, those who see Straussians as a politically motivated camp sometimes ignore their arguments or dismiss them on grounds of the Straussians' own supposed biases and elitism or the antiquated worldview that (arguably) dominated ancient Greeks like Plato, Xenophon, and Thucydides. Such aristocratic, European, male, patriarchal, religious individuals from the pre-postmodern world, some of the Straussians' critics seem to maintain, cannot speak to our generation with anything but hollow and bigoted voices. Implicitly, the argument condemns as reactionaries or worse those who do take ancient political thought seriously.[32]

Obviously, I do not endorse postmodern criticism's implication that the ancient thinkers cannot speak with relevance to us today (unless we reinterpret them as democrats or as "contestatory" or "discursive" elements), but neither do I accept the supposed Straussian tenet that Plato is not, to a significant degree, deeply influenced and even somewhat restricted by his own historical context.[33] Thus I do not intend either to dismiss the Athenians' criticisms of their own regime or to defend the ancient critics of *demokratia*. Rather, I wish to ask *what happened* in Athens that could have led to the views expressed by Plato, Thucydides, and Aristophanes, given these authors' predispositions and historical circumstances.

The approach employed in this volume rests on a belief in the necessity of examining important events and practices in the history of Athens if one wishes to draw conclusions relevant to modern government and society. This requires that we relegate ancient and modern opinions about the Athenian regime and rhetorical stances employed within the regime to secondary status. We can neither simply accept the modern view that democracy is the best form of government nor assume that Plato's critique of democracy and Thucydides' sarcasm about the Athenian people are justified. Rather, we shall analyze events in Athenian history and then attempt to draw historical lessons for ourselves from the Athenians' practical experience of democracy. A direct confrontation with these events will cause us to question the popular view that democratic practices tend to result in good government.

Underlying this approach to Athens is the belief that our society is similar enough to the Athenians' to make the exercise useful, and different enough to make it interesting. Madison himself wrote that he was

> not unaware of the circumstances which distinguish the American from other popular governments, as well ancient as modern; and which render extreme circumspection necessary, in reasoning from one case to the other. But after allowing due weight to this consideration it may still be maintained that there are many points of similitude which render these examples not unworthy of our attention.[34]

While Athenian history calls into question the popular view that democratic practices usually result in good government, Athenian society and government do offer positive lessons and perhaps even models for the modern world. However, these lessons usually do not buttress contemporary democratic ideals. Instead of resulting from democratic government or ideology, the "success" of Athens depended to an important degree on nonpolitical factors. By illustrating a society's need for at least some shared fundamental beliefs and the resulting extrapolitical restraints on action, Athens's history may help teach us how to limit or control the negative aspects of modern democratic theory and practices.

WHO KILLED SOCRATES?

The Athenian people's execution of Socrates in 399 serves as a useful touchstone, not so much because it was typical of Athenian democracy as because modern discussions of Athenian democracy so often ignore Socrates' execution or treat the event almost as if the philosopher took his own life. If a democratic ancient regime was capable of trying, convicting, and executing one of the most influential and brilliant thinkers in all of Western history (not to mention carrying out other equally appalling actions), surely we should confront the factors that led to this deed. Instead, readers of works on Athenian democracy are far more likely to encounter hymns to Athenian "liberty and equality" based on Pericles' famous Funeral Oration than frank analysis of Socrates' execution and other disturbing aspects of Athenian history.[35]

Ironically, even M. I. Finley, who called for the adoption of moral goals in politics, showed a reluctance to criticize certain Athenian policies based on moral factors:

> The Athenians made mistakes. Which governmental system has not? The familiar game of condemning Athens for not having lived up to some ideal of perfection is a stultifying approach. *They made no fatal mistakes, and that is good enough.* The failure of the Sicilian expedition in 415–13 B.C. was a technical command failure in the field, not the consequence of either ignorance or inadequate planning at home.[36]

The standard of judgment Finley adopts here (no "fatal mistakes" as "good enough") is surely too low. It is also historically inaccurate on its own terms: Athens survived the Peloponnesian War only because the victorious Spartans decided not to listen to the recommendation of their allies, who wished by destroying Athens's citizen population to inflict on the Athenians the same punishment that Athens had meted out to others. The Athenians' refusal to make peace earlier in the war (when offered favorable terms by Sparta) thus qualifies as a "fatal mistake," as do the series of mistakes made before and after Athens's defeat by the Macedonians at Chaeronea in 338 (see chapters 5 and 6 below). Moreover, the Athenians' decision in 415 to invade Sicily and attack Syracuse, as opposed to simply helping their Sicilian ally Egesta, was both demonstrably unwise and without moral justification, and it deserves criticism on both grounds.

To put the matter more bluntly, I maintain that the vision of Athens as the admirably democratic "school of Hellas" described in Pericles' famous speech commemorating the Athenian war dead in 431/0 (Thuc. 2.35–46) has now almost completely eclipsed the very different picture painted *by the actual events of Athenian history.* Pericles' patriotic and idealistic speech (recorded, to the extent not invented, by Thucydides) is treated almost as an accurate, historical account of Athenian society and virtues, while the fact of Socrates' trial and execution has become a virtual myth.[37] Plato, many moderns almost seem to believe, invented the trial and death of Socrates, just as he invented the myth of Er in the *Republic,* as a kind of fictional philosophical tool. In reality, Socrates' death—arguably the crucial event in Plato's life and thus in the creation of philosophy as practiced in the West—has been relegated to the classrooms of (one suspects increasingly few) philosophy departments, while Pericles' ideals and "democratic theory" are discussed seriously by historians and political scientists.[38] The reverse, I am suggesting, would be far more appropriate.

This mythologization of Socrates' life and death, encouraged (it must be admitted) by Plato himself, has had a dramatic and insalubrious impact on the study of Athenian history and society. It almost appears that once one accepts (and dismisses) the fact that the democratic Athenians voted to execute Socrates, any of the Athenians' other acts of injustice or political folly can be relegated to a rarely consulted mental appendix listing aberrations in Athens's illustrious democratic history.[39] After all, some might argue, Athens is the only state that can claim to have produced a Socrates. Surely, some might continue, we may simply write off events such as Socrates' execution as examples of the Athenians' failure to realize fully the meaning and potential of their own democracy.

The supreme irony of this attitude emerged most clearly in the only popular historical work devoted to Socrates' execution in recent years. In *The Trial of Socrates,* I. F. Stone came startlingly close to arguing that democratic Athens justifiably convicted and executed the philosopher.[40] For Stone, Socrates propounded a thoroughly antidemocratic and dangerous philosophy.[41] But even so, in Stone's view the philosopher might have avoided a trial if he had simply "demonstrated" a "reconciliation with democracy" and "paid some tribute . . . to the magnanimity of the majority in the peace settlement" that ended the strife between oligarchs and democrats after the Peloponnesian War.[42] If only Socrates had not consistently offended the democratic Athenian people, he might have been allowed to live![43] Stone's conclusion and Athens's action can, of course, be defended, on both technical and moral grounds. But surely the facts that the Athenians and their democratic political system could execute a Socrates (as well as other leaders), enslave or execute thousands of their fellow Greeks, and convert a league against Persia into a sometimes brutal empire over their former Greek allies (and others) demand that we consider the potentially negative effects of direct popular government.[44]

The misdeeds of the democratic Athenians are not only more frequent than moderns often care to admit; they also cannot be dismissed as anomalies themselves or as mere reflections of Athens's ancient Greek culture (since some of them were condemned even in antiquity).[45] Many of these events arguably occurred not just *when,* but—at least in part—*because* Athens was a democracy. Based on their own experience of Athenian government, many ancient critics of the regime adopted this line of analysis, and I would suggest that we cannot dismiss it unless we wish to betray the intellectual rigor and honesty we often claim to praise in the Athenians.[46]

What, I wonder, would Athens have become without its own public critics (like Aristophanes), its moderate and patriotic oligarchs (like Thucydides), and its intellectuals and teachers (like Socrates and Plato), whose works called into question the very basis of the regime?[47] Even the democratic hero Pericles acted as a critic of the Athenian people, standing in front of the demos and blaming the citizens themselves for their mutability. Like Socrates and Aristophanes, Pericles chastised the people of Athens, and like the philosopher and the comic poet, even Pericles incurred the demos's wrath (Thuc. 2.60–65). Yet what part does such public criticism of democracy, or of the citizenry itself, play in our society today? Has any politician in recent memory blamed "the American people" for national problems? Has any popular film ridiculed not only our leaders, but the people who elected them and the very system of election itself? Are we really satisfied with a public self-analysis that reaches its most philosophical and moralistic heights in the accusation "You mean you didn't *vote?!"*

ANCIENT LESSONS FOR MODERN SOCIETY?

By now some readers will expect that we are heading toward the conclusion that, if we moderns wish to produce a thriving and successful democratic regime, we must tolerate and encourage the kind of self-criticism practiced by the Athenians. We must, in effect, recapture the Athenians' critical attitudes toward their own government so that we too can have a "strong democracy."[48] By allowing us to keep democracy, or rather "true democracy," as our ultimate goal, this view presents an almost irresistible pull on contemporary sensibilities. Nevertheless, I believe it must be rejected.

We cannot test our democracy against the values of democracy. We cannot simply assume that the answer to any of democracy's apparent political or social shortcomings is "More democracy!" Instead, we must meet the basic challenge of setting goals and standards for our society that lie beyond a system of government. Modern democratic government is, after all, a tool created by human beings in order to achieve some end—an end such as a better or more just society. As a tool—and not a metaphysical principle—democracy deserves to be evaluated in terms of its ability to perform its task. For once a type of government becomes the goal of political action, the system of government may threaten to replace the values it was originally designed to foster, reflect, or permit. In short, treating democracy as an end rather than a means threatens to create a kind of popular faith centered on a political system (or the supposed values it generates) as the only true absolute.

American society may have reached this point. The worship of freedom through democracy seemingly has replaced other things as a goal for our lives and political system, things that may be more important to individual human beings and just societies. In essence, we may already have enshrined democratic political ideals as the tenets of a new religion. As support for this hypothesis, I would simply ask the reader to imagine a dinner party attended by any number of (say) businessmen, teachers, politicians, ironworkers, and journalists. A person at this party proclaiming, "I don't support the idea of marriage [or the family, God, the sanctity of human life, a citizen army, etc.]" is unlikely to raise an eyebrow. Let him, however, announce that he does not approve of *the vote* (or democracy itself), and the reaction is liable to be pointed. (If he lights a cigarette while making this announcement, it may even be violent!)[49]

On a scholarly level, political scientists now sometimes evaluate societal factors or government practices based on their ability to foster democracy. Statements such as "private property is the friend of democracy" and "private property furthers democracy only if ownership is widespread" betray a striking reversal of sociopolitical means and goals.[50] Democracy, or any form of government, should be acceptable or preferable because *it* furthers private property (or human excellence, social justice, or any other identified "good" sought by a society).[51] Conversely, if we deem ownership of private property to be just (or the attempt to take it away immoral and unjust),[52] we must defend the practice *on that basis,* and not on any supposed ability of private property "to further democracy." The Founders did not try to create an environment in which democratic government per se might prosper. Rather, they sought to address perceived injustices on the part of the British regime, first by revolting and then by establishing a representative and republican form of government that would prevent similar injustices, and under which justice, excellence, and the preexisting values of the American people might not be diminished (or, for some, might be encouraged).[53]

Yet my primary purpose is not to influence modern political scientists. What is needed in America, it seems to me, is serious criticism of representative government and democratic ideas *on a popular level.* Modern Americans need to confront the failings of their form of government and the absurdities of their political beliefs on a regular basis, as the Athenians did when they attended the theater, read history, or listened to certain political speeches. Modern Americans need to produce and watch films, read books and articles, and tell each other jokes that actually question the value of democratic practices or theory and that impugn the intelligence and moral rectitude of "the American people" themselves. How many jokes, one wonders, has the typical citizen of Massachusetts told or heard about Ted Kennedy, compared with the number he has told or heard about the people (including himself) who repeatedly reelect the senator? If we limit ourselves to making jokes only about particular political figures or actions, we in fact shield our political system, our society, and ourselves from criticism. The goal of such self-criticism is not a "better democracy," but rather the continual questioning and strengthening of our own extrapolitical values and the social and political means we choose to encourage them.

Athenian history illustrates the need for a society to foster such extrapolitical values. Although the Athenians instituted and expanded democratic practices with clearly deleterious effects (especially by extending the vote to those without property and making payments of public money to the citizens), they continued to hold a social ideal based on the performance of duties rather than the exercise of rights. These duties were primarily apolitical in the modern sense of the word *politics.* That is, these duties had nothing to with attending assemblies or casting votes, but rather bound Athenians to their gods, families, and fellow citizens. In fact, *politics* as we define the word played a very limited (but important) role in Athenian life. To put it simply, neither Athenian thought nor Athenian society ever became fundamentally democratic in the modern sense, with its emphasis on political rights rather than social duties.[54]

Nevertheless, despite the Athenians' emphasis on duties rather than rights, Athens did suffer from instituting specific democratic practices. The potentially negative effects of democratic practices in Athens look particularly ominous today, since contemporary America (like ancient Athens) has instituted potentially dangerous democratic practices but (unlike Athens) also has generated a society based on modern democratic theory and beliefs. Unlike Athens, *America today has no strong set of values against which to gauge democracy.* And, as Finley almost predicted, the ostensible rejection of explicit moral goals for society that are extraneous to the system of government and the ennoblement of democracy itself as politics's ultimate end has led in fact to the adoption of questionable "values" derived from that form of government.[55] Democracy and its ideological offspring—freedom, choice, and diversity—threaten to dominate American society and supplant older American ideals as moral goods, despite the constitutional and largely nondemocratic form of American government.[56] In short, without a strong set of nonpolitical values, modern America may run risks that the Athenians never confronted.

FACING UP TO ATHENIAN HISTORY

Athens's history offers bracing positive and negative lessons for modern citizens and their regimes. These lessons do not, however, fall readily under the comfortable rubrics of "liberty and equality." They rather stem from the Athenians' unwillingness fully to embrace ideas like absolute equality, political choice through election, and the rights championed by modern political philosophers. Athens's lessons for us derive more from an Athenian social matrix based on duty to gods, family, and polis, and from the economic realities in ancient Athens, than from the fact that Athenians without property could attend meetings of the assembly and cast their votes.

The Athenians' society and their conception of themselves do not always present an attractive image. Indeed, the Athenians held violent prejudices, easily condemned today. But their prejudices manifested themselves in more ways than elitism, sexism, and racism, all traits which the Athenians certainly possessed. Albeit with prejudice, the Athenians jealously guarded the privileges of citizenship, and continually asserted the importance of the duties of the citizen rather than the rights of the individual. Far from endorsing in actual fact Pericles' specious claims about Athens's respect for personal freedom (Thuc. 2.37), the Athenians demonstrated a real interest in influencing and even controlling certain choices of individuals, underscoring Socrates' admittedly exaggerated assertion that, in Athens, a just man who wished to survive had "to live a private, not a public life" (Pl. *Ap.* 32a).

To enjoy the potential benefits of studying Athenian history, we must face the possibility that *demokratia* had deleterious effects on Athens. We must also face the possibility that the city's "successes" rested on factors largely unrelated to Athens's democratic government. Beyond the fact that the Athenians enjoyed a strong and intricate social structure that preceded and then to some degree restricted the negative impact of *demokratia,* early in democracy's history the Athenians found themselves in unique and enviable circumstances stemming from their rich natural resources, the centralization of Athenian power (through a long and largely stable period of tyranny), the existence of a large disfranchised but free and economically beneficial class (the metics), and the successful advancement of Athenian imperialism.[57]

But democratic practices such as using public funds to make payments to those serving on Athens's juries arguably aggravated negative aspects of the Athenian character. In the fifth century, these democratic practices first encouraged the Athenians' martial and aggressive tendencies, fueling the Athenian empire. Athens's power and prosperity and its increasingly radical democratic government ultimately helped bring on the devastating Peloponnesian War and then encouraged its continuation for twenty-seven years. The factors inspiring this war and the long conflict itself fundamentally altered the fourth-century Athenians' historical circumstances and attitudes. Under these new conditions, Athens's democratic regime amplified existing problems and created others, weakening the Athenians' military and morale sufficiently to facilitate Macedon's victory over the southern Greeks, thereby contributing finally to the loss of Athens's independence and the end of classical Athenian democracy.

ONE

Athenian Society
and Government

THE HISTORY OF ATHENS DURING the period of classical democracy (ca. 507–322 B.C.) cannot be appreciated without a basic understanding of Athenian society and government. This chapter therefore attempts to describe the basic structure of Athenian government, to show how it resembled the governments of other Greek city-states, and to outline the intricate relationship between "society" and "government" in ancient Athens. Historians or classicists already familiar with Athenian government may wish to jump immediately to the discussion of voting and election in chapter 2. For others, I hope that this preliminary examination of the Athenian polis will make the treatment of specific issues in later chapters more comprehensible.

Our best sources of information about Athenian history and government derive from contemporary historians (especially Herodotus, Thucydides, and Xenophon), Athenian orators and intellectuals (especially Andocides, Plato, Isocrates, Demosthenes, and the anonymous author known as Pseudo-Xenophon), and Aristotle's works analyzing Athenian and Greek political life (especially the *Politics* and the *Constitution of the Athenians,* the latter possibly but not certainly written by Aristotle). Besides the references to older (but now lost) material found in such late authorities as Plutarch and the Hellenistic and Byzantine commentators, we also possess a significant number of decrees *(psephismata)* passed in the Athenian assembly. The Athenians often inscribed these measures on stone pillars (called *stelai*) and fragments of many of these decrees and other inscribed documents have survived. Combining the testimony from these sources, scholars over the past two centuries have put together a fairly detailed picture of Athens in the fifth and fourth centuries B.C. In the following survey, I have tried to present a conservative reconstruction. This procedure seems especially necessary for this work, since we desire that the conclusions drawn in later chapters rest on a reliable (if admittedly imperfect) historical foundation and not on tenuous interpretations of the evidence.

ATHENS AND POLIS GOVERNMENT

Ancient Greece, which the Greeks (Hellenes) called Hellas, was dominated by hundreds of independent, self-governing city-states known as *poleis* (singular *polis*).[1] The origins of the polis are controversial, but this form of settlement was firmly established in Greece by the eighth century B.C.[2] A typical polis comprised a town or city center *(astu)* surrounded by land *(chora)* farmed and owned by the polis's citizens. Goods were exchanged and formal and informal public interaction took place in the main square and marketplace *(agora)* in the city center. Some poleis possessed a citadel, often located on defensible and/or fortified high-ground. At Athens, this citadel came to be called the *akropolis* ("high city").

Greek poleis ranged in size from tiny villages with perhaps fewer than several hundred citizens to super poleis, of which Sparta and Athens were probably the largest. Athens covered an area (known as Attica) of approximately 1,000 square miles and probably had at least 30,000–40,000 adult male citizens for most of the classical period. Attica's total population is unknown and depends to a large degree on variables like the number of slaves or resident foreigners ("metics") living there at any given time, but it cannot have been less than about 100,000 souls and may have been as great as 400,000 or more.[3]

Other large poleis in Hellas included Thebes (to Athens's north in Boeotia), Corinth (located on the isthmus between Attica and the Peloponnese to the west of Athens), Argos (south of Corinth in the Peloponnese), and, of course, Sparta (also called Lacedaemon), which by around 600 B.C. had come to control the southern Peloponnese. Most of this land was not part of the Spartan polis per se. Rather, the Spartans dominated the poleis located in their immediate vicinity (inhabited by those they called *perioikoi,* or "dwellers around") and directly controlled other territory worked by an enserfed population known as "helots." The helots especially farmed the land in the southwestern portion of the Peloponnese known as Messenia.[4]

Despite the wide range of sizes among Greek poleis, so far as we are able to tell most possessed fairly similar governments by the classical period. Each

Map 1. Ancient Hellas

polis relied on an assembly of adult male citizens that acted as a more or less sovereign authority within the state. In the assembly, citizens of each polis might vote to elect magistrates; approve legislation, treaties, and decisions about war or peace; and, at least in some cases, render judicial decisions.[5] In Athens, this assembly was known as the *ekklesia* and it eventually consisted of all free citizen males, regardless of whether they owned property or not.

Most of the poleis' executive functions were fulfilled by magistrates elected by the citizenry (the *demos*) or chosen by lot, although some offices were restricted to the members of certain families or economic classes.[6] In Athens, the chief magistrates originally consisted of an annual board of nine archons (plus a secretary), at first elected but after 487 chosen by lot from a list of elected candidates.[7] Among these magistrates were the eponymous archon, who gave his name to the year and acted as chief magistrate; the *polemarchos,* or "war archon"; and a primarily religious official called simply the *basileus,* or "king" (sometimes translated as "king-archon").

After 487 and the advent of lot-based selection of Athens's archons, the elected office of general *(strategos,* plural *strategoi)* played an increasingly important political role in Athenian government. Pericles, for example, served as one of Athens's ten elected generals for fifteen consecutive years, making the office the formal basis of his power in the state. But in the fifth century, many other *strategoi*—including Themistocles, Aristeides, Cimon, Cleon, and Alcibiades—acted as both military and political leaders, proposing policies and addressing the people in the council or assembly and then commanding the armies that implemented those policies. Other famous Athenians, including the dramatist Sophocles and the historian Thucydides, also held the elected position of *strategos* and commanded Athens's armies or fleets.

A small council (often of elders or former magistrates) usually completed the tripartite arrangement of polis government. In Sparta this council consisted of twenty-eight elected elders plus the two Spartan kings.[8] In Athens the oldest (known) council was the Areopagus (named for the Hill of Ares, on which the council met). This body consisted of all former archons, who served for life, and it acted as a high court for certain kinds of offenses and served in a general advisory (and perhaps supervisory) role in early Athenian government.[9]

Of course, this composite picture of "typical" polis government, with assembly, council, and magistrates, must be adjusted when we possess enough evidence to describe any particular city-state in detail. For example, when around 507 B.C. Athens instituted the government that would become known as *demokratia,* the Athenians created a second council (the *boule*), this one of 500 citizens chosen (at least eventually) by lot from the citizen body and serving for one year.[10] This *boule* of 500, after 462/1, if not before, became the most important council of the Athenian state.[11] It prepared business for and provided members to preside over meetings of the assembly, heard embassies from foreign powers, supervised financial and military matters, and could act as a kind of court. For one-tenth of each year, the fifty members of the council representing one of the ten Athenian tribes[12] acted as a standing committee for the council as a whole, and these *prytaneis* ("presidents") had to remain in Athens for this entire period (thus known as a "prytany"). Again, the members of the Council of 500 (or *bouleutai*) were chosen by lot, apparently from all Athenian citizens that possessed a moderate amount of property, although by the fourth century, even the poorest citizens were apparently able to serve.[13]

Property qualifications for citizenship or office-holding were apparently common in Greek poleis, as they were in most parts of early America, even after the Revolution and the ratification of the U.S. Constitution.[14] In Sparta, the state seemingly provided equal plots of land for the limited numbers of full citizens (known as *homoioi,* or "equals"),[15] but in other poleis ownership of a small farm and the consequent ability to afford the arms necessary to fight in the infantry phalanx as a hoplite (i.e., one with a *hoplon*— a large shield) probably qualified one for citizenship.[16] However, one of the defining qualities of Athens's *demokratia*—a word combining the basic ideas of power *(kratos)* and the people *(demos)*—was the absence of a property qualification for citizenship. Thus at Athens even the poorest individuals had the opportunity to cast their votes in the assembly and (at least eventually and perhaps unofficially) to serve on the Council of 500.[17]

Nevertheless, both before and after the institution of *demokratia,* the Athenians did divide their citizen body into stratified groups based on the ownership of property and restrict certain offices to those reaching a given property qualification. According to Athenian tradition, the lawgiver Solon (ca. 594/3) separated the Athenians into four categories based on the agricultural production of their land: the *pentakosiomedimnoi* (possessing land yielding 500 *medimnoi* of dry or wet produce per year) formed the highest group, followed by the *hippeis* ("horsemen," with land producing over 300 *medimnoi*), *zeugitai* ("yokemen," from their style of fighting or their yokes of plow animals, with over 200), and *thetes* ("laborers," possessing land producing less than 200 *medimnoi* per year or no property at all).[18] Athenian archons initially had to belong at least to the class of *hippeis,* but after the year 457 the *zeugitai* also could hold this office.[19] The treasurers *(tamiai)* of the sacred wealth of Athena, in some ways Athens's highest financial position in the fifth century, had to belong to the highest property class, the *pentakosiomedimnoi.*[20]

As strange as it seems in the modern world, Solon's property qualifications represented a radical movement in Greek politics, because they formally separated the qualifications for office-holding from one's birth.[21] At an earlier point in Athenian history, perhaps even into the period just before Solon's reforms, it appears likely that only the members of Athenian families known as *eupatridai* (literally, the "well-fathered") were able to hold Athens's highest offices. After Solon, any citizen rich enough to join the *pentakosiomedimnoi* could (theoretically) hold any political position in Athens. Nevertheless, the members of the clans of the *eupatridai,* which claimed descent from the ancient Athenian aristocracy, continued to play a major role in Athenian government and society through their control of particular religious cults and their potential influence in the social groups that made up the demos as a whole.[22]

These smaller religio-social units represent another way in which the Athenian demos divided itself into component elements.[23] Membership in one of the aristocratic families or clans *(gene)* obviously provided advantages for those wishing to wield power in Athens, both in terms of the land and wealth these clans usually controlled and because of the supposed antiquity and religious associations of the families. The aristocratic clans in turn apparently wielded significant influence in the phratries ("brotherhoods"), poorly understood organizations based at least theoretically on common descent and connected through religious cults. It seems likely that the phratries approved citizenship for individual Athenians before the institution of *demokratia,* and thus the aristocratic clans probably played a crucial role in determining who was and who was not considered an Athenian citizen.[24] Larger than the phratries were the original four tribes *(phylai)* into which the members of the demos were divided. These tribes also related (theoretically) to descent, and most Ionian Greeks (the ethnic/linguistic subgroup of Hellenes into which the Athenians fell), whether they lived in mainland Greece, the islands, or Asia Minor, were divided into similar *phylai.* For some, this suggests that these tribes originated before the polis form of government, and perhaps even before the migration of Ionian Greeks to the islands and Asia Minor during the early Greek Dark Age (ca. 1100–800 B.C.).[25] Like the phratries and the clans, these tribes were religious as well as social and military organizations, with their own cults, priests, and rituals.

The Athenian demos as a whole was thus divided in both economic and religio-social ways into subgroups that played particular roles within the polis (and in most cases probably resembled similar divisions in other poleis). Aside from their religious functions, the tribes and phratries, for example, almost certainly served (at least originally) as organizing units for the Athenian military.[26] Both in their state funerals and in the inscriptions recording those who died in battle, the Athenians divided the fallen according to tribe.[27]

But the demos as a whole also functioned as a unit, particularly in the worship of the polis's tutelary goddess, Athena.[28] The city came together to propitiate and celebrate the goddess in a festival known as the Panathenaea, held once every year and every four years with special splendor. The celebrations included a procession to the acropolis, where the temple of Athena was located and her sacred treasure was stored.[29]

Eligibility for Athenian office-holding did not depend only on the actual wealth of the would-be magistrate. Every Athenian chosen by lot or election for office went through a vetting process known as the *dokimasia*, in which his citizenship was checked and anyone who wished could lodge a complaint against him.[30] A prospective member of the Council of 500 or a candidate for the office of archon also answered certain questions put to him by the Council of 500, including whether he was enrolled in a cult of the gods Zeus Herkeios and Apollo Patroos (and where the shrines were located), whether he treated his parents well, and whether he had served in the military when called upon and paid his taxes.[31] Candidates for other magistracies answered similar questions before a court of Athenian jurors.[32] In this way, the Athenians placed formal checks on the persons who could hold their most important offices, even if the individuals were selected by lot from the citizen body. But one must emphasize that the questions the candidates were asked had nothing to do with their abilities to perform the tasks associated with their office. Instead, these questions sought information about the potential officeholders' citizenship and their previous performance of duties. That is, prospective Athenian officials faced questions about their *character* and behavior and not about their knowledge, intelligence, experience, or technical skills.[33]

Many of the aspects of Athens's *politeia* (the customary "arrangement of the polis" and thus often translated as "constitution") discussed so far arose before the institution of democracy (ca. 507) and then continued under the new regime. They clearly illustrate the basic structure of polis government and the various kinds of connections between individual citizens and between groups of citizens (from families to tribes) that existed within Athens. The social bonds that tied Athenian to Athenian before and after the institution of democracy are particularly well exemplified by the questions asked of the candidates for the Athenian archonship, which basically sought to determine whether an individual had performed his duties to the gods, his family, and the polis. Moreover, every subgroup of the polis, from the family to the demos as a whole, had a religious character, with particular rites to be performed and gods to be propitiated. This reminds us that for the ancient Greeks, religion pervaded society and government and was usually a corporate affair, consisting largely of rites or sacrifices carried out on behalf of the group (family, clan, phratry, tribe, demos) in order to secure the goodwill of the gods.[34] In turn, as we shall see, every group or corporate action in which the Athenians engaged had a religious aspect.

ATHENS AFTER SOLON'S REFORMS

Not long after the period of Solon's reforms (ca. 594/3), Athens fell under the control of the tyrant Peisistratus and his sons (ca. 561–511/10).[35] Like many Greek tyrants, Peisistratus was simply an "unconstitutional" ruler, someone who had seized power in a polis and had done so outside the normal avenues of political action. The position of tyrant in sixth-century Greece did not carry the particularly negative connotations later associated with the term. In fact, to some later Athenians, the period of Peisistratus's rule seemed to have been a "golden age." Peisistratus was said to have left the traditional Athenian constitution in place, only ensuring that his own supporters held the most important offices (such as that of eponymous archon).[36]

The period of Peisistratid rule is especially crucial for this study, because so many of the trends that developed under the *demokratia* seem to have their origins under the Athenian tyrants. Coming to power during and in part because of conflict between rival aristocratic factions, Peisistratus perhaps styled himself a kind of champion of the demos: one who claimed to protect the common people of Athens from the aristocrats that controlled so much of Athenian political and social life and drew the members of the demos into their struggles. Besides suppressing these conflicts, Peisistratus seems to have opened up avenues of citizenship to those of questionable birth or connections, thereby increasing the ranks of his supporters while undermining his aristocratic would-be opponents.[37]

Other important trends that began under Peisistratus include the expansion of Athenian power into the Aegean, especially in the area around the Hellespont, the stretch of water leading into the Black Sea and its grain-rich coast.[38] Peisistratus (or his sons) apparently also constructed a major temple to Athena on the acropolis (later destroyed by the Persians and then replaced by the Parthenon and Erechtheion), and may have offered loans to poor farmers, as well as instituting the first tax on agricultural produce in Attica.[39] He also used economic power apparently derived at least partly from mines in Thrace and in Attica to fund the military support on which he relied. In all these ways, Peisistratus and his sons set important precedents for fifth-century, democratic Athens.[40]

The overthrow of the Athenian tyrants in 511/10 was accomplished not by the Athenians themselves but by the Spartans. Peisistratus's son Hippias had become a harsh ruler after the murder of his brother Hipparchus in 514 by a pair of insulted aristocratic lovers, one of whom had rebuffed the tyrant's amorous brother. After Hippias's subsequent expulsion of certain aristocrats from Athens, some of the exiles apparently then tried to oust the Peisistratids from power, but failed. Fortunately for these Athenian aristocrats, the sixth-century Spartans made something of a habit of destroying tyrannies, and their overthrow of the Peisistratids allowed the reestablishment of the more typical style of polis government in Athens. The Spartans apparently saw such nontyrannical regimes, usually dominated by the aristocrats but based on a citizen body of rough equals, as consistent with Spartan interests.[41]

After the Spartans removed the Peisistratids in 511/10, the Athenian aristocrats returned to power and apparently resumed the kind of internecine quarreling that had allowed Peisistratus to seize power in the first place. Eventually an Athenian named Cleisthenes (a one-time brother-in-law of the tyrant Peisistratus and the grandson of another tyrant, Cleisthenes of Sicyon in the northern Peloponnese) seemingly determined, in effect, to reconstitute the faction that had supported Peisistratus. By appealing to the demos for support against the other aristocrats, Cleisthenes was able to defeat his rivals and pass the reforms that would create the government eventually known as *demokratia*. The Spartans most probably took Cleisthenes' regime for a new form of tyranny (since the only forms of Greek regime known to them at that time were either rule by a tyrant or the typical aristocratic/timocratic polis government[42]), and returned to Athens to force Cleisthenes and his family (the Alcmeonids) from power. The Athenians dutifully expelled Cleisthenes and his relatives. But when the Spartans then attempted to dismantle Cleisthenes' political reforms, the Athenians balked and ejected the Spartans, who ultimately decided to accept Athens's new regime.[43]

Precisely what Cleisthenes accomplished ca. 507 and by what means he managed it are problematic questions. It appears that he partially separated control of citizenship from the potentially aristocrat-dominated phratries and gave more power in this and other areas to the individual residents of the villages/neighborhoods of Attica (the *demoi,* or "demes"). After Cleisthenes, a man's citizenship would be determined (at least in part) by his neighbors, and not (at least technically) primarily by his connection with aristocratic families or patrons.[44] At the same time, Cleisthenes created a new council of state, made up not of the aristocratic former archons (as was the Areopagus) but rather of five hundred citizens (at least eventually) chosen by lot.[45] These five hundred would be chosen through the increasingly important demes. The demes themselves were now allocated into ten new tribes, each containing some demes from the coastal region of Attica, some from the interior region around the city of Athens, and some from the city itself.[46] Each new tribe therefore represented a geographical microcosm of the polis as a whole, perhaps reflecting a desire to use these ten tribes as organizational tools for the Athenian military, as well as for the political and religious arrangement of the polis.[47] After 501/0, each tribe elected one of the polis's ten generals, although at some point in the fifth century, the specific allocation of one general per tribe was abandoned.[48]

By around 500 B.C. the structure of Athens's government had taken the basic form it was to have for nearly two centuries (apart from two brief periods of oligarchic rule). Like other poleis, the Athenians had an assembly of all citizens (the *ekklesia*), a smaller council (actually two: the *boule* of five hundred citizens and the older Areopagus), and a group of magistrates (the archons et al.). In Athens, the citizenry as a whole (the demos) was also divided into subgroups reflecting economic circumstances, local residence, and religio-social connections, and these subgroups had political, religious, and probably military significance.

The most unusual aspects of Athenian government at this time—what at least arguably made it *demokratia* as opposed to the type of polis government that might be called either *aristokratia* (rule by the *aristoi* or "best") or *oligarchia* (rule by the rich *oligoi,* or "few"), depending on one's point of view—was the absence of any property qualification for participation in the assembly and the influence on citizenship and the Council of 500 (and thus on government policy) of the neighborhood demesmen. At least at this early stage, both the assembly and council probably consisted primarily of the middle-class hoplite-farmers that dominated the Greek countryside. By helping determine citizenship and by providing the members of the new council, the demes (in which these citizens resided) became in some ways the most significant subdivision of the Athenian polis.[49] But beyond these obviously important distinctions involving property qualifications and the selection of councilmen by lot, Athenian polis government circa 500 B.C. at the structural level resembled that practiced elsewhere in Greece (including even Sparta).

We know very little about precise legislative and judicial procedures in this early period of *demokratia*. The Athenian assembly passed decrees *(psephismata)* by majority vote on issues placed before it by the Council of 500. The council had the option of putting an actual measure before the assembly (which might then be amended), or simply placing an issue on the agenda, a procedure that permitted specific proposals from the floor of the assembly.[50] Although fourth-century Athenians distinguished between permanent and general "laws" *(nomoi)*—regulations either laid down by a lawgiver like Solon or (later) created by a special process of lawmaking—and particular "decrees" passed in the Athenian assembly, this may not have been true in the early fifth century. At that time, whatever the assembly decreed by vote seems to have had the same force as Solon's (or Drakon's) law code.

However, by at least 415 the Athenians had adopted the position that one could not propose a decree in the assembly that was contrary to a standing law *(nomos)*. Anyone proposing such a measure could be indicted on the charge of introducing an illegal decree *(graphe paranomon)*.[51] Moreover, in the years between 410 and 399 the Athenians undertook a complete revision and republication of their laws. After this, laws *(nomoi)* were formally distinguished from the decrees of the assembly, and the *nomoi* could only be changed through a process *(nomothesia)* involving a special court selected by lot for this purpose. For this reason, some scholars have argued that Athens moved from the "popular sovereignty" of the fifth century (where decrees of the demos were equal in force to laws and thus limited only by themselves) to the fourth-century "sovereignty of the law" (where the assembly was formally constrained by preexisting *nomoi*).[52]

The distinction between these periods should probably not be overemphasized. The Athenians apparently never had public prosecutors or any regular procedure for reviewing the legality or "constitutionality" of a measure proposed in the Council of 500 or assembly, and thus the ability of the *nomoi* to enforce themselves (and constrain the assembly) depended heavily on the voluntary actions of individual citizens.[53] Like modern Americans, the ancient Athenians apparently had widely divergent ideas about what was or was not "unconstitutional," and indictments for making proposals contrary to the law were often brought by citizens as much for personal and political reasons as out of constitutional concern. Our own experience of the sometimes questionable extent to which the U.S. Constitution actually controls modern American government or legislation also might make us leery of inter-preting Athenian "rule of law" or "sovereignty of the law" too literally.

The Athenian judicial system also underwent significant changes during the period of *demokratia*. The assembly itself could apparently act as a huge court (the *heliaia*) in certain matters, while the ancient and much smaller Areopagus council heard cases involving homicide (and probably other mat-ters).[54] But in 462/1 the Athenian Ephialtes put forward proposals to restrict the Areopagus's powers, and thereafter most cases were heard before courts *(dikasteria)* made up of larger numbers of Athenian citizen-jurors ("dicasts," numbering from 200 to 2,500 for each court). These jurors were chosen by lot and allocated to particular courts each day from a roster of 6,000 selected each year.[55] Probably in the late 450s, Pericles proposed that these dicasts should be paid, and eventually they received three obols (one-half of one drachma, perhaps about a day's wage for an unskilled laborer in the mid fifth century) per day for their service.[56] Payment of jurors undoubtedly encour-aged participation in the judicial system by a large number of Athenians. It also led to payment for other public services, including membership on the Council of 500 and (in the fourth century) attendance at the assembly.[57]

Because of the tripartite arrangement of polis government (including Athens's *demokratia*), with assembly, council (and later other courts), and magistrates, it is tempting to conceive of such a regime in terms of the mod-ern legislative, judicial, and executive "branches of government." But this conception seriously misrepresents the Athenian system, first because the Athenians recognized nothing like the modern separation of powers, and sec-ond because the word *government* itself betrays a modern and un-Athenian view of the *politeia*.

It is clear that no "separation of powers" existed in Athens. The assembly passed legislation and could also act as a court. The juries themselves were made up of those who voted on the decrees in the *ekklesia*.[58] Indeed, it is more than likely that many jurors sitting on a case involving an allegedly illegal de-cree would have themselves voted for or against this decree in the assembly. Such a juror thus had the opportunity to condemn and fine an individual who had proposed a decree the juror himself might have voted to support. Likewise, members of the Council of 500 and Athenian magistrates also par-ticipated in the assemblies (and presided over them if they were *prytaneis*). Particular "executive" officials like the *polemarchos* and *thesmothetai* also acted as supervisory officials in Athenian courts (and perhaps originally in the as-semblies), while generals could propose or oppose (before the Council of 500 or the assembly) specific military actions they themselves would then command.[59] Thus each of the three basic parts of the Athenian regime participated in both judicial and legislative matters.

Moreover, there was no ancient Athenian term equivalent to the modern *government* (which may be divided into "branches" with separate powers). Since the Athenian citizens themselves voted on issues of taxation and spending, and war and peace (often including the details of diplomacy and strategy), as well as electing their generals and serving as magistrates on important boards after having been chosen by lot, the Athenian demos literally *was* the Athenian government. Few Athenians would have understood a modern American's conception of the government as an entity separate from (much less hostile to!) the citizen body itself.[60] Today, we speak of protecting ourselves from "the government," of "government intrusion," or of allowing "the government" to pay for programs or take on other responsibilities. Particular government bureaus are given independent and almost anthropomorphic existence: "the IRS" is said, for example, to harass citizens, or a local Department of Social Services is said to provide assistance to the poor, while "the military" is often discussed as if were an entity entirely separate from the American citizenry itself. In ancient Athens, it was "the Athenians" (or the demos) who voted for war and then fought the battles themselves, who raised taxes and (if they were wealthy enough) paid them, who passed decrees and convicted or acquitted individual citizens. Like other Greeks, the Athenians usually referred to their city (and its government) in terms of the collective citizenry. Some scholars have pointed out that an ancient Greek polis might thus be called a "citizen-state" as much as a "city-state."[61] As the Athenian general Nicias remarks in a famous passage in Thucydides: "men make a polis, and not ships or walls without men in them" (Thuc. 7.77).[62]

ATHENIAN HISTORY IN THE CLASSICAL PERIOD

In the period just after the institution of *demokratia* ca. 507, Athens withstood threats from its Greek neighbors. Both the Boeotians and the Chalcidians (the inhabitants of Chalcis, a city on the great island of Euboea off central Greece's eastern coast) apparently wished to test the new Athenian regime, and according to Herodotus, the Spartans also planned to overthrow the new government and reinstall a tyrant.[63] The alleged Spartan invasion fell apart because of discord between the two Spartan kings and the withdrawal of Sparta's Corinthian allies. The Athenians then defeated the Boeotians and Chalcidians, even seizing prime land on Euboea from the latter and settling

Athenians there (Hdt. 5.75–77). In a well-known passage describing Athens's victories over these forces ca. 506, Herodotus comments that this success showed how quickly Athens became a military power after achieving *isegoria* ("equality of speech").[64]

Athenian self-confidence appears to have continued to rise, because in 498 Athens sent twenty warships to Asia Minor to help the (largely Ionian) Greek cities there in their rebellion against the Great King of Persia. Although the Athenians withdrew after only one campaign (and the Ionian revolt eventually ended in disaster), Athens's brief participation in the failed action led ultimately to Persian retribution. In 490 a large Persian force (accompanied by Hippias, Athens's former Peisistratid tyrant) landed at Marathon, located in northeast Attica about twenty-seven miles (a "marathon" distance) from the city center of Athens. The Athenians, apparently fearing possible betrayal of the city to Persia if they remained within their city walls, marched out to meet the Persians. First awaiting Spartan assistance (which came only too late), the 10,000 or so Athenians (assisted by about 600 allies from Plataea) eventually determined to attack the much larger Persian army. Making their assault on the run, surely to give the Persian archers less time to weaken their force with missiles, the Athenian infantry won a great (and very unexpected) victory. According to Athenian tradition, 192 Athenians fell, while 6,400 Persians were killed. The Athenian hoplites then hurried back to Athens in time to prevent a Persian landing there.

For the moment, Athens had been saved from Persian domination.[65] Nevertheless, in the next decade the Athenians carried out reprisals against leading citizens suspected of supporting the Peisistratid tyranny or medizing (taking a stance sympathetic to the Medes and Persians), voting to exile certain individuals from Athens for a period of ten years.[66] This procedure for temporary banishment (called "ostracism," from the broken potsherds, or *ostraka,* on which the Athenians wrote the desired victim's name) allowed the banished individual to reclaim his property (and resume his political activities) after his return to Athens, and it continued to be an important part of the Athenian political landscape through the late fifth century. Some of Athens's most famous statesmen, including Aristeides, Themistocles, and Cimon, were forced to leave the city by vote of their fellow citizens.

In addition to several significant ostracisms, the 480s also saw an epochal change in Athenian public finance and national defense. In 483/2 the Athenians struck a particularly rich vein in the public silver mines located in southern Attica. Previously, profits deriving from the mines had apparently been distributed to the citizens at large. But in this year, the Athenian

Themistocles proposed that the polis collectively use this money to construct a larger fleet as protection against Athens's island neighbor and enemy Aegina (which had a large fleet) or against the expected return of the Persians.[67] Voting to follow Themistocles' advice, the Athenians practically overnight became a naval superpower and soon possessed a fleet of two hundred or so warships.

When the Persians under their new Great King, Xerxes, did invade again in 480, the now publicly enriched Athenians provided the bulk of the allied Greek fleet that opposed them. Nonetheless, only about thirty Greek poleis chose to stand against the tens and probably hundreds of thousands of invading Persians and their subjects (including other Greeks). At the head of the allied Greeks were the Spartans, who as the greatest Hellenic power commanded both the land and sea operations against Xerxes.[68]

In a series of battles and with the aid of some timely storms, which wrecked much of the Persian fleet, the Greek allies repulsed the Persians in 480–479 and expelled them from mainland Greece. Early in the invasion, the famed three hundred Spartans (including one of their two kings) held the pass into central Greece at Thermopylae (in 480) and died to a man, allowing the other allies time to fall back. Shortly after this, at the island of Salamis off the coast of Attica, the allied Greek fleet won a great victory over the Persian forces. Xerxes himself thereupon returned to Persia, leaving a substantial body of elite troops behind. In the following spring (479) at Plataea, the allied Greek infantry defeated this force and effectively ended the Persian invasion of mainland Hellas.[69]

Seaborne operations against the Persians continued on the coast of Asia Minor and around the Hellespont, freeing eastern Greek states that had been compelled to join the Persians. However, the Spartans seem to have been unwilling to continue campaigning overseas during the winters of 479/8 or 478/7. Meanwhile their commander Pausanias had made himself obnoxious to the allied Greeks, allegedly in part by adopting Persian habits. Connected with many of the freed Greeks of Asia Minor by their Ionian heritage and providing most of the allied fleet in any case, the Athenians now seemed the logical choice to lead any continuing actions against Persia in the eastern Aegean. By spring 477 the Spartans acquiesced to this situation, probably because they were troubled by their regent Pausanias's actions and happy to be rid of naval operations that took them far away from the Peloponnese.[70]

After the Spartans withdrew, the Athenians and other Greeks formed a new alliance, often called the "Delian League" by moderns because it held its meetings and initially stored its common funds on the island of Delos, a center of Ionian Greek cult. The Athenian Aristeides received the task of determining the amount of annual contributions (*phoros,* or "tribute") the Greek allies that did not provide ships would pay to the league, while Athenian treasurers (called *hellenotamiai,* or "Greek treasurers") were selected to steward the money. The ostensible purpose of these payments, the historian Thucydides tells us, was the plan "to ravage the Persian Great King's land" as an act of vengeance for all he had perpetrated against the Greeks.[71] But, in the coming years, the Athenians seemingly launched few campaigns against the Great King's territory. Instead, other Greek states were forced into the league and Athenian settlements were established in the Aegean.[72]

By the mid 460s, some members of the alliance were seeking to leave the league. But the Athenians refused to allow this, even after a great Hellenic victory over Persian land and sea forces at the Eurymedon River in southern Asia Minor (ca. 466) effectively ended the immediate threat of Persian activity in the Aegean.[73] Subsequently, the large island of Thasos (a member of the league) and Athens apparently disputed the Thasians' control of certain mines and markets located in the northern Aegean region. When Thasos attempted to leave the alliance and retain its control over these mines, the Athenians blockaded and then reduced the city (ca. 465–463).[74]

Perhaps equally discomforting to some members of the Delian League, which had been designed at least in part to punish the Persians, in 462/1 the Athenians abandoned their alliance with Sparta against Persia, made a new alliance with previously medizing Thessaly and Argos (the latter Sparta's bitter enemy), and ostracized the pro-Spartan Athenian general Cimon.[75] At the same time, and apparently in connection with this foreign policy volte-face, the reforms of Ephialtes radicalized the Athenian democracy, removing at least some power from the more conservative Areopagus and ultimately (if not immediately) distributing power to the courts made up of common Athenians (the *dikasteria*).[76] Hostilities against Athens's former allies Corinth and Sparta were opened ca. 460, while the Athenians concurrently sent a major expedition to Egypt (which was in revolt from Persia).

Athens's expedition to Egypt ended in disaster in 454,[77] around the same time that the Athenians decided to move the common treasury of the Delian League to Athens. Subsequently Athens's public expenditures seem to have ballooned, with payments to jurors on Athenian courts and funding for an expensive building program, centered on the acropolis, but affecting other parts of Attica.[78] In 451/0 Pericles proposed that Athenian citizenship be restricted to those with Athenian mothers as well as fathers, a law that effectively limited the aristocratic practice of marrying sons to the daughters of

wealthy non-Athenians, and that probably also reflected the financial benefits (through public payments) now attaching to Athenian citizenship.[79]

Despite Athens's failure in Egypt, the so-called First Peloponnesian War
against Sparta and Corinth resulted in Athenian gains in central Greece
(Boeotia) and even in the Peloponnese. After Cimon returned from ostracism, he effected another policy reversal in Athens, negotiating a five-year
truce (451) with the Spartans that confirmed Athens's gains.[80] Cimon then led
a major campaign against Persian forces in Cyprus but died before the Athenians won a great victory. This success apparently led to negotiations between
the Persian Great King Artaxerxes and the Athenians, and to the end of actual hostilities between Athens and Persia.[81]

Whether a formal "Peace of Callias" (as the alleged Atheno-Persian treaty
that followed the Cyprus campaign is sometimes called, after the Athenian
credited with the negotiations) existed or not, the de facto state of peace that
followed Cimon's victory and death allowed Pericles to focus the Athenian
demos's attention on consolidating what had become a Greek empire.[82] The
Athenians embraced this mission with great enthusiasm, as several decrees of
the assembly from the early to mid 440s demonstrate.[83] And although Athens
lost most of its holdings in central Greece and the Peloponnese after a major
defeat in 447/6 forced it to accept a thirty-years' truce with Sparta in 446/5,
the Athenian grip on the allied states continued to produce rich rewards in
the form of yearly tribute payments. With this source of wealth added to their
native supply of silver, the Athenians were able to maintain a great stockpile
of ready cash in the city, pay their jurors and other officials, and continue to
erect new buildings, statues, and walls.[84] Meanwhile, in 441/0 Athens intervened in a conflict between Samos and Miletus—two of the larger and more
powerful members of the Athenian alliance—taking the side of the Milesians
and imposing a democracy on formerly autonomous Samos. When the Samians resisted, the Athenians besieged the city for nine months, and having
taken it, they compelled the Samians to pay the costs of the war.[85]

In 433 the Athenians received a request for alliance from the Corinthian
colony of Corcyra, a powerful island in the Adriatic off the northwestern
coast of Greece. The Corcyreans and Corinthians had come to blows over another city, Corcyra's own colony Epidamnus. The Corinthians, for their part,
suggested that an Athenian alliance with Corcyra would break the spirit of
the treaty of 446/5 between Athens and Sparta. This treaty had included
Sparta's allies, of which Corinth was by far the most important and powerful. Apparently already eyeing possible expansion into the central Mediterranean, the Athenians nonetheless concluded a defensive pact with Corcyra.[86]

This ultimately resulted in their participation in a naval battle between Corcyra and Corinth on the Corcyrean side. Shortly after this, in 432 the Athenians took aggressive steps against another Corinthian colony, Potidaea, which happened to be a tribute-paying member of the Athenian empire. Fearing Corinthian reprisals over Corcyra, the Athenians demanded that the Potidaeans destroy part of their city wall, give hostages, and dismiss their Corinthian magistrates. In response, the Potidaeans revolted from Athens and accepted Corinthian assistance. The Athenians besieged the city, located in the northwest Aegean on the westernmost prong of the Chalcidice (see map 3).[87]

Corinth, along with other Peloponnesian allies, now complained to Sparta that Athens had grown too powerful and must be checked. The Spartans were ultimately compelled to agree, and in 431 they invaded Attica, beginning the well-known Peloponnesian War, which would last for twenty-seven years. In the first years of this war, Athens endured a devastating plague and expended most of its ready cash. By 428, Pericles was dead and the Athenian demos determined to levy a tax on wealthier Athenians' property in order to continue the war and pay the democracy's expenses. The first phase of this war continued until the year 421, when Athens and Sparta agreed to a treaty (called the Peace of Nicias, after its Athenian negotiator).[88] Despite this treaty and a brief period of alliance, in 418 an Argive-Athenian army fought (and lost) a major land battle against Sparta at Mantinea in the Peloponnese. In 416 the Athenians besieged and reduced the Spartan colony on the island of Melos, killing all the men and enslaving the women and children.[89] The next year, the Athenians launched their major invasion of Sicily, aimed ultimately at the Corinthian colony Syracuse, a Peloponnesian ally and the dominant power on the great island.

Blunders in command and the failure of the city to support the expedition adequately led to the disastrous defeat of the Athenians in Sicily in 413. Virtually the entire invasion force was lost. Meanwhile, the Athenians had provoked renewed hostilities with Sparta in mainland Greece.[90] The Spartans responded by occupying the Attic village of Decelea, using it as a base to raid Athenian territory. Some twenty thousand slaves now deserted Athens to the Spartans, and the Athenians found themselves largely bereft of the profits of their silver mines.[91] Enriched by Persian subsidies, the Spartans now built a fleet and began campaigning in the eastern Aegean, leading to revolts among Athens's most important allies.

By 411 the Athenians had completely exhausted their once vast monetary reserves, and had begun relying entirely on the yearly income from their subjects' tribute payments and local taxation to fund the war effort. In this environment, the exiled Athenian general Alcibiades, who had at first cooperated with the Spartans and then assisted the Persians, now suggested that he could bring Persia (and the Great King's money) over to Athens's side if the Athenians would agree to alter their form of government. Alcibiades' promise would prove to be overly optimistic (if not duplicitous), but the offer nonetheless set in motion the oligarchic revolution of 411. In response to Alcibiades' offer, a group of Athenians proposed and carried measures to suspend public pay for jury service and the like, to select a new Council of 400 to replace the Council of 500 previously chosen by lot, and to restrict the citizen body to the five thousand or so Athenians who could afford to serve as hoplites in the Athenian army.[92]

The Athenians passed these reforms in a special meeting of the assembly, with many members of the demos present undoubtedly believing that such measures offered the hope of defeating Sparta and maintaining the empire. But the actual citizen body of five thousand never materialized, and the Four Hundred in fact dominated Athens (even assassinating some of their enemies) for about four months in mid 411. Eventually a few of the Four Hundred (especially Theramenes) and some agitated hoplites began to suspect pro-Spartan sympathies among the core oligarchs, and this led to a public movement to replace the oligarchy with a more inclusive regime. The Athenians voted to remove the Four Hundred from power and install a "moderate" government based on a limited (but real) citizen body of about five thousand. Those of the Four Hundred who remained in Athens were tried and executed; most fled the city, including Plato's cousin Critias.[93] The moderate regime lasted only a little longer than the Four Hundred, and by 410/9 Athens's demokratia—including citizenship for all free Athenian males and payments for public services—had been reinstituted.[94]

In the last years of the war, the Athenians received offers of peace based on the status quo from the Spartans. However, Alcibiades was once more acting as an Athenian general, and he and other commanders won important victories in the northeastern Aegean that restored Athenian confidence. The Athenians consequently refused Sparta's proffered peace treaties, choosing even to melt down the gold statues of their goddess Athena Nike (Athena "Victory") to coin the money necessary to continue the war. Only in 405, when the Athenian fleet was caught off guard and almost completely annihilated at Aegospotami in the Hellespont and Athens's grain supply was subsequently shut off, did the Athenians seriously consider treating for peace. After enduring a blockade of several months, they agreed in 404 to terms dictated by the Spartans: Athens's empire and the walls connecting the city to its harbor were to be dismantled and its fleet reduced to a paltry twelve ships. Athens's foreign policy was to be under Spartan control. But this treatment was lenient; Sparta's allies Corinth and Thebes had apparently wanted Athens to suffer the same fate it had imposed on the Melians and others—namely, execution of the men and enslavement of the women and children.[95]

In the year 404/3 a group of thirty Athenian conspirators backed by the Spartan commander Lysander once again revolutionized Athens's government. This government of "the Thirty" ostensibly represented a restricted citizen body of 3,000 individuals, but in fact the Thirty and their comrades eventually acted as virtual tyrants.[96] Apparently headed by the Socratic follower Critias and including other veterans of the Four Hundred (from 411) such as Theramenes, the Thirty even sought to implicate the aged philosopher Socrates in their crimes by asking him to bring an innocent man to Athens for execution. Socrates did not comply. Theramenes himself came to oppose the Thirty's trumped-up trials and property confiscations, and he was tried and executed by his former fellow conspirators.[97]

Meanwhile, a group of Athenian exiles and democrats led by Thrasybulus put together a force and invaded Attica. Making war on the Thirty and their supporters, they killed Critias in battle, but the oligarchs still held the city. At that time, a Spartan king (Pausanias) arrived on the scene and after defeating the democratic insurgents nevertheless decided to reconcile the two Athenian factions. The core oligarchs still living were to be held liable for their actions, but a general amnesty eventually was declared for everyone else. *Demokratia* was restored in Athens in 403, and a revised Athenian law code was published not long afterward.[98]

Although he probably should have been immune from prosecution for his actions before 403 under the terms of the declared amnesty, Socrates' association with Critias and Alcibiades encouraged his prosecution in 399 on charges of corrupting the youth, introducing new gods, and not believing in the state's gods. An Athenian jury convicted the philosopher and sentenced him to death.[99] Among Socrates' surviving followers, some now apparently abandoned any hope of a political career. Plato first left Athens but then returned and devoted himself to the study of philosophy, while Xenophon had already departed to lead the life of a military adventurer and author.[100]

In the early fourth century, the Athenians made some effort to reestablish their power, first allying with Thebes, Corinth, and Argos against Sparta. The so-called Corinthian War (395–387/6) that resulted from this alliance culminated in a peace treaty essentially imposed on the Greeks by the Great King of Persia. It helped ensure Spartan supremacy in mainland Greece while abandoning the Greeks of Asia Minor, who once more came under Persian control.[101] In the period that followed this ignominious truce, the Spartans proved to be as predatory as the fifth-century Athenians, imposing their will on previously independent states and even installing a garrison in the city of Thebes (382–379). Sparta's activities allowed the Athenians to organize a new alliance, often called the Second Athenian League, this time with Sparta, rather than Persia, as its object (378/7).[102]

Restrictions on Athens's actions and other factors made the second league much weaker than the first, thus providing scope for other Greek states.[103] The Thebans unexpectedly increased in power under their superb general Epaminondas, even defeating the vaunted Spartans at Leuctra in 371. The shocked Athenians (fearing a suddenly powerful Thebes to their immediate north) now turned away from Thebes and toward Sparta for an alliance. The Theban army under Epaminondas actually campaigned inside the Peloponnese several times during the 360s. In these campaigns, Thebes succeeded in freeing helot-tilled Messenia from Spartan control, thereby destroying the economic foundation of Spartan power. However, Epaminondas's death at Mantinea in 362 ended Thebes's brief period of hegemony, the most lasting effects of which were the destruction of Sparta as an international Greek power and the military inspiration that the young Philip of Macedon likely received in the 360s from his Theban hosts.[104]

By 359 this Philip was king of Macedon, and by 357 he had ended most internal unrest and pacified his barbarian neighbors sufficiently to allow him to begin looking to the Aegean coastline and areas formally controlled or claimed by Athens.[105] The Athenians themselves suffered from a war brought on by rebellion among their allies, and this Social War (357–355) to some degree diverted their attention from Philip's growing power in the northwestern Aegean, although they did declare war on the king.[106]

Between 357 and 341 Philip moved repeatedly east and south from Macedonia, extending his control or influence into Thrace, Thessaly, and central Greece by using a combination of military action, opportunism, and diplomatic sagacity. In the last area, Philip was particularly adept, repeatedly assuring the Athenians that his intentions were not hostile, even as he encroached on or actually seized Athenian holdings or interests. This complex and difficult period of Athenian history is analyzed in detail in chapter 6. Suffice it to say here that, despite a formal state of war between Athens and Macedon after 357 and Demosthenes' repeated calls for a serious and concerted effort to thwart Philip, the Athenians took no vigorous actions against him until at least 343/2. These actions followed an attempt to ally with Philip (the Peace of Philocrates in 346), which had in fact only strengthened the Macedonian's position and weakened the Athenians'. But even the efforts of 343/2 suffered from the Athenian citizens' unwillingness to make the financial and personal sacrifices necessary to support their military adequately.

Finally, in 339/8, the Athenians voted to transfer their surplus funds from the treasury for public payments into the military treasury, while they also sought and gained their former enemy Thebes's alliance against Macedon. Nevertheless, Philip's forces defeated those of Thebes and Athens at Chaeronea in central Greece (338). Athens was allowed to keep its *demokratia* at the Macedonian king's pleasure, but the defeated Greeks were compelled to appoint Philip as commander *(hegemon* or *strategos autokrator)* and declare war on Persia.[107]

Philip's great ambitions (and more) were to be fulfilled by his young son Alexander. Succeeding his assassinated father in 336, Alexander dealt harshly with a Theban revolt, razing the ancient city to the ground. The Athenians had refused the Theban request for assistance before this revolt, and they must have been horrified and chagrined at the fate of their former ally against Philip.[108] While Alexander campaigned in Asia and destroyed the Persian empire, the Athenians watched passively as the Spartan king Agis III attempted to unite a Greek force against the Macedonian overlords.[109] After Agis's revolt failed (331–330), neither Sparta nor Thebes was capable of offering any viable support when Athens itself chose the moment of Alexander's untimely death to attempt to break away from Macedonian control. The resulting Lamian War (323–322) ended in Athenian failure. Demosthenes took his own life, and Athens fell under the power of a Macedonian-backed oligarchy. In the same year (322), classical Athenian democracy and independent Athenian government both ended.[110]

TWO

Democracy and Demagogues
Election, Voting, and Qualifications for Citizenship

But I consider it right as a citizen to set the welfare
of the state above the popularity of an orator. Indeed,
I am given to understand—and so perhaps are you—
that the orators of past generations, always praised but
not always imitated by those who address you, adopted this
very standard and principle of statesmanship. I refer to the
famous Aristides, to Nicias, to my own namesake, and to
Pericles. But ever since this breed of orators appeared who
ply you with such questions as "What would you like?
What shall I propose? How can I oblige you?" the
interests of the state have been frittered away
for a momentary popularity. The natural
consequences follow, and the orators
profit by your disgrace.

DEMOSTHENES 3.21–22
trans. J. H. Vince

We must realize that it is very hard to save a
civilization when its hour has come to fall beneath
the power of demagogues. For the demagogue has been
the great strangler of civilization. Both Greek and Roman
civilizations fell at the hands of this loathsome creature who
brought from Macaulay the remark that "in every century
the vilest examples of human nature have been among
the demagogues." But a man is not a demagogue simply
because he stands up and shouts at the crowd. There are
times when this can be a hallowed office. The real
demagogy of the demagogue is in his mind and is
rooted in his irresponsibility towards the ideas

that he handles—ideas not of his own creation,
but which he has only taken over from their
true creators. Demagogy is a form of
intellectual degeneration.

JOSÉ ORTEGA Y GASSET
History as a System, *trans. Helene Weyl*

"The will of the nation" is one of the phrases most
generally abused by intriguers and despots of every age.

ALEXIS DE TOCQUEVILLE
Democracy in America, *trans. George Lawrence*

IN THIS CHAPTER, I SEEK to test the modern democratic faith in election, voting, and low qualifications for citizenship.[1] Analysis of the Athenians' practices in these areas will demonstrate the negative impact of their reduction of property qualifications for full citizenship and of their use of the vote to determine policy, while outlining the positive effects of continued noneconomic qualifications for citizenship. An examination of Pericles' career will illustrate the benefits and dangers of charismatic leadership in an environment of popular rule. I hope to suggest that the vote—especially in an environment with few social restraints or civic responsibilities—represents a threat to, as much as an instrument of, justice.[2]

The vote has not always served as the defining feature of democracy. As strange as it may seem to moderns, Aristotle considered election to be an oligarchic or aristocratic element in government.[3] As Aristotle noticed, even in regimes with no property qualifications for citizenship or office, wealthier citizens tend to dominate elected positions. The philosopher thus identified democracy not with the act of voting but rather with popular control of the courts, the absence of a property qualification for citizenship, the use of the lottery to fill public offices, and the rule of the poor in their own interests.[4] Nor was Aristotle's view completely idiosyncratic. Since even nondemocratic classical Greek poleis used votes by the citizen body to select at least some important officials or to determine policy, the Greeks understandably did not see voting itself as a defining quality of *demokratia*.

Nevertheless, most moderns consider the casting of ballots in free elections the defining element of democratic government, and the Athenians did make policy and choose fellow citizens for particular state offices through votes in an assembly open to all citizens. Analysis of their electoral practices thus offers us a potential analogue for modern regimes.

Perhaps most important, the Athenians elected ten men annually to hold the office of *strategos*. These *strategoi* were Athens's highest military officials, acting as generals on land and admirals at sea and wielding significant political power in the city during the fifth century. Of course, successful military leaders have always had the opportunity to exert political influence, regardless of the type of government they have served. But in Athens, the close connection between Athens's empire and its democracy's funding, as well as the people's direct role in managing the empire, offered great scope for the elected *strategoi*. The political aspect of the generalship was emphasized and developed by statesmen like Pericles, who held the office for fifteen consecutive years.[5]

By Athenian reckoning, Pericles held not only the official position of *strategos,* but also the informal place of *rhetor* (political orator), making proposals in the council and assembly and thus acting as what the Athenians would later call a *demagogos* (plural *demagogoi*), literally a "leader of the demos." The Athenians initially seem to have used the term *demagogos* without pejorative intent, and it has been well said that the so-called demagogues served a necessary function in the Athenian regime.[6] Such men served not merely as the voices of various political interests but also as remarkably free critics of the very populace they sought to influence. That is, the best *demagogoi* attempted *to change* popular opinion and thus, as Thucydides puts it in his praise of Pericles, to lead the people "rather than to be led by them" (2.65). Indeed, since the term *demagogos* explicitly denotes someone who leads or shepherds the demos, the eventual use of this word as the primary epithet for a political panderer represents a virtual reversal of its original meaning.[7] The word *demagogos* in fact implies that the people need someone to lead them and that political power, at least in part, is exercised appropriately through this leadership.

As early as Pericles' day, some Athenians apparently expressed or implied reservations about allowing a citizen body including even those without property to choose Athens's leaders and make policy via votes in the assembly.[8] Although justifiable as a way of permitting all citizens to participate in their government, such a practice obviously enabled the poorer citizens to empower leaders who had improperly ingratiated themselves with them, placing the interests of a faction above those of the polis as a whole.[9] The latent dangers in allowing greater participation to those without property began to emerge after Pericles proposed that Athens begin to pay citizens for jury duty.[10] These payments led to others: if jurors deserved daily payment, why not members of the Council of 500 or those holding other magistracies?[11]

After the mid fifth century, payment for public service served as a fundamental and defining characteristic of Athenian democracy.[12] In the years following Pericles' innovation, it undoubtedly became increasingly difficult for a leader opposed to this use of public money to win out over Pericles and his supporters. Although many Athenians were willing to consider ending payment for public service beyond the military (at least temporarily) as late as 411,[13] after the Peloponnesian War and the discredited oligarchic regimes of 411 and 404 (which had curtailed state pay), only proposals to increase public payments seem to have had political viability in Athens.

That these conditions encouraged the rise of what we call "demagogues" is entirely comprehensible. In an environment where a public figure can help secure his own election to office or the success of his legislation by proposing the distribution of more public money to a large enough portion of the electorate, and where there is no strong feeling among the populace that such a distribution is shameful or morally wrong, leaders proposing increased payments possess a tremendous advantage over their opponents.[14] Nevertheless, Athenian government did not collapse immediately after the institution of public payments, nor did the Athenians immediately vote themselves into public bankruptcy. Indeed, not until the 420s do we begin to see evidence of the potentially harmful effects of these practices.

Several factors in Athenian society and government apparently slowed the debilitation of the people's morale through political pandering. Since we know of no laws restricting the Athenians' actions in this area, informal social constraints (deriving from the Athenians' ideas about the propriety of distributing public money) apparently limited both the extent to which the people would support leaders seeking to ingratiate themselves by distributing public funds and the number of leaders attempting such ingratiation. In addition, the fact that the office of *strategos* was a burdensome and life-threatening position probably helped diminish the rate at which mainly self-interested individuals became powerful political voices in Athens: *strategoi* gained political power or glory while literally risking life and status, both of which could be lost at the hands of the enemy (in battle) or the Athenian demos (in court or through ostracism). Finally, the system of selection by lottery for members of the Council of 500 and other officials (like the treasurers of the sacred funds) provided a potentially significant check on the dangers of demagoguery. That is, many important Athenian offices simply were not filled by election, but instead relied on individuals chosen by lot serving their fellow citizens for short periods of time.[15] Despite these checks, our sources indicate that "leaders of the demos" after Pericles increasingly pandered to the electorate and (unlike Pericles and some others) often told the people only what they wanted to hear.[16]

The election of leaders represents only one of the important votes cast by members of the Athenian assembly. As we have noted, the citizen assembly also acted as a court, policy-making body, and sovereign legislature, limited in authority (until the late fifth century) only by itself and deciding the most important issues of the state, including issues of war and peace. Under this system, to vote was to rule one's neighbor in a very direct and public fashion. By raising his hand in the assembly, a citizen openly demonstrated his own desire to make war or peace, to tax other men's property, to impose rules on his fellow citizens, or to elect a corrupt person to office. But again, most Greek city-states had citizen assemblies or councils in which members of the citizen body voted on at least some important matters. What made Athens's system odd was its payments for public service and its low property requirements for full citizenship, both of which encouraged greater participation by the common people in political decision-making and administration.

QUALIFICATIONS FOR CITIZENSHIP

Most Greek poleis in the classical period seem to have had property qualifications for full citizenship. These qualifications apparently tended to coincide roughly with the amount of property necessary to enable someone to provide his own weapons and thus serve in the citizen militia of hoplites. Similar property qualifications were also common in the United States, even after the Revolution and the ratification of the Constitution.[17] Thus economic limitations on full participation in the political life of a regime are not inconsistent either with the ancient Greek ideals of *eleutheria* and *isonomia* ("liberty" and "equality of the law") or with the principles embodied in the American Constitution.

Nevertheless, by the 450s the Athenians had removed all but the most nominal economic restrictions on free Athenian males for full (or almost full) participation in political life. Athenians of the lowest property class, the *thetes*, could vote in the assembly and (probably) serve on the Council of 500. And although the property qualification for the office of archon remained at the approximate level of the hoplite-farmers (the *zeugitai*) after 457, Aristotle suggests that in the fourth century this restriction was not enforced.[18] Thus by the mid fifth century even the poorest free Athenian males could vote, and by the end of the century they could hold most of the major public offices in the polis.[19]

The Athenians' removal of property qualifications for citizenship might encourage us to analogize citizenship in democratic Athens and citizenship in modern democratic regimes, in which property qualifications long ago passed out of use. But this analogy is very misleading, first, because moderns tend to associate citizenship primarily with the rights and privileges this status guarantees rather than with the qualifications it requires or the duties it implies. Moreover, many of these protections for citizens (e.g., the right to own property and the protection of one's person or free speech) are thought to be virtually universal "human rights" that do not—or, rather, should not—depend on a particular form of regime or on a distinction between citizens and resident aliens. (Neither, of course, do they sanction a class of slaves living alongside citizens, as in ancient Athens.) Thus many Americans value their citizenship because it ostensibly ensures rights they believe are due to everyone, and not because the duties they perform as citizens entitle them to privileges that distinguish them from other persons. The analogy between ancient and modern democratic citizenship also fails because, despite the lack of a property qualification in classical Athens, Athenian citizenship—unlike its modern American counterpart—did entail very real obligations and requirements.[20]

First, after Pericles' citizenship law of 451/0, all Athenian citizens were required to be sons of free Athenian parents; neither parent could be a foreigner or a slave.[21] Young men were presented to their fellow deme members for enrollment on the citizen list at the age of eighteen. The demesmen voted under oath, confirming both that the prospective citizen had reached the legal age and that he had been born "in accordance with the laws," apparently a reference to the parents' citizenship.[22] The Athenians obviously took these hereditary requirements for citizenship very seriously, since the attempt to pass off an ineligible individual as a citizen seems to have resulted in the city selling the impostor into slavery.[23]

Having been enrolled as a citizen on his deme's register, the eighteen-year-old Athenian entered a two-year period of state service known as the *ephebeia*. The young "ephebes" received military training and acted as a kind of home guard for the polis. During this period they received a stipend from the city and were immune from prosecution, "so that there might be no reason to leave their duties."[24] Scholars are uncertain when the formal system of *ephebeia* began in Athens, although very young and very old citizens had acted as a home guard since at least the mid fifth century (see, e.g., Thuc.

2.13).[25] In any case, the formal system existed by the mid fourth century, and it followed a long-standing tradition of mandatory military service by young citizens. However, we should note that scholars disagree about whether the members of the lowest property class in Athens (the *thetes*) were required or allowed to participate in the *ephebeia,* which consisted largely of training for the (traditionally middle-class) hoplite infantry.[26]

All the ephebes swore an oath, which has come down to us in various ancient sources:

> I shall not disgrace the sacred weapons (that I bear) nor shall I desert the comrade at my side, wherever I stand in the line. And I shall fight in defense of things sacred and non-sacred and I shall not hand down (to my descendants) a lessened fatherland, but one that is increased in size and strength both as far as [it] lies within me [to do this] and with the assistance of all, and I shall be obedient to those who on any occasion are governing prudently and to the laws that are established and any that in the future may be established prudently. If anyone tries to destroy (them), I shall resist both as far as [it] lies within me [to do this] and with the assistance of all, and I shall honor the sacred rites that are ancestral. The witnesses (are) the gods, Aglauros, Hestia, Enyo, Enyalios, Ares and Athena Areia, Zeus, Thallo, Auxo, Hegemone, Herakles, (and) the boundaries of my fatherland, the wheat, the barley, the vines, the olives, the figs.[27]

Along with the citizen's sworn duty to protect the laws, the military and religious aspects of the oath are striking, in particular the promise to pass on to one's descendants a fatherland "increased in size and strength." The oath also nicely demonstrates the way social, military, and religious issues came together in the lives of Athenian citizens, who were expected to perform duties in each of these areas throughout their lives.[28]

The Athenian citizen's liability for military service did not end after his two-year stint as an ephebe. All citizens could be called up for service until about the age of sixty.[29] The citizens' continuing duties in this area (and others) are emphasized in the questions asked of prospective candidates for the Athenian office of archon, a position filled by lot after 487:

> When [the members of the Council of 500] are checking qualifications [for archonship], they ask first: "Who is your father, and what is your deme? Who was your father's father, and who was your mother, and her father and his deme?" Then they ask whether the candidate is enrolled in a cult of Apollo Patroos and Zeus Herkeios, and where the shrines are, then whether he has family tombs and where they are; whether he treats his parents well, pays his taxes, and has

gone on military campaign when required. When these questions have been asked, the candidate is required to call witnesses to his answers.[30]

All prospective Athenian officials, whether chosen by election or by lot, faced the same or similar questions before either the Council of 500 or a regular Athenian court. This vetting process *(dokimasia)* served to test the candidate's formal qualifications and personal conduct, not his supposed technical competence for a particular office.[31] Any citizen could make accusations against a candidate during the *dokimasia,* and such accusations could result in the candidate's rejection (by vote) before the examining body. Rejections may have been rare; we know of only a few cases from the classical period.[32] But even if candidates rarely failed to pass their examinations, the questions put to hundreds of Athenians each year by their fellow citizens made a strong public statement about the values of the demos and the duties expected of each Athenian.

Every Athenian citizen faced obligations that included military service, participation in the religious life of the polis, and taking care of his parents. But beyond these positive duties, citizens also risked the imposition of fines, loss of citizen privileges (a penalty called *atimia*), banishment, and even death if they violated certain formal or informal standards of conduct set by the polis. In the political arena, fifth-century Athenian political leaders who fell afoul of the demos for any reason could be ostracized, and many of the best-known Athenian statesmen endured this punishment.[33] In the fourth century, fines, *atimia,* and the death penalty seemingly increased in frequency and replaced ostracism as the punishment for failed or unpopular political or military leaders.[34]

Citizens were also expected to meet certain standards of private conduct. In particular, "an Athenian who prostituted himself or caused another to prostitute himself was punished with death or *atimia*."[35] The seduction of a free woman could result in severe penalties including the seducer's summary execution by the woman's relative (if the man was caught in the act), physical torture, or a fine. Seduced women themselves had to be divorced by their husbands and were excluded from civic religious functions.[36] Failure to care for aged parents, to give them appropriate funerals, or to maintain the cult at their graves after death also incurred the penalty of *atimia.* A citizen who squandered his inheritance was liable for the same penalty.[37] Any citizen, moreover, who committed an act of overweening arrogance *(hybris)* against another individual—a provision that included but was not limited to dishonoring him in some way—became liable for prosecution.[38]

By these means, citizen status at Athens was tied directly and closely to very real hereditary requirements, as well as to a set of public and private obligations imposed by other citizens. In return for fulfilling these obligations, the Athenian citizens enjoyed the opportunity not only to vote in the assembly, but also to serve in office as magistrates, other officials, or members of the Council of 500, and to earn pay as public officials or as jurors on the large Athenian courts. In the fourth century, they could also receive pay for attending the assembly and (eventually) even a subsidy for the cost of their theater admission. By that time, disabled citizens were also eligible to receive a small pension, while the orphaned sons of those who died in battle had been brought up at public expense since the fifth century. Citizens obviously could own property in Attica, although foreigners could not (unless they received special dispensation from the polis). Certain crimes received harsher punishments if committed against citizens than if they were committed against metics or slaves. Citizens could not be beaten or tortured, although slaves could be flogged and both metics and slaves were subject to torture. In fact, a slave's testimony had to be obtained under torture before it became admissible in an Athenian court.[39]

In contrast to citizen rights in modern America, the privileges of citizenship in ancient Athens carried with them serious responsibilities and duties. Before the mid fourth century, these duties meant that most Athenian men at least occasionally risked their lives in military service. Athenians also expected their fellow citizens to maintain standards of personal conduct in order to retain their privileged status, and they could withhold privileges (such as office-holding) or impose punishments for failure to meet these expectations. Obviously, therefore, Athens's removal of property qualifications for citizenship does not indicate that the Athenians set no standards for participation in the sociopolitical life of the polis. The citizens of Athens continued to perform public and private duties and meet standards of personal conduct in exchange for their citizenship throughout classical Athenian history.

DID THE DEMOS RULE WELL?

Although the Athenians continued to insist on personal qualifications for citizenship, they did remove most economic restrictions on participation in the polis's government. Those without property could participate in the Athenian assembly and sit on Athenian juries.

Many Athenians apparently had confidence in the poorer citizens' ability to rule wisely through voting. Pericles claimed that the common members of Athens's electorate—the whole demos—were "not insufficiently knowledgeable" in public affairs and that all Athenians were "able either to originate or, at least, to judge policies astutely" (Thuc. 2.40).[40] Indeed, the principle that all men received justice *(dike)* in equal shares from the gods and thus could act as "capable judges" in public matters (including trials) seems to have been one of the ideas used to justify democratic government.[41] But does an evaluation of classical Athenian history bear out this proposition? Did the Athenian citizens in assembly tend to make just or wise decisions about ruling themselves and others? Surely any honest critique of democracy must confront this basic question: do the people rule well?

The major events of Athenian history are rarely examined as expressions of the Athenians' electoral justice, wisdom, or skill. Perhaps this stems from the fact that, if one treats Athens's actions as the results of ballots cast by a free people in assembly, Athenian history makes a poor argument for popular rule. Athens's history under *demokratia* shows the Athenian people voting repeatedly to make war on their former friends and allies (as well as enemies), to conclude alliances with their recent enemies or with Greeks that had collaborated with Persia, to execute or exile their own leaders, to extort monetary payments from allied states that wished to be free of Athenian hegemony, to use this extorted money to fund Athenian projects (including the extortion of more money), to impose their own form of government on formerly autonomous states by force, to execute and enslave thousands of non-Athenian Greeks, to invade foreign states with massive force in order to expand Athenian power, to usurp or undercut taxes formerly paid by foreign citizens to their own states, to require religious oaths of loyalty from their allies, to refuse requests for assistance from allied states or to send only token or mercenary forces to these allies, to continue and even increase state payments to themselves in the face of pressing need elsewhere, to refuse to help other Greek states resist Macedonian hegemony, and to grant honors to the very dynasts who imperiled their form of government. All this, again, resulted from majority votes in the Athenian assembly.

Of course, we may attempt to balance these expressions of the popular will by juxtaposing them with the Athenian votes to send aid to the Ionian Greeks during their revolt from Persia (499), to stand against the Persians at Marathon and Salamis (490, 480), to crush the Persian forces in southern Asia Minor at the Eurymedon (ca. 466), to assist their Spartan allies during a helot revolt (462/1), to reestablish *demokratia* (in 410), to stand (at last) against Philip of Macedon (in 339/8), and to honor citizens, foreigners, or other states that had done good services for Athens. But it would certainly be difficult to construct a list of praiseworthy or wise Athenian votes in the classical period that could rival in number those ballots that to many moderns (and at least some ancient Greeks) have seemed unjust, belligerent, or simply foolish. Moreover, most of the Athenian assembly's more admirable decisions appear very early in the period of *demokratia,* before the radicalization of the regime in the late 460s. After that time, very few votes of the demos reflect anything but a rather narrow view of Athens's (or rather, individual Athenians') self-interest.[42] In fact, after the vote in 462/1 to assist Sparta during the helot revolt, we rarely see the Athenians voting to support policies that could not be painted as profitable for the citizens or the city.

Let us remind ourselves once again of certain specific decisions taken by the Athenians in assembly in the early years of *demokratia.* Shortly after Cleisthenes' reforms, the Athenians rejected an alliance with Persia.[43] Athens remained independent of Persian control thereafter, the citizens voting to send aid to Ionian Greeks revolting from Persia in 499 and then electing to resist Persian invasions of mainland Greece in 490 and 480–479.[44]

With the creation of the Delian League in 478/7, the Athenians entered a new period, in which their assembly was called upon repeatedly to make decisions about their empire and the fate of non-Athenian Greeks and others encountering Athens's power. Scholars differ on the extent to which the Athenian assembly governed the alliance in its early years. Thucydides reports that the league had its own congresses (1.96), and thus the allies presumably had some say in league affairs in the years just after 478/7.

However, by the mid 460s, the Athenians were voting to use force to prevent their former allies from withdrawing from the league. This continued even after their victory over the Persians at the Eurymedon in Asia Minor ca. 466, when the Persians ceased to be a real threat in the Aegean. As a tangible sign of this, in the year 462/1, the Athenians "released their alliance [with Sparta] against the Persians" and elected to make treaties with the friends of Persia and enemies of Sparta (Argos and Thessaly).[45]

This year 462/1 was epochal in several ways, for it also marked one of the last times the Athenians voted to send a major force to assist an ally without any real expectations of increased Athenian power or profit. The Spartans had endured a damaging earthquake several years before this and had been attempting to put down a helot revolt ever since. The Athenian general Cimon persuaded the assembly to send a large hoplite force to assist the Spartans. But (apparently) after Cimon and his infantrymen had left the city, his political enemy Ephialtes passed revolutionary measures in the assembly that, among other things, restricted the powers of the conservative Areopagus Council. Learning of this revolution and (probably) of Athenian negotiations with the Argives, the Spartans dismissed their friend Cimon.[46] The general returned to Athens, where the Athenians now voted to ostracize him. Whatever Ephialtes had done (combined with Cimon's abortive mission to Sparta) had created sufficient support for the new regime to produce the exile of Athens's greatest leader after the Persian Wars.[47]

With Athens now exerting force to retain its current allies and rejecting its previous alliance with Sparta in favor of the medizing Argives and Thessalians, the members of the Delian League by the late 460s undoubtedly recognized that this "alliance" had become a tool of Athenian power rather than a weapon against the Persians. As if to underscore this fact, in 454/3, the Athenians voted to transfer the league treasury from the island of Delos to Athens, and they subsequently voted to use this money for Athenian projects like the building program on the acropolis.[48] At least one prominent Athenian, Cimon's relative Thucydides son of Melesias, seems to have opposed Pericles' program of spending the allies' money in this way. But the Athenian demos voted to ostracize him too (ca. 444/3) and continued to support expenditures for buildings for Athens and payments for themselves as jurors.[49]

Around the same time that the Athenians instituted jury payments— probably in the late 450s[50]—Pericles also persuaded them (in 451/0) to vote to limit Athenian citizenship to those whose mothers and fathers were both Athenian.[51] The increasing benefits of citizenship were thereby restricted to "native" Athenians, and aristocrats were forced to seek marriages inside the city rather than making inter-polis alliances of the kind that were common among their class.[52]

Once we come to the 440s, we reach the period of Pericles' clear dominance of the Athenian political scene.[53] Although we know of only a few particular decrees proposed by the statesman after the citizenship law of 451/0, his name or influence is associated with many of Athens's most famous or infamous acts in this period.[54] We also know the names of some of the other Athenian leaders who made significant proposals before the people in this period, because they are included as part of the prescript of the Athenian inscriptions that record the assembly's decrees. Virtually all these documents begin with the same basic formula:

> Resolved by the Council [of 500] and the demos [in assembly]: X was the tribe in prytany, X was the secretary [of the Council of 500], X presided [over the assembly], and X made the motion [here recorded].[55]

Although the dates of many of these inscriptions remain controversial, there is general agreement that at least some of them go back to the 440s (and earlier), and that they thus reflect the period of Periclean leadership in Athens.[56] Given the popular association of Pericles and Athens with the ideals of humanism and democracy, these documents would seem particularly troubling. For in them we have recorded on stone not the dictates of an emperor or tyrant to his subjects but rather the decrees of a free people in assembly, an assembly including (if not dominated by) the poorest members of Athenian society.

It is rarely emphasized that each inscription records an actual vote of the Athenian people: that is, each directly reflects the Athenian popular will (or rather the will of the majority present at a given meeting of the assembly). Each of these documents thus presents a snapshot of the Athenian electorate, and the image preserved is often less than flattering. From one of the earliest examples of Athenian rule (and several that follow), we see that the Athenians voted to impose their own form of government on other Greek states, to install garrisons in other cities, and to require particular religious sacrifices of their subjects.[57] The Athenian demos also voted to create colonies on foreign soil and to send out Athenian settlers to occupy lands formerly owned by others.[58] In their assembly, the Athenians voted to reduce their revolted allies and to force them to swear oaths of loyalty to the Athenian demos, and sometimes even to swear "to love the demos of the Athenians."[59] A majority of the Athenians decided that certain legal disputes involving Athenians and their subjects should be heard in Athens by Athenian jurors, rather than locally, where non-Athenians would make decisions.[60] The demos threatened and imposed fines and other punishments on foreign allies and on Athenian officials who failed to fulfill their duties.[61] Indeed, it would seem that the Athenian demos voted to threaten and punish their fellow citizens (with fines, exile, execution) as frequently as their foreign subjects.

Athenian hegemony and imperialism—whatever we think of them—flourished in the environment created by democratic government. At the same time that the Athenians were voting to impose their form of government on and exact tribute payments from formerly autonomous regimes, they were voting to pay themselves from public funds and erect fabulous new buildings.[62] Of course, the people who cast their votes are only one side of this equation. The options that they have are partially restricted by the leaders they support, and thus an examination of the most famous and admired of Athens's democratic leaders would seem in order.

Pericles casts a long shadow. Undoubtedly the most important figure in the history of Athenian democracy, he nonetheless suffers from mythologization similar to that which has colored modern Americans' opinions about George Washington and Abraham Lincoln. The legends surrounding these men arguably shroud adequate popular appreciation of them as real human beings and political figures. The disaster of George Washington's reputation is demonstrated almost every year when I ask my students, "What did George Washington do?" The answer is immediate and disturbing: "He chopped down a cherry tree." Even the moral of the children's story ("I cannot tell a lie . . . ") has been obscured by the humorous image of young George wielding his trusty hatchet, presumably making an early start on the construction of his wooden teeth.

In reality, Washington was a complex and fascinating figure. Although he was perhaps the single man most responsible for America's victory in the Revolutionary War, Washington nevertheless rejected the pseudo-royal titles and perquisites offered by some of his contemporaries. Since he set the precedent for future presidents, Washington arguably acted as the founder of actual American *government* (as opposed to political theory). He presided over the Constitution's creation without intervening until the last day of the Congress, when his one suggestion was accepted without further debate by the previously contentious delegates. A superb horseman and charming dancer with an impressive physique, even in middle age he could throw an iron bar further than younger challengers without so much as removing his coat. Washington's real talents and achievements explode the hollow myth surviving in the popular mind and on our one-dollar bills.[63]

Like Washington, Pericles has become both larger (and smaller) than life. To moderns, he often seems a kind of disembodied or dehumanized spokesman for democratic values, transmitted to us through less than careful readings, summaries, or decontextualized quotations from Thucydides' account of Pericles' Funeral Oration. Many people know that Pericles in that address called Athens the "school of Hellas," and that he praised Athenian government and society in contrast to the Spartans' regime. Yet few authorities have emphasized the primary thrust of the speech, which is thoroughly militaristic, collectivist, and unstintingly nationalistic.[64] Behind Pericles' image in the popular mind, and at times clouding the very picture of him, are the famous buildings on the acropolis of Athens, built as part of the "Periclean" program of construction. In fact, the Parthenon and (a very small part of) Pericles' speech stand together as the most concrete modern images of ancient democracy and classical Athens.[65]

This is a strange situation. For, like Pericles' career, the Parthenon is not a testament to Athenian democracy, humanism, or liberalism, although some scholars still hold versions of this view.[66] A temple to Athens's patron deity, Athena, the building was financed in part by money the Athenians had exacted from other Greek states.[67] Its frieze depicted the Athenian festival known as the Panathenaea (i.e., sacred rites that were "All Athena" or "All Athenian").[68] Inside the impressive structure, a colossal gold and ivory statue of Athena held the image of "Victory" (Nike) in her hand, while her sandals rested on images of the myth of Pandora, who had released troubles innumerable to man.[69] The Parthenon is first and foremost a monument to Athenian power, glory, and victory over both barbarians (like the Persians) and, by implication if not direct representation, other Greeks. The building was a dedication to and housed a representation of the goddess that presided over and ensured Athenian superiority. The temple proclaims "Athena and Athens!" without so much as a hint of Panhellenism or "democratic" values. As one eminent scholar recently concluded, "To say that the Athenians built the Parthenon to worship themselves would be an exaggeration, but not a great one."[70]

Many fifth-century Greeks would have expected nothing else. After all, what would have been more bizarre than if the Athenians had actually chosen to build a temple showing Athens as merely one part (or even the leading part) of a larger Greek confederation, or making Athena merely one god within the Hellenic pantheon? Instead, Pericles and the Athenians sang their own praises and those of their goddess.[71] Some other Greeks undoubtedly did not approve of the Athenians' dominant position in the Aegean, but all understood it, and many of those who visited Athens must have admired the beauty and magnificence of Athenian art and architecture, no matter how they had been funded.

A close examination of Pericles' Funeral Oration in Thucydides reveals a monument perhaps an even more "nationalistic"—as opposed to "democratic"—than the Parthenon. After briefly dilating on Athens's open society and implicitly contrasting this with the control of individual lives putatively found in Sparta, Pericles passes quickly to the issue of Athens's power and the need for Athenian citizens, literally, to become "lovers" of the city or its power.[72] Even Pericles' famous proclamation that Athens was a school, or "education" for Greece, rests on a military foundation:

In short, I say that as a city we are an education for Hellas, and I doubt if the world can produce a man, who where he has only himself to depend upon, is equal to so many emergencies, and graced by so happy a versatility as the Athenian. And that this is no mere boast thrown out for the occasion, but plain matter of fact, *the power of the state acquired by these habits proves.* For Athens alone of her contemporaries is found when tested to be greater than her reputation, and alone gives no occasion to her assailants to blush at the antagonist by whom they have been worsted, or to her subjects to question her title by merit to rule. *Rather, the admiration of the present and succeeding ages will be ours, because we have not left our power without witness, but have shown it by mighty proofs;* and because far from needing a Homer for our panegyrist, or other of his craft whose verses might charm for the moment only for the impression which they gave to melt at the touch of fact, *we have forced every sea and land to be the highway of our daring, and everywhere, whether for evil or for good, have left imperishable monuments behind us.* Such is the Athens for which these men, in the assertion of their determination not to part with her, nobly fought and died; and well may every one of their survivors be ready to suffer in her cause. (2.41; trans. R. Crawley, adapted, with emphasis added)

Such ideas are echoed later in the last speech of Pericles presented in Thucydides' work:

Remember, too, that if your country has the greatest name in all the world, it is because she never bent before disaster, and because *she has expended more life and effort in war than any other city, and has won for herself a power greater than any hitherto known,* the memory of which will descend to the latest posterity; even if now, in obedience to the general law of decay, we should ever be forced to yield, still *it will be remembered that we held rule over more Greeks than any other Greek state, that we sustained the greatest wars against their united or separate powers, and inhabited a city unrivaled by any other in resources and magnitude.* These glories may incur the censure of the slow and unambitious; but in the breast of energy they will awake emulation, and in those who must remain without them an envious regret. *Hatred and unpopularity at the moment have fallen to the lot of all who have aspired to rule others; but where odium must be incurred, true wisdom incurs it for the highest objects.* Hatred also is short-lived; but that which makes the splendor of the present and glory of the future remains forever unforgotten. Decide, therefore, for glory then and honor now, and attain both objects by instant and zealous effort: send no heralds to Lacedaemon, and do not betray any sign of being oppressed by your present sufferings, since they whose minds are least sensitive to calamity, and whose hands are most quick to meet it, are the greatest men and the greatest communities. (2.64; trans. Crawley, adapted, with emphasis added)

Modern sensibilities recoil (or rather *should* recoil) from the naked nationalism of Pericles' orations, a nationalism that one cannot dismiss as merely empty or patriotic rhetoric. The Parthenon's symbolism and Athens's consistent drive to Aegean hegemony after the 470s confirm this aggressive sense of national superiority as a guiding principle of Athenian interaction with other states and a fundament of the Athenians' self-image.[73] In contrast, one might speculate that in introducing "democratic values" into the Funeral Oration, Pericles was making a significant innovation, asking the Athenians to conceptualize themselves in a new or unusual way.[74] But even Pericles does not allow his image of Athens as a unique or superior state to rest primarily on its democratic form of government. For Pericles, *Athens's superiority to other states stemmed from its power* and from its citizens' character—a character that had facilitated the acquisition of that power.[75]

Pericles' speeches and career thus provide important evidence of the Athenians' martial self-image and of their early efforts to conceptualize their polis—but only in part—as a state with an unusual and superior government/society *(politeia)*. Nevertheless, and despite his crucial role in the radicalization of Athenian democracy, Pericles himself has attracted relatively little scholarly attention in the past few decades. One suspects that this stems in part from his semi-mythologized character, which makes a "book about Pericles" appear to be a less than completely scholarly enterprise.[76] In fact, grappling with the problems of Pericles' biography, his political career, and his long-term influence must be central to any study of Athenian history in the second half of the fifth century.

From the work that has been attempted, Pericles has emerged as both a man of his time and a kind of aberration. Pericles' family background certainly made him unusual. His mother came from one of the most famous (and infamous) aristocratic families in Athens. This clan (the Alcmeonids) had produced the founder of Athenian *demokratia* (Cleisthenes). But it also suffered from the stigma of an apparently state-sanctioned curse incurred sometime in the late seventh century B.C., when an Alcmeonid official executed would-be revolutionaries after they had sought protection of the gods as suppliants at a sacred altar. These actions resulted in the family's expulsion from Athens and the subsequent purification of the city by a Cretan soothsayer.[77]

After this event the Athenian populace and the Alcmeonid family had a tumultuous relationship. Having secured their return from exile by the early sixth century, the family sought power by aligning themselves through marriage with the Athenian tyrant Peisistratus in the mid 500s. At the time, this must have been seen as a "popular" and antiaristocratic move, since the Peisistratid tyrants apparently sought power as champions of the people against some of the aristocrats that dominated Athens. This tactic clearly worked, because the tyrants' subsequent fall in 511/10 resulted from hostilities between the Peisistratids and certain aristocratic families and from the Spartan policy of overthrowing tyrannies, and not from any hostility toward the tyrants within the Athenian demos at large. A few years later, it was the Alcmeonid Cleisthenes—Peisistratus's former brother-in-law and the grandson of another tyrant—who managed to pass the reforms in Athens that ultimately resulted in *demokratia* (ca. 507). Obviously a connection with tyrannical government or families in no way disqualified a leader from popular support in late sixth-century Athens.[78]

But Pericles' great-uncle Cleisthenes seems to have fallen from power shortly after the reform that created *demokratia,* perhaps because his government sought Persian protection in the face of possible Spartan interference in Athenian internal affairs. (The Spartans, having removed the Peisistratid tyrants, had returned to Athens and attempted to overthrow the regime instituted by the Peisistratids' relation Cleisthenes. The Athenian people successfully resisted their attempt, but then rejected an alliance with Persia apparently supported by Cleisthenes.)[79] Later, Pericles' Alcmeonid relatives found themselves under suspicion of pro-Persian sympathies. After the battle of Marathon they were accused of collaboration with the Persian invaders, and Alcmeonids and those close to them were ostracized by vote of the Athenian demos.[80] Included in this banished group were Pericles' father, Xanthippus (who was married to an Alcmeonid), and his Alcmeonid uncle Megacles. Pericles thus spent important adolescent or early adult years during the mid to late 480s as the son of an exile, probably returning to Athens with his father only after those ostracized had been recalled in 481/0.

It has been reasonably suggested that all this left an indelible mark on Pericles' later political persona. Tainted by the religious curse on his mother's family, Pericles seemingly sought out the company of the growing number of rationalist philosophers present in Athens—men who were unlikely to treat such a stigma with anything but disdain.[81] The Spartans' role in the attack on Cleisthenes and Pericles' own dubious relations with philo-Spartan political forces in Athens (represented by Cimon and his allies) must have contributed to Pericles' virulently anti-Spartan foreign policy. His family's apparent inability to consolidate its power (or, rather, achieve supremacy) through typical aristocratic means (especially through land and cults) and their subsequent need to seek popular support—first through connections with the tyrants and then through *demokratia*—laid the groundwork for Pericles' own radicalization of the democratic regime and the demos's subsequent empowerment.[82]

About Pericles' early political career we know very few specifics. It appears likely that he entered politics somewhat late in life, perhaps fearing ostracism, given his father's experience, the curse on his mother's family, and their connections with the Peisistratids.[83] He certainly served in Athens's military in the 470s, and we know he acted as the producer *(choregos)* of Aeschylus's *Persians* in 473/2. After his restrained prosecution of Cimon in 463,[84] Pericles most probably attached himself to the faction supporting Cimon's political enemy Ephialtes. When Ephialtes seized the opportunity presented by Cimon's expedition to the Peloponnese to put through his reforms (462/1), Pericles almost certainly supported him. After Ephialtes' subsequent murder, Pericles apparently emerged as the leader of the progressive faction.[85]

Unfortunately, we confront a virtual vacuum in the sources for Pericles' career between 463 and 451/0. Aeschylus's *Eumenides* may suggest that Pericles was seen as a major force among the reformers by 459/8, the year of the play's production,[86] but there is no direct evidence of his political activities in this period. We may infer from his later policies that Pericles favored the rejection of the Athenian alliance with Sparta against Persia (Thuc. 1.102) and supported the subsequent First Peloponnesian War, which pitted Athens against Sparta and its allies (especially Corinth) ca. 460–446. It is difficult to say the same about Athens's ultimately disastrous expedition to Egypt (459–454), apparently launched to assist Egypt's attempt to break free of Persian control and (surely) also in the hope of establishing Athenian influence in the rich lands of northeastern Africa.[87] Pericles' later actions and Plutarch's testimony suggest that the statesman probably would have preferred to focus Athens's attentions on projects closer to home, foregoing the war against Persia in favor of extending Athens's Hellenic empire in the Aegean and on the Greek mainland.[88]

Pericles' desire to expand Athens's Greek holdings may also help explain the events surrounding the so-called Peace of Callias, an apparent agreement (formal or informal) between Athens and the Persian Great King Artaxerxes ca. 449 that ended Atheno-Persian hostilities in the Aegean. Pericles undoubtedly supported this agreement, which had been brought about by a renewal of active war with Persia after Cimon returned to Athens from ostracism ca. 451. In Cyprus, Cimon's forces won a major victory, which apparently brought Artaxerxes to the bargaining table, while Cimon's death allowed his political rivals like Pericles to take advantage of the situation.[89]

The Cyprus campaign suggests that Cimon briefly dominated Athenian foreign policy after his return in the late 450s; Pericles at that time apparently focused on domestic questions.[90] In 454/3, the treasury of the Delian League had been transferred to Athens, and increased expenditures on Athenian projects followed in short order.[91] As we have seen, Pericles' proposal to begin the payment of jurors from public funds probably occurred during this period, and the statesman's legislation to restrict Athenian citizenship to those with two Athenian parents in 451/0 suggests a reasonable historical context for the measure. When the benefits of Athenian citizenship were on the rise, it might seem both economically and politically expedient (from Pericles' standpoint) to limit this citizenship to those of strictly Athenian descent.[92] Since the law also effectively ended the Athenian aristocrats' practice of marrying into aristocratic non-Athenian families, it would tend to diminish any inter-polis aristocratic ties and/or feelings of "Panhellenism." We may assume that Pericles intended and welcomed both results.[93]

The peace with Persia ca. 449 allowed Pericles and the Athenians to turn their attentions fully to Greece itself. Unfortunately for Athens, the peace also confirmed the allies' fears that tribute payment to Athens and Athenian domination of the Aegean were ultimately unrelated to any continuing war against Persia. Apparently, some states demonstrated resistance or revolted, and the Athenians resorted to force to keep the "alliance" together.[94] Meanwhile, Athenian gains in central Greece were challenged by renewed hostilities with Sparta and a Boeotian coalition led by Thebes (448/7–447/6). When cities on the great island of Euboea also revolted, Pericles led a force there to reduce the poleis, only to learn that Megara had now revolted and murdered its Athenian garrison, opening the isthmus to a Peloponnesian invasion of Attica.[95] According to one tradition, Pericles solved the Spartan problem by bribing the advisers of the Spartan king Pleistoanax, who then failed to attack Athens and was himself forced to leave Sparta.[96] Nevertheless, the Athenians' loss to the Boeotians at Coronea in 447/6 signaled the end of Athens's land empire in central Greece, and, combined with the troubles in Euboea and elsewhere in the empire, led to a peace treaty with Sparta in 446/5 that was intended to last for thirty years.[97]

Despite the limited success of his presumed foreign policy initiatives in the early to mid 440s, Pericles enjoyed increasing influence in Athenian domestic affairs. Work on the Parthenon began in 447/6, and the Periclean building program as a whole poured large sums of money into Athenian pockets and Athens's economy.[98] Pericles' opponents apparently raised objections to the use of the funds paid by the members of the Delian League for such expenditures, but the program was obviously lucrative for the Athenian portion of the builders, artists, and workers involved, and thus popular. After the demos finally ostracized Pericles' chief political rival and opponent of the program, Thucydides son of Melesias,[99] Pericles began his impressive run of fifteen consecutive years (444/3–429/8) as one of Athens's elected *strategoi*.[100]

Pericles supported, participated in, and probably proposed Athens's intervention in the conflict between its allies Samos and Miletus in 441.[101] Having taken the Milesians' side, the Athenians ultimately voted to impose a democracy and a garrison on Samos and took Samian hostages. When the Samians balked, and some of their anti-Athenian exiles sought the assistance of a Persian satrap, the Athenians besieged the city for nine months before reducing it and then executing many Samian opponents of Athens's actions (440–439).[102]

A faction in Athens clearly resented the brutal Athenian treatment of an ancient and powerful ally like Samos, and Pericles seems to have endured some criticism over his policy.[103] However, the statesman's enemies only succeeded in slandering Pericles' consort Aspasia and possibly indicting, exiling, or ostracizing one or more of his associates.[104] Meanwhile, contemporary jibes at Pericles and his associates may have been responsible for the decree the Athenians apparently passed in 440/39 prohibiting the comic abuse of individuals.[105] This measure, repealed in 437/6, and numerous fragments of lost comedies suggest that Pericles and his associates served as frequent butts of the comedians' jokes. (A favorite topic was the size and shape of Pericles' head, which was said to resemble a sea-onion, and which one poet claimed was large enough to hold "eleven couches.")[106] If comic poets' attacks on Pericles precipitated the measure, the decree nonetheless shows that Pericles could still muster real support in the assembly.[107] And the fact that the Samian War did not do any lasting harm to Pericles' overall popularity with the demos may be suggested by the fact that he was chosen to deliver a funeral oration for the Athenians who died in the war.[108]

Pericles' arguably greatest political success occurred in the late 430s, when he persuaded the Athenian populace to refuse all concessions to the Peloponnesians (thus bringing on the Peloponnesian War in 431) and then persuaded the hoplite-farmers of Attica to move inside the city walls and allow their lands to be ravaged by Spartan invaders.[109] Even after the war continued into its second year and the Athenians were suffering from a devastating plague, Pericles continued to support the conflict and the Athenian dominance that he seemingly believed it would ensure, albeit in the face of great popular opposition. Although the demos fined Pericles and apparently removed him from office in this year (430/29), the Athenians subsequently re-elected him. Pericles once more was serving as *strategos* when he died (probably from the plague) in 429/8.[110]

Pericles' political convictions and even the particular program he pursued as a result of those convictions—including peace (or at least détente) with Persia, imperial expansion into mainland Greece and tightened controls on the allies (all actions that risked hostilities with Sparta and its allies), and payments made to poorer Athenians in return for their participation in public service—seem comprehensible, if not predictable, given his family background and personal history. But it is less easy to explain the kind of abstraction that appears in Pericles' thoughts about Athens in the speeches Thucydides attributes to him. That Thucydides has colored these addresses with his own language and thought cannot be doubted, but the historian—who expresses his admiration of Pericles' political character in glowing terms—is unlikely to have invented the basic thoughts contained in these orations.[111]

While many have studied or cited limited sections of these speeches as examples of "democratic" values, the orations as a whole have rarely been examined carefully as documents of Pericles' thought (in part because of the question of Thucydides' involvement in their composition). But at worst they represent what Thucydides thought people would believe Pericles had said or might have said, and they are therefore, even on the minimalist view, the reflection of an acute contemporary observer's opinions about Pericles' ideas.

What these orations show, beyond a rhetorical brilliance that surely stems from Pericles at least as much as Thucydides,[112] is a fervent nationalism based on an intense belief in Athenian superiority—or rather, the belief that Athens could be superior given the right actions. The Athenians, in Pericles' view, needed to accept his belief both in the superiority of the state to the individual and in the related moral value of public service and its ability literally to act "as a cloak to cover a man's other imperfections."[113] Such ideas stood in stark contrast both to the older aristocratic ideal of individual *arete*—manly excellence exhibited to assert individual superiority and to gain the honor and rewards *(time)* such superiority produced—and to the newer Socratic conception of excellence, which emphasized individual ethics.[114]

Of course, the ideal of civic responsibility and public service was hardly unknown to fifth-century Athenians. Indeed, I have suggested that it permeated every aspect of Athenian society. But Pericles seemingly had taken this concept—ultimately based on utility, community of religious and other sentiments, and natural patriotism—and developed it into a fervent nationalism designed to underpin Athenian power and superiority and ensure Athens's place in history. That is, Pericles' abstract ideal looks toward Athens's future reputation even more than to its present situation or its inherited past. It is, therefore, explicitly *not* a utilitarian or moral view of duty and service. As Pericles states in Thucydides, "even if now, in obedience to the general law of decay, we should ever be forced to yield, still it will be remembered that we held rule over more Greeks than any other Greek state" (2.64). These views, perhaps less than remarkable in modern societies, which are focused on the future and thus obsessed with "progress" and creating a better world "for our children," made Pericles a very unusual thinker for fifth-century Greece.[115]

In short, Pericles apparently believed that individual Athenians' contemplation of their state's future reputation (as opposed to their own personal safety or honor) actually should comfort citizens suffering from the loss of their children and bolster their morale in the face of a war now aggravated by the outbreak of a deadly plague. Yet the statesman perhaps somewhat overestimated the Athenians' willingness to sacrifice themselves for the sake of history, since the people eventually fined him. Nevertheless, taken as a whole, Pericles' career demonstrates his ability to sell his conception of Athens to the demos. As Thucydides put it, Pericles was able to lead the people, and thus to persuade them to take unpopular actions.

> Pericles indeed, by his rank, ability, and known integrity, was enabled to exercise an independent control over the multitude—in short, to lead them instead of being led by them; for as he never sought power by improper means, he was never compelled to flatter them, but, on the contrary, enjoyed so high an estimation that he could afford to anger them by contradiction. Whenever he saw them unseasonably and insolently elated, he would with a word reduce them to alarm; on the other hand, if they fell victims to a panic, he could at once restore them to confidence. In short, what was nominally a democracy became in his hands government by the first citizen. With his successors it was different. More on a level with one another, and each grasping at supremacy, they ended by committing even the conduct of state affairs to the whims of the multitude. This, as might have been expected in a great and sovereign state, produced a host of blunders. (2.65; trans. Crawley)[116]

In Thucydides' opinion, Pericles' accomplishments, skill, and integrity separated the statesman from the demagogues who followed him—men who pandered to the demos by inciting their baser passions or by simply telling them what they wished to hear. Pericles, on the other hand, turned the populace toward policies *he* deemed appropriate, policies he honestly believed were best for Athens's present power and, especially, for the city's future reputation.

The events of Pericles' career offer manifold positive and negative lessons about political leadership in a democratic environment. His success demonstrates unequivocally that a voting populace can be led into difficult, treacherous, or simply unpopular political territory by an individual with sufficient persuasive powers and personal character—an individual who is willing to risk removal from office or the loss of power by contradicting majority opinion. But Pericles' career also shows the political advantages that can accrue to democratic leaders that promise the electorate profits, glory, and power.[117] It is surely no coincidence that Pericles' more "popular" acts—including the building program and the creation of jury pay—came in his early or middle career, while he was still establishing himself. Subsequently, Pericles became a leader able to push the citizenry into a deadly and far from universally popular war with Sparta.

Pericles' leadership should also give us pause because both his popular and his unpopular policies seem to have rested on ominous theories of the Athenian people's special destiny, theories suffused with intense nationalism and a belief in the supremacy of collective over individual morality that in turn served this nationalism. If such ideas resonated and then took hold in Athens, this may have been in part because Pericles' political actions had resulted in real economic gains for many segments of the Athenian electorate. Payment for public service and the massive building program helped earn him the basic support of the poorer members of the demos, whose service in the Athenian navy (in turn) took some military pressure off the hoplite-farmers who made up the infantry. This last group, like the sailors and even many aristocrats, also enjoyed the benefits Athens's empire brought to the city, including the markets it opened for their surplus produce and the lands it provided for their occupation.[118] Pericles' support of imperial policies like the planting of Athenian colonies around the Aegean and the collection and use of tribute from "allied" Greek states never seems to have wavered.[119] The idea that the Athenians were thereby ensuring a place in history for their city, as well as material advantages for themselves, undoubtedly encouraged the natural view that their polis was special and perhaps helped allay any fears that their empire was unjust.

If one extrapolates from the reports about Pericles' lack of sociability and his apparent unwillingness to express much basic human sympathy for the parents of Athens's dead soldiers in the Funeral Oration, at least one potential motivation for Pericles' political actions in favor of the demos disappears.[120] No evidence suggests that Pericles loved the common members of the demos (any more than he loved his fellow aristocrats) or that he sought to improve their conditions out of humanitarian concerns. Rather, in the landless mass of citizens Pericles saw an untapped source of Athenian power and the crucial support for Athenian dominance. In short, Pericles seems to have believed that it was necessary to raise the demos (even at the expense of the aristocrats) so that his policies might succeed and so that Athens might thus triumph (both then and in history).

This essentially nonpolitical goal of ensuring Athens's place in history and Pericles' own personal integrity separate him from the demagogues who came after him. Where they looked for success in the assembly or on the battlefield in order to gain power in the present, Pericles sought to make Athens powerful in order to ensure the city's future reputation. And Pericles' ideals, his integrity, and his personal charisma, combined with his ability to abstract himself and other individual Athenians from their real political environment in order to focus on Athens's position in history, made Pericles both the greatest and the most dangerous leader Athens ever produced.

If unmitigated praise for Pericles is therefore unjustified, we may pause to focus on one of his admirable qualities that stands out most starkly in the modern democratic world. Even if Pericles' proposals sometimes stemmed in part from a plan to ingratiate him with the demos at large (as a means to achieve his greater goal), the evidence we have demonstrates clearly that he occasionally spoke harshly and critically to the Athenian people. Confident in his own powers of persuasion and loyal to his own ideals, Pericles felt no compunction about telling the Athenian demos that they were wrong. "If you are angry with me," he states early in his last speech in Thucydides, when the Athenians were enduring a plague that increased the suffering caused by the Peloponnesian War, "you are angry with a man who is, as I think, second to no man either in knowledge of the proper policy or in the ability to expound it, and who is moreover not only a patriot but an honest one" (2.60; trans. Crawley, adapted). In the same speech, Pericles reminds his audience that *they* had voted for the very war for which they now wished to blame him. One is hard pressed to imagine a modern elected leader in the midst of an unpopular war or economic recession (much less a plague!) proclaiming to the electorate (in essence), "I am smart and honest; if you are angry with me, it is because you are neither smart nor honest with yourselves, since you have become fickle, while I have remained the same." Let us remember that by speaking in this way and by proposing and then supervising politically dangerous policies (like war with Sparta), Pericles risked immediate removal from office, fines, ostracism, *and even execution* by the populace he addressed. The timid modern statesman, afraid even to suggest that "the American people" might be misguided, only runs the risk of losing his bid for reelection and thus being forced to return to a lucrative position in the private sector.

Contrary to what Thucydides suggests in his summary of his career (2.65), Pericles was not the last elected Athenian leader willing to risk criticizing the populace. His successor Cleon, often seen as the prototypical demagogue (in the modern sense), apparently also upbraided the Athenian people. In a speech presented in Thucydides, Cleon abuses the citizens for their inability to rule an empire effectively and their obsession with political debates, which Cleon maintains they treat like sporting events rather than serious considerations of policy (modern journalists and pundits, who treat politics as entertaining fodder for the nightly cable television programs, should take note):

> The persons to blame [for the difficulties Athens faces in ruling her empire] are you [members of the Athenian assembly] who are so foolish as to institute these contests, who go to see an oration as you would to see a sight, take your facts on hearsay, judge of the practicality of a project by the wit of its advocates, and trust for the truth as to past events not to the fact which you saw more than to the clever strictures which you heard; the easy victims of new-fangled arguments, you are unwilling to follow received conclusions, slaves to every new paradox, despisers of the commonplace; the first wish of every man among you is that he could speak himself, the next to rival those who can speak by seeming to be quite up with their ideas by applauding every hit almost before it is made, and by being as quick in catching an argument as you are slow in foreseeing its consequences; you ask, if I may say so, for something different from the conditions under which we live, and yet you comprehend inadequately those very conditions; you are very slaves to the pleasure of the ear, and more like the audience of a professional public speaker than the council of a city. (Thuc. 3.38; trans. Crawley, adapted)

Like Pericles, Cleon here sought not to align himself with perceived popular opinion but rather to teach the people that their actions and beliefs were unwise. This attempt highlights a clear line of distinction between real political leaders and the worst kind of demagogues. And although later Athenian politicians also sometimes criticized the people, by the fourth century this criticism had become not only formulaic and hollow, but also seemingly ineffective.[121]

Of course, a populace that has been empowered politically through the vote or public payments will probably begin to have an increasingly high opinion of itself. This, we may speculate, can lead ultimately to the confirmation or even encouragement of this high opinion by politicians (who wish to gain the people's approval). This inflated self-image can also lead to unwillingness on the part of the people to hear itself criticized by those to whom it grants authority, especially if elected officials repeatedly tell the people that they (their leaders) are mere conduits for the popular will. Thus, for example, American politicians find it impossible to *lead* the people when they are constantly claiming that they seek to reflect or implement what "the American people" want.[122]

One may justifiably doubt whether a thoroughly democratized populace will frequently elect those who stand in opposition to the electorate's view of itself. This doubt points to one of the inherent dangers facing modern democratic regimes, which define and defend themselves primarily through the existence of free elections. The vote allows individuals in effect to rule their neighbors and thus makes them think of themselves as rulers. Eventually this self-image may tend to supplant other considerations when the people evaluate candidates. Those candidates who seem to assert any superiority to the people (intellectual, moral, or otherwise) become less acceptable than those who confirm what the people already think of themselves.[123]

The observation that a democratically empowered populace may begin to think too highly of itself underlines the need for a people to elect those individuals—like Pericles—who can be respected by the electors themselves. Only leaders of integrity and/or those who have accomplished significant feats in their own (nonpolitical) lives are likely to influence the populace through criticism, through telling the people that *their* views are incorrect or unjust. In short, Pericles' career and Thucydides' analysis suggest that democratic societies benefit from leaders who can command the people's personal respect and who possess the character required to risk the populace's disapproval.

The Athenians' fifth-century tendency to look to their elected military commanders for political leadership may have provided a check on the speed with which the vote could corrupt the electorate's morale. The Athenians' respect for their generals at the least reflects their implicit belief in the important connection between an individual's accomplishments, experience, and character and his ability to advise the people. In the fourth century, Athenians turned increasingly to those outside the board of generals for political leadership. Thus orators like Demosthenes, Eubulus, and Aeschines replaced generals like Themistocles, Cimon, and Pericles as the chief advisors to the Athenian demos.[124] Besides other social, political, and military factors that led to this situation, it is possible that an Athenian populace that itself became less directly involved in waging its own wars (i.e., relying more and more on mercenary troops) also became less willing to listen to those who actually participated in the often nasty business of rule. Moreover, there may be a tendency for a democratic people, again, once they have been empowered politically, to seek out not only leaders to whom they feel no collective inferiority but even leaders to whom a significant part of the people can feel superior (morally or otherwise). As the collective morale of a democratic society declines, the people may decide to sacrifice real leadership in favor of their own psychological comfort, and while it cannot be proved that this occurred in fourth-century Athens, modern experience suggests that it is a real possibility.

At the very least, Athenian history demonstrates the need for democratic politicians to be able to criticize the electorate. This necessitates that those willing to risk political defeat and those of perceived character and accomplishment hold office. As the Athenians showed, one way to help achieve this goal is to connect political leadership with onerous and dangerous duties like those required of an Athenian general. Based on the Athenians' experience, Americans may justifiably ask whether there is not a need for qualifications for political leadership beyond the age of the candidate.

Although a formal requirement of military service, volunteer work, or some other nonelectoral public service for certain elected officials might go part of the way toward addressing this issue, such a formal solution cannot instill in the electorate a desire to choose leaders of character who are willing to criticize and thus lead the people. Any such formal requirements would therefore only solve one side of the problem. Ultimately, the populace also must come to value the qualities that define real leaders. For without electing individuals it can respect and then listening to them, an electorate is likely to get precisely the caliber of leadership it deserves.

MODERN CONFUSION ABOUT ELECTION

The common Athenians' ability to cast ballots in assembly did not lead to a particularly just or peaceful regime. In fact, it would be much easier to argue the opposite—that Athens's use of the common citizens' votes to determine policy aggravated martial and nationalistic tendencies and eventually empowered individuals more interested in their own advancement than in the good of Athens or its citizens.

To the extent that moderns have seized on voting as the defining act of de-

mocracy, we have enshrined an aspect of the Athenian regime that is potentially dangerous and that the ancients themselves did not even consider particularly democratic. Because voting demands little of us, and allows us by
extension to rule our neighbor, tax his property, or limit his smoking—all
from the anonymity of the voting booth (as opposed to the public, open-air
ballots by show of hands in the Athenian assembly)—it provides both a
cheap salve to our civic conscience ("I am a dutiful citizen since I vote") and
a philosophical and moral justification for any current regime ("the people
voted for it"). Meanwhile, modern voters themselves remain free from more
onerous duties of citizenship (like military service) and avoid the difficult decisions and risk that a real choice about the form of government would entail. Since election also intensifies the tendency for citizens of a modern regime to shift the blame for any action onto "the government" or elected
officials, the vote serves conveniently to shield the electorate from both criticism and responsibility.

As we have noted, the Athenians did not use the secret ballot in their assembly. Jurors in Athenian courts, however, could disguise their votes for or
against conviction even from their fellow jurymen.[125] Is it not strange that
modern America has chosen almost the very opposite arrangement? We tend
to hide our personal preferences regarding our leaders, voting in tiny, private
booths and often considering the question "Whom did you vote for?" somewhat rude. Meanwhile, our jurors discuss their views openly among themselves (since they often seek unanimity) and, more than infrequently in major
cases, eventually appear in interviews for newspapers or television programs,
explaining why they voted for guilt or innocence. But surely the question of
a citizen's preference in an election should be a more public affair than a
juror's determination about the guilt or innocence, and thus even life or
death, of another individual. The fact that asking another citizen about his
preference in a national election could be considered impolite in fact demonstrates the extent to which the modern idealization of politics has distorted
our conception of the appropriately public and the private aspects of our
lives. Since a citizen's vote has the potential to affect the lives of all other citizens in a very real and concrete way, only *not answering* questions about one's
vote should be considered offensive.

Strangely, many Americans ostensibly put more emphasis on the act of
voting than on the issue of whom one supports. But since the purpose of voting presumably is to elect particular individuals, who will then carry out particular policies or represent particular ideas, this reverence for the very act of
voting itself seems perverse. Many Americans have apparently come to be-

lieve that the democratic "process" is more important than the "product." [126] (And is this not an idea one actually hears in numerous contexts today, where discourse and consensus are so often praised over particular decisions?) The idea that voting and free elections are the principal condition necessary for the existence of good government has become a modern dogma. A means of reaching a definable end ("voting" in order to empower individuals who are just and will do specific things) has become an end itself.

To rectify this situation, we must first ask ourselves what goal we actually seek by allowing individual citizens to vote. If, in fact, our only goal is simply voting itself, we might as well admit that the American political system has little purpose other than to ensure its own moral justification.[127] In such a situation, any immoral or unwise act—whether it is executing a great philosopher or killing civilians while making undeclared war on Serbia or Iraq—can be defended on the grounds that it reflects the results of the democratic process. Ironically, in America—because of our representative constitutional government—this may be true whether a majority of the electorate actually favors a policy or not. That is, American policies may be defended on "democratic" grounds even if they do not in truth represent the people's will.

I fully recognize that many people are not sincere when they say that "participation in the democratic process" is the most important product of elections. Such individuals almost always desire a particular end, and simply believe that the participation of a greater number of voters will ensure the victory of their camp.[128] However, one only rarely hears politicians or other interested parties say that because they believe their view represents a minority position, they actually hope *fewer people will vote*. That is, the established public faith in the process of voting compels even those who know they hold a minority view to pretend that they would like to see a high voter turnout. This fact demonstrates that participation in the act of voting irrespective of the result it might produce has become one of the fundamental professed tenets of the modern faith in democracy.[129]

Finally, those who do vote sometimes seem to consider themselves morally superior to those who do not. But it surely reflects the sad state of modern America's concept of civic duty when one is hard pressed to produce any other aspect of participation in public life beyond voting that can be equated with a moral responsibility. Even jury service, the democratic action par excellence to Aristotle, is frequently treated by Americans as an onerous imposition on one's time, to be avoided at all costs by anyone "with a life."

The modern emphasis on voting as the fundamental act of modern democracy betrays a significant difference between our conception of democratic citizens' duties and that of the Athenians. To recover the Athenian conception would require that the vote be made simply one part of a larger set of public and private duties citizens would be expected to perform. Without the controls on voting and election that Athens enjoyed—including the influence of officials chosen by lot instead of by ballot, serious and weighty requirements for citizenship, and the responsibilities and risks attaching to political leadership—modern representative democracies continually face the dangers posed by leaders who primarily seek to empower themselves by pleasing the people.

Voting obviously permits the exercise of actual political authority over one's fellow citizens and is therefore a public act of enormous consequence. It also provides unscrupulous politicians with an opportunity and means to ingratiate themselves with the electorate and thus cannot be seen as an unmitigated good for any society. Only elections resulting in officials willing to risk removal from office by criticizing the populace that elected them—in short, that result in real leaders—should be considered beneficial. To the extent that voters elect only those who will in turn hold them up to no standard of conduct, the practice of election should be seen as potentially harmful.

Modern representative governments looking to ancient Athens for lessons or examples must face up both to the need to change the electorate's opinion about the significance and effects of the act of voting and to the need to limit its deleterious effects on government and society. The ancient Athenians addressed this problem by limiting the ability to vote and the ability to lead to those members of the populace who met the collective populace's high standards for citizenship. It would thus seem obvious, if we wish to treat the Athenians' experience seriously, that we should not casually jettison such standards or warmly endorse a system that allows persons not meeting them to serve in office or to cast a ballot. Nevertheless, a better system by itself seems unlikely to solve all the problems voting presents; for whatever the historical situation, popular election would seem to tend to result in leaders who reflect the character of the functional majority of the electorate. It is, therefore, the character of that electorate, and not the particular form of government, that will always be the central "political" issue facing any people that relies on the vote.[130]

THREE

Public Finance

Democracy and the People's Purse

> . . . a democratic government is the only one in which
> those who vote for a tax can escape the obligation to pay it.
>
> ALEXIS DE TOCQUEVILLE
> Democracy in America, *trans. George Lawrence*

MOST AMERICAN POLITICIANS AND CITIZENS (of whatever political persuasion) seem to agree that the national debt and the government's frequent budget deficits threaten the economic well-being of the nation. If economists disagree about the extent to which such debt presents a significant economic problem, Americans and their leaders often *speak* as if deficit spending were potentially harmful.

This situation seems counterintuitive. For how can a people in basic agreement that there should be no, or at least less, public debt continue to support political leaders or policies that create or tolerate it? To address this question, I wish to show how certain public actions and attitudes led to Athenian overspending and public debt during the fifth century, when Athens was a very wealthy state. In the less prosperous fourth century, the Athenians refused to adapt their political regime to the realities of their fiscal condition, public morale, and foreign policy needs. The history of democratic Athens illustrates the willingness of people to vote themselves into difficult financial circumstances, even in the face of imminent threats to their national interests and security.

We are fortunate to possess significant documentation of Athens's fiscal life. By the fifth century B.C., the Athenians had begun inscribing a significant number of their public documents on stone. Many of these inscriptions treat matters related to imperial or public moneys, and thus state finance remains one of the few areas of Athenian governmental practice about which we are relatively well informed.[1]

Our sources suggest that two fundamental factors continued to influence Athenian financial practice throughout the classical period. The first was the democracy itself, which placed actual control of the state's income and expenditures in the hands of an electorate including even the poorest citizens and which required significant funds for its operation. Athenian citizens in assembly heard proposals to distribute, expend, or collect public money, and then cast their votes for or against these measures. Although most Greek city-states possessed citizen assemblies that probably passed legislation on at least some financial matters, the absence of a property qualification for voting and holding important offices and the consequent involvement of the poorer citizens in the state's fiscal management helped distinguish Athens's democracy from other Greek regimes.[2]

The second factor consistently influencing Athenian financial practices were the silver mines located in Laurium in southern Attica. By the early fifth century the Athenian demos collectively owned these mines, and the public revenues derived from this silver made Athens a very special polis.[3] None of the other major Greek powers (Corinth, Sparta, Argos, Thebes) possessed such a ready source of wealth. The famous "owls" the Athenians minted from this metal (named for the bird of Athena, which, along with the goddess herself, appeared on the coins) became one of the standard coins of the Aegean, and eventually even Persian authorities in Asia Minor imitated this coinage (see fig. 1).[4]

THE SPOILS OF BATTLE AND
THE FRUITS OF THE EARTH (483/2–431)

Athens's native silver first appears above the historical horizon in a rather odd way. Herodotus tells the story in his description of Athenian preparations before the Persian invasion of 480:

> The Athenians [in 483/2], having a large sum of money in their treasury, the produce of the mines of Laurium, were about to share it among the full-grown citizens, who would have received ten drachmas apiece, when Themistocles persuaded them to forbear the distribution, and build with the money 200 ships, to help them in their war against the Aeginetans. It was the breaking out

FIGURE 1. This Athenian silver tetradrachm (four-drachma piece) was produced ca. 450–440 B.C. and illustrates the characteristics common to Athens's famous "owl" coinage: on the obverse, helmeted Athena; on the reverse, the owl, with olive sprig and crescent moon and an abbreviation for "Athens." The silver mines in southern Attica (Laurium) and the wealth the fifth-century empire generated allowed the Athenians to issue such coins in great numbers. Photo courtesy the Wriston Art Gallery, Ottila Buerger Collection, Lawrence University, Appleton, Wis.; inv. 91.069. All rights reserved.

of the Aeginetan war which was at this time the saving of Greece, for hereby were the Athenians forced to become a maritime power. The new ships were not used for the purpose for which they had been built, but became a help to Greece in her hour of need [in 480]. And the Athenians had not only these vessels ready before the war, but they likewise set to work to build more. (Hdt. 7.144; trans. G. Rawlinson)

Here and elsewhere, Herodotus suggests that the few Greek states with mines normally distributed the wealth from this source directly to the populace. The polis's government (i.e., the citizens collectively) did not regularly retain this money as a surplus, available to be spent for public purposes. Such a distribution of mining revenues arguably reflects an archaic practice, by which the state (or, rather, the demos collectively as opposed to individual citizens) made no claim on such money.[5]

Understandably, when a society first recognizes the idea of property ownership, it will probably attach such ownership to concrete entities like individual citizens, tyrants, or deities rather than to abstractions like "the state."[6] After all, in the absence of an existing tradition of "state funds," why would any people retain the silver from mines in a *public* treasury? In sixth- and early fifth-century Athens there were few major public expenditures to fund. The expenses of government, such as they were at that time, usually fell to the lot of wealthy Athenians, who performed "works for the people" *(leitourgiai)* like the command and upkeep of an Athenian warship for one year (the trierar-chy).[7] The early Athenian army consisted of a citizen militia made up of those wealthy enough to provide their own weapons.[8] The religious observances and rituals that made up such a large part of Greek life were undoubtedly funded by wealthy Athenians and the deities involved, since the Hellenes often maintained temple treasuries to stockpile the gods' wealth.[9]

Thus when the Athenians struck a particularly rich vein of silver, the citizens naturally expected the resulting windfall to be distributed to them individually, and not stored away for some "public" need. In persuading the Athenians to forgo this distribution in order to construct a larger fleet, Themistocles probably created the first substantial public wealth in Athens. The demos itself, and not just individual citizens or deities, would now retain and employ (at least some) surplus wealth, and such money would come to play an increasingly important role in Athenian history.

The revenues of the silver mines, once they had been converted to public purposes[10] resulted in Athens immediately becoming a naval superpower. Previously maintaining a fleet of probably 70 or so warships, the Athenians now could put to sea with a fleet of almost 200.[11] This required a greater number of captains ("trierarchs") for these ships (*triereis* or "triremes"), which, with their three banks of oars also required a large number of rowers *(nautai),* about 170 for each ship (see fig. 2).[12]

Since the *nautai* most often were drawn from the ranks of the *thetes*—citizens below the middle class of the hoplite-farmer (the *zeugitai*)—it was necessary that their daily sustenance be provided by the state. Paying the rowers thus followed logically from the creation of the fleet itself (and by the mid fifth century, hoplites were also receiving a daily allowance).[13] When we add in the shipwrights, dockworkers, day laborers, and support personnel such a fleet and its harbor required, it becomes obvious that Themistocles' proposal resulted in radically new economic and social conditions in Athens. The Athenians became not only a naval people but also a people with great responsibilities of public finance. With an assembly in which both the hoplite-farmers and the *nautai* (as well as the wealthy trierarchs) cast their votes, they also became a people for whom public financial issues took on very immediate political significance.

By the time the Persian Great King Xerxes had been routed at Salamis in 480, Athens was the leading sea power in Greece. When the Spartans ap-

FIGURE 2. The Athenians dominated the Aegean sea in the fifth century by virtue of their expensive fleet of warships (*triereis*, or "triremes," named for the three banks of oarsmen on each side of the vessel). This reconstruction, called *Olympias*, was created in the 1980s to test several theories about trireme construction and performance. (See J. S. Morrison, J. F. Coates, and N. B. Rankov, *The Athenian Trireme: The History and Reconstruction of an Ancient Greek Warship* [Cambridge, 2000].) Like the ancient vessels on which it is based, this ship is approximately thirty-five meters in length and about five meters wide. It can be propelled either by 170 oarsmen or by sails (although the latter were often removed for battle in antiquity). A trireme's primary weapon was its bronze beak or ram, which was designed to pierce the hull of an enemy vessel. While common Athenians (and non-Athenians) rowed the vessels for pay, each ship was usually under the command of a well-to-do Athenian captain (the trierarch), who also paid part of the ship's upkeep costs during his year of service. Over the course of the fifth century, the Athenians not only built and maintained the largest fleet of triremes in the Greek world, but also became very skilled in the ships' employment in battle. Photo courtesy J. F. Coates and the Trireme Trust.

peared less than enthusiastic about continuing operations against the Persians in Asia Minor and the Hellespont, it probably seemed only natural that the Athenians should take over the command of what was, after all, largely a naval affair in any case. Thus in 478/7 the Delian League was formed, with Athens at its head, and this organization ultimately became the formal basis of the Athenian empire.[14]

Other Greek states in the new league agreed to supply ships or make annual monetary payments to support the alliance's actions. However, much if not most of the "tribute" they paid apparently accumulated on the island of Delos, where Athenian officials *(hellenotamiai)* took charge of the funds' management.[15] Moreover, as far as our sources allow us to gauge, the new allied fleet seemingly spent more time attacking other Greek states (some of which had sided with the Persians) and compelling the league's own members to continue supplying manpower for the fleet or paying tribute than it did making war on the Great King. By 460 the Athenians were actually at war with Corinth and Sparta, their former allies against Persia.[16] And although hostilities with Persia continued for a few more years,[17] around the year 449 the Athenians and Persians seem to have concluded some kind of agreement ending open hostilities.[18]

From a financial perspective, this peace with Persia marks an important watershed. For it removed the Athenians' last excuse for collecting tribute at around the same time that they apparently decided to use the money they had accumulated from their allies' tribute payments for their own purposes. Probably in the year 454/3, the Athenians had transferred the treasury of the Delian League from Delos to Athens and had begun to take one-sixtieth of each year's tribute off the top and dedicate the money to Athena.[19] As we have seen, at about this time, they also began to pay Athenian citizens for serving on the large juries *(dikasteria)* that heard cases in Athens. Payment from public funds for other public offices (like service on the Council of 500) would follow. By the early 440s, the Athenians had begun the massive and expensive building program that centered on the acropolis and resulted in such constructions as the Parthenon. This project also featured a colossal gold and ivory statue of Athena designed by the Athenian sculptor Pheidias. Other work included a new temple to Hephaestus in the agora, the Odeion (a public building designed at least in part for musical performances), another four-mile wall connecting Athens with its harbor at the Peiraeus, and other public buildings.[20]

Even for wealthy Athens, this was an ambitious and expensive program. When we recognize that this building activity coincided with the new payments for public service and the maintenance of the costly Athenian fleet, it becomes obvious that the Athenians had begun to draw on the tribute collected by the Delian League for operations against Persia.[21] Explicit inscriptional testimony to this use of the league money does not appear until the 430s. However, our sources suggest that even before this the Athenians had placed a good deal of the Delian League's surplus funds in their own goddess Athena's treasury, from which they made withdrawals for at least some military costs and part of the building program.[22] In fact, in his biography of Pericles, Plutarch reports that the great Athenian statesman came under severe criticism for using other states' money to adorn Athens:

But there was one measure above all which at once gave the greatest pleasure to the Athenians, adorned their city and created amazement among the rest of mankind, and which is today the sole testimony that the tales of the ancient power and glory of Greece are no mere fables. By this I mean [Pericles'] construction of temples and public buildings; and yet it was this, more than any other action of his, which his enemies slandered and misrepresented. They cried out in the Assembly that Athens had lost her good name and disgraced herself by transferring from Delos into her own keeping the funds that had been contributed by the rest of Greece, and that now the most plausible excuse for this action, namely, that the money had been removed for fear of the barbarians and was being guarded in a safe place, had been demolished by Pericles himself. "The Greeks must be outraged," they cried. "They must consider this an act of bare-faced tyranny, when they see that with their own contributions, extorted from them by force for the war against the Persians, we are gilding and beautifying our city, as if it were some vain woman decking herself out with costly stones and statues and temples worth millions of money."

Pericles' answer to the people was that the Athenians were not obliged to give the allies any account of how their money was spent, provided that they carried on the war for them and kept the Persians away. "They do not give us a single horse, nor a soldier, nor a ship. All they supply is money," he told the Athenians, "and this belongs not to the people who give it, but to those who receive it, so long as they provide the services they are paid for. It is no more than fair that after Athens has been equipped with all she needs to carry on the war, she should apply the surplus to public works, which, once completed, will bring her glory for all time, and while they are being built will convert that surplus to immediate use. In this way all kinds of entertainment and demand will be created which will provide inspiration for every art, find employment for every hand, and transform the whole people into wage-earners, so that the city will decorate and maintain herself at the same time from her own resources." . . .

Thucydides [the son of Melesias] and the other members of his party were constantly denouncing Pericles for squandering public money and letting the national revenue run to waste, and so Pericles appealed to the people in the Assembly to declare whether in their opinion he had spent too much. "Far too much," was their reply, whereupon Pericles retorted, "Very well then, do not let it be charged to the public account but to my own, and I will dedicate all the public buildings in my name." It may have been that the people admired such a gesture in the grand manner, or else that they were just as ambitious as Pericles to have a share in the glory of his works. At any rate they raised an uproar and told him to draw freely on the public funds and spare no expense in his outlay. Finally, Pericles ventured to put matters to the test of an ostracism, and the result was that he secured his rival's banishment and the dissolution of the party, which had been organized against him. (Plut. *Per.* 12, 14; trans. Ian Scott-Kilvert)

The historicity of the precise events described in these passages has been justifiably questioned. But the reliability of the actual details found in Plutarch's account is largely immaterial, because even without it—based merely on Pericles' attested connection with the building program, public payments, and the empire in general—we could reasonably infer that Pericles and his camp endured something like the kind of criticism appearing in Plutarch's account.[23]

As we have seen, ancient tradition associated Pericles both with the building program and with the institution of public payments. According to the Aristotelian *Constitution of the Athenians,*

[f]orty-eight years after the battle of Salamis, in the Archonship of Pythodoros [432/1], the Peloponnesian War broke out; during this citizens were shut up inside the city walls, and grew accustomed to earn their living by military service, and decided, partly consciously and partly through the force of circumstances, to run the state themselves. Pericles [had previously] introduced pay for those serving in the *dikasteria* as a political move to counter the effects of Cimon's wealth. Cimon possessed a kingly fortune, and not merely performed his public liturgies magnificently but also maintained many of the members of his deme, for any member of the deme Lakiadai who wished could come to him every day and receive adequate maintenance, and all his estates were unfenced so that anyone who wished could help himself to the fruit. Pericles' wealth was not adequate to match such liberality, and Damonides of Oa [= Damon], who was thought to have suggested most of Pericles' measures, and was later ostracized for this very reason, suggested to him that since he could not match Cimon in private resources, he should give the people what was their own; Pericles accepted his advice, and arranged pay for the *dikastai* [jurors]. Some say that the quality of the *dikastai* declined, since it was always the ordinary people rather than the more respectable who took care to ensure that their names were included in the ballot for places on the juries. This was also the beginning of corruption of the *dikastai*, the first instance being Anytus after he was *strategos* at Pylos; he had been accused over the loss of Pylos, but bribed the court and was acquitted. (*Ath. Pol.* 27.2–5; trans. J. M. Moore)

Again, we may justifiably doubt the specifics of this story. Damon is a rather romantic figure, a philosopher associated with Pericles as well as a musical theorist cited by Plato.[24] Moreover, the precise need for Pericles' use of public money presumed in this passage is absurd: Pericles was a wealthy member of a very aristocratic Athenian family, and if he had less ample resources than Cimon, he certainly had enough to make a political mark by private means had he so chosen.[25] This passage betrays the influence of fourth-century authorities who desired to make Pericles a politician of significantly more modest means than Cimon. Nevertheless, only Pericles' motivation for the introduction of jury pay receives an explanation in the passage—his responsibility for the creation of public payments is taken for granted, and this detail thus probably goes back to a fifth-century tradition.

Whatever one concludes about Pericles' personal involvement, the Athenians did begin to make payments to their own citizens for public service by the mid fifth century. At this time, awash in the wealth of silver mines and imperial tribute, the Athenians apparently foresaw no end to their massive annual income. Indeed, in 454/3, they had erected a giant stone pillar *(stele)* on which to record the portions of the annual tribute payments from the allies that they had dedicated to Athena. Since the first inscribed list occupied less than 10 percent of the available space on the huge monolith—while the rest remained blank, awaiting the inscription of future lists—the Athenians clearly were making a statement that their empire and the payments of tribute would go on indefinitely.[26] Under these conditions, Athenians like Pericles understandably would have felt free to propose programs that depended on the surplus revenues the empire provided, apparently without much consideration of the effects such policies would have if the Athenians' external revenues somehow decreased in the future.

A famous passage in Thucydides well illustrates the vast public wealth of Athens in this period. The historian tells us that at one point—probably the early 440s—the Athenians had almost ten thousand talents of silver in their reserve (2.13.3–5). The modern equivalent of a silver talent in fifth-century Athens cannot be fixed precisely, but the ancient talent contained six thousand silver drachmas, and the average wage of a day laborer or rower in the fifth-century Athenian fleet ranged from about one-half to one drachma, while jurors in the mid fifth century eventually received half a drachma per day for their service. One talent, therefore, represented (at some points in the fifth century) something like the wages of six thousand or more men for one day and thus was truly a fortune by ancient standards.[27] By the year 431, again according to Thucydides, the Athenians still possessed some six thousand talents of coined money in their reserves.[28]

Athens's vast monetary reserves played a major role in its ability to make war

FIGURE 3. The Athenians often published their laws or the assembly's decrees by inscribing them on stone tablets *(stelai)* and placing them in public places. Records of certain kinds were also published in this fashion. In the year 454/3 B.C. the Athenians began to subtract one-sixtieth of the tribute paid annually by their allies and dedicate this money to Athens's tutelary goddess, Athena. At the same time, they determined to inscribe the lists of cities paying these sums on a stone tablet, which was probably placed on the acropolis. However, this tablet was far larger than other Athenian inscriptions, standing over three meters in height. Most of the surviving fragments of the stone (often called the "first stele," or *lapis primus*) were assembled in the 1920s in the Epigraphical Museum in Athens. The resulting reconstruction, pictured here, provides some idea of the sheer mass of this monolith, which would have dwarfed other Athenian stone inscriptions. Since the first year's tribute quota list occupied only a small fraction at the top of the stone, leaving the rest blank, this massive stone advertised to all who viewed it that the Athenians intended to keep collecting tribute indefinitely. Photo courtesy of the Epigraphical Museum, Athens.

and manage the empire. By the late 440s the Athenians often expended large sums from their reserves for particular military actions. Although these expenditures were apparently supplemented by payments made directly from the annual tribute income, the Athenians of the mid fifth century seemingly often preferred to expend money from the sacral treasury of Athena for warfare. Such money was usually taken out as loans at interest from the goddess to Athens; repayment of these loans (presumably from resources including tribute payments and booty)[29] provided a way for the goddess both to participate in wars and to profit from them. Now loans from temple treasuries (even to private citizens) were not uncommon in ancient Hellas, and in principle such borrowing would have seemed in no way impious or sacrilegious to the Athenians. Thus the Athenians laid up vast amounts of wealth in Athena's treasury not because they wanted to seclude this money from public use: rather, they placed money in the goddess's treasury so that it might be put to public use in special ways, either through the construction of sacred buildings or statues or through loans of sacred funds for war. Athenian finance, religion, and warfare all met in the Athenians' use of Athena's treasury.[30]

While this view of Athenian financial practice remains somewhat controversial, there can be no doubt that Pericles and other Athenians recognized that only vast reserves of wealth could prepare a state that depended on an expensive navy for warfare. (Infantries in Greece, we may recall, were small and relatively inexpensive, at least as long as they relied on those who could provide their own arms, while naval expeditions required expensive warships, thousands of rowers, and from half a talent to one talent per month just to pay a single trireme's crew.)[31] Pericles himself supposedly said that wars were won through careful and intelligent planning *(gnome)* and surplus funds *(periousia chrematon).*[32] The surplus wealth Athens accumulated in the mid fifth century, both the money simply resting in Athena's treasury and that expended to adorn the city itself or fund Athens's wars, must have helped engender a feeling of confidence among the Athenians. Thus, when the great crisis between Athens and Sparta arose in 432–431, Athens made few serious efforts to avoid this conflict, which many Athenians must have considered a lamentable if not frightening prospect.[33] When Pericles sought to encourage the Athenians before the first Spartan invasion of Attica in 431, he concentrated on the tremendous wealth the Athenians had laid up on the acropolis and the yearly income the imperial revenues provided:

> [Pericles] encouraged [the people] to take heart, since 600 talents, for the most part of tribute, were coming into the city annually from the allies, apart from

the other income, and since there were still at that time 6,000 talents of coined silver resting on the acropolis (the highpoint had been 9,700 talents, from which expenditures had been made for the Propylaea of the acropolis and the other buildings and for Potidaea), not to mention the uncoined gold and silver in the private and public dedications, and the sacred equipment used for the processions and contests, along with the Median spoils and anything else of this type, (amounting to) not less than 500 talents. In addition, he appended the treasures from the other temples, which were not few in number and which they might employ; and (he added) that if they were bereft all other resources, (they could also use) the gold adorning the goddess (Athena) herself. He pointed out that the statue consisted of 40 talents of pure gold, and it was all removable. And if they should ever use (these things) for their salvation, he said, it was necessary to put the same amount back again. (Thuc. 2.13.3–5)

In Pericles' opinion, Athens could afford to expend the money necessary for its democracy and its public payments, its buildings and statues, *and* a war with the greatest land power in Greece. Thus Athens's vast wealth, accumulated through the exploitation of its fellow Greeks and the Laurium silver mines, encouraged not only the radicalization of the democracy through public payments but also the continuation of imperial policies (including more tribute collection) and the outbreak of the Peloponnesian War. Indeed, since control of the empire and the resultant tribute collection made payments to Athenian jurors and magistrates conceivable, the empire had the effect of directly fueling the democracy's radicalization by providing Athenian politicians like Pericles with the motive and opportunity to "give the people their own money." And since the Athenian demos was perfectly well aware that its stipends derived in part from tribute collected from other Greeks, *the citizenry encouraged the extension or more efficient exploitation of the empire*.[34] It follows that the belligerent face of the fifth-century Athenian democracy was not a historical aberration or betrayal of supposed Athenian ideals of "liberty and equality"; rather, it was one result of the democratic Athenian citizens' determination to enrich and empower themselves and achieve greatness at the expense of other Greeks.

This competitive, "agonistic" spirit in the Athenians was in no way unusual for classical Greece. Indeed, some Greeks believed that all states (or individuals) sought to rule others by their very nature.[35] But the Athenians' democratic political system intensified aggressive attitudes by connecting voting Athenian citizens' economic condition directly to money generated through war and empire.[36]

Nevertheless, the Athenians' ability to generate imperial wealth and sustain the political system that relied on it upset a kind of balance that had previously existed in the (eastern) Hellenic world.[37] Before the Persian Wars and rise of Athenian sea power, certain factors had tended to make wars between Greek states extremely brief and of little consequence in terms of the exchange of territory or wealth.[38] The typically poor regimes that relied on hoplite-farmers for their armies had no efficient means to dominate and exploit their fellow Greeks, and the few Greek states that had developed systems of exploitation were unlikely to upset this balance. The Spartans, who relied on the semi-enslaved helots to work their lands and to provide surplus wealth for their Spartan lords in the form of agricultural produce and who were the strongest force in Greece before Athens's rise, proved unwilling or unable to engage in the kind of foreign operations necessary to maintain an empire outside the southern Peloponnese.[39] Meanwhile Thebes (and the on-again/off-again Boeotian confederation in central Greece) possessed no apparent means of generating surplus wealth and thus usually remained unable to project its power very far beyond its immediate surroundings.[40]

But the Spartans—who by dominating Lacedaemon and the surrounding area came closest to forming a Greek "empire" before Athens, and who occasionally engaged in short-lived foreign projects like the attempted overthrow of tyrants in Naxos or Samos—never controlled even all of the Peloponnese. The stronger members of their alliance (like Corinth) sometimes resisted Spartan overlordship, and the Spartans showed neither the ability nor the desire to extract direct monetary payments from the members of this league. Moreover, the Spartans' decision to rely on helots to work their lands acted as a kind of tether connecting the Spartan warrior-citizen caste to the southern Peloponnese: the possibility of a helot revolt, innate Spartan conservatism, and orientation toward the land kept them near Sparta. Although extremely powerful, they were, as Thucydides puts it, "slow to go to war" (1.118).

Athens was different. Even before the rise of the Athenian empire, Athens enjoyed financial benefits (from the Laurium silver mines) and a particular species of polis government that had tended to place somewhat more power in the hands of those below the middle class than this group possessed in other poleis. Still, without Themistocles' radical proposal to construct a larger fleet and the Persian Wars (resulting in a new Greek league), Athens might simply have continued as another nonimperial Greek polis.[41] It might well have maintained relatively friendly relations with Sparta—which had overthrown Athens's tyrants—and would perhaps have fought periodic wars with neighboring Thebes to the north, thus mimicking in central Greece the almost generational conflicts between Argos and Sparta that determined the (im)balance of power in the Peloponnese.

But what Athens in fact became was a hypermartial and expansionist imperial city, fueled by a political system that demanded a steady and indeed increasing stream of revenue. Meanwhile, political success in Athens became connected directly to the military office of *strategos,* an elected position held by every successful Athenian statesman about whom we know anything in the fifth century. Some leaders undoubtedly sought to discourage the Periclean policy connecting the empire and its revenues with political success. But they failed, and Pericles' chief rival—Thucydides son of Melesias—was ostracized. The demos had chosen. It was to be Pericles, *demokratia* (including the distribution of public funds), and *arche* ("rule" over others).

WAR, TAXES, DEBT, AND REVOLUTION (431–399)

One result of the Athenians' preference for Pericles and his policies was Athens's war with Sparta, a devastating affair lasting 27 years and exhausting Athens financially. From a fiscal perspective, Pericles' death in 429/8, a little more than two years after the Peloponnesian War began, came at a fortuitous moment for the leader. For contrary to Pericles' apparent expectations, the Spartans did not give up invading and ravaging Athenian territory after a couple of years. Vast amounts of Athens's reserves flowed out of the city in the first four years of the war, and by 428 the Athenians felt compelled to institute a property tax *(eisphora)* to raise two hundred talents.[42] Since most of the property owners who paid such taxes undoubtedly resented them, the *eisphora* alone should alert us to the reduced status of Athenian war reserves by 428: citizens of a polis like Athens, which possessed surplus wealth from its silver mines, were not likely to impose such a tax on themselves without extraordinary reasons. Our inscriptional evidence for the period confirms that, by about the year 428/7, the Athenians had expended the greater part of their once-formidable monetary reserves.[43]

Despite their financial condition, the Athenians resolved to go on fighting, proving that their desire for empire did not rest on a purely economic foundation. For even if the poorer citizens (who did not pay the *eisphora*) wished to continue the war simply to provide for their own employment as rowers in the fleet (and we may certainly doubt this), other Athenians had strong motives to end the conflict. The upper classes in Athens after 428 had been compelled to endure the unpopular war tax, and the middling hoplite-farmers had seen their farms repeatedly ravaged by Spartan invaders.[44] One such farmer, Aristophanes' hero Dicaeopolis ("Just City") in the *Acharnians* (produced in 425 B.C.), comically seeks to make his own peace with Sparta if Athens as a whole will not end the war. Near the beginning of the play, Dicaeopolis arrives at the Pnyx hill for an assembly meeting:

> But never since my first bath have my brows been as soap stung as they are now, when the Assembly's scheduled for a regular dawn meeting, and here's an empty Pnyx: everybody's gossiping in the market as up and down they dodge the ruddled rope [i.e., marked with red dye and used to force people to attend the assembly]. The Presidents *[prytaneis]* aren't even here. No, they'll come late, and when they do you can't imagine how they'll shove each other for the front row, streaming down en masse. But they don't care at all about making peace. O city, city! I am always the very first to come to Assembly and take my seat. Then, in my solitude, I sigh, I yawn, I stretch myself, I fart, I fiddle, scribble, pluck my beard, do sums, while I gaze off to the countryside and pine for peace, loathing the city and yearning for my own deme, that never cried "buy coal," "buy vinegar," "buy oil"; it didn't know the word "buy"; no, it produced everything itself, and the Buy Man was out of sight. So now I'm here, all set to shout, interrupt, revile the speakers, if anyone speaks of anything but peace. (ll. 17–39; trans. Jeffrey Henderson)

Despite the farmer Dicaeopolis's desire for peace, we may safely conclude that it was the wealthier Athenians who most wished to end hostilities with Sparta. Paying the property tax and serving as trierarch were expensive and danger-ous propositions, and Athens was waging this war against the state that many Athenian aristocrats admired as the most well-governed (possessing *eunomia*) and moderate (possessing *sophrosyne*) in all of Hellas. Aristocratic youths aped the Spartan fashion of long hair and adopted other "laconisms." Cimon had named his son Lacedaemonius, "the Lacedaemonian" or "the Spartan."[45]

Given this fact, Athens's continuation of the expensive war with Sparta after Pericles' death must relate in part to the need for upper-class Athenians seeking political power to adopt a "hawkish" position. Apart from Aristo-phanes' comedic appeals, we hear of no serious talk of peace with Sparta until the mid 420s. Even then, only after 422 and the death of Pericles' political successor Cleon—an arch-imperialist and anti-Spartan—did a peace policy become a viable political position in Athens. Significantly, Cleon's death oc-curred during Athens's failed attempt to recapture the strategically crucial city of Amphipolis and coincided with the depletion of Athenian war reserves.[46] Economic, military, and political motives thus combined to encourage an end to the war, and the conservative Athenian general Nicias arranged peace with Sparta in early 421.[47]

I have suggested that the desire by some portions of the Athenian demos to continue receiving the benefits Athens's empire generated contributed to the outbreak and protracted length of Athens's war with Sparta. However, it would seem that by the late 420s, a new political dynamic had emerged: Aristophanes suggests that by that time, an Athenian politician proposing the use of public money for warships instead of public payments found himself at a disadvantage. In his *Knights,* when the demagogic character Sausage-Seller describes the earlier actions of the Athenian people (personified by a character called Mr. Demos), he remarks, "and if two politicians were making proposals, one to build long ships and the other to spend the same sum on state pay, the pay man would walk all over the trireme [warship] man."[48]

Aristophanes' humor here relies in part on the Athenian audience's recognition that their politicians *could* sacrifice military concerns in favor of gratifying the demos through public payments (and that the citizens themselves had encouraged such tactics). It therefore testifies to the way Pericles' policy of public payments (probably instituted by ca. 450) had altered the Athenian political environment. By the 420s these payments, in part a product of the wealth generated by Athens's empire and the triremes that policed it, were apparently seen by some as a virtual entitlement, unconnected with the work (especially in the form of military action) and sacrifice (in the form of funding trireme construction instead of other projects) that were necessary to maintain Athens's empire. Once established, this idea encouraged the view that public payments were necessary whether the empire that originally had helped fund them existed or not. Eventually, some Athenians decided that more frequent taxes on Athens's richer citizens could serve to supplement the city's diminished external revenues, with the added benefit that relying on local taxes would make extensive military service to maintain the empire less necessary.

But these developments occurred some time after the Peloponnesian War ended in 404. Although the attitudes that would lead to them had already begun to emerge in the 420s, in the immediate wake of the treaty in 421 ending the war's first phase, the Athenians determined to repay their massive debt to Athena and to the other Attic deities that had "loaned" their wealth for the war effort. The unprecedented and unanticipated length of this war had resulted in a huge debt of some seven thousand talents (in principal and interest) owed to the gods. The Athenians apparently decided to repay this money to the sacred treasuries in small installments, using only a portion of their annual imperial revenues. The rest of this income they chose to store in a nonsacral treasury managed by the *hellenotamiai,* from which they could make expenditures without incurring debts to the gods. The Athenians thus determined to abandon their previous practice of financing wars largely through loans from sacral treasuries.[49]

Of course, the Athenians' expenditure of money borrowed from their gods' treasuries does not equate in economic terms with the modern practice of borrowing money from the future through deficit spending. Nevertheless, for the purpose of this study, the psychological and political effects of this debt were significant. For, whatever the economic realities of the situation, *the Athenians considered themselves literally in debt to their gods* as a result of their massive war expenditures. Their readiness to vote to incur such debt thus provides a telling comment on public finance in a democratic environment. And if we feel surprised that the Athenians so willingly incurred this debt, let us recall that the Athenians' debt stemmed from the expenditure of an existing surplus. Modern public debt, on the other hand, actually *represents money taken by one generation from their own descendants.* Despite the ubiquitous public rhetoric about the great concern we feel for our children and grandchildren, through deficit spending we contemporary Americans saddle our descendants with higher interest rates and the necessity to spend public funds on debt servicing rather than public projects. If deep concern "for the children" really motivated this generation, surely we would look for ways to remove this economic albatross from our descendants' necks, instead of spending vast amounts of *their* money on ourselves.[50]

Democratic Athens's accumulation of a massive debt was accompanied by the deaths of thousands of Athenians and others in the Peloponnesian War between 431 and 421. The Athenians, it should also be emphasized, did not incur this debt in order to protect themselves from domination or takeover, but to perpetuate the imperial lifestyle to which they had become accustomed. And we should keep in mind that the Peloponnesian War was waged by a state ruled by an assembly in which all citizens regardless of property qualifications were eligible to vote and by a Council of 500 citizens chosen by lot: the Athenian demos could at any point have chosen to make peace by majority decision. In fact, the Spartans offered peace on favorable terms in 425, but the Athenians, led by Cleon, rejected the offer.[51]

Thucydides characterizes the Athenians when they rejected this peace with Sparta in 425 and on other occasions as driven by *pleonexia,* a kind of overreaching, or literally, "grasping for more."[52] His judgment is amply borne out by the Athenians' decision to renew major military operations only six years after the Peace of Nicias. In 415 Athens launched a major expedition into the western Mediterranean, ostensibly to help Egesta, an allied state, against its enemies, but in fact aimed at the conquest of the city of Syracuse, the greatest power in Sicily.

Thucydides calls the initial invasion force "the most expensive and splendid fitted out by a single polis up to that time" (Thuc. 6. 31). It included over 100 warships and thousands of hoplites, and its size and expense clearly demonstrate how far Athens had repaired its financial condition by 415. As we have seen, the Athenians could not finance their costly naval operations by means of modern war bonds or the like, borrowing from the future to make payments today. Only surplus wealth deposited in their temples and state treasuries or direct taxes on their wealthy citizens could fund such an effort. A vote for this kind of expedition was therefore a vote to expend the state's and the citizens' resources immediately and directly, not a vote to spend imaginary money to be repaid by later generations.

Despite the sacrifices the Sicilian expedition entailed, the war also held out the promise of profit for individual citizens (through booty and pay) as well as for the state itself. According to Thucydides, the Athenian leader Alcibiades emphasized such material profits and glory, as well as the need for empires to expand continually, when he supported the expedition to Sicily in the Athenian assembly:

> Let us therefore be convinced that we shall augment our power at home by this adventure abroad, and let us make the expedition, and so humble the pride of the Peloponnesians by sailing off to Sicily, and letting them see how little we care for the peace that we are now enjoying; while at the same time we shall either become masters, as we very easily may, of the whole of Hellas through the accession of the Sicilian Hellenes, or in any case ruin the Syracusans, to the no small advantage of ourselves and our allies. (Thuc. 6.18; trans. Crawley, adapted)[53]

Although the Athenian general Nicias attempted to dissuade the citizenry by stressing the size and expense of the undertaking they were contemplating, the Athenians voted to launch the Sicilian expedition. Thucydides' description of the scene is memorable and chilling:

> All alike fell in love [eros] with the enterprise. The older men thought that they would either subdue the places against which they were to sail, or at all events, with so large a force, meet with no disaster; those in the prime of life felt a long-

ing for foreign sights and spectacles, and had no doubt that they should come safe home again; while the idea of the common people and the soldiery was to earn wages at the moment, and make conquests that would supply a never ending fund of pay for the future. With this enthusiasm of the majority, the few that liked it not, feared to appear unpatriotic by holding up their hands against it, and so kept quiet. (Thuc. 6.24; trans. Crawley)

In the event, the Sicilian expedition failed miserably and thus did not result in endless pay for the multitude. Instead, the invasion depleted Athens's resources through the expenditure of thousands of talents and the deaths of thousands of citizen-soldiers and rowers. Of the tens of thousands of Athenians and allies serving in the initial Athenian fleet of 415 and the ships sent out subsequently, most were killed or sold into slavery by their Syracusan captors. Since the overconfident Athenians had also reopened hostilities with Sparta in mainland Greece in 414, the news of the ultimate disaster in Sicily in 413 resulted in near panic conditions in Athens.

Amazingly, even after the news of the Sicilian disaster reached them in 413, the majority of the Athenian electorate still rejected any idea of peace with Sparta. Instead, Athens's citizens voted to install a special commission of ten elder statesmen *(probouloi)*—including the tragedian Sophocles—to make recommendations to the state and oversee the economy *(euteleia)* of operations: that is, the *probouloi* apparently sought to find ways to cut Athens's expenses.[54] Thucydides describes this decision as the kind of move toward moderation *(sophrosyne)* that the demos "loves to make" when confronted with difficulties. The spendthrift demos, Thucydides implies, only seeks to control itself when real problems arise. Of course, Thucydides earlier makes it clear that leaders like Pericles, Cleon, and Alcibiades had incited the populace to action (in the last two cases in part because of personal ambition): ultimate responsibility for Athens's actions must be shared by both her leaders and her citizens.

The movement toward moderation and fiscal retrenchment in Athens in 413 hints at an increasing dissatisfaction with Athenian policy among some citizens. Over the next year, moreover, conditions worsened as Athens's allies began to revolt and the Athenians were forced to break into the 1,000-talent reserve set aside in 431. Having expended these funds, the Athenians thereafter fell back on income from tribute or taxes on wealthy citizens, whose resources were themselves reduced by the expenses of trierarchies and service abroad in the ongoing war. An abortive attempt in 413 to replace the tribute paid by the allied states with a tax of 5 percent on all goods moving through imperial ports apparently failed to produce the increased revenues needed.[55] Moreover, after 413 the Athenians lost access to their silver mines as a result of the Spartan occupation of the Attic village of Decelea.[56] To make matters worse, the Persians reentered the picture as allies of Sparta, providing the kind of monetary resources the Spartan war effort had never before enjoyed. The Spartans now dispatched a large fleet to the eastern Aegean, encouraging revolts among Athens's allies and further weakening Athens financially.[57]

This was the situation by winter 412/11, when the Athenian fleet operating in the eastern Aegean received communication from the exiled Alcibiades, who was now acting as an advisor to a Persian governor in Asia Minor.[58] Alcibiades suggested to the leaders of the Athenian fleet that he could bring the Persians and their money over to the Athenian side in the war if the Athenians would only alter their form of government: Alcibiades obviously believed that a more restrictive regime would allow him to return to Athens and continue his career as an Athenian leader.[59]

Alcibiades' offer combined with Athens's dire fiscal conditions ultimately resulted in the city's first oligarchic revolution.[60] But this revolution initially took the form of a constitutional reform, carried out peacefully in the Athenian assembly.[61] The fundamental principle underlying the reformers' program was that the Athenians could not continue to fund both their democratic public payments and the war effort. Thus, in order to continue the war, the voting citizen body would be restricted to those with enough property to serve as hoplites—the polis would no longer provide pay for any public service outside the military. This, at least, was the openly expressed plan of the reformers, and it would not have seemed radical in a fifth-century Greek context (outside Athens). In fact, it probably brought Athens's constitution into line with those of most other Greek poleis.[62]

The Greek political environment and Athens's military and financial situation provide a context in which the Athenians' actions in 411 are understandable. Yet the Athenian populace's support of the oligarchic reform— first by voting to allow its proponents to put any matter they wished before the assembly, and then by voting for the reform itself—deserves careful attention. It may seem surprising that the Athenian demos agreed to alter their form of government in order to continue the war with Sparta, given their supposed attachment to democracy and the drastic measures of economy seemingly needed in order to secure an Athenian victory. Some may attribute the vote to the intimidating tactics used by the conspirators behind the reforms (Thuc. 8.64–66). But this explanation is insufficient, because after overthrowing this first oligarchic regime established in 411, the Athenians voted to establish *another* less than fully democratic government, including a property qualification for full citizenship (Thuc. 8.97). Even if one argues that most of the Athenians supporting the reforms saw them as a temporary expedient necessary to win the war and preserve the empire (Thuc. 8.54), their willingness to limit or abolish the democracy *even for a time* demonstrates that fifth-century Athenians did not conceive of their peculiar form of regime as something sacred or inalienable.

DIGRESSION: DEMOCRACY AND THE ATHENIAN SELF-IMAGE

From these popular votes to alter Athens's form of government, we can draw certain important conclusions about Athenian attitudes toward themselves and *demokratia* in the late fifth century. In early 411, at any rate, many Athenians did not believe that their current form of polis government *(demokratia)* was the only legitimate or practicable form of regime. A good number of Athenians were willing to contemplate a major change in their political system, a change that would in fact almost totally remove what had become two cardinal principles of Athenian democracy: pay for public service and the absence of a property qualification for full (voting) citizenship. Even if many Athenians saw the replacement of democracy as a temporary measure, it would seem that their view of themselves as a unique and superior people at this time was not tied primarily to the idea or practice of *demokratia*.[63]

That the Athenians did consider themselves a superior and extraordinary people can be amply demonstrated through Athenian literature and architecture. This view rested in part on a belief in superiority that is observable in most "national" groups. But in Athens's case, this opinion was buttressed by the Athenians' claims of autochthony (i.e., their status as the original inhabitants of Attica, literally sprung "from the ground"); their self-proclaimed position as citizens of the mother country of all the Ionian Greeks, who had migrated (at least in myth from Athens) to the islands and the eastern Aegean; their victories over the Persians at Marathon in 490 and thereafter; their consciousness of their own artistic and aesthetic superiority (vividly expressed in Athenian architecture, sculpture, and dramatic performances);[64] their belief in their ancient status as the protectors of suppliants (undoubtedly emphasized, if not created, after Athens took over the league against Persia at the "request" of the other Greek allies) and as the destroyers of barbarians like the Amazons (again, undoubtedly emphasized after the Persian invasion); their native silver mines and the "owls" they produced; their special relationship with Athena (the goddess after whom the city was named); and the fact that their *politeia* rested ultimately on the lawgiving of Solon, one of the sages of archaic Greece and the individual most Athenians apparently considered the real "founding father" of Athens's government.[65]

Obviously, the Athenians had no need of *demokratia* to define themselves or to justify their own national pride. Even Pericles' Funeral Oration as reported by Thucydides (2.35–46) treats democracy as merely one facet of the Athenian character and claim to superiority. Indeed, it is the *power* of the city and its military prowess that Pericles emphasizes above all other aspects (in this speech as in the two others attributed to him by Thucydides: 1.140–44, 2.60–64). Modern Americans' treatment of "democratic" government and the freedom it ensures as the most important aspect of the American condition and the Athenians' *later* emphasis on this factor arguably prevent us from viewing the situation in 411 clearly.[66] Having endured the unpleasant effects of the revolution of 411, another oligarchic revolution in 404, and the Athenians' defeat by nondemocratic Sparta, fourth-century Athenians eventually came to view democracy itself as one of the more important defining characteristics of the Athenian polis.[67] The Athenians in 410/09 instituted a famous law against overthrowing the *demokratia,* simultaneously an expression of some Athenians' growing attachment to the idea and of their political insecurity about democracy's future.[68] Eventually, Demokratia became a goddess in fourth-century Athens, marking the culmination of a process by which a political form became an Athenian dogma.[69]

Given the actual conditions Athens faced in 411, we can surely forgive if not praise the Athenians' attempts to reform their constitution, replacing their expensive democracy with a more restrictive and frugal regime. Unfortunately, certain leaders of the reform quickly seized the opportunity to empower themselves and even to assassinate their enemies. History has therefore justifiably passed harsh judgment on the resulting regime of the Four Hundred—named for the new council of four hundred members that replaced the old Council of 500 chosen by lot. Even Thucydides, who praised one of the reformers of 411 (Antiphon) as the most intelligent man of his time (8.68), stated that oligarchic regimes arising out of democracies are unlikely to succeed, since individual oligarchs will inevitably turn to the disfranchised people to increase their own power (8.89). In the case of the Four Hundred, Athens's middle-class hoplites apparently also came to believe that the Four Hundred planned to make accommodations with Sparta and perhaps even that their own citizenship was in question. Both ideas were intolerable to them: the citizens who provided arms had to be allowed a real voice in the regime, and the war against Sparta had to be continued (8.90–98).

Encouraged by one of the Four Hundred (Theramenes), a group of hoplites determined to march into the city and confront the leading reformers (8.92–93). Promises by members of the Four Hundred to moderate their regime prevented a possible clash between the factions in the city, and the Athenians met subsequently in the assembly and abolished the Four Hundred, voting to replace it with a less restrictive regime: the assembly would consist of five thousand citizens, who were required to meet the hoplite property qualification and who would receive no pay for public service (8.94–97). Virtually all the conspirators among the Four Hundred fled rather than face trial for their actions. An exception was Antiphon, who, Thucydides reports, delivered the greatest defense speech given in his day (8.68); he was nonetheless executed.

The oligarchic reforms of 411 have required attention because of the financial motivations behind them and the fact that they demonstrate the relatively low status of *demokratia* in the Athenian self-image long after democracy's creation. Less needs to be said about the revolution of 404, which was headed by a core group of thirty oligarchs. Far more than that of 411, this movement reflects the attempt by a small number of Athenians to install themselves in a position of power, execute their enemies or other wealthy Athenians in order to confiscate their property, implicate others in their crimes, and generally act as "tyrants."[70] Moreover, this government received support from a Spartan commander (Lysander) and a Peloponnesian garrison, and was therefore as much a reflection of Sparta's (or Lysander's) policy of installing friendly (oligarchic) regimes in other states after the Peloponnesian War as of Athenian desires for a more conservative government.

It is nonetheless telling that, despite the fact that the thirty oligarchs who dominated this revolution restricted citizenship to only 3,000 individuals, many Athenians present in Athens apparently supported this restrictive regime for some time, even in the face of a military assault by exiled or disaffected Athenian democrats.[71] In the end, it took a Spartan army and king (Pausanias), who was apparently worried about Lysander's growing power in Athens and elsewhere, to remove the oligarchs completely from power and reconcile the Athenians in the city (who had supported the oligarchy) with the democratic forces.[72]

From a financial perspective, Athens never recovered from the 27-year-long Peloponnesian War. If Athens's great wealth before the war encouraged the undertaking, the war itself exhausted the Athenians' reserves and destroyed the empire that had generated them. Even the Athenians' gods felt the strain. In the last years of the war, the Athenians chose to melt down sacred dedications in their gods' treasuries in order to fund their military. Most ironically, gold statues of Athena Nike (Athena "Victory") were converted into gold coins. By the time this had begun (407/6), we can be assured that almost all of Athens's more liquid resources had already been expended.[73]

The Athenians resolutely faced up to the situation after 403. Having reestablished *demokratia,* they completed the revision of their law code and declared an amnesty for all but the few dozen core oligarchs involved in the tyranny of the Thirty.[74] The huge monetary debt owed to the gods was simply canceled, although the Athenians made efforts to replace sacred treasures that had been liquidated. While Athenian financial practice underwent significant formal changes in the fourth century, it always rested on one very basic principle. There was to be no termination of state pay for public services like jury duty or service on the Council of 500. Although scholars disagree about whether magistrates (like the Athenian archons) received salaries in the fourth century, the populace at large—serving on juries, in the council, and in the army or navy—certainly received regular payments.[75] Moreover, soon after the Peloponnesian War, Athenian politicians began to extend the concept of public payments, first supplying money for attendance at the assembly and ultimately even granting subsidies for theater tickets during Athenian festivals. Eventually, an Athenian could receive as much as one and a half drachmas for attending certain assembly meetings and casting his vote.[76] Athenian experience suggests that a similar proposal to encourage voting (perhaps beginning with mandatory vacation time or government "subsidies" for lost wages on election days) may not lie too far off in America's future.

EPILOGUE: PAYING THE PUBLIC OR
FUNDING THE MILITARY? (399–322)

Since Athens's income both from its overseas holdings and, it would seem, from its silver mines decreased significantly in the early fourth century, the Athenians had to find other ways to fund the payments required for the democratic regime. Besides its empire and mines, Athens's only other source of such funding was taxation, and the fourth century thus saw a marked increase in the property taxes levied on property-owning Athenians.[77] Richer Athenians found themselves in the unenviable position of either paying the taxes regularly and fully (as well as performing other expensive duties such as providing a chorus for dramatic festivals or assuming a trierarchy) or risking the wrath of the demos if they found themselves on trial before an Athenian jury. Wealthy Athenians who wished to pursue a political career and succeed in the Athenian assembly felt an even more pressing need to show their fiscal support for the demos.[78] In short, fourth-century Athenians taxed their wealthier citizens to supplement the diminished revenues from Athens's subjects and silver mines, which by themselves were now incapable of funding the democracy and foreign policy.

Despite these tax revenues, fourth-century Athens faced serious fiscal constraints. Even after the Athenians created the Second Athenian League in 378/7, the "contributions" *(syntaxeis)* from their allies never resulted in a massive surplus—the kind of reserve necessary to fund the manifold undertakings of Periclean Athens.[79] Choosing to continue public payments rather than repay their massive debt to the gods and unable to stockpile large sums, the Athenians made a regular distribution *(merismos)* of annual public funds to various boards of officials, who then made payments for specific purposes. By the mid fourth century, any public surpluses usually accrued either to the "stratiotic" (military) or "theoric" (festival payment) funds, neither of which normally contained any major reserve.[80]

After the Athenian statesman Eubulus convinced the Athenians that all surpluses should flow perforce into the theoric treasury (which Eubulus administered for some time), it became increasingly difficult for the already underfunded Athenian military to deal with unforeseen contingencies.[81] Athenian generals in the fourth century frequently found themselves without funds to pay their rowers or infantrymen (who were often mercenaries by this time), and they were thus forced to rely on their private resources or on the virtual extortion of money from other cities.[82]

The attempt to rectify this situation occupied some years of the great Athenian orator Demosthenes' life. Early in his career, Demosthenes recognized the threat to southern Greece posed by Philip of Macedon (with his superb cavalry, the new Macedonian phalanx, and other military innovations).[83] However, since Demosthenes' views required the payment of property taxes and movement of significant amounts of money out of the theoric fund and into the military treasury in order to defend Athenian interests in the northern Aegean more vigorously, they long went unheeded. By the time the Athenians took aggressive steps to confront Philip, they were incapable of fielding a sufficient force or forming a large enough coalition to prevent his domination of central and southern Greece.[84]

How much did the weakness in the Athenians' public finances contribute to their failure to preserve their independence? The question is sometimes ignored, and Athens's defeat attributed to something like the "irresistible military might of Macedon."[85] Admittedly, Athens's own hoplite army in the fourth century was inferior in experience and caliber, if not in size, to that of the fifth century. The fourth-century Athenians relied increasingly on the numerous mercenary troops drifting around Greece after the Peloponnesian War, and these troops apparently did not compare in quality with citizen armies.[86] But surely a citizen infantry and an adequately funded Athenian navy might at least have delayed Philip's expansion into the Chalcidice and Thrace in the late 350s and early 340s, while the Athenians worked to form a strong alliance against the king.[87]

However, Athenian leaders like Demosthenes (once he began a concerted effort to foster popular support for an aggressive policy against Philip) found themselves on the horns of a dilemma. Sufficient funding for the military could only be found by levying property taxes and touching the theoric fund and thus threatening the payments made to individual Athenian citizens. Such a move—already politically unpopular in the 420s when the imperial and mining revenues were still able to compensate for extra expenditures on triremes—appears to have been almost completely untenable by the 340s. The Athenian people, who in the 480s had sacrificed their own income from the silver mines for purposes of national defense, by the mid fourth century had become unwilling even to give up their theater tickets or payments for attending the assembly in order to provide for the protection of Athenian interests.[88]

Obviously the Athenian political fabric and the Athenian people's psychology and morale had changed drastically between 483/2 and the mid 340s. Athens's silver mines and the tribute payments by Athens's allies had initially provided Athenian politicians with a means to achieve power unavailable in other poleis. These extraordinary financial conditions in fifth-century Athens facilitated the radicalization of the democracy through payments for public service. For the first time in Western history, individual citizens without property were able to participate directly in the government of their own state by serving on juries and the ruling council and by holding other (now paid) positions.

But this system developed within an unusual historical environment, created by Athens's unique natural resources and the Athenian people's willingness and ability to dominate and exploit other Greek states. In this environment, Pericles and his camp essentially taught the Athenian demos to shift the cost of their new regime onto others. But by the time the empire was lost and the silver mines had become less productive, it had become politically impossible to wean the Athenian people from the benefits these resources had provided. Since the Athenians had apparently lost the will or technique necessary to recreate their empire and exact the necessary funds for their regime from other states, they sought revenues from increased taxation on property-owning Athenians and money-collecting raids or other extraordinary measures by Athenian commanders (including renting out their services to foreign powers).[89] At the same time, real financial reform became less possible, because it was not politically viable to propose either a significant decrease in the financial claims made on the wealthiest Athenians or the reduction of public payments to the poor and middle class—payments the taxes helped make possible. The Athenian example suggests, therefore, that once people are allowed to vote themselves an income—whether from revenues confiscated from other states (or future generations), from natural or public resources, or from the property of their fellow citizens—and once they have become inured to the receipt of such funds, it becomes increasingly difficult to reverse the situation via democratic processes. One imagines that a political leader of tremendous character and charisma would be necessary to convince such a populace to vote to give up their stipends.

No such leader emerged in fourth-century Athens. As much as we may admire Demosthenes' oratorical skills or his early recognition of the danger Macedon posed to Athens, his initial warnings gained few adherents, and his ultimate crusade came too late. But it hardly seems possible that the state that in the fifth century had produced Themistocles, Aristeides, Cimon, Pericles, and Alcibiades—not to mention Sophocles, Socrates, and others—was incapable of producing equally talented or brilliant leaders a mere century later. Is it not much more likely that such individuals actually did exist in fourth-century Athens, but that they often chose not to enter the public arena?

Our fifth-century sources hint that such an attitude among some wealthy Athenians was already developing in the mid fifth century.[90] By the fourth century, state service as a general or political advisor to the demos carried increasing risk to one's person and property.[91] According to Plato, Socrates stated in 399 that it was impossible for a just man to live a public (i.e., political) life in Athens (*Ap.* 32a). After his teacher's execution, Plato himself eschewed Athenian political life and devoted himself to philosophy, although he made abortive and futile attempts to assist would-be philosopher-kings in Syracuse.[92] Talented men like Xenophon and other Socratics also either left Athens or abandoned politics. We may again note the increasing separation in the fourth century between the political careers of Athenian orators/diplomats and the military careers of Athenian generals.[93] Men like Demosthenes and Eubulus did not normally command armies, as Pericles, Cleon, and Themistocles had done. Is it too much to surmise that this separation of duties had a deleterious effect on the character of Athens's leadership, although perhaps not on the quality of its leaders' speeches?[94]

If some men like Aristeides or Cimon *did* enter the political arena in fourth-century Athens, they failed to achieve notable success, probably because their spirits and policies were simply out of tune with the contemporary political environment.[95] A political orator who told the Athenians that they must either give up their long-established public payments or risk Athens's security and autonomy simply could not acquire a following. Demosthenes' career and speeches suggest that the hard realities of public finance and foreign policy provided a poor platform for political aspirants in fourth-century Athens. Demosthenes more than once warned the Athenian people that they were unwilling to listen to a speaker who did not tell them what they wanted to hear.[96] Perhaps he was right.

FOUR

Foreign Policy I
Democracy Imperial

Of the gods we believe, and of men we know,
that by a necessary law of their nature they rule
wherever they can. And it is not as if we were the first
to make this law, or to act upon it when made: we found
it existing before us, and shall leave it to exist for ever
after us; all we do is to make use of it, knowing
that you and everybody else, having the same
power as we have, would do the same.

THE ATHENIANS TO THE MELIANS
(Thuc. 5.105; trans. R. Crawley, adapted)

A STUDENT ONCE SAID TO ME, "*The people* never want war." However, fifth-century history repeatedly illustrates the martial tendencies of the free Athenian citizenry, a group possessing vast resources and driven by an intense nationalism, self-confidence, and the desire for public enrichment. Although compelled by the Persian threat to become a great military power, the Athenians then used this threat as a pretext for the construction of a Greek empire. While Athens's citizens compelled their "allies" to remain part of an ostensibly anti-Persian league, the Athenians themselves rejected their alliance with Sparta and made agreements with states that had assisted the Persian invaders. By midcentury, the Athenians arranged for peace with the Persians, while nevertheless voting to continue the collection of tribute, to pay themselves for public service, and to construct the Parthenon and other brilliant reminders of their successes over both the "barbarians" and other Hellenes.

Athenian nationalism has been underappreciated in studies of Athens's history, although it certainly surpasses *demokratia* as a theme in fifth-century art, architecture, and literature.[1] Even most conservative Athenians, who had no love for the radical democracy and who wished to see Athens remain an ally of Sparta, apparently had few objections to Athens's creation of a Hellenic empire. Thus fifth-century Athenian statesmen of widely divergent views—including Themistocles, Aristeides, Cimon, Pericles, Cleon, Nicias, and even the tragedian Sophocles and the historian Thucydides—all willingly exercised brute force at the demos's orders to further Athenian control over other Greek states.

This chapter analyzes the Athenians' systematic exploitation of the states that had initially joined them in an alliance against Persia in 478/7. Fifth-century Athenian foreign policy presents a complicated story, set against the backdrops of Athens's own aggressive history before the institution of *demokratia* and the unsettled nature of Greek inter-polis relations during the classical period. I cannot hope to treat adequately many of the issues raised. But examination of critical events in the mid fifth century will serve to illustrate the way democracy aggravated an already aggressive Athenian foreign policy.

EARLY ATHENIAN AMBITIONS
IN THE AEGEAN (CA. 561–490)

Like important roots of Athenian democracy, the origins of Athenian imperialism lay partly in the period of Athens's rule by the Peisistratid tyrants (ca. 561–511/10).[2] In many Greek poleis, the emergence of tyrants coincided with and encouraged the consolidation of state power, increased militarism, and new foreign entanglements, deriving in part from the tyrants' desires to foster relations with friendly regimes, especially other tyrannies.[3] In Athens, Peisistratus pursued an aggressive foreign policy designed to extend Athenian power and strengthen his position through influence in important regions and connections with other tyrants.

Peisistratus's efforts to gain influence in crucial parts of the Aegean basin foreshadowed democratic Athens's foreign policy in the fifth century. In the southern Aegean, Peisistratus established his associate Lygdamis as tyrant on the large island of Naxos.[4] In the north, the tyrant apparently possessed connections in the Thraceward region, one of the only areas in Hellas (besides Attica) that possessed significant mines. Peisistratus's ability to assemble a mercenary force and install himself as tyrant undoubtedly profited from this connection, just as the fifth-century Athenians drew on the region's timber and precious metal resources.[5] The tyrant also apparently sought to control the Hellespont and the grain route from the Black Sea region. Peisistratid holdings in Sigeum near the straits' southern side complemented the Peisistratid-tolerated (and almost certainly sponsored) Athenian tyranny of the Cimonid family on the northern side (the Chersonese).[6] Islands that linked Athens with the northeastern Aegean were eventually seized and colonized. Cimon's father, Miltiades, had taken Lemnos from his base in the Chersonese by ca. 500, and Imbros may have been taken about the same time.[7] In these ways, the Peisistratids and their associates established a guiding principle for all Athenian foreign policy after the mid sixth century: influence in the northern Aegean and control of the Hellespont were crucial to Athenian strength.

The Cimonid family, who served Peisistratid interests as tyrants in the Chersonese and continued their own operations in the northeast Aegean after the Peisistratids' overthrow (511/10) and the introduction of *demokratia* (ca. 507), provide the crucial link between Athenian foreign policy under the tyranny and under democracy. Having gained crucial islands for Athens, Cimon's father, Miltiades, was nevertheless unsuccessfully prosecuted on charges of tyranny when he returned to Athens ca. 493.[8] After becoming the hero of Athens's victory over the Persians at Marathon (490), Miltiades led a failed expedition against the Greek island of Paros.[9] Miltiades' son Cimon continued his family's (and Athens's) aggressive Aegean policy in the 470s, grabbing the island of Scyros, expelling its native population, and establishing an Athenian colony there.[10] The three islands of Lemnos, Imbros, and Scyros thereafter were considered Athens's principal Aegean holdings, and their geographical significance (basically forming a line between Athens and the Hellespont) can hardly be coincidental.[11] Cimon also attempted to maintain (or reestablish) Peisistratid/Athenian interests in the Thraceward region, paving the way for an (unsuccessful) Athenian colonization effort on the Strymon River, reducing Thasos, and seizing the mainland mines the Thasians controlled.[12] Under Cimonid leadership, Athens's Aegean ambitions, which clearly originated before the institution of democracy, had continued unabated after the new regime took power.[13]

Athens's policy toward Persia under the tyrants also presaged that of the later democracy. Like many other tyrants, the Peisistratids apparently maintained friendly relations with the Persian empire, and their Cimonid proxies in the Chersonese cooperated with the Persian Great King Darius during his invasion of Thrace and Scythia ca. 514.[14] After the Peisistratids' expulsion from Athens by the Spartans in 511/10, the tyrant family sought refuge at

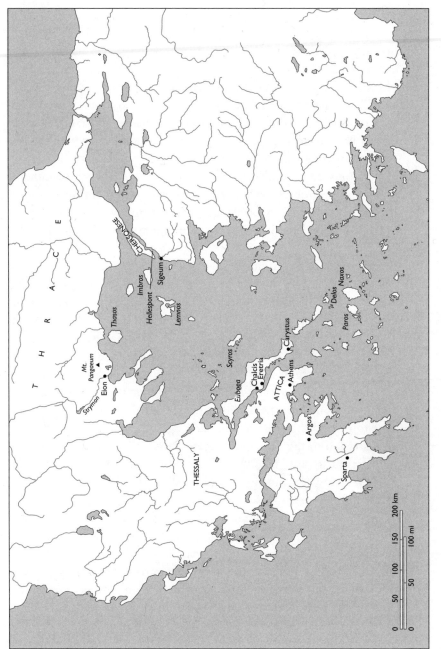

Map 2. Peisistratid-Cimonid foreign policy interests

Sigeum near the south coast of the Hellespont and eventually at the Persian court, where Cimon's half-brother had already received a warm welcome.[15] The friendly Peisistratid and Cimonid relations with Persia explain why, after the Spartans removed Peisistratus's former brother-in-law Cleisthenes from power in Athens and attempted to abolish the nascent *demokratia*, the Alcmeonid Cleisthenes and his allies also sought protection from Spartan control via a relationship with the Persians. But Cleisthenes apparently failed to appreciate that most Athenians desired no further connection with the Persians or the Peisistratids. Athens's citizens rejected the proposed Persian alliance and punished the ambassadors who had secured it, while Cleisthenes himself disappears from Athenian history, either banished or simply ignored by the regime he had created.[16] Athenian *demokratia* would pursue an independent course, reliant on neither foreign support nor particular political leaders.

Athenian expansion continued in the first years after the establishment of *demokratia*. Attacked by powers to their north, the Athenians defended themselves successfully and even secured holdings on the great island of Euboea to their northeast (ca. 506).[17] Herodotus writes that the Athenians' institution of "equal speech" *(isegoria)*—probably a euphemism for the more partisan term *demokratia*—coincided with the emergence of Athens as a formidable military force in central Greece.[18] Although the historian here ignores earlier Athenian expansion under the tyrants, he correctly surmised that the institution of *demokratia* encouraged the Athenians' militarism and attempts to expand their power. And although one may attribute Athens's earlier aggression to the Peisistratids themselves (rather than the Athenian people), after the tyrants' fall, Athens's expansionism clearly stemmed from the Athenian populace, which now expressed its will directly through votes in the assembly.[19]

A complex set of factors combined to make Athens an imperial force in the early fifth century. *Demokratia* was only one element—and perhaps not even the most important—contributing to Athens's foreign policy profile in this period. Athens's geographical position (jutting into the central Aegean like a massive island), the extensive Attic coastline with its excellent port near Athens, and the relative ease of travel by sea in antiquity provided Athens with as many natural ties to the Aegean islands as to mainland Greece. The Athenians' tyrannic period had already involved them in foreign projects in the Aegean (especially around the Hellespont) and in diplomatic entanglements that would continue for two centuries. Athens's possession of publicly owned silver mines eventually allowed her to create and maintain an unusually large fleet. Into this mix was thrown a new form of government, in which propertyless men—who would row the ships in this fleet and profit (through pay and perhaps booty) from their service—would cast the votes determining Athenian foreign policy. When we add in Athens's practice (again stretching back to the tyranny) of establishing Athenian settlements on seized lands—settlements that allowed those with little or no property to become members of the hoplite-farmer middle class—the Athenian demos's desire to continue Athens's Aegean expansion becomes quite explicable. Many Athenians benefited in tangible and important ways from Athens's aggressive policy. Thus, far from placing any restraints on Athenian aggression, the direct participation of the poorer citizenry in Athenian government through *demokratia* aggravated a preexisting martial and expansionist tendency in Athens. Democracy, while not the only cause of Athenian imperialism, provided crucial fuel for Athenian hegemony and ultimately helped make Athens the most aggressive Greek state of the fifth century.

THE PERSIAN WARS AND THE CREATION OF THE ATHENIAN EMPIRE (CA. 490–463)

It is hard now to grasp the incredible upset that the Greek victories over the Persians in 490 and 480–479 constituted. As the great Mediterranean and west Asian superpower in the sixth and fifth centuries, the Persian empire had swallowed whole most of Asia Minor (540s), Babylonia (539–538), and Egypt (525–522). The Persians' push westward brought them up against the fragmented, poor, and contentious Hellenic world, which boasted Sparta as its most formidable military force, a state without a significant navy, foreign holdings (beyond the Peloponnese), or even its own coinage.

When the Greek cities in Asia Minor rebelled against Persia in 499, the Spartans refused to send assistance over such a distance. The citizens of Athens, which claimed to be the mother country of the Ionian Greeks (many of whom were participating in the revolt), dispatched twenty ships, probably a little less than a third of the city's fleet at that time, to aid them. Surely feelings of *syngeneia* ("kinship") as well as Athenian interests in the eastern Aegean combined to make this expedition attractive, although Herodotus wryly comments that it seemed "easier to deceive a multitude than one man," since thirty thousand Athenians had been won over by an Ionian appeal for assistance rejected by the Spartan king Cleomenes.[20]

After merely one season of fighting and the allied Greeks' failed attempt to capture the citadel of Sardis (the Persian governor's capital), the Athenians returned home.[21] A brief reversal in their foreign policy may perhaps be reflected in subsequent domestic politics: in 497/6, the demos elected an apparent relative of the Peisistratid tyrants (who were now with the Persians) to hold the Athenian office of eponymous archon for the next year.[22] If this election was an attempt to assuage Persian anger at the Athenians' involvement in the Ionian revolt, it proved unsuccessful. The Great King Darius launched a failed invasion of Greece from the north in 492, followed by the expedition he sent across the central Aegean in 490. After a landing and assault on Naxos, the Persian force attacked the city of Eretria, located on the island of Euboea near Attica. (The Eretrians had sent five ships to aid the Ionians' revolt.) After Eretria was betrayed to the Persians, the latter turned their sights on Athens.[23]

The former Athenian tyrant Hippias (the son of Peisistratus) accompanied the invading Persians, who probably intended to reinstall him at the head of a puppet regime. The Persians and Hippias landed at Marathon in northeast Attica, where the Peisistratid tyrants apparently had support, and then waited several days, perhaps expecting an Athenian attack or the city's betrayal. Meanwhile, Athens's request for aid went unheeded due to the Spartans' religious strictures, which prevented an immediate march.[24] The upshot is well known: the Athenian infantry under the general Miltiades and the war archon Callimachus, aided only by a few hundred Plataean allies from Boeotia, met the great Persian force on the plain of Marathon and routed it. The Athenian soldiers then rushed back to the city and prevented an attack there. The Persians sailed home, and the legend of the Athenian *Marathonomachai* ("Marathon-fighters") was born.[25]

The Athenian victory at Marathon carried symbolic importance far beyond the simple expulsion of an invading force from the motherland. It was a victory of Greek over barbarian, with Athens standing (basically) alone against the *barbaroi*. Thus, it was also a kind of Athenian moral triumph over other Greeks, and, perhaps more important, it seemed to legitimize the Athenians' strange new form of government, which was not tyranny but not quite traditional polis government either. As a great infantry victory, it also provided the Athenians with a ready response to any later suggestion that they were only a naval power, reliant on a mob to row their ships and incapable of meeting the great Greek hoplite powers (Sparta and sometimes Thebes) on equal terms. For these reasons, Marathon (even more than the naval victory at Salamis in 480 or the combined land and sea defeat of the Persians at the Eurymedon ca. 466) would forever occupy a hallowed place in the Athenian mind.[26]

The immediate result of Marathon was not the creation of an Athenian force to seek retribution from the Persians. Such an idea would undoubtedly have seemed ludicrous to most Athenians in the 480s. Instead, Miltiades launched an assault against the Greek island of Paros (which under Persian compulsion had provided a single ship for the invasion of Attica).[27] Following this, the demos began to ostracize individual Athenians thought to have collaborated with the Persians (especially Alcmeonids and their connections) or connected with the Persian-sponsored Peisistratid family,[28] including Pericles' father, Xanthippus, and his uncle Megacles. Since Miltiades himself died in disgrace after his failure at Paros in 489, the years immediately following Athens's victory at Marathon saw the pool of potential Athenian leaders significantly depleted.[29]

While the battle of Marathon represents a crucial stage in the development of the Athenians' self-image, an arguably more important factor in the rise of Athenian power occurred in 483/2, when Themistocles proposed that Athens use a windfall from the public silver mines to construct a larger fleet.[30] Athens's new fleet made the Athenians' participation vital to the anti-Persian alliance formed in 481/0. Although serving under Spartan command, the Athenians provided the largest contingent to the allied fleet and played essential roles at the battles of Artemisium and Salamis in 480.[31] The next spring (479), a hoplite force led by the Spartans defeated the remaining Persians at Plataea, in central Greece, and expelled them from mainland Hellas.[32] Meanwhile, the allied Greek fleet operating off the coast of Asia Minor, with Pericles' father, Xanthippus (recalled from exile before Salamis), acting as the Athenians' commander, defeated Persian forces there.[33]

Spartan and Athenian actions in the wake of these victories illustrate a basic fissure in the Hellenic alliance. The allies' supreme commander in the east (the Spartan king Leotychides) returned to Sparta with his forces for the winter of 479/8. At the same time, the Athenians under Xanthippus continued operations against Persian outposts in the Hellespont.[34] The Athenians' actions obviously reflect their long-standing interests in the northeast Aegean, and these interests and Athens's forward policy contrast with the Spartans' decision to winter at home. Sparta was concerned primarily with removing the Persian threat from mainland Greece; the Athenians sought also to maintain and extend their preexisting interests in the Aegean (at the expense of the defeated Persians and any medized Greeks or others who opposed them).

In 478, when Pausanias, the new Spartan commander in the eastern Aegean, outraged the allies through his high-handed actions and then himself fell under suspicion of medizing, the Athenians seized the opportunity to assume leadership of the allies. Even the pro-Athenian Herodotus notes that the Athenians used these circumstances to establish themselves as the new leaders of continuing Greek actions against Persia.[35] Unhappy in their role as leaders of this largely naval affair and pleased enough with the Athenians at this time, the Spartans accepted the situation. After spring 477 they sent out no further commanders, and they did not press their formal claim to leadership of the alliance.

Perhaps because a larger organization was needed to carry out offensive operations against Persia, the Athenians and other Greek states formed a new league over the winter of 478/7. Thucydides reports that the "ostensible purpose" of this Delian League was to "retaliate for the things they had suffered by ravaging the Great King's land." The war would be carried into Persian territory, and many of those involved undoubtedly expected profits and glory to result.[36]

The Delian League had certain unusual features almost from the very beginning. First, as we have seen, while some states provided ships for the fleet to be used against Persian interests, others agreed to make payments of money, presumably to fund the fleet. However, at least a good portion of the money paid by the other states simply accumulated in a treasury kept on the island of Delos and overseen by Athenian officials *(hellenotamiai)*.[37]

Perhaps stranger still is the fact that in the league's first years, we hear of no operations directly against Persian territory. The fleet operated in the northern and western Aegean, removing Persians from outposts, expelling or enslaving alleged collaborators or pirates, collecting tribute payments from Greek states, and forcing at least some into the new league.[38] Some similar actions apparently occurred on the mainland; probably in 478 the Spartan king Leotychides led an expedition to Thessaly, perhaps in order to punish medizers there.[39] But the oddity of the Athenians' actions is underscored by the membership of many Greeks from Ionia and the eastern Aegean in the new league. Although the Ionians (under compulsion) had sailed along with the Persians in 480, as part of the new Athenian-led alliance they were now participating in the reduction of other Greeks—Greeks who certainly were no more guilty of assisting the Persians than the Ionians themselves. That is, the new league was *not* an alliance of those Greeks that had always opposed Persia now making war on the Persians and the Greeks who had helped them. The significant distinction between states in and outside the new alliance was simply their membership in the league. Previous history became largely irrelevant to the purposes of Athens and its new allies: after 478, other Greeks would be punished for refusing to join or attempting to leave the Delian League, *not* for having assisted the Persians in 480–479.[40]

From its first decade of operation, the new league provided the Athenians with opportunities to extend their power. Sometime in the 470s the Athenians under Cimon seized and colonized the island of Scyros, thereby completing the chain of islands that linked the mainland with the Hellespont. As we have seen, Cimon's action represented the culmination of a program begun under his Peisistratid-sponsored Cimonid ancestors. The pretext given for Cimon's act was that the Dolopian inhabitants of Scyros were pirates—probably not an unusual or even particularly outrageous occupation in the early fifth-century Aegean. But Cimon's responsibility for Scyros's capture and his father's management of the seizure of Lemnos and probably Imbros betray earlier Athenian designs on the island and the underlying motive for the action.[41]

By the early 460s, certain Greek allies apparently had grown weary of an alliance used for furthering Athenian hegemony rather than making war on the Persians. The great island of Naxos sought to leave the league (ca. 467), only to find that it was not free to do so. The Athenians brought the league fleet to bear on their now unhappy ally, and when the Naxians resisted, their walls were pulled down and their warships seized. Thereafter, the Athenians compelled Naxos to make payments to the league treasury.[42] As Thucydides comments, this was the first time the Athenians "enslaved" an ally, "in contravention of what was established."[43] But, as he also notes, other examples followed almost immediately. When Athens made some claims on holdings of Thasos in the northern Aegean, the Thasians also attempted to revolt. Besieged for two years (465–463), they eventually capitulated and suffered the same fate as the Naxians, except that the Thasians also lost control of their mainland mines.[44] This gave Athens a virtual monopoly on the precious metal supplies in the Aegean.[45]

Shortly after Naxos's revolt, the Athenians and their allies under Cimon met and defeated Persian forces in southern Asia Minor at the Eurymedon River.[46] This battle effectively ended any real Persian threat in the Aegean for the foreseeable future. It thus forms the only known example of the Athenians' partially living up to Thucydides' description of the Delian League's professed purpose: to seek revenge by ravaging the Great King's land. The clearing of the Aegean of Persian forces and the victory at the Eurymedon also suggest that most potential Athenian justifications for continuing the league and the collection of tribute were invalid by ca. 465 (unless the Greeks now intended to anticipate Alexander's march deep into Persian territory).[47] Yet, rather than disbanding the league, the Athenians reduced Thasos and seized its mines, sending a clear message to any other "allies" who wished to leave the alliance. The Delian League was by this time unquestionably an Athenian empire. And although it took the Athenians many years to develop the techniques necessary to exploit their position efficiently, by the 460s, they were openly demanding money and service from other Greek states. Modern historians often date the conversion of the league into the Athenian empire to the early 440s or even later, but *no* ancient source places the beginning of Athens's *arche* ("rule") any later than the 460s, and most Athenians themselves identified Athens's empire directly with the Delian League and therefore dated the empire's creation to the 470s.[48]

The democracy's role in fashioning Athenian policy in the mid fifth century is not palpable in our best sources (Herodotus and Thucydides), which largely ignore the period between the Persian (490–479) and Peloponnesian (431–404) wars. However, Athens's known actions during this period and the better-documented events before and after it show that the *demokratia* not only did not restrain Athenian ambitions, it actually heightened them.

After 478 the dominant political figure in Athens appears to have been the Athenian general Cimon, who maintained close relations with the Spartans and successfully pleaded for Athenian aid to Sparta after an earthquake and a helot revolt.[49] Like his father, Miltiades, Cimon sought to expand Athenian control over other regions and peoples of Hellas. For men like Cimon, friendship with aristocratic Greek states like Sparta or Chios implied no special treatment for subject Greeks in Thasos or Naxos, and his policies thus cannot be fairly characterized as "Panhellenic." He nevertheless favored a program of offensive action against the Persians, demonstrated by his victory at the Eurymedon and his command against Persian forces in Cyprus just before his death ca. 450.[50]

We may infer from Cimon's popularity before 462/1 that his imperialist views comported with those of the majority of the Athenian electorate, a conclusion supported by an unusual anecdote. When Cimon returned from the successful siege and reduction of Thasos in 463, the general was prosecuted by Pericles and others on a charge of accepting a bribe intended to prevent an Athenian attack on Macedon.[51] This report, which is well known because of the personalities involved, deserves study because of what it implies: if a Macedonian king could be thought to have bribed an Athenian general *to prevent him from invading Macedon,* such an attack must have seemed a real possibility to Macedonians and Athenians alike. Indeed, Plutarch *(Cim.*

14) explicitly reports that some Athenians lamented the fact that Cimon had not seized this opportunity for expansion. Whatever the truth of the charge, the whole story floats in a historical context that demonstrates the Athenian demos's desire for expansion into new territories in the mid 460s and Athens's neighbors' fears that they might be the Athenians' next victim.

REVERSED ALLIANCES AND CONTINUING EXPANSION (CA. 462/1–430S)

A series of events in the late 460s led to radical changes in Athenian domestic and foreign policy. After a major earthquake rocked the Peloponnese around the year 465/4, Sparta's helots and certain *perioikoi* revolted. Cimon's proposal to assist Sparta resulted in an Athenian expedition to the Peloponnese in 462/1. While Cimon and his associates were away, Ephialtes carried through a plan of reform that brought about a significant change in the way *demokratia* functioned and accomplished an almost complete reversal in Athenian foreign policy.[52] The Athenians "dissolved their alliance with the Spartans against the Mede" (Thuc. 1.102) and made treaties with Argos and Thessaly,[53] powers tainted with medism and—in the Argives' case—bitter enemies of the Spartans. The Athenians now ostracized Cimon himself and opened hostilities with Sparta's ally Corinth (another member of the old Greek alliance against Persia). The resulting conflict with Sparta and its allies, often called the First Peloponnesian War (ca. 460–446/5), saw Athens attempt to establish a land empire in mainland Hellas to accompany her domination of the Aegean.[54]

Conservative reaction to these changes apparently brought Athens to the brink of civil war in the early 450s. Ephialtes was murdered shortly after his reforms, and in 458 or 457 a group of Athenians hostile to the democracy and/or its new policies contemplated betraying the city to a Spartan force then in central Greece.[55] The prospect of an Athenian civil war is reflected in Aeschylus's *Oresteia* (produced in 458). The last play of the trilogy *(Eumenides)* warns against internal strife *(stasis)* and encourages the Athenians to turn their energies outward. On one view, the play also sought to reconcile more conservative pro-Spartan Athenians to Athens's new alliance with Argos and to provide support for a young leader of the democratic faction (Pericles) now that Ephialtes was dead.[56]

The ostracized Cimon did not attempt to return to Athens forcibly or exploit the volatile situation in the city for his own purposes. At very least,

Cimon might have appealed to Sparta for aid against the now anti-Spartan regime in Athens.[57] Nevertheless, Cimon took no action to encourage internecine strife in Athens.[58]

If Cimon took any solace in these years of exile, it may have derived from the anti-Persian bent of Athens's foreign policy immediately after 461. Around 460, the Athenians accepted a request to assist in Egypt's rebellion from Persia, and from 459 to 454, they campaigned in and around the Nile Delta.[59] Of course, it is possible to see this action simply as the continuation of Athens's antagonism to Persia. But given the fact that Pericles and his supporters would soon advocate giving up the Persian war in favor of consolidating Athens's Greek empire, the Athenians' efforts in Egypt perhaps derived as much from their desire to gain booty, influence, and even territory as from hostility to Persia. The expulsion of Persian power from rich northeastern Africa would create a power vacuum that some Athenians may have felt they would be in a position to exploit, if not fill. Unfortunately for Athenian hopes, the expedition ended in utter disaster, with the loss of as many as 200 to 250 triremes and thousands of lives.[60]

Athenian foreign policy immediately after this disaster suggests a period of retrenchment and consolidation. We hear of no offensive operations on Athens's part until Cimon returned from ostracism, apparently ca. 451.[61] The Athenian losses in Egypt, the helot revolt, and the protracted if desultory First Peloponnesian War between Athens and the Spartan confederation had apparently softened Athenian and Spartan attitudes somewhat. Cimon arranged for a five-year peace treaty with the Peloponnesians on favorable terms for Athens: the Athenians were able to retain most of their gains from the First Peloponnesian War, including the island of Aegina (made a tributary member of the league ca. 456), interests in Boeotia to the north, and even a foothold in the Peloponnese itself.[62] In terms of mainland power, Sparta's acquiescence to Athens's gains in the Five Years' Truce represents the highwater mark of Athenian imperialism. After negotiating this truce, Cimon then led a great expedition against Persian forces and holdings in Cyprus. In the course of this expedition, which resulted in a major victory for Athens, Cimon fell ill and died, ending his career as he had begun it, campaigning to expand Athenian power and crush the Persians.[63]

How Pericles viewed all this is unknown. Apart from noting his support of the law restricting citizenship to those with two Athenian parents (451/0),[64] the sources are virtually silent about him in these years. Certainly Pericles in the late 450s was not yet the unquestionably dominant force he was to become in the next decade, and he may have thought it prudent not to oppose

Cimon's proffered peace with Sparta and the expedition against the Persians for any number of reasons.[65]

But Pericles must have realized that Cimon's death and the Athenian victory at Cyprus ca. 450 offered him an unprecedented opportunity to set Athens on a new course. Frustrated by the defeat of his forces, the Great King of Persia could now be brought to the bargaining table. Thus Pericles and his associates, especially Callias son of Hipponicus,[66] apparently secured some kind of arrangement that ended hostilities between the two powers in the Aegean. The nature and precise date of this so-called Peace of Callias has been one of the most hotly disputed questions in Greek history for half a century, but at the minimum, aggression on both the Persian and Athenian sides clearly was curtailed after about 449.[67] Pericles and Athens were now free to turn their attention back to mainland Greece and to the consolidation of the empire. Meanwhile some of the Athenians' "allies," probably in part either reacting to a real treaty between Athens and Persia or simply suspecting that some kind of accommodation had been made, attempted to break away from the empire. The specifics of events in this period are very cloudy, but our sources suffice to show that in the early 440s the Athenian assembly passed measures intended to tighten Athens's control of its recalcitrant Aegean subjects.[68]

As the direct expressions of a democratic electorate's desire to exert control over other states, these decrees *(psephismata)* of the Athenian demos regarding control of the empire are remarkable documents. Through votes in the assembly, the Athenians installed garrisons in other states; converted hostile oligarchic governments to democracies on the Athenian model; ordered Athenian officials to keep tabs on allied actions; regulated or usurped taxes normally paid in allied states; transferred at least some legal cases involving Athenians and the allies to Athens, where they would be tried before Athenian juries; designated certain cooperative allies as official friends *(proxenoi)* of Athens and threatened anyone who did them harm; and compelled citizens of allied states to swear oaths of obedience and allegiance. As we have already noted, these were not the decrees of tyrants or dictators, but the orders of a free people meeting in assembly, each one put before the people and subjected to majority vote. Each decree opens with a statement of this fact: "Resolved by the Council [of 500] and the demos [in assembly]." Whatever one thinks about democracy's role in creating the Athenian empire, there can be no doubt about its direct involvement in ruling it.[69]

Ultimately the Athenians' attempt to consolidate control over both their island empire and their mainland holdings in the early 440s proved too am-

bitious. After a major defeat in central Greece at the hands of certain Boeotians in 447 (after which Athens withdrew from central Greece) and the partial reinvigoration of Spartan policy, the Athenians were compelled in 446/5
to conclude a Thirty Years' Treaty with Sparta and its allies. By the terms of
this truce Athens gave up most of its mainland possessions, including those
in the Peloponnese.[70] For the next decade and a half, Athens's attentions
would be focused on domination of the Aegean.

In the year 441 the Athenians received a request to intervene in a conflict
between two large and important states within their empire, and as a result
entered a major war with a former ally. The great island of Samos and its
neighbor Miletus, located on the coast of Asia Minor and one of the most illustrious cities in all Hellas, had come to blows over control of the smaller
city of Priene. At the request of the bested Milesians and certain political exiles from Samos, the Athenians sent a force to the island and overthrew the
Samian government, installing *demokratia* in its place. Samos was one of the
three large island states (along with Chios and Lesbos) lying just off Asia
Minor, all of which had managed to retain a degree of independence within
the Athenian empire, in part by continuing to provide contingents of ships
for the imperial fleet. Thus, if any members of the Delian League in the 440s
could still be considered real *allies* (rather than subjects) of Athens, it was
these three islands. The Athenians' decision not only to take Miletus's side
in this dispute with Samos, but even to settle the matter by removing
Samos's traditional government and installing one modeled on their own regime, therefore constitutes one of the grosser examples of Athenian imperialism in the mid fifth century.[71]

Gossip blamed the Athenians' intervention on the fact that Pericles' notorious consort Aspasia hailed from Miletus.[72] But whatever Pericles' personal
motives for supporting the action, let us recall that the measure had to be put
before the Athenian assembly. Like other Athenian military moves, the decision to destroy Samos's government and forcibly replace it with democracy
was approved by the majority of Athenians present for the vote and then implemented by leaders representing a wide range of political views (the generals in charge of the "revolution" and/or the subsequent war with Samos included Pericles himself, the tragedian Sophocles, and a certain Thucydides).[73]
When some Samians refused to accept the new regime and resisted Athens
by force (assisted by mercenaries and a Persian satrap), the Athenians besieged their city for nine months (440–439). When it was finally taken,
demokratia was probably reinstituted, Samos's city walls were destroyed,
hostages were taken, and the city was saddled with the massive expenses in-

curred by Athens for the whole operation.[74] According to a dubious tradition, the Athenians crucified some Samian prisoners; however, the leaders of the Samian resistance were probably simply executed.[75]

The Samian War exemplifies the democratic Athenians' sometimes brutal imperial style: the Athenian demos voted to overthrow the government of one of Athens's theoretically sovereign allies. Although it was not the first time that this had happened, Athenians earlier seem to have sometimes used alleged medizing or internal strife as an excuse to intervene and install an Athenian-style regime.[76] In the case of Samos, it was Athens's intervention in a Samian-Milesian quarrel and the subsequent imposition of *demokratia* that apparently led to violence on the island. And although certain political exiles from Samos apparently encouraged the Athenians' actions in 441, no evidence suggests that anything like a civil war had erupted before the Athenians' intervention. The existence of such exiles provided no special justification for Athens's action. Many of the larger Hellenic states had political exiles, including Sparta and—most notably—Athens itself, which expelled Cimon in 462/1 and ostracized Pericles' conservative nemesis Thucydides son of Melesias around 444/3.

There is some evidence that certain Athenians hostile to Pericles resented Athens's harsh treatment of Samos. Among those appalled at Samos's fate we would expect to find the more aristocratic Athenians, who were also those most likely to have friends (or even relations) among the Samian elite.[77] As we have seen, gossip attempted to attach the reason for the war to Pericles' personal life. Moreover, associates of Pericles like the philosophers Damon and Anaxagoras and the sculptor Pheidias seemingly also came under attack in the 430s.[78] These oblique assaults on Pericles demonstrate both the hostility his policies elicited in some quarters and the utter inability of Pericles' opponents to launch a successful *direct* attack on the great statesman. The assaults therefore tend, ironically, to confirm the popularity of Pericles and the Athenians' policy toward Samos, once more spotlighting the harsh face of the imperial demos.

Herodotus (5.78) to the contrary, the Athenians did not first overthrow their tyrants, install a democratic regime, and only then become a formidable military force. Athenian aggression predated the creation of *demokratia*. After the creation of the new government, Persian expansionism and a fortuitous silver strike gave Athens both the motive and opportunity to develop a naval force of unprecedented size (for the Greek world).

Presented with the opportunity to rule themselves and others, the Athenian people not only did not turn Athens toward peace; they in fact embraced and nurtured the aggressive tendencies they had inherited. Voting repeatedly to make war on their former allies, reduce their subjects, and exact payments from states too small to refuse, the Athenians created a system for enriching their public institutions while rebuilding and adorning their city. At Athens, democracy fostered an empire, and the empire in turn made democracy practicable and profitable.

Admittedly, Athens's *demokratia* was born and reared in a atmosphere of nationalism and warfare. Perhaps it is no surprise that this regime, like the warrior goddess the Athenians worshipped, so frequently bore a martial visage.

FIVE

Foreign Policy II

The Peloponnesian War

In peace and prosperity states and individuals have
better sentiments, because they do not find themselves
suddenly confronted with imperious necessities; but war
takes away the easy supply of daily wants, and so
proves a rough master, that brings most men's
characters to a level with their fortunes.

THUCYDIDES 3.82

trans. R. Crawley

THE EFFECTS OF THE PELOPONNESIAN WAR

The Peloponnesian War stretched on for almost three decades and arguably
inflicted a mortal blow on the system of independent poleis that had dominated Hellas for three centuries. The war necessitated revolutions in military
tactics and strategies, and its conclusion unleashed a mercenary generation
on Hellas. If scholars continue to debate the war's ultimate causes and precise effects, it is indisputable that it and the civil strife it inspired ended the
lives of tens of thousands of Greeks and deprived fourth-century Athens of
many valuable leaders and citizens.[1]

As a result of the war, the Athenian empire and its revenues were lost, and
the democracy largely fell back on its own wealthy citizens and the silver from
the Laurium mines to fund its operations. During the war and just after it,
Athenian revolutions spawned two reactionary regimes, both ultimately
dominated by unscrupulous oligarchs and culminating in executions during
the oligarchs' reigns and acts of revenge after their fall. One of the casualties

of these revolutions was Socrates, who had served courageously and repeatedly in the Athenian army during the war.

The war also had devastating effects on Athenian literature and drama. In the late fifth century, Athenian tragedy and comedy continued to flourish, with Aristophanes, Sophocles, and Euripides all producing masterpieces down to the last years of the conflict. However, the two great tragedians did not survive the war, and Aristophanes' work from the period after 404 suggests that either Athenian tastes had changed or Athens's poets had lost their muse, or both.[2] By the early fourth century, the Athenians were reproducing the tragedies of the fifth-century masters and entering a period of literary decline from which they never emerged.[3] Athens's more creative minds turned to history, philosophy, and oratory. The giants of post–Peloponnesian War Athens are Plato, Isocrates, and Demosthenes, all in their ways products of an imperial-democratic polis that had fed freely on the world around it only to turn inward after it was forced back on its own means. But Plato and Isocrates, like Thucydides and Xenophon, at least experienced the great war and the world in which Socrates spoke, Sophocles and Euripides wrote, and Aristophanes lampooned politicians and the demos itself. Demosthenes and his contemporaries could only read of such things. The effect is palpable.

The rehabilitation of fourth-century Athens has become fashionable in contemporary scholarly circles. Many classicists and historians have understandably turned away from the much-plowed fields of the fifth century in order to focus on the less cultivated territory of fourth-century sources and history. A need to defend this perfectly reasonable strategy may have inspired overly optimistic evaluations of Athens's government, art, and literature in the 300s.[4] Certainly it has been shown that the old view of a "crisis of the polis" in the fourth century was overstated.[5] Isocrates, Demosthenes, and others arguably took oratory to a higher technical level in the fourth century, and the study of the century's voluminous rhetorical material has opened new windows onto Athenian politics and society. Nevertheless, comparison of these orators with their predecessors (and Thucydides' speeches) suggests to me that refinements in rhetorical technique or style can only be thought to compensate for inferior substance in a society that has already embraced its own decline. The tragedians Aeschylus, Sophocles, and Euripides have no fourth-century rivals except the reproductions of their own works. Thucydides begat Xenophon and a host of inferior and non-Athenian descendants. The heritage of fifth-century statesmen-generals like Pericles, Nicias, and Alcibiades was split between political orators like Demosthenes, on the one hand, and relatively apolitical generals such as Iphicrates and Timotheus, on the other.[6] The fourth-century Athenians' desire to recreate the fifth-century empire ultimately combined with democratic hunger for public payments and unwillingness to make personal sacrifices to produce a weakened military incapable of achieving its goals and resentment among the wealthy Athenians who provided funding for both this military and the democracy. The fourth-century Athenians lacked not the desire to impose their will on other states, but rather the ability and character to do so. The sometimes vaunted stability of Athenian government in the fourth century culminated in crushing defeats by the Macedonians and the destruction of the democracy itself.

Athens's democratic empire and the Peloponnesian War it spawned are arguably the principal historical factors responsible for the condition of fourth-century Hellas, for the war set forces in motion that would debilitate Sparta even more thoroughly than they did Athens. Explaining why this war was contemplated, undertaken, and extended thus becomes the fundamental task of historians of ancient Greece. Thucydides understood this well, and devoted the long and complex first book of his history to such an explanation. Unfortunately, he failed in his stated goal to put the matter to rest (1.23). Conclusions about the war's causes since Thucydides' work have ranged from outright condemnation of Sparta for invading Athenian territory to theories of Corinthian or Periclean miscalculation to the view—apparently most popular in antiquity—that the Athenians brought the war on themselves through their own aggression.[7]

DIGRESSION: HISTORICAL CAUSATION
AND THE AESTHETICS OF HISTORY

As Thucydides recognized, complex historical events like major wars are not susceptible of simple explanations, easily summarized in a few sentences. All such events have significant prehistories, which combine with rational and irrational factors motivating individual human beings; the economic, social, religious, and political environments of the contending parties; and other forces that the Greeks would have attributed to the goddess Chance or Fortune (Tyche). It is therefore hardly surprising that modern journalists and historians cannot agree about the "real" causes of even well-documented contemporary occurrences. One is sometimes tempted to reject any search for the factors responsible for major historical events as hopeless and jejune.

But to despair of our abilities to address questions of causation in history is to regress to the status of mere chroniclers or statisticians, little better than postmodern versions of our cave-dwelling ancestors, who recorded enemies destroyed or bison brought down by means of crude images on a rock wall. Establishing events, their proper chronology, and then attaching explanations and meaning to them is in fact the task par excellence of the historian.[8] Added almost as an afterthought to the statement of his purpose in the first paragraph of Herodotus's account of Greco-Persian hostilities,[9] this idea of causation is preeminent in Thucydides' long introduction to his own work (1.1–23). Here Thucydides both addresses the historical and prehistorical factors affecting Greece before the Peloponnesian War and lays out a sophisticated theory of historical causation.

Thucydides' approach focuses on the stability, material conditions, and wealth of a people, their acquisition of naval power, and issues of "fear, honor, and self-interest," which the historian suggests play the greatest role in motivating individual historical actors (be they persons or cities).[10] Since Thucydides believed that man's nature was (basically) fixed, the study of history can prove useful for those who would seek to know what is likely to happen in the future in given circumstances:

> The absence of romantic elements in my history will, I fear, detract somewhat from its interest; but if it be judged useful by those inquirers who desire an exact knowledge of the past as an aid to the interpretation of the future, which in the course of human things must resemble if it does not reflect it, I shall be content. In short, I have written my work not merely as the exploit of a passing hour, but as a possession for all time. (Thuc. 1.22; trans. Crawley, adapted)

Thucydides thus established the goal of serious historical inquiry as description of the past as an aid for the present and future: history was to be useful. But he also laid down many of the most important technical and methodological foundations for such work.[11] Thucydides' history, whether or not it always met the disciplinary standards he himself established, also set the aesthetic standards for historiography until the nineteenth century. The best historical works, until the scholarly revolution of the 1800s, would be imitative (or "mimetic," from the Greek *mimesis*), reproducing events for the reader in a way that allowed him to experience them in his mind, as well as providing explanations for them. Historians thus sought to recreate battles and speeches in vivid fashion, and this procedure was not seen as any sacrifice of the work's historical value.[12]

Thucydides' complex conception of history (involving his aesthetic, methodological, and utilitarian standards) encouraged a few imitators but no real successors. Subsequent historians rather quickly divided into roughly three camps: those who simply pursued "the facts" of history and tended toward the chronicle, those who primarily sought out explanations of events through self-conscious application of "scientific" standards, political-philosophical theory, and avoidance of overly imitative or dramatic accounts (e.g., Polybius), and those who emphasized the imitation of human disaster or triumph (and often focused on the vagaries of Fortune), sometimes augmenting potential emotional or moral effects of the narrative at the expense of accuracy.[13] Perhaps Thucydides had set a standard combining all these elements in a way that was simply unattainable for later authors; in any case, most did not even make the attempt. Nevertheless, it must be emphasized that historians from all these camps were expected to produce beautiful (and in most cases useful) literature.

The nineteenth-century and largely German revolution in historical writing ultimately (if unintentionally) relieved the "scientific" or scholarly *(wissenschaftlicher)* historian of any remaining formal burdens of *mimesis* and the creation of "literature." By the mid twentieth century, serious historical writing was no longer expected to be beautiful. During the same period, the development of academic disciplines such as archaeology, anthropology, and sociology distanced the historian proper from the material conditions and psychology of his human subjects by making him an amateur in fields where he had once trodden confidently, but where—many now began to think—special expertise and training were necessary. It is a telling fact that the academy treated the twentieth century's application of anthropological and sociological method and theory (and most recently, literary theory) to historiography as something of a revolution, understandably and sometimes justifiably resisted by more traditional scholars.[14] Too often, many historians trained in the nineteenth–early twentieth-century school of history believed, those developing or wielding the new theories or methods did not possess sufficient grounding in purely historical data and technique to use their tools responsibly. And the members of the "old school" foresaw that such dubious use of social-scientific and literary theory or techniques could lead to the kind of anti-history often written today, in which logic, facts, evidence, and narrative are sometimes denigrated or ignored in favor of theory or individualized "stories" based less on the ancient sources than on the theories themselves.[15]

But the attempted modern combination of historical scholarship with anthropology, sociology, and archaeology is in fact nothing more than a return to fundamental principles of the first historians. Herodotus was an anthropologist every bit as much as a historian, and Thucydides relied heavily on a largely implicit but deep theory of human interaction based ultimately on his acute observation of real human beings. Modern historians should therefore welcome the recombination of the original elements of historiography (while nevertheless drawing attention to those who use such elements less than responsibly). For this recombination may not only allow us to address causation in a more sophisticated fashion; it may also encourage the pursuit of the aesthetic standards for history set by the ancients. We may, in short, see more history that is both useful and beautiful.

In their failure to hold themselves to ancient aesthetic and utilitarian standards, postmodern historical theoreticians are perhaps even more guilty of offense than the (few remaining) academic authors of traditional narrative history. For much of what theorists compose does little to nourish the reader's sense of beauty. For example, Josiah Ober writes:

Historical studies grounded in contextual specificity can gain purchase in contemporary debates when informed by the concerns of normative theory. And theory will be both tempered and strengthened by a confrontation with the pragmatic consequences of political thought and practice in a society that developed norms strikingly similar to those of modern liberalism, but predicated those familiar norms on radically unfamiliar grounds.

Professor Ober also draws heavily on theory in his discussion of the "revolution" in Athenian government ca. 507, here using an interpretation of events in the French Revolution to establish a principle:

According to the brilliant interpretation of these events by Sandy Petrey, the Third Estate's renaming of itself, and Louis' declaration that the renaming was void, set up a confrontation between speech acts—both the Third Estate and Louis made statements that were intended to have material effects in the real world of French society; both sides were attempting to enact a political reality through the speech act of naming (or, in Louis' case, "unnaming"). In the normal environment of prerevolutionary France, the king's statement would have been (in the terminology of J. L. Austin's speech-act theory, on which Petrey's interpretation is based) "felicitous" or efficacious—the Assembly would be dissolved because a sovereign authority had stated that it was dissolved. Yet, as Petrey points out, in a revolutionary situation, speech acts are not, at the moment of enunciation, either felicitous or infelicitous ipso facto. Rather, their felicity or efficacy is demonstrated only in retrospect.[16]

Such scholarship probably has little chance of exciting the aesthetic sensibilities of most human beings. But the humane and literate side of historical writing *and* the historian's interest in causation and traditional narrative must be recaptured and then fostered if the discipline is to fulfill its ultimate mission of preserving the past as a lesson for the present and window into the future.

Since the devastating and lasting effects of the Peloponnesian War on Greek history and culture make attempting to explain its causes one of the most important tasks in all of ancient historiography, it is something of an embarrassment that only two scholarly books in English have been devoted to the subject in the past half-century, and that both appeared within a few years of 1970.[17] The situation is understandable, however, given the fact that modern scholars' reactions to "another" book on such a subject often amount to "It's already been done." But those who react to a subject like the Peloponnesian War's causes with such a response betray either their view of historiography as merely the accumulation of raw data (which, once collected, become authoritative), their postmodern interest in the dead ends and backwaters of history (as opposed to central issues or major trends), or their lack of interest in the utility and potential beauty of well-done history. A more important question about any historical topic than "Has it been done?" is "Has it been done beautifully and well, and in a way that fulfills all the goals of historiography, including addressing the present and the future?" Primary even to this is the question, "What benefits could derive from study of this subject?"[18] With a subject like the Peloponnesian War, the potential benefits are enormous.

Nevertheless, the current need to ignore major (and often-studied) events while discovering uncharted historical territory in order to justify scholarship (and academic career advancement) and the postmodern interest in marginalia and in rediscovering ourselves in the past have spawned innumerable works on subjects that barely deserve mention in the lecture hall, much less years of painstaking research and documentation.[19] I once heard a lecture by an eminent scholar on the subject of Italian marriages and dowries in the fifteenth century. One of his theses appeared to be that the size of dowries had a major influence on marriages during this period. Was this detailed and formidable work of scholarship really necessary? Could one not have reasonably *inferred* the conclusion based merely on (even an imperfect) knowledge of human nature? And even if one wished to confirm this inference via research, would such confirmation merit presentation as a scholarly paper or article?

Should not every historian be forced to ask, at the outset of his task, "What is the *point* of this work?"[20] And if modern historians recoil at this impertinent question and wish simply to accumulate historical data or manipulate sociological models while leaving the interpretation, contextualization, or justification of their work to others, let them show no surprise when the resulting interpretations are disturbingly shallow or flawed,[21] or when the public and their colleagues respond with a collective (if unspoken) "So what?" when their work is done.[22]

PRELUDE TO WAR

By the late 430s Pericles' influence in Athens had risen to unprecedented heights. Having weathered the storm brought on by the controversial Samian War, the Athenian leader apparently felt able to pursue an implicit goal of his foreign policy since the 450s: Sparta must be compelled to accept Athenian predominance in Hellas (outside the Peloponnese). Pericles undoubtedly would have been delighted if the Spartans had yielded to Athenian expansionism without a fight. This might even have been a real possibility, given Sparta's sluggish foreign policy, had the Athenians not chosen to impinge on Corinth, Sparta's most important ally.[23]

Like the Athenians, the Corinthians were a great naval power with foreign projects and colonies and the extraordinary source of wealth necessary to support their ambitions. This wealth derived from the city's advantageous location: sitting astride the isthmus joining central to southern Greece and connecting the Corinthian and Saronic gulfs, Corinth served as a center for trade. Long known as "wealthy Corinth,"[24] the city provided the Spartans with a considerable fleet and, almost certainly, with much of the naval skill necessary to operate it. Situated closer to Sparta's enemies Athens and Argos than to Sparta, Corinth also guarded the land approach to the southern Peloponnese. In short, Corinth was the most important member of the Spartan alliance, which moderns call the "Peloponnesian League" and which the ancients called "the Lacedaemonians and their allies."

Between 435 and 433 the Corinthians had become involved in a war with their colony Corcyra (modern Corfu), which ultimately attracted Athenian interest. Located off mainland Greece's northwest coast and on the major sea route to the west, Corcyra was a wealthy naval power, frequently experiencing troubled relations with its mother city and rival sea power, Corinth.[25] In 433 both Corinth and Corcyra sent embassies to Athens, the Corcyreans to request Athenian aid against Corinth and the Corinthians to persuade Athens not to assist a state that fell within Corinth's sphere of influence (as a Corinthian colony). The Thirty Years' Treaty (446/5) between the Peloponnesian League and Athens stipulated that neither side was to make treaties with the other's allies. While the Corcyreans themselves were not signatories of the Thirty Years' Peace or formally allied with Corinth (and thus were technically neutral), the Corinthians asserted that assisting Corcyra against Corinth would break the spirit of the truce. For their part, the Corcyreans reminded the Athenians of Corcyra's advantageous situation for a power like Athens interested in westward expansion. Moreover, the Corcyreans maintained, an Athenian war with the Peloponnesians was inevitable, and if the Athenians did not assist Corcyra now, Corcyra's fleet would be added to that of the Peloponnesians in the coming conflict.[26]

Ultimately the Athenians voted for a defensive alliance with Corcya, by which each state would protect the other from attack but would not join in offensive actions against other states. Cimon's son Lacedaemonius was dispatched to Corcyra as general with an Athenian fleet, either because the Athenians believed this choice might allay Spartan concerns or because Pericles and his supporters wished to embarrass Lacedaemonius and/or implicate him in the new policy.[27] In the event, the Athenians at Corcyra became involved in a battle between the Corinthians and Corcyreans, and the stage was set for open Athenian-Corinthian hostilities.

In this tense environment, the Athenians demanded certain concessions from Potidaea, another Corinthian colony, but located in far northern Greece. Athens's demands included an order for the Potidaeans to pull down part of their city's walls and to give hostages. Rather than accede to Athens's dictates, the Potidaeans determined to break away from the Athenian empire. Certain Corinthians offered Potidaea assistance, and the Athenians dispatched another force northward in 432/1 to control the situation.

Meeting Athenian opposition on two fronts, the Corinthians now made a direct appeal to the Spartans for assistance. Other members of the Peloponnesian League also made complaints against the Athenians. The trade-oriented Megarians complained that they were shut out of Athenian-controlled harbors and the profitable marketplace in Athens, while citizens of the island of Aegina, strategically situated between Athens and the Peloponnese, lamented that their autonomy—supposedly ensured by the truce of 446/5—had been infringed upon.[28]

Given the anger of the Spartans' most important allies, their continued reluctance to attack Athens well demonstrates the conservative nature of

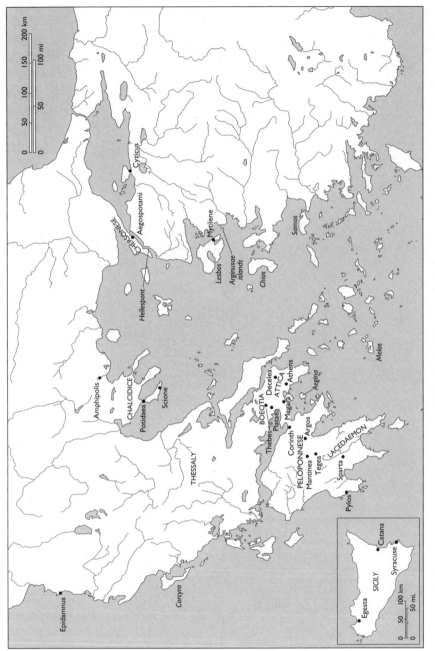

Map 3. The Peloponnesian War

Sparta's foreign policy in this period. Indeed, even after the Spartan assembly in 432 had voted that Athens had broken the treaty of 446/5 and after the synod of the Peloponnesian League had voted to make war on the Athenians, the Spartans continued to send embassies to Athens attempting to seek terms on which peace could be made.[29] At one point in the course of these negotiations, the Spartans made it clear that war could be avoided if the Athenians removed their ban on the Megarians' use of the empire's harbors and marketplace. But even this small matter, Pericles said in a speech before the Athenians, warranted a war with Sparta and its allies, since conceding on this point would lead inevitably to future concessions.[30]

Pericles' own intransigent policy toward Sparta appears ominously in the first words he speaks in Thucydides' history: "I always hold the same view, Athenians. No concessions to the Peloponnesians." The extreme unreasonability of this policy is rarely noticed: according to Thucydides, Pericles opposed not just *strategically damaging* concessions or *unjustifiable* concessions but *any* concessions. Did this policy, considering the fact that Athens was the aggressor where Corinthian/Peloponnesian interests were concerned, drive Athens and Sparta to war in 431?[31]

PERICLES AND THE CAUSES OF
THE PELOPONNESIAN WAR

If we now turn in earnest to analyzing the causes of the Peloponnesian War, earlier chapters and indeed the thesis of this book might lead us to expect to find its origins in Athens's acquisitive and belligerent democracy. I hope that what has been said about the complex causes of major events makes such a conclusion immediately unpalatable to the reader. Still, one might argue easily that the forces within Athens's *demokratia* continued to aggravate aggressive and martial Athenian tendencies until a kind of Hellenic "world war" was inevitable. But I find this view unsatisfactory too, because of my belief that political forms and other impersonal factors rarely serve as the primary or efficient cause of such major events as the Peloponnesian War, and (more important) because of Thucydides' own unwillingness to draw the conclusion that, loosely speaking, Athenian democracy caused the war.

Thucydides himself divides the causes of the war into two groups: first the *aitiai* ("reasons, blames, complaints") and *diaphorai* ("differences, points of disagreement"), and second what he calls the *alethestate prophasis* ("truest cause"). The former he gives us to understand as the conflicts between

Corinth and Athens and the other Peloponnesian complaints against Athens.³² The latter, the "truest cause," he identifies explicitly, although he says it was least spoken about openly at the time: "having become great and inspiring fear in the Spartans, the Athenians compelled them to go to war" (Thuc. 1.23).

Scholars have expended a great deal of effort to clarify what would seem, at first glance, to be a relatively straightforward statement by the historian.³³ To some degree, it would appear that this effort arises from the uncomfortable (and usually unspoken) feeling among democratically minded modern scholars that Thucydides here blames (democratic) Athens for the war, even though the (oligarchic) Spartans actually attacked Athens first. But in fact, Thucydides attaches not the slightest moral evaluation to his judgment about the "truest cause" of the war. Nor, we may speculate, would most Greek readers of the fifth century have concluded that it was unexpected, much less "wrong," either for the Athenians to have grown as powerful as possible or for the Spartans to have felt compelled to prevent Athens's further aggrandizement (which, at some point, must come at Spartan expense). But perhaps few Athenians would have claimed openly to other Greeks that Athens's goal was to become as great as possible and thus to diminish or even challenge Sparta's authority with their Peloponnesian allies, just as few Spartans would have admitted that fear of Athens's power motivated their actions. Thus the Spartans needed another reason for the war that they could state publicly, beyond their view that Athens had simply grown too powerful for Spartan comfort.³⁴

If we reasonably conclude that *demokratia* increased the Athenians' desire and perhaps even their ability to become powerful and impinge on the Spartan sphere of influence, we should not forget that Athenian aggression arose under Athens's predemocratic tyranny. Athenian ambitions existed before the institution of democracy, and the status of Sparta as the greatest power in Hellas, Athens's rich silver mines, and its proximity to the (largely Dorian) Peloponnese and Sparta probably made some kind of conflict between these two states as close to "inevitable" as anything in ancient Greek history. On the other hand, there were powerful states lying between Athens and Sparta (Corinth, Argos, and Aegina), one of which was Sparta's inveterate enemy (Argos) and another of which was a sometimes recalcitrant ally and a major sea power (Corinth). Such states could either buffer or encourage Atheno-Spartan hostilities. Moreover, Sparta's primary interest in the control of the Peloponnese and Athens's focus on the Aegean and surrounding coasts gave the two cities naturally divided spheres of interest, which offered at least the potential for peaceful coexistence. In addition, the presence of the mighty

Persian empire to the immediate east of Hellas posed a threat to the independence of all Greek states and therefore sometimes encouraged alliances between otherwise unfriendly poleis. Thus, even if we conclude that some sort of hostility between Sparta and Athens was likely in the fifth century, other factors suggest that Spartan-Athenian conflicts need not have been frequent or unusually protracted.

These considerations dictate that the most penetrating question to ask about the Peloponnesian War's causes is not simply why it occurred but rather why the war broke out precisely when it did, and then, why it lasted so much longer and spread so much further than other classical Greek wars.[35] Thucydides apparently found the answer to the first question in his *aitiai* and *diaphorai*, especially in the conflicts arising between Athens and Corinth— conflicts themselves stemming from a war between Corinth and Corcyra. Why did the war happen just then, in the late 430s? For Thucydides, it was partly because civil war had broken out in Epidamnus and the Corinthians had intervened in the affairs of that Corcyrean colony, leading to Corcyra's requests for Athenian assistance and Athens's subsequent alliance with the island.

But, of course, the Athenians might have voted *not* to involve themselves with Corcyra (as a majority did when they considered the matter in assembly on the first day, only to reverse their decision at the following day's meeting) or to accept any one of the Spartans' numerous peace proposals before spring 431. Thus even Thucydides' *aitiai* and *diaphorai* provide only the historical conditions within which the Athenians faced a choice about war. Athens's actions suggest that, under Pericles' guidance, the greater part of the demos felt that the situation in 432/1 ultimately warranted risking a conflict with Sparta.

As regards the Corcyrean alliance specifically, Thucydides provides no explanation for the Athenians' changed votes beyond acceptance of the Corcyreans' arguments: war with the Peloponnesians was inevitable, and this alliance was expedient for this reason and because of Athens's interests in the western Mediterranean. Despite the differing votes in successive assemblies, Thucydides does not even imply that this change resulted from the fickle nature of the demos, a theme that he chose to highlight elsewhere in his work, or from the leadership of a particular politician.[36] But Thucydides also neglects to inform us how many Athenians needed to change their votes to alter the policy (the number could have been quite small). Nor does he name the Athenian politician or group who proposed the acceptance of an alliance with Corcyra. Through these omissions, Thucydides in fact places the responsibility for the decision squarely on the collective Athenian demos.

Thucydides does provide a clear reason for the failure of Sparta's diplomatic efforts to secure peace by extracting some kind of concession, even a largely symbolic one, from the Athenians before war actually erupted. In this case, so far from not providing the name of the relevant political leader, Thucydides reproduces Pericles' famous speech beginning with his stated policy of "No concessions to the Peloponnesians" (Thuc. 1.140–44). Following that speech, Thucydides continues:

> Such were the words of Pericles. *The Athenians, persuaded of the wisdom of his advice, voted as he desired, and answered the Lacedaemonians as he recommended,* both on the separate points and in general: they would do nothing on dictation, but were ready to have the complaints settled in a fair and impartial manner by the legal method [i.e., arbitration], which the terms of the truce [of 446/5] prescribed. So the [Spartan] envoys departed home, and did not return again. (1.145; trans. Crawley, emphasis added)

In this passage, Thucydides goes out of his way to attribute a particular Athenian decision to a single individual, who is able to persuade the demos to follow him even against their own natural desires or judgment.[37]

Later in his narrative the historian goes even further to establish Pericles' responsibility for the war's outbreak in 432/1. When the Spartans, upon actually marching toward Athenian territory, sent out a herald to test the waters for peace one last time, their spokesman found himself prohibited from addressing the Athenian people, "for a proposal of Pericles that they should not admit either herald or embassy from the Lacedaemonians after they had marched out had already passed" (2.12). This passage is followed immediately by the report of the speech Pericles made to encourage the Athenian people as they faced the Spartan invasion (2.13).

Putting all these passages together with Thucydides' praise of Pericles as one able "to lead the demos rather than to be led by them" (2.65), we may conclude that, for Thucydides, Pericles himself served as the *sine quo non* for the outbreak of the Peloponnesian War in spring 431. Impersonal conditions (the *aitiai* and *diaphorai*) admittedly created the historical environment within which Pericles' abilities and policies could bring about this war (at this time). But when Aristophanes and others later joked that Pericles had started the war for personal motives (such as desiring to divert attention from his potential legal problems), they were simply adding a comic twist to the obvious responsibility Pericles bore for the war's outbreak in 431.[38] The democracy, in this instance, must bear the responsibility for repeatedly electing Pericles and then voting to follow his policies, but Thucydides' narrative suggests that the statesman himself led the Athenians to adopt an intransigent position that few men could have made acceptable to the demos.

I do not wish to be misunderstood. Thucydides expresses not the slightest condemnation of Pericles for encouraging the Peloponnesian War's outbreak. Moreover, Thucydides seems to have believed that Pericles' emphasis on naval power and surplus wealth had placed Athens in the best position to win the war once it started. No rational person, not even Pericles, Thucydides almost seems to say at one point, could have predicted a war that would go on for twenty-seven years.[39] Elsewhere he comments that even given the disasters that befell Athens over the war's course and the Athenians' violations of Pericles' strategy, Athens still came close to prevailing (2.65). Thucydides' amazing ability to separate himself from his personal views about the war (which there can be little doubt that he thought ultimately disastrous for Athens and Greece as a whole) allowed him to calculate coolly that Pericles, despite everything, had almost been right. Athens could have won![40]

The outbreak of the Peloponnesian War in 432/1 demonstrates the dangers of a persuasive, nationalistic, charismatic, and idealistic leader as much as the dangers of democratic government. The event suggests that a man like Pericles is sometimes capable of altering or using the political tools available to him to bring about even unpopular policies. And while democracies may offer tremendous scope for such individuals, other regimes also provide ample opportunities. As it was, Athens's fifth-century *demokratia* was particularly well suited to Pericles' style and temperament. Later demagogues like Cleon were perhaps more a function of the radicalized *demokratia* that Pericles, to some degree, had molded into a mechanism to accomplish his larger purpose. Pericles' only real successor as an extraordinary leader was his one-time ward Alcibiades, who, like his mentor, proved himself capable of remaking his own political environment and of persuading any stratum of the Athenian political body. Unfortunately for Athens, Alcibiades lacked his mentor's patriotism and scrupulous public morality.

THE PELOPONNESIAN WAR (431–404)

Pericles' death provided great opportunities for Athenian leaders wishing to capitalize on the environment created by the ongoing war with Sparta. Our sources suggest that Cleon used the empire, the war, and anti-Spartan feelings to empower himself, and perhaps to line his own pockets.[41] Under his leadership, the Athenians raised the amount of tribute demanded from their allies to at least twice its previous levels, tightened control of that tribute payment and management of the empire in general, began to tax Athens's wealthier citizens when the immense war chest established under Pericles began to dissipate, voted for the mass execution of all male citizens and enslavement of the women and children of states revolting from the Athenian empire, and refused Spartan offers of peace on favorable terms.[42]

When we compare Thucydides' (and Aristophanes') unflattering portrait of Cleon with the historian's treatment of the similarly radical and "democratic" Pericles, we are led to conclude that Cleon supported and encouraged such policies because it brought him power rather than because he held any particular ideal of Athenian supremacy. Thucydides found no occasion to praise Cleon's public morality as he had Pericles', despite the latter's democratic policies and Thucydides' own self-proclaimed preference for a moderate oligarchy over democracy.[43] Thus, even if we can excuse the Athenian demos to some degree for its willingness to follow a man like Pericles (even into a disastrous war against Athens's former allies), we are hard pressed to issue such a pardon for the demos's captivation by Cleon and his supporters. Fortunately for Athens, Cleon met his end in 422 in the battle of Amphipolis, which also took the life of Brasidas, a leading Spartan proponent of war. Peace with Sparta followed almost immediately, arranged by the moderate Athenian leader Nicias in early 421. The terms of the Peace of Nicias in 421 returned Greece to its prewar political conditions, with minor exceptions.[44]

To the extent that Athens had persuaded Sparta to accept the Peace of Nicias (and thus prewar conditions), the ten-year war had been an Athenian "success." We may well question whether the Megarian Decree—the Athenian revocation of which might have achieved the same end in 431—justified a decade of warfare with Sparta. The Athenians, however, seem to have had few such misgivings. In fact, what is most surprising about the period following 421 is the swiftness with which the Athenian demos resumed hostilities with Sparta and then took on a new war of conquest in the west. The ten-year war with Sparta had not, in fact, hardened Athenian opinion against aggressive and extensive military operations. The Athenians of the period from 420 to 416 were not a people exhausted or thoroughly disgusted by the prospect of war, despite the thousands of lives and thousands of talents expended over the previous decade. If anything, Athenian militarism rebounded and then increased during the brief cessation of hostilities.

For a short period of time after spring 421 the Athenians actually allied with the Spartans against other Greek states unhappy with the peace (Thuc. 5.23). But by 419 Athens was once more hostile to the Lacedaemonians, supporting the Spartans' bitter rival Argos in the Argives' Peloponnesian adventures. The result was a major hoplite battle in the central Peloponnese in 418 (Mantinea), at which the Spartans resoundingly defeated an Atheno-Argive force and reestablished their Peloponnesian supremacy and their reputation as the greatest land power in Hellas.[45]

Even this defeat did not soften Athenian imperialist designs, which by 416 were once more growing. In that year the island of Melos, a Spartan colony and one of the only Aegean islands not already a part of the Athenian empire, was surrounded and ordered to pay tribute to Athens.[46] Melian support of the Spartans during the ten-year war probably provided the pretext for this, but in Thucydides' famous "Melian Dialogue" the Athenians brazenly admit that they require no more justification for their action than the simple fact that they *can* reduce Melos to tributary status.[47] Not to do so, the Athenians maintain, would be evidence of Athens's weakness. The Melians' appeals to justice and their faith in the gods and their Spartan relations are dismissed as folly by the Athenians in a famous passage:

Melians. You may be sure that we are as well aware as you of the difficulty of contending against your power and fortune, unless the terms be equal. But we trust with the help of the gods that our fortune may be as good as yours, since we are just men fighting against unjust, and that what we want in power will be made up by the alliance of the Lacedaemonians, who are bound, if only for very shame, to come to the aid of their kindred. Our confidence, therefore, after all is not so utterly irrational.

Athenians. When you speak of the favor of the gods, we may as fairly hope for that as yourselves, neither our pretensions nor our conduct being in any way contrary to what men believe of the gods, or practice among themselves. Of the gods we believe, and of men we know, that by a necessary law of their nature they rule wherever they can. And it is not as if we were the first to make this law, or to act upon it when made: we found it existing before us, and shall leave it to exist for ever after us; all we do is to make use of it, knowing that you and everybody else, having the same power as we have, would do the same as we do. Thus, as far as the gods are concerned, we have no fear and no reason to fear to have the worse. But when we come to your notion about the Lacedaemonians, which leads you to believe that shame will make them help you, here we bless your simplicity but do not envy your folly. The Lacedaemonians, where their interests or their country's laws are in question, are the worthiest men alive; of their conduct toward others much might be said, but no clearer idea of it could be given than by shortly saying that of all men we know they most indubitably consider what is agreeable honorable, and what is expedient just. Such a way of thinking does not promise much for the safety which you now unreasonably count upon.[48]

The Melians nevertheless resisted and were destroyed. As Thucydides bluntly writes, the Athenians "put to death all the grown men whom they took, and sold the women and children for slaves, and subsequently sent out five hundred colonists and inhabited the place themselves" (5.116; trans. Crawley). This infamous example of Athenian brutality, which became paradigmatic for all those wishing to cast aspersions on Athens or its democracy, speaks for itself.[49] For our discussion of Athenian and democratic foreign policy, this action underscores (as much as, if not more than, Athens's alliance with Corcyra in 433) the Athenian willingness to put Sparta in an extremely difficult position vis-à-vis its Peloponnesian allies. The Spartans, an Athenian could reasonably have held, would be virtually compelled to react to Athens's destruction of Melos (if not the island's investment) or risk serious embarrassment with their allies. That is, the Athenians had every reason to believe that their treatment of Melos might result in the renewal of war with Sparta. Thus, when the Athenians discussed the operation against Melos in the assembly—and they must have done so, especially since the siege of Melos went on for some time before the island's capitulation—some Athenians must have warned the demos that this aggression risked reigniting the war with Sparta. This devastating war had ended only five years earlier (in 421) and had almost resumed in 418 with the battle of Mantinea. Thucydides does not report this debate over Melos, perhaps because Sparta in the end reacted in a sluggish fashion and proved, as the Athenians had warned the Melians, that of all men the Spartans most readily considered "what is agreeable honorable, and what is expedient just."

But our own knowledge of the events following Melos's destruction should not deflect our focus from what must have been discussed in the Athenian assembly before these events. In 416 the Athenian people in assembly contemplated risking another war with Sparta so that they might impose their will on the island of Melos. The Athenian demos concluded, in the end, that the risk was justified. The Athenian democracy's martial character in the period could hardly be demonstrated more clearly.

Ironically, modern studies usually treat Sparta as the archetype of Greek militarism, characterizing it as "a perpetual armed camp."[50] But this evaluation echoes *fourth-century* judgments of the Spartans and thus reflects the Lacedaemonians' own period of hyperaggression and militarism, which followed the Peloponnesian War and ultimately spawned a Greek alliance against Sparta in 378/7.[51] In fact, Thucydides' history and the Athenians' own actions clearly show that fifth-century Greek states considered the Spartans' *reluctance* to undertake military action (especially outside the Peloponnese) to be their foreign policy's defining quality.[52] Surely the fact that fifth-century Spartan citizens actually trained for warfare does not make them more militaristic than the Athenians, who trained less but voted repeatedly in open assembly to impose their will on other Greeks, and who then carried out their own democratic decrees with brutal efficiency. Table 1 illustrates the relative militarism of Sparta and Athens in the five decades or so before the Peloponnesian War.[53]

A final example will buttress this demonstration of Athenian hyperaggression, aggravated by its democratic government. Usefully, it occurs in the same historical environment as Athens's decision to risk war with Sparta in 416. In that same year, the Athenians received a request for assistance from the city of Egesta, an Athenian ally in Sicily. The Egesteans sought aid against an enemy state that happened to be allied with Syracuse, a colony of Corinth and the greatest Greek power in the western Mediterranean. Athenian ambassadors were dispatched to Egesta, where the Egesteans tricked the Athenians into believing that they could provide significant financial support for an Athenian expeditionary force. The Athenian demos ultimately approved the request for assistance, which would almost certainly involve them in hostilities with Syracuse, and then held a second assembly to consider the details of the expedition. Thucydides provides a vivid account of this second meeting, reporting speeches by Nicias (against the action) and Alcibiades (favoring an expedition to Sicily).[54] The historian also begins his account of these matters with a long digression on the antiquity, size, and power of the Greek and non-Greek settlements of Sicily, thus foreshadowing statements made by Nicias about the magnitude of the undertaking the Athenian demos was contemplating.[55]

Nicias's final rhetorical strategy designed to dissuade the Athenians from embarking on an expedition to Sicily resulted in disaster: he not only failed to discourage the Athenians by detailing the very great size of the force necessary, but actually assuaged their fears that a smaller force might run significant risks. Thus his speech, combined with Alcibiades' optimistic and charismatic account of Athens's undoubted success and the need of an empire to continue growing or else die, resulted in the Athenian electorate's overwhelming vote supporting the invasion of Sicily.[56] As we have already seen, Thucydides describes the scene chillingly, emphasizing the reluctance that those who opposed the expedition felt about raising their hands to vote

TABLE I
Athenian and Spartan Military Action in the Mid Fifth Century

	Athenian Actions	Atheno-Spartan Relations	Spartan Actions
470s (after 479/8)	Eion besieged and captured Scyros taken and colonized Carystus forced into league	Spartan-Athenian expedition against Cyprus, Byzantium (478)	Expedition to Thessaly (478?: Hdt. 6.72) Tegea (?: Hdt. 9.35)
460s	Naxos reduced Eurymedon (ca. 466) Campaign in/colonization of Chersonese (?: Plut. Cim. 14) Thasos reduced (465–463) Attempt to colonize Ennea Hodoi (?) Naval sweeps by Ephialtes (and Pericles?: Plut. Cim. 13) Cimon's expedition to Sparta (462/1)		Dipaea (?: vs. Arcadians except Mantinea (Hdt. 9.35) Ithome (vs. helots/ Messenians, 465–456?: Hdt. 9.35 with Thuc. 1.101–3) Stenyclerus (? in Messenian War: Hdt. 9.64)
450s	Occupation of Megara Attack on Cyprus (ca. 459) Invasion of Egypt Attack on Halieis (vs. Corinth) Cecryphalea (vs. Pelop. fleet) War with Aegina Other actions vs. Corinth/Megara (Thuc. 1.105–6)	First Peloponnesian War (ca. 460–446) Corinthian actions vs. Athens (459–455)	Battle of Oenoe (?: vs. Argives/Athenians: Paus. 1.15.1, 10.10.4)
	Tanagra Oenophyta (vs. Boeotians) Aegina forced to surrender Tolmides' attacks on the Peloponnese Capture of Naupactus (?) Attack on Sicyon Final defeat in Egypt (454?) Thessaly invaded to restore Orestes	Battle of Tanagra (Sparta/Boeotians vs. Athens: 458/7)	Expedition to Doris; Tanagra Spartans capture Halieis (?: Hdt. 7.137.2)

TABLE 1 *(continued)*

Athenian Actions	Atheno-Spartan Relations	Spartan Actions
	Attack on Sicyon and Acarnania	
	Five Years' Truce (451)	
	Expedition to Cyprus and Egypt	
440s	II Sacred War (vs. Delphians)	II Sacred War (in favor of Delphians)
	Expedition to Chersonese (?: *CAH* V².127–28)	
	Revolt and invasion of Boeotia; Coronea (447/6?)	
	Expeditions to Euboea and Megara (after revolt)	Abortive invasion of Attica (446)
		Thirty Years' Truce (446/5)
	Democracy imposed on Samos (441)	
	Samian revolt and war (440–439)	
430s	Colonization of Amphipolis (437/6: Diod. 12.32.2, schol. Aeschin. 2.31)	
	Actions in Acarnania and Ambracia (?); Pericles' expedition to Black Sea (?: Plut. *Per.* 20.1–2 with *CAH* V².145–46)	
	Battle of Sybota (vs. Corinth: 433)	
	Siege of Potidaea (after revolt)	
	Siege of Potidaea continues	Peloponnesian War (431–404)	Spartans invade Attica (431)

against it and the desire for pay and adventure that motivated many of those who supported it.[57] Thucydides' eloquent description of the dangers inherent in making foreign policy by majority decision resonates because everyone reading it has felt the compulsion to raise his hand (at least metaphorically) when those of others were raised.

Poor generalship and the failure of the demos to support its forces adequately or make good decisions about the expedition's command resulted in utter disaster for the Athenian troops and their allies in Sicily. After failing to fight their way out of the Syracusan harbor, the surviving trireme crews and thousands of Athenian and allied infantrymen—no fewer than forty thousand men, according to Thucydides (7.75)—abandoned the dead and wounded and determined to try to march across Sicily toward what they thought was safety. On this horrific death march, the Syracusans harassed the hungry and exhausted Athenians and their allies for several days and nights, until those still alive reached the Assinarus River in southeast Sicily. Thucydides completes his account of the expedition with the most memorable passage in his entire work:

> As soon as it was day [the Athenian general] Nicias put his army into motion, pressed as before by the Syracusans and their allies, pelted from every side by their missiles and struck down by their javelins. The Athenians pushed on for the Assinarus, impelled by the attacks made upon them from every side by numerous cavalry and the swarm of other arms, fancying that they should breathe more freely if once across the river, and driven on also by their exhaustion and craving for water.
>
> Once there they rushed in, and all order was at an end, each man wanting to cross first, and the attacks of the enemy making it difficult to cross at all, since they were forced to huddle together, and so fell against and trod down one another, some dying immediately upon the javelins, others getting entangled together and stumbling over the articles of baggage, without being able to rise again. Meanwhile the opposite bank, which was steep, was lined by the Syracusans, who showered missiles down upon the Athenians, most of them drinking greedily and heaped together in disorder in the hollow bed of the river. The Peloponnesians also came down and butchered them, especially those in the water, which was thus immediately spoiled, but which they went on drinking just the same, mud and all, bloody as it was, most even fighting to have it.
>
> At last, after many dead now lay piled one upon another in the stream, and part of the army had been destroyed at the river, and the few that escaped from there had been cut off by the cavalry, Nicias surrendered himself to [the Spartan commander] Gylippus, whom he trusted more than he did the Syracusans, and told him and the Lacedaemonians to do what they like with him, but to stop the slaughter of the soldiers. . . . [Most of the Athenians still alive were now taken prisoner, although some were secretly sold into slavery and some managed to escape.]
>
> The Syracusans and their allies now mustered and took up the spoils and as many prisoners as they could, and went back to the city [of Syracuse]. The rest of their Athenian and allied captives were deposited in the quarries, this seem-

ing the safest way of keeping them; but Nicias and [the other Athenian general] Demosthenes were butchered, against the will of Gylippus, who thought that it would be the crown of triumph if he could take the enemy's generals to Lacedaemon. One of them, Demosthenes, was one of her greatest enemies . . . and the other, Nicias, was . . . one of her greatest friends, owing to his exertions to [persuade the Athenians to make peace in 421]. For these reasons the Lacedaemonians felt kindly towards him; and it was in this that Nicias himself mainly confided when he surrendered himself to Gylippus. . . . [Nevertheless, certain Syracusans secured Nicias's execution.] This or the like was the cause of the death of a man who, of all the Hellenes in my time, least deserved such a fate, from his exact attention to virtue *[arete]*.

The prisoners in the quarries were at first harshly treated by the Syracusans. Crowded in a narrow hole, without any roof to cover them, after being tormented by the heat of the sun and the stifling closeness of the air, during the day, the violent change to the nights, which came on autumnal and chilly, undermined their health; besides, as they had to do everything in the same place for want of room, and the bodies of those who died of their wounds or from the variation in the temperature or from similar causes were left heaped together one upon another, intolerable stenches arose; and hunger and thirst never ceased to afflict them, each man during eight months having only half a pint of water and a pint of corn given him daily. In short, no single suffering to be apprehended by men thrust into such a place was spared them. For some seventy days they thus lived all together, after which all except the Athenians and any Sicilian or Italian Greeks who had joined in the expedition were sold. The total number of prisoners taken it would be difficult to state exactly, but it could not have been less than seven thousand.

This was the greatest achievement of any in this war, or, in my opinion, in Hellenic history; it was at once the most glorious to the victors, and most calamitous to the conquered. They were beaten at all points and altogether; all that they suffered was great; they were destroyed, as the saying is, with a total destruction; their fleet, their army—there was nothing that was not destroyed, and few out of many returned home.

Such were the events in Sicily.[58]

We may speculate that practically every Athenian family in 413 was touched directly by the disastrous end of Athens's expedition to Sicily. Most must have lost a brother, a father, an uncle, or at least a cousin in this campaign. Despite this fact, *the Athenian people determined to continue the war against Sparta,* making changes in their system of tribute collection and eventually in the form of government itself in an attempt to press on when their financial resources had been exhausted.[59]

Some of the most infamous acts committed by the Athenians occurred during the Peloponnesian War's final years. These events are usually associated most directly with the oligarchic revolutions of 411 and 404 (examined in chapter 3), and the assassinations and injustice ultimately flowing from both. But as Socrates reminded the Athenians in his defense speech in 399, it was the demos itself *during the democracy* that chose to violate Athenian custom and execute an entire group of generals without separate trials or customary defense.[60] Eight generals, it was alleged, were responsible for allowing shipwrecked Athenians and dead bodies to go unrecovered after the Athenian victory at the Arginusae islands (near Lesbos) in 406. The assembly voted to execute all six generals then in Athens—two had chosen not to return—among them Pericles' son by Aspasia, Pericles II, who had been granted citizenship by a special law by the same demos that now passed a sentence of death on him.[61] Xenophon describes the Athenians' decision to execute the generals in his *Hellenika:*

Euryptolemus, the son of Peisianax, and a few others now intervened with a summons against Callixenus for putting forward an unconstitutional proposal [that the Athenians should vote on the guilt of the generals in assembly without the normal legal procedures], and some sections of the Assembly clearly backed them in this. However, the great mass shouted out that it was an intolerable thing if the people were not allowed to do what it wanted to do. Lysicus took up this theme and proposed that unless the sponsors of the summons withdrew it, they too should be judged by the same vote as the generals. They were thus forced to withdraw the summons.

Next some members of the presiding committee [the *prytaneis*] declared that they would not put the motion to a vote, since it was an illegal one. Callixenus then mounted the platform again and put forward the same charge against *them,* and the crowd shouted out that, if they refused, they [the *prytaneis*] should be prosecuted. At this all the members of the committee except Socrates, the son of Sophroniscus, were terrified and agreed to put the motion to the vote. Socrates said that he would do nothing at all that was contrary to the law. . . .

[The Athenian Euryptolemus now made a speech in favor of following traditional legal procedures in the case of the generals.] After making this speech, Euryptolemus put forward a motion that each of the men should be given a separate trial in accordance with the decree of Cannonus. The Council's motion, of course, was that they should all be tried together by one vote. When a vote was taken on these two motions they at first decided in favor of the proposal of Euryptolemus. Menecles then lodged an objection under oath; another vote was taken, and this time the Council's proposal was approved. Then they voted on the eight generals who had taken part in the naval action and found them guilty. The six who were in Athens were put to death.

Quite soon afterwards the Athenians regretted what they had done and voted that complaints should be lodged against those who had deceived the people; that those against whom complaints were lodged should have to provide sureties for themselves until their case came up for trial, and that Callixenus should be included among them. Complaints were lodged against four others apart from him and all were put in confinement by their guarantors. Late, however, in the course of the disturbances in which [the demagogue] Cleophon was put to death, they escaped before being brought to trial. Callixenus did come back again at the time [in 404/3] when the [democratic] Piraeus party returned to the city; but everyone loathed him and he died of starvation.[62]

The execution or exile of failed Athenian commanders or other officials was hardly an unusual event.[63] But the mechanism employed in 406 and the blanket nature of the generals' convictions (as well as Socrates' refusal to put the matter before the people for a vote while serving on the assembly's presiding committee) mark this event out as unorthodox even by Athenian standards.[64]

While such actions by the demos may have been aggravated by the ongoing war, which most Athenian voters continued to support, these matters do not fall properly under the rubric of foreign policy. One must note, however, that even after the almost complete destruction of the Athenian fleet at Aegospotami in the Chersonese in 405, the Athenians continued to refuse to make peace until they were blockaded for several months and starved into submission.[65]

The Peloponnesian War stretched over the course of an entire generation. It was waged by a free people for their own aggrandizement—rather than their protection—and resulted in the deaths of countless Athenians and other Greeks, the temporary collapse of *demokratia,* and the permanent loss of the empire that had funded it. Although the Athenians had refused offers of peace from Sparta on favorable terms earlier in the war (and although the Spartan general Lysander supported the oligarchic regime of the Thirty that ruled Athens in 404–403), the Spartans themselves prevented the destruction of Athens in 404, and a Spartan king ultimately fostered the reconciliation between rival factions that led to the reinstitution of *demokratia* in 403.[66]

Had the Spartans acceded to their allies' wishes in 404, they would have executed a truly illustrious group of Athenians, including almost certainly

Aristophanes, Socrates, Plato, Xenophon, Isocrates, and perhaps even expatriates or exiles like Andocides and Thucydides, *all of whom, with the exceptions of Aristophanes and Socrates, had yet to write or publish their now famous works.*[67] The Spartans, we must emphasize, need only have done to Athens what the Athenians (with far less justification) had done in Melos and Scione—executing the entire male population—to have destroyed crucial fundaments of classical culture, philosophy, and the Western tradition.[68] And the Athenians rightly feared that they *would* suffer this punishment at the hands of their enemies.[69] Are we unjustified in showing considerable gratitude to Sparta for our classical heritage, and in asking what kind of men *did* die in the war (on both sides) and what we have lost because of their deaths?

The Peloponnesian War devastated Athens and brought forces into play that seriously undermined the system of independent poleis dominating the classical Greek world. And even those who would deny that Athens's democratic regime bears some responsibility for starting this war cannot deny that the democracy played no role whatsoever in ending it.

SIX

National Defense
Democracy Defeated

Hope, danger's comforter, may be indulged in
by those who have more than ample resources, if not
without loss at all events without ruin; but its nature is to
be extravagant, and those who go so far as to put their all
upon the venture see it in its true colors only when they
are ruined; but so long as the discovery would enable
them to guard against it, it is never found wanting.

THE ATHENIANS TO THE MELIANS
(Thuc. 5.103; trans. R. Crawley, adapted)

A FOURTH-CENTURY EMPIRE?

The history of Athenian foreign policy in the fourth century is complex and
sordid. It reflects, almost down to the very moment before Athens's defeat by
Macedon in 338, an understandable, if unjustified, Athenian confidence in
their status as an independent, sovereign, and democratic polity. Having survived the Persian invasions and the Peloponnesian War, few Athenians seem
to have worried that Athens might actually come under a foreign power's
sway. Alliances were made and then ignored or dissolved with unsettling
swiftness. The Athenian people, at first attempting to protect themselves
from Spartan hegemony (395–371), then sought to assist Sparta in the face of
a new threat presented by the Thebans' rise to power (370–362). Meanwhile
the alliance formed by Athens (initially) against Spartan aggression and
known as the Second Athenian League (378/7) failed to produce the revenues

or attitudes needed to reestablish real Athenian supremacy in the Aegean. The Athenians' efforts to rebuild their power suffered from domestic resistance to the necessary sacrifices and from restrictions on Athens's freedom as the league's leader—restrictions Athens accepted in an attempt to assure its allies that the fourth-century league would not go the way of the fifth-century alliance. Athens's fourth-century allies understandably sought to avoid becoming subjects of any renewed Athenian imperial power.

The fifth-century Athenians bequeathed to their fourth-century descendants the expensive form of government called *demokratia,* but denuded of the imperial revenues that had supported it; Athens's record of domination, which made the reestablishment of old alliances and imperial revenues difficult; and a public morale that made individual citizens less willing to make sacrifices to empower (or protect) the state. Pericles' contemporaries and immediate successors had also squandered the thousands of talents built up as a war chest during the fifth century. Fourth-century Athens would never possess the surplus wealth that Pericles and Thucydides believed was necessary for successful warfare in antiquity (especially naval warfare). To make matters worse, the Attic silver mines seem to have become less productive in the fourth century.[1] In the years after 404, Athens found herself on a financial footing resembling that of other large Hellenic cities.

In terms of leadership, too, fourth-century Athens seems to have found itself at something of a disadvantage when compared with the fifth-century polis. In part, this undoubtedly derived from Athenian losses during the Peloponnesian War. No lineal descendants of Cimon or Pericles seem to have inherited the mantle of their fathers, grandfathers, and great-grandfathers. In fact, few leaders of fourth-century Athens could boast ancestors who had commanded Athenian forces during the Peloponnesian War, much less before it.[2] The Athenian leadership's ranks, dominated in the fifth century by families with connections to the sixth-century tyrants, had been another casualty of the long war and the demos's exiling and execution of its own generals, a practice that obviously had deleterious effects on wealthy Athenians' desire to serve.

Leaders from new families emerged in and after the Peloponnesian War to take up the reins of political leadership and military command.[3] And while these families were obviously capable of producing brilliant or capable leaders, these men did not bring a long tradition of leadership with them into office. While one may reasonably doubt whether this lack of family tradition actually affected their abilities or skills, there can be little question that the new leaders' lack of inherited standing affected the way the Athenian people viewed them. And once we admit that the people are not likely to have viewed Cleon or Demosthenes in the same way they did a grandson of Miltiades, it becomes fair to suppose that these new leaders looked for some means to compensate for their lack of ancestral standing.[4]

The fourth-century trend toward separating the informal position of *demagogos*—a rhetor who advised (and in the best cases led) the demos—from the elected position of general also had a potentially debilitating effect on Athenian leadership, encouraging men who had not taken on the onerous duties of command to make proposals to the people about foreign policy.[5] Meanwhile, the dangers that attended a military or political career, and that came in the form of trial, fines, exile, and execution at the hands of the demos, certainly discouraged some capable Athenians from seeking either to advise or to command the demos.[6] At least one promising Athenian commander— Xenophon—joined the adventurers accompanying Cyrus in his attempt to overthrow the Persian Great King in 401 and went on to serve under the Spartan king Agesilaus and spend much of his life as a Spartan retainer.[7] Plato and a few others like him took up philosophy and retreated to the Academy. Both men had been associates of Socrates, and the execution of their friend and teacher left an indelible mark on their attitudes toward democracy and state service, and probably on the attitudes of many other young noblemen.[8]

Of course, many others did seek to advise the demos in assembly and to command in the field. Yet the loss of one or two men of brilliance can be devastating to any regime. If we look back on the fifth century, removing (let us say) either Cimon or Pericles, Themistocles or Alcibiades, the history of Athens in that period becomes far more difficult to picture clearly. (The same might be said of removing Winston Churchill or Franklin Roosevelt from the twentieth century's history.) Lifting a potential Cimon or Themistocles out of a pool of leaders in the fourth century therefore represents far more than the loss of just one man: it may in fact represent the loss of *the* man crucial to a certain line of history. Thus the withdrawal of Plato and Xenophon in itself constituted a potentially monumental drain on Athenian leadership. Since, moreover, they are only the best-known representatives of a larger group of disaffected or displaced Athenians, and since Athens was a minuscule state (by modern standards) with a correspondingly small pool of leadership talent, the crisis of leadership in fourth-century Athens may have been acute.

Unfortunately for Athenian foreign policy, the demos took no actions to alter the policies that continued to discourage wealthy and capable individuals from entering state service. Failing generals continued to be prosecuted in public suits by private enemies and public rivals. Athenian policy was tested in Athens's courts before hundreds of paid jurors as frequently as it was decided in the field or in the assembly. Generals were tried and fined or condemned to death with shocking frequency.[9] By one estimate, as many as one-fifth of Athenian generals faced indictment after their service through a procedure known as *eisangelia,* and this usually resulted in conviction and a sentence of death.[10] Since the Athenians had other procedures besides *eisangelia* by which to bring their generals to trial, the peril faced by those choosing to serve as *strategoi* appears to have been great.[11] As a leading scholar has written,

> No matter whether the generals deserved the sentences passed on them or not, the numerous *eisangeliai* cast a shadow over the Athenian democracy and indicate that a direct democracy may employ the same judicial methods as a totalitarian state. So the Athenians behaved as *tyrannoi* not only against their allies but also against their own leaders.[12]

Even a general who found himself unharassed by the demos or his political enemies faced financial constraints that might make it necessary for him to rent out his forces to foreign powers, take out personal loans, or raid other states to secure pay for his troops.[13] For these reasons, commanding Athenian forces in the fourth century often proved to be a grim and frustrating affair. Athens's most able commanders in this period, men such as Timotheus and Iphicrates, spent a considerable portion of their careers in voluntary or state-imposed exile, even serving as mercenary commanders under Persian or Thracian dynasts.[14] Timotheus and Iphicrates also waged private wars on each other through the courts until finally contracting a marriage alliance.[15] But this alliance could not save Timotheus from the Athenian jurors; he ultimately fled Athens and died in exile after his conviction and a fine of 100 talents.[16]

The Athenians' willingness to prosecute and condemn their own commanders had begun to take a toll on Athens's military efficiency at least as early as the 420s. Pericles was fined and probably removed from office as *strategos* in the first years of the Peloponnesian War, and the fifth-century general Demosthenes also feared the demos's wrath early in his career and may have been removed from a command.[17] Phormio, perhaps Athens's greatest naval commander at that time, apparently dropped out of public life after his own run-in with the Athenian demos.[18] During the Athenians' invasion of Sicily in 415–413, the general Nicias refused to adopt certain policies at least in part because he feared the demos's wrath upon his return to Athens, despite the special powers that he and his colleagues had been granted before they left Athens.[19] After the destruction of most of Athens's fleet in 405, the Athenian general Conon elected not to return to the city with the few ships that had survived the disaster because he dreaded the people's wrath.[20] Thus, although the wholesale execution of Athenian generals in 406 after Arginusae became infamous, it represents merely a particularly egregious example of the troubled relationship between the Athenian demos and its chosen commanders.[21] The Athenians' elected generals served as a convenient focus for the citizens' disappointment with the failed policies that they themselves had endorsed via vote in the assembly.

Athenian practice in this area surely hampered Athens's war efforts on more occasions than Nicias's failed withdrawal from Sicily. Unfortunately, since it is usually impossible to determine when a general took (or did not take) a specific action primarily because of his worries about later prosecution, we cannot clearly trace the effects of these trials on particular campaigns. But to deny their effects would be like denying the effects of malpractice suits on the modern practice of medicine. And while contemporary physicians have developed protection through malpractice insurance and are hardly (like the Athenian generals) in fear of their lives in the event of a mistake, the only protection available to Athenian *strategoi* was flight from office or from Athens.[22]

A decline in leadership was only one of the many factors that prevented the Athenians of the fourth century from recreating the fifth-century Athenian empire or defending themselves against Macedonian aggression. Not only had the silver mines apparently become less productive, but Athenian citizens had become less willing to serve abroad in order to ensure their public and private incomes. Taxation of wealthy Athenians proved to be a far less dangerous way to supplement public revenues, even if it alienated the wealthy and failed to generate the income necessary for public payments *and* imperial ambitions. In addition, given Athens's imperialism in the previous century and its failure to provide effective aid to its allies in the fourth, the other fourth-century Greek states were much more circumspect about committing themselves to an Athenian alliance and serving under Athenian generals. A picture emerges of a people desirous of power and income, but unwilling to make the personal and public sacrifices necessary to secure either.

THE RISE OF MACEDON AND
THE END OF ATHENIAN DEMOCRACY

I intend to pass over the shifting alliances of the earlier fourth century in order to focus on the great crisis Athens faced around midcentury. At that time, Hellas saw the rise of a new Aegean "superpower," emerging from a very unlikely location in the foothills of far northern Greece. The Macedonians inhabiting this country had always been considered backward and even semi-barbaric by the Greeks to their south.[23] For although (at least some) Macedonians spoke Greek and their kings traced their heritage back to Argos, they did not practice polis life like most other Greeks.[24] They therefore had no long tradition of free and sovereign cities governed by citizen assemblies and magistrates that were either elected or chosen by lot. Indeed, Macedonian government probably resembled Homeric kingdoms of the *Odyssey* or *Iliad* more than regimes governing classical poleis.[25]

Although the Macedonian kings had been important, if secondary, players in the northern Aegean at least since the early fifth century, they had played no crucial role in inter-Greek relations south of Thessaly before the 350s. Indeed, one scholar has called Macedon before 360 a "banana monarchy," remarking that, given Macedon's problems, when a Macedonian ruler came to power, "the Athenians knew that they need scarcely take the new king more seriously than a figure in a comic opera."[26]

But in 360 or 359 Philip II became king of Macedon and swiftly and forever altered the balance of power in the Balkan peninsula. Having spent some of his formative years in Thebes during the period of that city's greatest military achievements, Philip apparently had absorbed the advances in infantry tactics engineered by the Thebans Epaminondas and Pelopidas.[27] Reforming the Macedonian ground troops into a new phalanx of tremendous mobility and speed and armed with a longer lance (the *sarissa*), he combined this deadly infantry with the already superior Macedonian cavalry, lightly armed mercenaries, and new technologies like catapults to create a superb military force.[28] In defeating the barbarian tribes to his north and west, Philip largely ended the raids that had sometimes preoccupied and weakened previous Macedonian kings. Moving eastward against western Thrace, he seized the crucial mining district around Crenides and renamed the city after himself (Philippi).[29]

Scholars have questioned why Macedon became so powerful at this moment in history. Surely, it has been suggested recently, this rise should be attributed largely to something other than Philip's own ingenuity or charisma.[30] However, given Macedon's previously lackluster history, the answer must lie—at least in part—precisely in Philip himself. His personal circumstances, skills, and ambition led him to adopt and improve the latest military innovations in Greece and the East.[31] Philip then combined these advantages with the acquisition of a ready stream of income from the Thracian mines seized early in his reign. As we have already noted, such mines were rare in Hellas. By seizing them, Philip immediately put himself in a position of financial superiority over every other Greek state.[32] The new army, the new money, and the ambitious and talented king together converted Macedon into a real (if initially underappreciated) Balkan power by the mid 350s. In those years, Philip began to encroach directly on territories along the north-western Aegean coastline where the Athenians had long-standing interests.

What was the condition of Athens around the mid fourth century as the citizens contemplated this new development to the north? Superficially, Athens seemed to have recovered some portion of the power and status it had lost after the Peloponnesian War ended in 404. By the mid 390s, the Athenians had forged an alliance with Corinth and Thebes against Sparta, and had begun attempting to regain holdings in the Aegean and the Hellespont. The Corinthian War (395–387/6) ended with a peace imposed on the Greeks by the Great King of Persia and enforced by the Spartans. The "King's Peace" ensured Spartan supremacy in mainland Hellas, but at the cost of abandoning the Greeks of Asia Minor, who once more came under Persian sway.[33] Moreover, the Athenians and other Greeks, both in and outside the Peloponnese, grew increasingly uneasy about Spartan aggression, which reached its peak in the late 380s, when the Spartans installed a garrison in Thebes. By 378/7, the Athenians had brought together a group of allies including Thebes and Chios in the so-called Second Athenian League. Explicitly designed to protect its members from Sparta, the league rested on a charter that contained provisions intended to prevent the Athenians from converting this alliance (like the fifth-century Delian League) into their own imperial tool: Athens was to collect no tribute; it was to seize or occupy no territory in the allied states, and the league would be governed by a council *(synedrion)* with two houses: allied representatives on the one side and the Athenian assembly on the other.[34]

In terms of finance alone, the Second Athenian League was incomparably weaker than the old Athenian empire. Despite the fact that the Athenians eventually began to collect "contributions" *(syntaxeis)* from the allies and taxed their own wealthy citizens with increasing frequency, Athenian generals often found themselves without funds for their expeditions.[35] To make matters worse, as we have seen these generals frequently faced prosecution and condemnation upon their return to Athens if their underfunded expeditions failed.

The rise of Thebes as a major power led to a radical change in Athenian policy.[36] The Thebans defeated the Spartan infantry at Leuctra in 371, and the Athenians quickly decided that a powerful Thebes (to their immediate north) posed a greater threat than Spartan imperialism, especially since Sparta now seemed weakened. Reversing their field, the Athenians in the early 360s allied with Sparta against Thebes, while maintaining the second league (obviously now without Thebes as an active member).[37] While attempting to help the Spartans resist Theban aggression on the mainland, the Athenians also began to renew their efforts in the northern Aegean. In the northeast, the Persians threatened Athenian interests around the Chersonese, while in the northwest, instability in Thessaly and the continued weakness of Macedon led to renewed Athenian attempts to regain the city of Amphipolis, an Athenian colony and a crucial source of timber and money that had been lost to Athens in the Peloponnesian War.[38] Although Athens failed to acquire Amphipolis, in the late 360s Timotheus captured many important cities along the northwestern coast, including Methone, Pydna, and Potidaea.[39]

The battle of Mantinea in 362/1 and the "common peace" agreed to by the major Greek states signaled the end of Sparta as an international power.[40] It had refused to join in the peace, which recognized the independence of the formerly Spartan-dominated and helot-tilled territory of Messenia. Nevertheless, in the following years the Spartans proved unable even to recover their recent losses. Meanwhile, the Athenians suffered a setback of their own, when several of their most important allies revolted from the second league. The resulting "Social War" (i.e., a war between *socii,* Latin for "allies") centered in the eastern Aegean and continued from 357 to 355 (when the Persian Great King's threat to assist Athens's revolting allies led to peace).[41] This war also arguably hindered Athenian reactions to events in the northwest, where Philip showed increasing aggression. But it was in this condition—with a relatively powerful Thebes to their north, enduring a revolt of their most important allies, and with less than ample public revenues—that the Athenians first came into conflict with the new Macedonian king.

In 357 Philip seized Amphipolis and Pydna, the first claimed and the second actually held by Athens. The Athenians declared war on the king, but took no measures to recover either city.[42] We may usefully compare Athens's actions in the fifth century, when the city frequently pursued major operations on two (or more) fronts even while enduring or running the risk of Spartan invasions of Attica. In the 350s Athens seems to have felt incapable of or uninterested in such a policy. When Philip besieged Athens's recent acquisition of Potidaea in 356, the Athenians reacted too late to save the city. In the same year, they made an alliance with three barbarian kingdoms moving against Philip (Illyria, Paionia, and western Thrace), but they took no action in concert with their new allies, whom Philip reduced by 355. The Macedonian king next seized Methone, another city in the northwestern Aegean under Athenian sway.[43]

As perceptive a scholar as Raphael Sealey has recently downplayed the significance of these losses to Athens (apart from Amphipolis), emphasizing their supposed irrelevance to Athenian vital interests. Perhaps, he has suggested, the Athenians would not have reacted vigorously to Philip in the mid 350s even if they had not been distracted by the Social War.[44] I believe this view to be somewhat problematic. Amphipolis and the other Athenian holdings in the northern Aegean provided Athens with direct access to crucial timber supplies for its fleet (as Sealey recognizes). Moreover, Athens's inaction allowed Philip to acquire the rich mines in western Thrace in 356, or at least to gain them more quickly than he might otherwise have done. Philip's actions in the mid 350s thus both harmed Athens and improved the Macedonian's own position substantially. But even if Sealey is right and Athens's vital interests were not harmed significantly in this period, many Athenians themselves undoubtedly would not have agreed. Their holdings in the northwest Aegean (especially Potidaea, Methone, and Amphipolis) had played a major role in the first Athenian empire and the Peloponnesian War. That is, control of this area was crucial to the Athenians' own perception of their power in the fourth century. Macedonian control of these coastal cities was therefore an affront to Athenian naval supremacy and Athenian pride.[45]

It is therefore a telling fact that, *despite* Athens's real or perceived interests in the northwest Aegean, even after the Social War ended in 355 the Athenians took no vigorous actions against Philip.[46] The king, indeed, made protestations of friendly intentions toward Athens, but he backed these claims up with no overt actions in Athens's favor. Instead, he continued to expand eastward into Thrace and southward into Thessaly, while the Athenians seemed more concerned about renewed Persian aggression than about Philip's expansion.[47]

Nevertheless, by 352 the Athenians felt compelled to occupy the pass into central Greece at Thermopylae in order to forestall a continued southern advance by the Macedonian king, who through hostilities with the state of Phocis had involved himself in the conflict in central Greece known as the Third Sacred War (355–346). In 352/1 Demosthenes began to make speeches warning Athens of the danger Philip presented and asserting the need for Athenian *citizens* (as opposed to mercenaries) to serve against him.[48] But Demosthenes was a relatively young orator, lacking significant influence in these years, and his insistence that Athens adopt a "worst-case scenario" policy regarding Philip was unpopular.[49] Most Athenians apparently preferred to believe Philip's protestations of goodwill, and to reject any call for the campaigns and expenditures Demosthenes' pessimistic views entailed. Demosthenes' warnings about Philip thus went largely unheeded, and the Macedonian continued operations in Thrace and along the Aegean coast against the Chalcidian League.

When the league's principal city, Olynthus, appealed to Athens for an alliance (which was granted) and then for aid against Philip in 349, Demosthenes urged the Athenians to send a major force. The orator maintained that such a force could be funded (even given Athens's weakened financial condition) if the Athenians would only pay the property tax, serve on campaign themselves, and expend their public funds on the military instead of their own theater tickets.[50] But the changes in Athenian public finance (discussed in chapter 3) that had led the fourth-century Athenians to enrich their "theoric fund" at the expense of the "stratiotic" or military treasury rendered Demosthenes' recommendations stillborn. By the early 340s, a law was apparently in place that explicitly prevented the transfer of surplus funds from the theoric chest to the military treasury except under very specific conditions. An Athenian orator who proposed a transfer in early 348 was tried and convicted.[51] The Athenian demos had taken strong measures to protect its theater subsidies.

Rejecting Demosthenes' advice, the Athenians ultimately responded to Olynthian requests with small forces: Olynthus fell to Philip and received severe treatment. Athens's failure to take strong action to prevent this has been defended as part of an Athenian policy based on protecting only vital or compelling interests. But even if one accepts that the Athenians developed or pursued such a policy, the fall of Olynthus irreparably damaged Athenian credibility in foreign relations. Athens's allies and potential allies would no longer put much faith in promises of Athenian assistance against Macedon.[52]

Moreover, this supposed policy of protecting only vital interests remains problematic. The Athenians did, after all, send limited forces to Olynthus. What purpose did such a force serve if the fall of the city was considered immaterial to Athens's vital interests? Would such a weak force comfort Athens's other allies (who thereafter might expect an equally impotent reaction)? In fact, the dispatch of this force suggests that Athens's policy rested on considerations other than vital interests: Olynthus (and control of the northwestern Aegean) was clearly important to the Athenians, and it would be saved, *but only if this could be done with a minimal expenditure of funds and citizen lives.* Like other Athenian actions, Athens's policy toward Olynthus depended on a cost/benefit analysis that set Athenian public distributions for assembly pay and theater subsidies against the military expenditures necessary to protect Athens's foreign policy interests.[53]

There was, therefore, no line of Athenian action or inaction based on *vital* interests. Rather, the Athenians calculated *how much* they were willing to give up to protect this particular ally and then spent only that much of their energy and resources. I do not wish to imply that such a cost/benefit analysis was in any way unusual. It had always been a part of Athenian foreign policy decisions.[54] But the relative weight allotted to the variables in the equation shifted in the fourth century, because the Athenians had grown less willing to serve on campaigns themselves or to sacrifice their public distributions in order to meet the costs of aggressive military actions to expand Athens's power or increase national security.[55]

The speeches of Demosthenes and Aeschines provide evidence for this conclusion (although one must attempt to correct for the orators' rhetoric through our knowledge of Athens's actions in this period and by a comparison with its policy and campaigns in the fifth century).[56] Simply put, the Athenians consistently refused to field a force of sufficient size or citizen makeup to provide a real check on Philip's ambitions. If we defend their choice by noting that Philip was continually professing good intentions toward Athens, then we endorse the adoption of a foreign policy based on "best-case scenario" calculations: that is, "Philip may be telling the truth (and we hope he is), so we need not take the actions we would take if he were lying." Such an attitude, encouraged by misguided or (as Demosthenes maintained) duplicitous orators, prevented the Athenians from acting aggressively in response to Philip.[57]

Surely it is unwise for any state to risk its own interests or security based on optimistic predictions about what *might* happen if everything turns out in the best way possible. Unfortunately for Athens, however, the attraction of such a policy was too strong to be resisted by most voters and speakers in the Athenian assembly. These speakers faced an Athenian demos that apparently *wanted* to believe that Philip had no designs on crucial Athenian holdings like the Chersonese or on central and southern Greece itself.

The belief that Philip's ultimate intentions toward Athens were benign proved extremely attractive to all classes of Athenians. It prevented the diversion of money to the military fund and the resulting reduction or end of public distributions, thus comforting poorer citizens. It also weakened any call for further trierarchies and increases in the property taxes levied on landowning Athenians, thus pleasing the wealthy. Finally, it seemingly diminished the need for middle-class farmers to risk their lives as hoplites far from Athens. As Demosthenes learned, in the political environment of the late 350s and early 340s, "it took little to persuade the Athenians to do nothing."[58] Athenian orators who stood before the people and assured them that Philip and his friends meant what they said, and that there was therefore no need for expensive and dangerous military action, thus received more support than pessimists like Demosthenes, whose recommendations entailed very real personal and public sacrifices.

Perhaps the majority of any democratic electorate will usually prefer leaders who tell them what they want to hear or believe.[59] Statesmen like Pericles, therefore, who sometimes succeed in persuading the electorate that the majority's opinion is wrong, are probably the exception rather than the rule. Pericles also had significant advantages over Demosthenes and other fourth-century leaders when it came to encouraging Athenian military actions. *Pericles addressed an Athenian populace more than happy to serve on campaigns in order to expand Athens's hegemony.* The Athenians of Pericles' day readily voted to expend their resources and lives in attempts to conquer new territory (Egypt, Sicily) or to maintain their empire through the suppression of revolted or recalcitrant allies (Naxos, Thasos, Samos). In the fifth century, the pessimists with the unpopular message were those who tried to dissuade the Athenians from military actions (like Nicias before the Sicilian expedition), while the optimists—those advocating a best-case scenario policy—assured the demos that glory and profit would attend the proposed operation.[60]

By the mid fourth century, most Athenians' attitudes had apparently changed. While the fifth-century citizens were often pleased to hear plans for expensive military campaigns, in which they themselves would serve, the fourth-century electorate preferred to hear that such actions and expenditures were unnecessary.[61] Successful political leaders in the fifth century advocated war and aggression; in the fourth, they advocated putting public payments before military expenditures. Why risk one's life in military actions, many fourth-century Athenians apparently thought, when one could earn public payments in the assembly or courts, hire mercenary forces to serve the state, and collect property taxes from the wealthy and *syntaxeis* from the allies to provide the necessary funding?

After Olynthus, diplomatic efforts to secure Athenian interests (particularly in the Chersonese) continued, especially in 347/6, when a formal embassy of ten Athenians (including Demosthenes) was elected and sent to Philip.[62] Peace with Philip was already supported by the optimists, who trusted Philip or at least maintained that he had no hostile intentions toward

Athens. Others, like Demosthenes, perhaps believed that the right kind of treaty could secure Athenian interests at least temporarily (or, at the very least, provide a casus belli if it were broken).[63] After their consultation with Philip, the ambassadors returned to Athens, where the Athenians held two assemblies on successive days to consider peace terms, while Philip's ambassadors were present in the city.[64]

One important matter at issue in these assemblies was the inclusion of other Greek powers (beyond the members of the Second Athenian League) in the terms of the treaty. Athens's allies in the second league had passed a resolution (which was read out in the first assembly) that supported peace with Philip, but which would allow other states to join in the peace after it was concluded. Such a peace might have offered some protection to the central Greek state of Phocis and the Thracian king Cersebleptes (ruler of eastern Thrace). Both were allied with Athens, but neither was a member of the second league. Philip had opposed Phocis in the Third Sacred War, and his gains in western and central Thrace seemed to threaten Cersebleptes' kingdom, now the only buffer between Macedonian-controlled territory and Athenian interests in the Chersonese and Hellespont. In the first assembly, Demosthenes and others seem to have supported the allies' resolution, despite the apparently common belief that Philip would not approve of these terms. In any case, on the second day of deliberations, the Athenians decided to approve a treaty with Philip (proposed by the Athenian Philocrates) that would not remain open to other states and which contained no written provisions for the Phocians or Cersebleptes.[65]

One interpretation of this evidence suggests that something had happened to undermine Athenian confidence before the second assembly. It is possible that the Athenians had learned that the Phocians holding the pass at Thermopylae had refused to comply with an earlier agreement and turn over that strategically critical location to an Athenian general.[66] This ominous news would have meant that forces now potentially unfriendly to Athens held the pass, increasing the Athenians' concerns about preventing Philip's entry into central Greece. Beyond this possible motivation, Aeschines and others apparently claimed that assurances could be obtained from Philip about matters not explicitly included in the proposed treaty between the Macedonian king and Athens. In fact, Aeschines continued to argue for Philip's goodwill even after the second embassy to the king (which obtained his oath confirming the treaty) returned to Athens with a letter from Philip containing only vague promises and without even (open) verbal assurances from the

Macedonian on specific issues.[67] Thus, led on by Aeschines and others and indulging their hopes that Philip might be sincere, the Athenians took no actions to protect their Phocian allies.

The chronology and the precise nature of the machinations surrounding the Peace of Philocrates constitute one of the thorniest problems in fourth-century Athenian history.[68] Our evidence consists primarily of dubious claims and counterclaims made in the self-serving speeches of Aeschines and Demosthenes. We cannot determine important facts, such as precisely when the Athenians learned that the Phocians had refused to surrender the pass at Thermopylae and precisely what was said at the assemblies held to discuss peace, and thus it is difficult to gauge public attitudes when the demos voted to accept Philocrates' proposal. (If they had just learned of the Phocian refusal, as Aeschines later claimed, it would say something important about fourth- as opposed to fifth-century Athenians. Previously, one might have expected the Athenians to react *militarily* to the Phocians' failure to live up to their agreement to turn over Thermopylae.)[69]

However these things may be, we do know that the Athenians felt threatened in 347/6 and that they had little prospect of assistance from other Greek states. Sometime in this year Philip had begun to harass the crucial Athenian holdings of Lemnos, Imbros, and Scyros, the three islands linking Athens with the Hellespont.[70] Such aggression was a direct threat to the Athenian grain supply, not to mention a stain on Athens's naval reputation.[71] These actions must have reinforced the view of those who believed that Athens could not simply pursue a policy of securing only "vital interests" in central Greece and the Chersonese.[72]

But envoys sent to the other Hellenes in 347/6 had not received favorable responses to Athens's invitation for deliberations about Philip. "Few Greek cities, if any, were willing in 347/6 to rely on the Athenians, or on a coalition led by the Athenians, for protection against Macedon," Sealey writes.[73] The real costs of Athens's failure to save or recover Potidaea and Amphipolis and of its refusal to send a large force to Olynthus were now painfully obvious. The Athenians had no credit with their potential allies and thus were unable to create a strong coalition against Philip when it was needed. If any Athenians had ever believed that their only vital interest lay in keeping Philip out of central Greece, the naïveté of this view now became clear. A state's interests cannot be measured only in terms of geography; protecting allies or others with little obvious "strategic significance" can play a very strategic role in foreign policy. The lesson of Olynthus's destruction had been learned well all over Greece. Athens's credibility was now shattered.

Athens's inability to secure allies and the belief (or hope) that Philip could be trusted undoubtedly encouraged some Athenians to support the Peace of Philocrates. Others may have been swayed by a particularly blunt assessment of the Athenians' position: during debate over the treaty, the Athenian statesman Eubulus warned the members of the demos that if they did not support the peace, they would be forced to levy a property tax on themselves, divert money from the theoric fund to the military chest, and immediately march down to the Peiraeus to man the warships.[74] Eubulus and his supporters thus contrasted the proposed peace with active military service, increased taxes, and lost public payments. In addition, Aeschines maintained that caution (and peace) was wiser than attempting to imitate the Athenians' heroic ancestors.[75] So much for Pericles' maxim that the Athenians must not fall short of their fathers, an idea sometimes echoed in fourth-century orations.[76]

The one Athenian leader we know to have opposed the peace was the elder statesman Aristophon, who spoke for resisting Philip on the basis of Athens's 300 triremes, 400 talents of income per year, and the support of its allies.[77] Whatever value we place on Aristophon's estimation of the strategic situation, the real problem he faced in the assembly lay in the fact that these were not the same Athenians who had marched to Marathon in 490 and had agreed to Themistocles' proposal in 483/2 to give up their silver distribution so that more triremes could be built. The Athenians now did not wish to man their warships or surrender their money in order to defend the state against a daunting enemy. Philocrates' decree carried.

The Peace of Philocrates proved to be a disaster for Athens, as even those who supported it and the Athenian demos itself soon recognized. Philip's actions in the treaty's aftermath led quickly to recriminations in Athens. So far from fulfilling Aeschines' hopes and those of the others who thought Philip would support Athenian interests in central Greece, Philip ultimately destroyed Athens's ally Phocis and thus settled the Sacred War in a way that pleased Athens's enemy Thebes, which had been at odds with the Phocians. Deluding themselves until the last moment, the Athenians had sent no assistance to their Phocian allies. Rather, they threatened to join the Phocians' enemies and march against Phocis if it did not surrender Delphi to the Amphiktyons (i.e., Philip's allies and Phocis's enemies).[78] The Athenians also voted to add Philip's descendants to the peace treaty, a symbolic move toward Philip that Demosthenes later claimed had encouraged the Phocians to capitulate. The Phocians, realizing that Athenian assistance would not be forthcoming, surrendered to Philip when he entered central Greece.[79]

Ensconced in the heart of Hellas, and having settled the war with Phocis according to his own desires, Philip was now obviously favoring Athens's enemy Thebes.[80] If this came as any surprise to the Athenians (as is sometimes thought), the demos and its leaders had been incredibly delusional. Philip had a long-standing relationship with the Thebans and had been at war with the Phocians (who had opposed his interests in Thessaly) since the late 350s. Philip therefore predictably favored Thebes in the settlement of 346. Only the dangerous reliance on best-case scenario thinking that we have seen in Athens's foreign policy in this period could have led anyone to expect otherwise.[81]

Once Philip had taken over the pass at Thermopylae and had destroyed Phocis's power, even politicians like Demosthenes briefly favored honoring the Peace of Philocrates and not provoking Philip now that Athens's strategic position had been undermined.[82] In addition to the destruction of Phocis, the Athenians also now faced the loss of their ally Cersebleptes in eastern Thrace, who (again) had stood as the only buffer between Philip and the Athenian interests in the Chersonese. Perhaps some Athenians had actually believed that Philip intended to leave the Chersonese unmolested.[83] But surely, all *should* have agreed to take precautions in case he did not. In the event, Philip had moved east against Cersebleptes while the Athenians were deliberating about the peace. Ironically, Philip had already completed his conquest before Athens rejected a request from the Thracian king to include him in the new treaty.[84]

Of course, the peace treaty with Philip did not result immediately in the Athenians' loss of independence or the destruction of *demokratia*. But the peace weakened Athens both strategically and diplomatically through the loss of allies and the concession of Philip's gains, with no real quid pro quo.[85] The political realities of Athenian democracy in the 340s that destroyed Athens's foreign policy credibility and then led to the treaty and to Athens's recumbent acceptance of its disappointing aftermath offer a bracing lesson for modern electorates that choose to heed only those politicians or diplomats with an optimistic or best-case scenario message. A free people unwilling to back up their vote with military service and personal financial sacrifice place the very liberty that they cherish in jeopardy. At least some Athenian orators recognized this. Even Aeschines supposedly claimed that in Athens there were "many shouters, but few to serve as soldiers when needed,"[86] and Demosthenes had repeatedly called for citizen service on campaigns and financial sacrifice in favor of military expenditures.[87]

In 347/6 the Athenians lost considerable ground in their efforts to prevent Philip's direct intervention in central Greece and to recover their own holdings in the northwestern Aegean. Through the peace, their allies in Phocis had been destroyed and Amphipolis had been formally ceded to Philip. Moreover, their ally Cersebleptes had been overthrown, and Philip now directly threatened Athenian interests in the Chersonese/Hellespont. The optimists, of course, might temporarily "spin" Athens's new alliance with Philip as an Athenian gain. One scholar has concluded that at least after 346, "the Athenians knew that for the time being Philip would not invade their territory, or harass their overseas possessions . . . or encroach on the Chersonese."[88] But the scrambling done by Athenian leaders like Aeschines and Demosthenes in order to dissociate themselves from Philocrates' ignominious peace shows that such "knowledge" comforted few Athenians.

Over the next six years, the Athenians grew increasingly unhappy with their peace treaty and with Philip, as the Macedonian king's actions repeatedly belied his professions of friendly intentions toward Athens. Encroaching on the Chersonese and involving himself in Euboea and the Peloponnese, Philip continued to rely on best-case scenario thinking among some of Athens's leaders and the demos itself to forestall any vigorous actions against him. Athenian intellectuals like Isocrates and Speusippos engaged in friendly "diplomacy" with the Macedonian, recommending such actions as a "Panhellenic" war against Persia.[89] Having withdrawn from the city after his indictment in 343, Philocrates himself eventually was condemned to death (in absentia) by the same demos that had passed his decree for peace, demonstrating again how the system of *demokratia* was capable of defending the citizens themselves from self-reproach.[90] The proposing politicians' names attached to Athens's decrees "of the council and the demos" formed a convenient way to redirect blame for the Athenians' own policies.

By 342 the Athenians were attempting to strengthen their hold on the crucial Chersonese. Additional settlers were dispatched to the scene with the general Diopeithes. But he received insufficient funds for his operation and had to exact money on the spot to pay for his troops.[91] Demosthenes now spoke in favor of even more vigorous action against Philip, including sending money to the Athenian forces in the north.[92] But by the time he delivered his *Fourth Philippic,* probably early in 341/0, Demosthenes had realized that his earlier proposal to end public distributions in order to fund the military was not viable. He no longer opposed payments to the people from the theoric fund, although he continued to urge a vigorous policy, including seeking assistance from Persia against Philip.[93] After Philip had seized the Athenian grain fleet in winter 340/39, the Athenians finally took Demosthenes' advice. Early in 339/8, they passed a decree directing money normally flowing into the theoric fund into their military chest.[94]

When Philip marched into central Greece in 339/8 on the pretext of set-tling a minor squabble that moderns call the Fourth Sacred War, the Athe-nians began to look for allies against the Macedonian. In the greatest diplo-matic success of his career, Demosthenes persuaded the Thebans to take the side of their former enemies at Athens, and a coalition led by Thebes and Athens thus took the field against Macedon at Chaeronea in 338.[95]

On paper, the forces were relatively even: the allied Greeks may have out-numbered the thirty thousand or so Macedonians by five thousand. Never-theless, although the Macedonians did not utterly crush the southern Greeks at Chaeronea, the Atheno-Theban alliance lost the battle and then supinely accepted the result.[96] Philip was able to install a garrison in Thebes and dic-tate policy to the rest of Greece. At a synod in Corinth, he was "elected" com-mander *(hegemon* or *strategos autokrator)* of the Greek forces, and war was de-clared on Persia. The defeated Greeks swore an oath not to make war on one another or overthrow Philip's kingdom. Athens itself had received mild treat-ment, and Philip allowed the polis to retain its democratic constitution. The grateful Athenians responded by voting a crown for Philip in honor of his daughter's marriage.[97] They also tried and condemned to death the Athenian general Lysicles, who had commanded Athens's defeated forces at Chaeronea.[98]

The Athenians obviously felt no love for Philip, but in the immediately subsequent years they could not bring themselves to oppose him or his son Alexander openly. This policy has been praised by historians as intelligent or "realistic." Chaeronea, it is sometimes argued, proved that the Greeks could not stand up to the Macedonians so long as the latter remained a united power.[99] This is an odd conclusion for modern students of Greek history, which provides significant examples of smaller forces overcoming larger numbers and great odds to win surprising victories. Could anything have been less "realistic" than the Greek allies' stand against Xerxes and the Per-sian empire in 480–479, or the Athenians' decision to engage the Persians al-most by themselves at Marathon in 490? Are we to believe that the southern Greeks, capable of resisting armies of tens if not hundreds of thousands of Persians, simply could not withstand the threat posed by thirty thousand Macedonians?

There is no reason to conclude that the southern Greeks *could not* have de-feated the Macedonians, especially if they had put together a reasonable coali-tion of powers early enough in Philip's reign. This required leadership from states like Athens (and Sparta) and an Athenian foreign policy that did not supply only weak support to allies (like Olynthus) and underfund important

military forces. It thus required both military and economic sacrifices by individual citizens, like those sacrifices made by the Athenians and Spartans before and during Xerxes' invasion. The primary reason that the Macedonians
won the war against Greece arguably lies in the altered Greek and Athenian
morale, not in grossly superior Macedonian military tactics.[100]

In fact, Greek armies could defeat Macedonian forces, as the Athenian revolt against Macedon after Alexander's death would prove. But by that time,
the Macedonians as a whole had grown even more powerful, and the Athenians had no major Greek allies left to assist them. For their lack of allies, the
Athenians had only themselves to blame: after 338 Athens had stood by and
watched as the great powers of classical Greece resisted Macedon only to be
crushed in turn. Cowed by Philip's son and successor, Athens sent no forces
to assist the Thebans in 335 when they revolted and were subsequently destroyed, their ancient city razed to the ground. When King Agis III of Sparta
mounted a large-scale revolt in 331–330, the Athenians likewise remained on
the sidelines, once more choosing to save their money for public distributions
rather than expending it on military expeditions.[101] The upshot was that the
Athenians themselves eventually faced the Macedonians in the Lamian War
(323–322) without Theban or Spartan assistance. Even so, they enjoyed several successes against their Macedonian foes. When they lost the war, they
also lost their *demokratia*.[102] Demosthenes killed himself, and an oligarchy
once more ruled in Athens.

But Athens arguably lost the Lamian War long before its final capitulation
in 322. Repeatedly refusing to take vigorous action as their allies and interests fell before Philip after the early 350s, the Athenians preferred to listen to
those statesmen who promised "peace in our time" and the continuation of
public payments. Usually unwilling to take the field themselves in large
numbers, Athenian citizens too often relied on mercenary troops even when
they did vote for military operations. The limited forces they dispatched were
underfunded, and the generals actually available and willing to command
lived under constant threat of fine, exile, or death if they failed.

To those who see Macedon's triumph as inevitable, the Athenian demos
and Athens's leaders bear little responsibility for the loss of their independent
government. Such a conclusion betrays a fatalistic and deterministic view of
history that ignores the very "unrealistic" stand made by a few Greek poleis
against the mighty Persian empire. In fact, we simply cannot say whether the
Macedonian army presented an impossible opponent for the southern
Greeks, because the Athenians and other Greeks waited too long before op-
posing Macedon aggressively and then were unable to put together the kind

of coalition force that had withstood the Persians. Athenian democratic politics played a major part in both these failures and therefore deserves to be analyzed carefully as one of the reasons for Macedon's success.

It is easy to attribute the end of Athenian freedom to Philip and his successors—too easy and too comforting, and too reflective of the usually unstated desire to exculpate the individual Athenians and their democratic political system from the choices that led to their defeat.

SEVEN

Democracy and Religion

It was that sense of community, I suggest,
fortified by the state religion, by their myths and
their traditions, which was an essential element in
the pragmatic success of the Athenian democracy. . . .
Neither the sovereign Assembly, with its unlimited
right of participation, nor the popular jury-courts
nor the selection of officials by lot nor ostracism
could have prevented either chaos on the one
hand or tyranny on the other, had there not
been the self-control among enough of
the citizen-body to contain its own
behaviour within bounds.

M. I. FINLEY
Democracy Ancient and Modern

Of all the dispositions and habits which lead
to political prosperity, Religion and morality are
indispensable supports. In vain would that man claim
the tribute of Patriotism, who should labour to subvert
these great Pillars of human happiness, these firmest props
of the duties of Men and citizens. The mere Politician,
equally with the pious man ought to respect and cherish
them. A volume could not trace all their connections with
private and public felicity. Let it simply be asked where is
the security for property, for reputation, for life, if the
sense of religious obligation *desert* the oaths, which
are the instruments of investigation in the Courts of
justice? And let us with caution indulge the supposition,
that morality can be maintained without religion. Whatever
may be conceded to the influence of refined education

on minds of peculiar structure, reason and experience
both forbid us to expect that National morality can
prevail in exclusion of religious principle.

GEORGE WASHINGTON
farewell address (1796)

It is true that the American innovation in
religion has been to call democracy divine. "As He
died to make men holy, let us die to make men free":
is there a more perfect expression of the New World's
improvement upon the Old World than the equation
between holiness and freedom in the concluding stanza
of "The Battle Hymn of the Republic"? The anthem has
been moistening many eyes in the weeks since the black
day [of September 11]. My own eyes included, and I do
not believe that he died to make men holy. So it is worth
remembering that the religious motive for democracy holds
only for the religious, and we are not all religious, and we
are all democratic. I would say even this: democracy
understood as obedience to God is democracy
misunderstood. Democracy represents a rupture
in the theological account of authority. It promotes
the reality of freedom over the explanation of freedom.
Did God make us free? There are those who think so.
But if we are free, then we are free also against
God. And for this reason, too, let us
die to make men free.

LEON WIESELTIER
"The Incoherence"

MODERN RULES OF ETIQUETTE ONCE suggested avoiding the topics of politics and religion at social occasions.[1] This (admittedly often violated) convention suggests that these topics share the ability to provoke unpleasant controversy because of passionately held views or irreconcilable differences. If the
dialogues presented by Plato and Xenophon bear even the faintest resem-
blance to the social events (like *symposia* or religious festivals) at or around
which they are sometimes set, the Athenians had no such convention governing polite discussion. Moreover, the Athenians' tragedies and comedies,

which were performed in part at public expense and on the most public of occasions, frequently and directly confront political leaders, the gods, and fundamental cultural myths in ways that probably would seem shocking in many modern contexts. Only in its treatment of sex can popular American culture rival the openness with which the Athenians publicly examined their cherished beliefs, social conventions, and political practices.

Yet the freedom with which Athenians addressed these issues should not lead us to conclude that they rejected cultural norms and embraced something like modern "social tolerance." In fact, even the Athenians' famously frank public attitudes toward sex illustrate well-developed social conventions.[2] I think especially of the fact that, despite their treatment of the subject of rape in drama, Athenian comedies and tragedies (so far as we can tell) never actually depicted—much less glorified—acts of sexual violence or degradation. In comedies, it is the normal biological act of sex and its effects or the threat or insinuation of unacceptable forms of the act that usually provide the humor. Both types of humor depend on conventions about what is and is not "regular" or acceptable in society, and both therefore reinforce a clear social norm in the area of sexual relations. Far from demanding a particularly tolerant attitude about sexual activity, the Athenians' treatment of sex in their popular media continually reinforced the prevailing moral code, which differed from other societies' conventions but was a moral code nonetheless.[3]

The Athenians' public life and especially their civic festivals highlight stark contrasts between Athenian social conventions and those of contemporary America. These festivals—like the Great or City Dionysia held each year in the spring—were explicitly religious affairs, boasting sacrifices and processions in the god Dionysus's honor.[4] At the City Dionysia, Athenians gathered by the thousands in the theater of Dionysus to view comedies and tragedies. If the plays themselves could be criticized for having "nothing to do with Dionysus," this both confirms Athenian understanding that the festival as a whole *was* connected with the god and suggests that the playwrights and celebrants enjoyed a broad latitude for the god's propitiation.[5]

Within the theater of Dionysus itself, the stage of which featured an altar to the god, the Athenians viewed plays and participated in a range of activities that would baffle the modern theatergoer. Sacrifices and hymns to the gods combined with appearances by political figures like the archon and the generals (who made a sacrifice), the drinking of wine, the display of the yearly tribute payments made by Athens's allies/subjects (in the fifth century), a parade of Athenian war orphans dressed in military garb provided by the city, and, of course, the plays themselves—tragedies and comedies with pointed religious, moral, and political messages, as well as (in the case of comedies and satyr plays) bawdy sexual humor. All these plays—tragedies and comedies alike—were then subjected to the vote of citizen judges (chosen by lot), who awarded prizes for the best dramas.[6] The Athenian demos's experience in the theater combined modern Americans' experiences of popular film, live theater, religious services, talent contests, political lectures, reports on the economic condition of the nation, ribald satire, and patriotic rallies.

It is hardly surprising that we have difficulty conceiving of the popular spirit necessary to produce and enjoy such an event. Whereas the Athenians conceived of society as an integrated whole—that is, without strict divisions between religious, political, economic, and social spheres and unified by a set of ideas, conventions, and duties—contemporary Americans attempt to separate church and state, while praising such concepts as "choice" and "diversity." The idea of a bawdy spoof performed during a church service (say) or a prayer and blessing offered at a government-sponsored public meeting would make many Americans uncomfortable, if not angry. Introducing alcohol, feasting, and ribald political abuse at either would surely be considered inappropriate by most and outrageous by some.[7]

If we wish to treat the Athenians' experience seriously as a potential object lesson for modern democratic societies, it behooves us to examine this striking difference between Athens and America carefully. Study of Athenian society in fact suggests that in drawing our social distinctions as we have, moderns may have attempted to thwart or simply ignore a fundamental aspect of human nature.

DIGRESSION: MAN'S DESIRE FOR SOCIETY

Like the history of other pre-twentieth-century peoples, Athenian history suggests that human beings possess an innate desire to live in an integral *society:* that is, a community in which religious practices, politics, social activities, and even economic affairs all relate to one another through their connection or subordination to a set of fundamental beliefs or principles. In such a society, particular aspects of human interaction are ultimately evaluated against a conventional set of values and duties. These conventions thus provide definitions of what constitute "good" and "bad" actions in public and private contexts.[8] Such a set of beliefs could, for example, explain why business transactions are carried out in a certain way (by defining what is "good business" and what is "cheating," or how much profit or interest is "excessive"), dictate what kinds of actions are appropriate at given social occasions (like weddings, dates, or parties), and assert standards for familial responsibilities (of spouse to spouse, parent to child, and child to parent).[9]

What does this hypothesized aspect of man's psychology—man's desire to live in an association of human beings undergirded by unifying conventions and meaning—imply for modern democratic values like "choice" and "diversity" and their ability to serve as effective organizing principles or idealized values for a society? On the face of it, diversity per se as a goal seems inconsistent with the idea of a "society" as traditionally understood and as desired naturally, I am speculating, by human beings. The word *society* reflects the idea of alliance between individuals or groups based on shared goals (*socii* in Latin are "allies," those who share, follow, act together). One modern dictionary defines the term *society* as "a. The totality of social relationships among human beings. b. A group of human beings broadly distinguished from other groups by mutual interests, participation in characteristic relationships, shared institutions, and a common culture. c. The institutions and culture of a distinct self-perpetuating group."[10] As traditionally understood, a society seems incapable of comprising a set of individuals seeking diversity *as a goal* (while societies of certain types may produce diversity *as a result*). Nevertheless, many Americans would list diversity as one of America's particular identifying features and strengths.[11]

Human beings obviously tend to see the world in terms of "us" and "them" in any given context, which can be as small as the family and break down on gender or age lines—boys versus girls, children versus parents—or as large as nations or ethnic groups. This tendency probably reflects both our innate need for safety and a desire to be joined in a distinct society with other people.[12] That is, our much-discussed need for an "other" arguably stems in part from our desire for an "us." Americans today most often seem to associate "Americanism," and thus the American "us," with political and economic freedom, social diversity, and the choices that freedom and diversity provide. The "values" of freedom, choice, and diversity are in turn thought to be associated with, ensured through, or generated by democracy. What can Athenian history tell us about the potential for freedom, choice, and diversity to serve as the fundamental and unifying principles of a democratic society?

To answer this question, one must first recognize that modern study of classical Athens has arguably placed too little emphasis on the social and religious structures in Athens and too much on the alleged "primacy of politics" in Athenian life.[13] The popular view of Athenians (and other classical Greeks) as thoroughly "political" people can be traced to Aristotle, who called man a "political creature" *(zoon politikon)* by nature.[14] As others have noted, our word *political* seriously misrepresents the Greek *politikos,* an adjective that usually ties the word it modifies to the polis or community (and thus to ideas like citizenship rather than to institutions or practices like elections). For a "living thing" *(zoon)* to be "political" *(politikon)* was to be like, and therefore naturally suited to life in, a polis.[15] But the polis rested on a society with unifying beliefs and without the distinct zones of economic, political, and religious activity found in modern America. Indeed, this is precisely how Aristotle (and Plato) conceived of the city-state—as a true *society* in which individuals were joined by common beliefs for common purposes.[16] Aristotle's conception of man as a "political animal" simply emphasizes the close relationship between man's nature and the society reflecting it in a Greek polis.

One therefore cannot speak of the classical Athenians as particularly "political" without making careful allowances for the Greek conception of social and political life. In Athens, the purely "political"—in the modern American sense, that is, relating to government, elections, and opinions about both—formed merely one small part of the social whole, and not even a specially privileged part. To appreciate this fact fully, it will help to recall the religio-social structure of the polis itself, which depended on groups of individuals (families, clans, phratries, demes, and tribes) united first for common defense and for the maintenance of cult, and not to ensure the political rights of individuals.[17] In a very real way, the most "political" act (in the ancient sense) that many Athenian farmers ever performed occurred when they armed themselves as hoplites (at their own expense), observed sacrifices to the gods, and then stood shoulder to shoulder with their tribesmen in the phalanx, thereby protecting the polis, their families, and their farms. That most of them worried about the everyday activities of the Council of 500 or ordinary votes of the Athenian assembly (things moderns would consider to be in the particularly "political" realm of the polis) is belied by the difficulty of frequent travel to Athens from outlying Attic demes, the low capacity of the Athenian assembly's meeting place, and the explicit testimony of Aristophanes and Aristotle.[18]

Most Athenians had neither the time nor the inclination to travel long distances by foot in order to involve themselves in the vast majority of the strictly political activities taking place in the city center. The Pnyx hill in Athens where the assembly met could probably seat no more than six thousand or so in the fifth century, and Athens had at least twenty to thirty thousand citizens during the whole period of classical democracy.[19] Obviously the Athenians never expected or intended for even half of the citizens to participate in the assembly's meetings.[20] Yet compare the theater of Dionysus, a public edifice where Athens's dramatic performances took place and which was eventually able to seat over fifteen thousand, or the Athenian military, which potentially (and at times actually) included virtually the whole citizen population.[21] In Athens, religious and military activities enjoyed a much higher degree of public participation than voting in the assembly. Athens's *politeia*—that is, the constitution of a polis in the sense of the way the city-state operated and governed itself—reflected the primary purposes of the polis (defense and cult) and reinforced the social organs through which these purposes were carried out: subgroups of the polis starting with families and moving up to tribes.

It is therefore no surprise that Greek armies and religious rituals intended to ensure the gods' goodwill usually seem to have been organized around these subgroups.[22] The Athenian Council of 500 also relied on the smaller units of Athenian society (demes and tribes) for its organization, while the assembly (theoretically the whole citizen body in its political form) also reflected the tribal divisions.[23] Scratch the surface of almost any Athenian political, military, or religious organ, and one finds families, phratries, and tribes as organizational units. The Athenians themselves clearly believed this to be crucial, for when ca. 507 they designed the organs of their new regime (eventually called *demokratia*), they created new tribes mimicking those of the old system, even providing them with demigod tribal "founders" and religious cults.[24] The old tribes, moreover, which theoretically expressed relations stretching back into the distant past and which cut across polis boundaries to connect Athens with other Ionian Greeks, were allowed to remain intact and continued to play a role in Athenian religious life after 507.[25] But we must emphasize that even the new tribes and the Council of 500—created out of whole cloth by the Athenians—were invested with more than a logistical or military significance. *To function as organs within Athenian society, they had to have a religious foundation.*[26]

Perhaps no fact better illustrates the lack of boundaries in ancient Athens between (what many moderns consider) different areas of society than the way in which religion pervaded every aspect of Athenian life. In chapter 3 we saw how the Athenians used sacred funds and treasure dedicated to their gods to finance military activities, and in this chapter we have seen that their state theatrical performances occurred within a setting celebrating the god Dionysus. The Athenian polis itself "could be ordered by Delphi or Zeus's oracle at Dodona to institute new festivals or sacrifices, and the decision to introduce new cults might be subject to oracular approval."[27] But although direct state involvement with religion may seem unremarkable in certain contexts, in fact there was no regular part of Athenian social and political life that was not connected in some way with the gods. Assemblies of the demos for voting began with religious ceremonies and the religious items on the agenda,[28] battles began with sacrifices to the gods, merchants beseeched the gods before embarking on trading voyages across the sea, men at drinking parties said prayers and poured libations before calling in the flute girls for entertainment, and interstate treaties (the word for which literally meant "pourings") were solemnized with libations to the gods.[29] In truth, virtually every part of Athenian life had religious aspects and significance, and virtually every religious activity was tied to other aspects of social life.[30]

So thoroughly did matters relating to the gods suffuse Athenian life that there was no identifiable "secular" realm (in the modern sense) in this society. Recent scholarship has begun to recognize this fact, emphasizing that the conventional separation of societies into spheres labeled "sacred" and "secular" does not apply to the ancient Greeks.[31] For the Athenians, every acceptable aspect of their world was associated with the gods in some way. That is, everything acceptable was to some degree "sacral," at least to the extent of having the gods' sanction. A range of sacredness stretched, roughly speaking, from simple acceptability to the gods (those things the Athenians called *hosia*) to things owned by or consecrated to the gods but still available for human use (which they termed *hiera*) to things so closely connected with the gods and thus pure that they had to be separated from common human uses (which they designated as *hagna*).[32] Outside of these categories lay everything unacceptable to the gods or impure things (which they designated by such terms as *anosia*, etc.). Thus there existed no "secular" realm in the way moderns understand the term (an acceptable area of life or action *separated* from the divine). Rather, *everything could be categorized by its particular relationship to the gods.*

Athens's financing of certain fifth-century military operations with money and treasure dedicated to the polis's gods nicely illustrates the overlapping political, religious, economic, and military aspects of Athenian society. But the practice also highlights the improbability that one aspect of life would become dominant over the others in Athenian society. Such an imbalance was unlikely because the different elements in Athenian society were complementary rather than competing, and because the individual elements were less important than the total package that comprised them, a package that reflected what Jon Mikalson calls the "remarkable homogeneity and consensus of basic religious beliefs" in Athens.[33]

It would seem, therefore, that *demokratia*—the particular form of polis government in Athens—was not likely to dominate or define Athenian culture or society as a whole. Athenian society existed before *demokratia* was instituted around 507 and during the oligarchical revolutions of 411 and 404. It existed both before and after the institution of new cults or festivals in Athens and during war or peace, alliance with or against Sparta, and times of public wealth or public poverty.[34] Rather than stemming from *demokratia* or ideals of "liberty and equality," the unifying principles of Athens's citizenry derived from common beliefs about the gods, from a sense of national superiority, and from shared values regarding the importance of performing their duties to gods, family, and polis. We have seen that the performance of these duties—to maintain the favor of the gods through the performance of rites, prayers, and sacrifices; to take care of parents; and to defend family, homes, land, and fellow citizens—was required of every citizen.[35] Common duties and a common religion thus undergirded every *particular* expression of Athenian culture or society, including *demokratia*. For this reason, democracy, like the Athenian empire and Attic tragedy, is more properly seen as a *product* of Athenian society, the Athenian character, and the actions of certain Athenians at particular historical moments, rather than as a fundamental or defining principle of that society.

Many Americans may resist this conclusion, in part because we live in a world where democracy and freedom are so often treated as the defining or fundamental principles of our society. We thus find it difficult to conceive of democracy simply as one acceptable form our government might take. But few Athenians probably would have asserted (at least before the fourth century) that *demokratia* was the only form of "good government" *(eunomia)*. Admittedly, the Athenians eventually defended their *demokratia* jealously and proudly. Yet, as we have seen, as late as 411 many Athenians were willing to vote to change this constitution. Even if many believed that their vote to replace *demokratia* with another regime was only a temporary expedient, the vote still demonstrates that many Athenians did not consider such a change in political form as a violation of sacred Athenian ideals or as an alteration of or threat to Athens's basic *society*. In the fifth century, while the Athenians may have sometimes cheered *demokratia* as a mascot, they did not worship it as a god.[36]

Of course, Athenian society was not static. We have already identified certain changes in the Athenians' views about public duty and personal sacrifice that had begun to undermine some aspects of Athens's society by the end of the fifth century. Nevertheless, although such changes continued, and the Athenians eventually developed a goddess Demokratia and cults of Zeus and Dionysos Eleutherios ("of freedom"), such expressions of the psychological and emotional power of popular rule and liberty from outside control never completely undermined the overarching conception of duty that dominated Athenian life.[37] In fact, the way that the Athenians eventually treated Demokratia as (merely one) goddess ironically underscores her position as something less than the Athenians' defining characteristic or principle.

The cult of Demokratia emerged in fourth-century Athens along with cults of other abstract forces such as Eirene ("peace") and Agatha Tyche ("good fortune"). Although there was apparently a long tradition of treating similar forces as deities associated with the Olympian gods (as Dike, "justice," was associated with Zeus), Athens may have been innovating by creating new abstract deities without such Olympian connections.[38] But it must be emphasized that the cult of Demokratia had no claim on a unique or special place in the Athenian pantheon. In fact, in the case of both Eirene and Demokratia, particular historical events seem to have called forth the cults— a peace with Sparta in 375 resulting in the former, and Athenian insecurities about the future of their polis after the loss to Macedon at Chaeronea (338) perhaps accounting for the latter.[39]

In short, even the cults of Freedom, Peace, and Democracy in Athens seem to have been expressions of particular historical circumstances rather than of any beliefs that democracy or "liberty and equality" served as the underlying principles of Athenian society or government. In fact, the older fifth-century deities of Eunomia ("good laws" or "good government") and Eukleia ("good repute," "glory") have an earlier claim on Athenian sentiments than either Democracy or Peace and are arguably more expressive of fundamental Athenian values than the fourth-century gods. As already noted, Athens's power and the glory and fame that resulted from it are far more consistent themes in Athenian art and literature than democracy, liberty, or equality.[40] Only after the end of the Peloponnesian War and the discredited oligarchical revolutions did the word *demokratia* apparently begin to supplant *eunomia* as the term for "good government" in Athens. Even if fourth-century Athenian orators like Demosthenes sometimes equated *demokratia* with "freedom" *(eleutheria)* and "good government" *(eunomia)*, it was the fact that democracy could be attached to these higher values that made it special. Almost no one, it would seem, considered the virtue or goal of good government to be democracy itself.[41] It is very questionable whether the majority of Athenians ever came to the point of defining "good government" as "democracy" and "bad government" as "anything but democracy." Certainly Athenian intellectuals like Plato, Thucydides, and Xenophon did not hold this view, and neither did the non-Athenian Aristotle, an astute observer of Athens.[42]

If, therefore, the theory of democracy as it is generally conceived of today—resting on the principles of natural rights and "liberty and equality" (as interpreted by moderns), expressed through voting—never pervaded Athenian thinking (even in the fourth century), one might reasonably ask how is it possible (or fair) to *blame* Athenian democracy itself (at least in part) for such acts as the execution of Socrates or the loss to Macedon. Simply put, it is both possible and fair because the theory or ideology ostensibly supporting any particular regime or society may not be reflected in all the actual practices of that regime or society. Although the Athenians maintained their belief in the importance of a citizen's duties and never developed the ideological and philosophical notions associated with modern democracy, democratic practices—especially making payments to the public and allowing those without property to cast ballots in the assembly—eventually created a political environment at odds with the Athenians' preexisting ideals of duty and public service. Athens's citizen army became increasingly mercenary and less effective, while its navy was financially weakened due to public distributions. In short, one might argue that the Athenians ultimately failed to sustain their independent government in part because they employed democratic practices that weakened them militarily, placed onerous financial burdens on the polis and the citizens, and conflicted with their ancient and predemocratic notions of a duty-based society.

In the fifth century, one of the effects of democratic practices had been an aggravation of the Athenians' martial spirit, ultimately encouraging Athens to follow Pericles' advice and accept (if not provoke) the debilitating Peloponnesian War. Before that war, Athens's increased martial spirit had the benefit of augmenting the Athenians' income through tribute collected from Athens's subjects, thus masking the financial strains that democratic payments for public service placed on Athenian resources. But in the fourth century, changed economic circumstances and degenerating public morale combined with democratic practices to produce a much less forward military policy at just the time when Athens needed one.

Another effect of democratic practices in Athens had been a shift in the balance of power within the Athenian electorate. Recent work has justifiably emphasized the importance of the egalitarian spirit and the middling hoplite-farmer who exemplified that spirit in the success of Athens and classical Greek poleis in general.[43] But in vesting so much authority in an assembly of all adult male citizens regardless of property qualifications, Athens created an uneasy alliance between the middling farmers (who risked their bodies in ho-plite battle) and the more urban population of poorer citizens (who exercised significant electoral power). Both groups arguably benefited from the fifth-century empire, and both ran risks: even the members of the Athenian masses—the so-called sailing mob *(nautikos ochlos)* that helped row Athens's triremes—did not receive their public payments without dangerous service in the Athenian navy. Those voting to take aggressive actions against Pelo-ponnesian interests or invade Sicily in the fifth century voted to seek glory, power, and wealth at the cost of risking their own lives. (That this situation failed to bring out any significant pacifistic tendencies even during a long and bloody war surely provides one of the most brutal lessons of Athenian his-tory for modern free societies.)[44]

By the time Athens began to hire numerous mercenaries, tax its wealthy cit-izens' property with increasing frequency, and pay citizens to attend the as-sembly, a new attitude was obviously developing. This attitude stemmed at least in part from the democratic system, which encouraged the practice of shifting duty and responsibility from the citizen to the state itself and thus fos-tered the idea that the state existed to protect citizens' privileges, while mak-ing as few demands on them as possible. A clear example appears in fourth-century Athenians' attitudes toward their military—attitudes that seem not unlike those of many modern Americans: they were ready to dispatch limited numbers of (usually mercenary) troops but not willing to serve themselves or to spend the money necessary to support their forces.[45] However, this attitude of state versus citizen responsibility apparently gestated for an insufficient pe-riod of time to undermine the Athenians' older views about civic duty com-pletely. It also lacked the historical and intellectual context likely to bring forth something resembling the modern theory of individual rights to be ensured by the state.[46]

Throughout the classical period, every Athenian found himself located firmly within a nexus of responsibilities (to the gods, to his family, and to his fellow citizens) that allowed little room for the consideration of a concept like individual rights. Since this was true even in the fourth century, it would seem that democratic practices and the resulting change in Athenian morale weakened Athens even without the development of a thoroughgoing ideal of rights and personal freedom. Thus Plato, an Athenian who to some degree "dropped out" of conventional Athenian society by eschewing the political career that his birth and wealth made not only possible but expected of him, still conceived of the polis as an integral social unit, which citizens *served* and which inculcated the values necessary for making those citizens better.[47] That is, even an Athenian intellectual like Plato, who expressed heterodox religious views and rejected a life of political engagement in his native polis, never developed the idea that an individual possessed inalienable rights that were ensured by the state and that could shield him from the will of the society or (more important) its human and divine laws.

MODERN AMERICA AND THE RELIGION OF DEMOCRACY

Our argument has arrived at something of a paradox. Study of Athenian history and society has suggested that the ancient Greek polis—even a democratic polis such as Athens—organized itself around religious practices, moral principles, and duties that touched virtually every area of public and private life. Indeed, we have seen that religion pervaded Athenian society, to the point that Athens possessed no true secular sphere. Yet we have also noted the tendency of modern democratic societies to attempt to separate the religious and political arenas. This separation "of church and state" and the freedom it ostensibly ensures for religious, social, and political activity are often hailed as very clear ways in which the modern conception of good government has improved on the political systems of the ancient Greeks or Romans.

The stricture preventing the U.S. Congress from making laws "respecting an establishment of religion" in the first article of the Constitution's Bill of Rights has encouraged the idea that the "separation of church and state" should serve as a fundamental principle of American government and society. Indeed, the phrase "separation of church and state" comes readily to students' lips when they are asked to quote something from the Constitution. Of course, neither the idea nor the phrase appears in the Constitution, but many Americans' *belief* that it does (or certainly should) demonstrates how important the idea of church-state separation is in the American psyche.

Modern Americans have extended the "constitutional" separation of church and state to justify actions at the state and local level, using the principle to attempt to banish nativity scenes from public property, prayer from schoolrooms, and the words "under God" from the Pledge of Allegiance.[48] It lies outside my own field of expertise to trace how this interpretation of the Constitution's position on church and state became codified as both a working judicial principle and an article of American faith.[49] However, there is little doubt that the contemporary consensus about the separation of church and state reflects neither the actual words of our founding documents nor the realities of American government and society in the decades following the Constitution's ratification. In fact, many states continued to maintain established churches or religious qualifications for office well into the 1800s.[50] Clearly, the Constitution's First Amendment did not limit the power of a city or state to patronize religion or encourage a particular religious standard. Rather, the First Amendment limited Congress's ability to interfere in this matter at the national, state, or local level.[51]

Nevertheless, like the idea that democracy represents the best form of government, the view that good government depends in part on a "separation of church and state" has become an American article of faith. Again, we must leave aside the fact that the American Founders made no effort to restrict local religious establishments via the Constitution and that they largely distrusted democracy and did not seek to make the United States into one. Today, most Americans *believe* in a "constitutional" separation of church and state and maintain that their government is a democracy. Our politicians encourage this belief by talking about heeding "what the American people want" and designating those regimes of which they approve as "democratic" and those they would criticize as "undemocratic." Having lost most of its historical content, the word *democracy* has come to stand for the amorphous idea of "good government" centered around personal rights and the practice of casting ballots. In short, like many successful religions, democracy has been put into a palatable and easily digestible form—a form that is only loosely related to its historical origins and that requires a certain degree of faith within the followers.[52] And like many religions, too, democracy sometimes affects public actions and professed opinions more than real lifestyle or private beliefs.

To speak of democracy as a kind of national religion may seem absurd, especially since contemporary American democracy has made separation of church and state such a hallowed doctrine.[53] But let us consider the idea for a moment. Surely it is fair to say that democracy now represents a doctrine that few dare to challenge openly in any serious or fundamental way. Publicly expressed American views about government and society seem to reflect an almost absolute belief in the value of democracy, treating it as something more than a mere political system with certain properties that has existed at particular moments in history.

Let us return to the imaginary dinner party attended by businessmen, teachers, politicians, ironworkers, and journalists described in the introduction to this book, where I argued that scarcely an eyebrow would be raised if one of those present said: "I don't support the idea of marriage [or the family, God, the sanctity of human life, a citizen army, etc.]," whereas it is not difficult to imagine a rather different reaction if someone announced: "I don't approve of democracy [or freedom, or rights]" or "I don't approve of granting the vote to all adults regardless of qualifications." We also saw in the introduction that the contemporary attachment to democracy is not limited to popular culture; political scientists now sometimes evaluate particular programs, institutions, or policies based on their ability to foster democracy, rather than evaluating *democracy's* ability to foster sociopolitical "goods" (like private property).[54]

If, then, democracy has become an almost unimpeachable doctrine, we might seriously consider whether it has begun to function as something like an unacknowledged religion, essentially filling a void left by the diminishing presence of previous social values. Is it so outrageous to suggest that the vote now serves as a kind of Eucharist—as *the* privilege and duty that identifies one as a citizen and democrat in good standing? (Indeed, those who do not partake in this sacrament are often said to have "no right" to criticize American government.) As in a religion, in modern America various sects within democracy compete for followers and dominance. But, as if mimicking the competing denominations or branches found within other religions, all claim to be the "true" democrats, who are really interested in providing "what the American people want" and thereby guaranteeing as much freedom and happiness to "the American people" as possible.[55]

Obviously Americans' views on particular political issues differ significantly (just as the faithful in any religion differ on questions of theology or ritual). Yet even these differences tend to remain within a remarkably narrow band of political thought. Democrats and Republicans quibble over fairly small changes in rates of taxation and marginal alterations to social programs. Questions about the *principles* supporting such programs as the progressive income tax, public education, or Social Security are rarely heard (much less taken seriously). Moreover, in a land that continually praises "diversity," is it not somewhat odd that there is virtually no popular political opposition to the principle that whatever "the American people" want is an appropriate goal of our society? I do not mean to imply that everyone who uses the phrase sincerely believes that he knows or really cares about what "the American people" want. I only wish to emphasize that this is the rhetorical stance one must take to suggest that one is a good political leader.[56] The idea that American political figures should actually *lead* the people by telling them what they *should* want and why—that is, the idea that a politician should risk popular disapproval by attempting *to change the opinion of the majority*—has almost no currency in contemporary public debate. Can anyone imagine an American elected official or political candidate today actually *criticizing* the populace for their views (and succeeding in changing the electorate's minds), as Pericles, Cleon, and even (in the end) Demosthenes did?[57]

In the Athenian polis, a matrix of duties and responsibilities arguably limited the deleterious effects of *demokratia* on Athenian society and restricted its ability to dominate Athenian thought. In contrast, modern Americans' veneration of freedom through democracy manifests itself in virtually every aspect of life today through the politicization of social, religious, and economic factors. Whereas political, economic, and other factors once played a subsidiary role within society, which itself was ultimately organized around nonpolitical principles, in today's society—based on the idealization of freedom and the political form (democracy) that is supposed to ensure it—social factors are subsumed by "politics."[58] Since modern America venerates freedom and treats it primarily as a political value, it is the political manifestation (democracy) of this ideal that acts as the primary organizing force for society. However, other manifestations of freedom receive increasing social endorsement and political protection, including the chemical manifestation (mood-altering drugs), the economic manifestation (unrestrained capitalism), the sexual manifestation (promiscuity without responsibility), and the religious manifestation (spiritualism without morality and traditional ritual).[59] Americans' endorsement and the government's protection of these "freedoms" strongly suggest that modern American society is organizing itself around a new set of beliefs spawned by our democratic regime and ideals. These new beliefs require the evaluation of each area of life in terms of its connection to the principle of freedom as expressed through and ensured by democracy.

This book's examination of Athenian society, and my hypothesis that people wish to live in something like an integral society, may help explain why the manifestations of freedom listed above are increasingly protected politically and endorsed socially. Sexual promiscuity, to take but one example, is socially tolerated and even encouraged by providing birth control and means of "safe" or "safer" sex to younger and younger adolescents. Although often associated with public health concerns, the desire to make relationships safer through means other than increased teenage abstinence and adult monogamy seemingly reflects a belief that sex (and, indeed, especially sex outside of marriage) constitutes a powerful expression of one's freedom and therefore should not be limited. Through its connection to freedom, sex functions as one of America's new shared values, and it is not easily undercut even by the known disadvantages faced by children born (in increasing numbers) out of wedlock or to teenage mothers, or even by the sexually transmitted diseases that make a promiscuous lifestyle dangerous. In a society practicing the worship of freedom through democracy and lacking any other constraining social forces, promiscuous sex threatens to become a protected sacrament despite the economic, psychological, and physical risks it entails.[60]

Modern America's current culture suggests that personal happiness is the proper goal of life, and that only freedom—indeed, the political and social "freedom to choose" how to live one's life, expressed through the increasingly politicized areas of life listed above—can make one truly happy.[61] We may pause for a moment to demonstrate the weakness of this premise, for it has important ramifications for the modern idealization of freedom and rights. Most human beings in recorded history have not been "free" politically or socially in the sense that we mean by the word *freedom* today. Many, in fact, have been slaves, literally held as the property of other human beings. Do we believe that all, or even most, of these politically unfree (or even enslaved) individuals were unhappy? Is it actually reasonable to believe that virtually all human beings before the eighteenth century lived unhappy lives because they did not possess democratic freedom? Can we really sanction the idea that only the modern condition of political and social freedom produces or maximizes happiness in individual human beings? Surely, we must admit, those in our own society with the most political and social freedom are the extremely wealthy or powerful. Do we believe that they are also the *happiest* (or least unhappy) individuals in society?

But if the state of happiness does not result directly from the condition of freedom, how, then, can we explain the pervasive view that freedom will or can make one happy? Arguably, it is derived largely from its negative: the lack of freedom (life in slavery or under political tyranny) *can and often does* make one unhappy. It seems reasonable, therefore (although it is strictly illogical), to conclude that it is freedom that makes one happy.

If we associate happiness not with political or personal freedom (from tyranny or enslavement) but with the modern "freedom to choose" how to live and thus to enjoy pleasures, we reach a similar result. Let us honestly examine those of our acquaintances who enjoy the most pleasures, or think of the times in our own lives when our active pleasures were maximized—should we conclude that those (including ourselves) enjoying maximum pleasure are also the happiest? I would suggest that to confuse maximized pleasure or maximized freedom from control by others with real happiness is to accept either an infantile (happiness = maximum pleasure) or adolescent (happiness = maximum freedom from control) conception of happiness. Thus, even if one agrees that happiness is the appropriate goal of human life, and that society should attempt to maximize it for individuals, there is little reason to believe that freedom or pleasure will produce this result. On the other hand, since life under tyranny or in slavery can make one *unhappy* and—more important—*because enslaving or tyrannizing over others is morally wrong,* members of any society have a duty to their fellow citizens to fight against these forces.

The idea that opposition to tyranny or slavery rests on a moral foundation contrasts sharply with the popular view that we oppose them because they infringe upon rights that exist separately from any system of moral obligations.[62] And yet such moral obligations seem necessary to support any attempt to protect individuals from those who would harm them. For, despite the long-standing attempt in political philosophy to provide a firm foundation for the idea of "natural rights," I cannot see any way that rights can exist except as the reciprocal effects of socially endorsed duties based on moral principles. That is, no one has a right to property: such a thing as a "right to property" simply does not exist.[63] But we all should be duty-bound not to steal something that belongs to another person and to protect others from those who would steal *because we believe stealing is immoral.* As Washington implied in his farewell address (quoted in an epigraph to this chapter), only duties based on moral principles of right and wrong can provide any secure environment for the protection of what moderns call an individual's "rights."[64]

To someone who would contradict this conclusion—arguing, for example, that the proposition "stealing is immoral" already rests on a "right to property" (which therefore can be stolen)—one may respond that it is also sometimes morally wrong to allow someone to retain his property (e.g., an individual who would harm himself or others with his own gun or knife). Thus it is the moral duty to our fellow man that is fundamental to the idea of rights and not vice versa. Such moral principles must undergird any society that wishes to protect rights in fact and not just in theory.

By demonstrating the important role society and extrapolitical values play in limiting the potentially dangerous effects of democratic practices and ideas, Athenian history should encourage us to ask whether it is wise to enshrine modern democratic ideals like freedom, choice, and diversity as values or establish them as goals without any other social framework of moral obligation. Can freedom, choice, and diversity, *when set up as goals or values,* actually undermine the very notions of values, individual responsibility, and morality, and thus fail to foster even themselves? Is it possible that those things many modern democrats claim to admire most—freedom, choice, and diversity— developed and continue to exist primarily as the by-products of moral principles and individual duties, such as the duty to protect others from violation, oppression, or prejudice because each of these acts is immoral when judged by the once conventional standards of our culture (itself based on the long Judaeo-Christian tradition)? In short, is it more likely that a society based on duties and moral principles will generate a significant amount of freedom, choice, and diversity, or that a society based on the latter will generate sound moral principles?

Recent events in American politics and society suggest that these questions deserve serious thought. Consider, for example, the violent and often brutally anti-woman attitudes expressed in popular music and acted out by the attendees at Woodstock III in July 1999 or in New York City during the Puerto Rico Day celebration in June 2000. In both cases, men mauled and molested young women in broad daylight and in view of hundreds of others. Media commentators and others justifiably complained about lax security and incendiary musicians in the first case and the ineffective police in the second. But the most troubling aspect of both incidents was that *they occurred within large crowds of bystanders who simply watched (or cheered!) while their fellow citizens were abused.* [65] The perpetrators judged (accurately) that they had little or nothing to fear from those around them. *There were no social constraints on them,* and surprisingly few analysts after the fact expressed significant consternation about the total breakdown in such constraints.[66] Instead, the musicians and organizers (at Woodstock) and the government institutions charged with protecting the populace (especially the police) received most of the blame.

But unless one wishes to create a totalitarian regime, institutions such as the police cannot be everywhere at once, and thus they cannot act as a consistent check on misbehavior and crime. Such a check is imposed most effectively not by government institutions but by communal moral standards and resulting individual action. However, in a world with few communal standards beyond freedom, choice, and diversity, if a man chooses to hold a low view of women, express these ideas profitably to a catchy tune, and/or treat the women around him accordingly, what is there to stop him? And even if we agree that noxious ideas must be tolerated by the state (in order to prevent political tyranny), can we justify the failure of individuals and society as a whole to condemn and oppose such views and the actions reflecting them on moral grounds?

I suggest that contemporary democratic thought is actually encouraging this situation, because, as we have already seen, the freedom that is idealized by modern society is not in fact the passive "freedom from being enslaved, tyrannized over, or violated" (Greek *eleutheria*), but rather the active "freedom to choose for oneself" based on personal desires and largely irrespective of moral obligation. Choice itself—instead of particular choices—thus forms an essential virtue and tool of modern democratic faith. Moral judgments and whatever else impinges on choice are often treated as potentially harmful if not evil, and that which encourages choice is deemed virtuous. "Pro-choice" is a moniker worn proudly by both "liberals" supporting abortion rights and "conservatives" supporting school voucher programs, while "anti-choice" is universally avoided.

America's democratic ideology and lack of a strong moral matrix—which would designate some choices as good or just and others as bad or unjust—mean that modern Americans have few standards by which to judge their actions and choices other than freedom itself.[67] And in this environment, whatever choices appear most free will seem most likely to produce happiness and therefore will exercise a powerful pull on individual minds and hearts, with little consideration of their effects on others within the society or the chooser's own character or soul. Thus social ills like divorce, family abandonment, and abortion (three things that I do not mean to equate morally), which can be characterized as choices expressing the freedom of the individual, are not only tolerated but sometimes actually encouraged, even if subtly.[68] And once a society has come to this point, surely we must admit that any theoretical connection between choice or freedom and the creation of a just and healthy society has obviously broken down. Deprived of a moral foundation, freedom's value rests largely on its status as an environment for choice, which itself can be evaluated only against the freedom that permits it. As Finley saw, freedom and democracy, which were once seen as *means* of achieving a *just* society, have transformed themselves into the definition of justice.

The idealization of freedom through democracy has led modern America to a precipitous position. Implicitly denying man's desire for a society based on beliefs and duties that lie beyond a system of government and the rights this government (democracy) is designed to protect, we have replaced society's extrapolitical goals with the potentially antisocial political doctrines of freedom, choice, and diversity.[69] These words have been made to resonate in the citizens' hearts in a way that God, family, and country once did in America (or gods, family, and polis in Athens). At the turn of the twenty-first century, freedom, choice, and diversity represent America's absolute "moral" goods and have become the would-be unifying principles of American society. They cannot be questioned in polite company, while God, family, and country are fair game.[70] What could more clearly demonstrate America's apparent conversion to this new religion than the fact that basic elements of traditional American society—such as the Pledge of Allegiance or the prayers opening Congress—seem to cause embarrassment to many intellectuals, media figures, and even politicians, who seem at most other times to be virtually incapable of embarrassment (much less shame)?[71]

Despite modern Americans' veneration of freedom and diversity, there is little sympathy or tolerance for those members of society who would make judgments about the moral worth of others' actions. While it seems perfectly acceptable in some circles to upbraid someone for holding politically "incorrect" views, the act of informing another person that his or her actions are morally wrong and socially unacceptable is itself considered rude if not immoral![72] The "freedom" to make such a statement about immoral actions, the "choice" to hold such beliefs, and the "diversity" that such differences produce do not seem welcome in contemporary America.[73] But no society with real values (that is, values beyond the anti-values of freedom, choice, and diversity) can continue to exist under strictures that prevent the reaffirmation of those values through the public and private disapprobation of individuals who violate them. Without the ability to inspire shame in those who violate societal norms and reward those who uphold them, a society possesses no effective means to reproduce its own values and structures.

America's loss of cultural structures that reinforce moral values has not gone unnoticed. The American political theorist Jean Bethke Elshtain, in her youth a "Nixon loather," who was surprised upon finding herself with feelings other than hatred of the former president after he died, concluded that in his own way, this complex man, humiliated and disgraced, struggled for the last two decades of his life to regain a measure of respect from his fellow citizens. *If we no longer create in America men and women who can be shamed* and made to pay a price for dishonoring the public trust, but *who, in turn, strive to recover just a few moments of civic grace,* we will have lost a culture that is strong enough to censure presidents and kind enough to permit them to recover their dignity through civil accomplishment.[74]

Those words, penned in April 1994, seem strangely prescient (and ominous) in view of the past decade of American history. It is no longer surprising if a president, a corporate executive, or even an archbishop—admittedly or obviously guilty of antisocial and immoral behavior—instead of seeking the public's forgiveness, rather trusts in its indulgence. One cannot help feeling that we may have already crossed into an age when public shame, collective kindness, and the moral notions that generate both are disappearing from American society.

In stark contrast, the classical Athenians never lost the ability to pronounce or enforce their collective standards of morality and thus to produce shame in individuals. Even the democratic icon Pericles spoke of those "laws which, although unwritten, yet cannot be broken without acknowledged disgrace" (Thuc. 2.37).[75] The negative and positive requirements for Athens's citizens analyzed in chapter 2 show that the Athenians placed real strictures on one another and could not have endorsed modern Americans' idealization of freedom, choice, and diversity. Respect for the laws, obedience to magistrates, and shame or disgrace for those who violated society's written and unwritten codes always formed a central part of Athenian life, which exhibited significant amounts of freedom, choice, and diversity as a result.[76]

In the United States today, the anti-values of freedom, choice, and diversity have become so powerful (and dangerous) in part because—note the supreme irony—they admit of no philosophical opposition. One simply cannot oppose treating these ideas as society's appropriate goals without risking being labeled a reactionary, heretic, or worse, as if it had been empirically proven that only peoples or regimes that worship these deities can produce justice or happiness. Has America seen the amount of social justice and personal happiness increase proportionately with its rising estimation of this trinity?

Finally, does real religious freedom actually exist in this society ostensibly based on the principles of choice and diversity? Would, for example, serious or organized dissent from the church of freedom (if any actually arose) be welcomed or even tolerated? It may seem to some unlikely that the state itself would suppress such opposition. But such suppression by the state is unnecessary where the people themselves enforce their own social (anti-)values. Dissent from freedom, choice, and diversity is suppressed informally at virtually every turn, and this as much as anything else demonstrates that our society has already reorganized itself around new principles. In short, our society still attempts to impose shame on its members, but only on those who violate the now sacred tenets of democratic ideology.[77]

It thus seems true that even a society that ostensibly rejects unifying ideals or morals will inevitably organize itself around some defining principles. For the United States in the early twenty-first century, those principles arguably derive from freedom, choice, and diversity expressed through democracy. Contemporary Americans become "democrats" in the same ineluctable way that serfs or cobblers in the Middle Ages became Christians, and ultimately we may be just as subservient to our church as was the medieval shoemaker.[78] Our priestly caste in the media and government speaks ex cathedra to the people, who, however unsatisfied in their daily existence, can at least comfort themselves with the belief that theirs is the one true faith.

In classical Athens, religion suffused every aspect of public life, from the theater to the military to the political assembly. The state (that is, the citizens) sponsored religious festivals and actively participated in the propitiation and worship of the gods. This fact well illustrates the way the various aspects of Athenian society—religious, political, economic, and social—overlapped with and affected one another, and the way every Athenian found himself set firmly within a matrix of duties to the gods, to his family, and to his fellow citizens. The principle of necessary duties (especially to protect the family, to serve the polis, and to propitiate the gods) formed the basic structure of Athenian society, and gave meaning to each religious, economic, military, and political act. In such an environment, it was impossible for the Athenians abjectly to worship a form of government, *demokratia,* even after they had made it a goddess. The idea that the "freedom to make choices" or "diversity" were absolute goods and thus could serve as goals or ideals (on a level with, much less above, family, gods, or polis) contradicted the very premises of Athenian society. Thus while democratic practices ultimately had a marked and deleterious effect on Athenian national strength and public morale and arguably contributed to the loss of Athenian independence, Athenian society managed to stave off the most harmful aspects of democratic theory. Even after they lost their democracy and autonomy, there is little evidence that the Athenians completely lost their fundamental conception of a society based on the principle of duties.

American history suggests that the Athenians might not have been able to withstand indefinitely the threat posed by the ideal of virtually unbounded freedom (had they ever developed it). Confronted with perceived tyranny from England, and enjoying what was (at worst) a semi-integral society, the American Founders constructed a regime that praised freedom (from that English tyranny) and reflected the modern liberal idea that individual human beings possess inalienable rights (even if most of them associated these rights with a creator). But, as some of the Founders may have recognized even at the time, they were largely free to encourage this view of rights because *they were grafting a government onto a society whose values had been long established.* For this reason and others, American government could theoretically be designed to interfere as little as possible in American society, which already enjoyed a firm foundation in civic duty, faith in God, and the belief that work would bring rewards.[79] And even those Founders most committed to separating the government from any religious establishment never doubted the need for the beneficial social by-products of Americans' religious practices and beliefs.[80]

As the nineteenth century wore on, a philosophical and social democratization occurred within America, whose form of government eventually came to be known as democracy, a concept that had given Madison and other Founders serious misgivings.[81] The supposed ideals of democracy eventually began to supplant older ideals, which the American Constitution theoretically had been designed to leave untouched. The twentieth century's breakdown in social forces derived from extrapolitical sources (especially basic ideas of duty, personal responsibility, and Judaeo-Christian morality), which initially were capable of restraining the latent dangers in the American system and the emerging democratic ideology, and the development of a thoroughgoing theory of rights and freedoms to be ensured by the state, expressed through active choice, and (theoretically) leading to diversity, have provided new fundamental beliefs for American society.

If, in the end, democracy has become a religion and the attempt to separate church and state in America has therefore failed, it may be because human societies have such a strong tendency to organize themselves around a set of interlocking principles and beliefs. A church of freedom has arisen amid the ruins of previous American ideals, and the message proclaimed from its pulpit is clear:

Choose anything but not to believe.

Conclusion

Socrates, Pericles, and the Citizen

THIS BOOK HAS SOUGHT TO set aside ancient (and modern) opinions about democracy in order to focus the reader's attention on Athenian history and the relevant lessons it offers for modern society and government. However, for a moment I would like to address two of the most well-known ancient characterizations of Athenian democracy and society, namely, Pericles' Funeral Oration and Plato's *Apology of Socrates*.

For several years I have asked my Greek history students to write essays criticizing Pericles' oration (Thuc. 2.35–46) from the standpoint of Socrates as expressed in the *Apology* (or vice versa). The topic is fruitful because the two works treat many of the same issues, but from radically different perspectives. Of course, neither of these works presents a verbatim account of the historical speech recreated. The text of Pericles' Funeral Oration (delivered in 431/0) may largely reflect only what Thucydides thought Pericles said or could have said (or even what other people would believe he could have said), and Plato's version of Socrates' defense speech (delivered in 399) also demands a critical approach. But even on a minimalist view of these speeches' historicity, they represent the views of two very distinct schools of thought about Athenian democracy and human society.[1] Those schools might be loosely described as a "statist" view (Pericles') and a "moral" view (Socrates').

Pericles values a citizen's service to the state above all other qualities. Indeed, "steadfastness in his country's battles should be as a cloak to cover a man's other imperfections; for the good action has blotted out the bad, and his merit as a citizen more than outweighed his demerits as an individual" (Thuc. 2.42; trans. Crawley). Moreover, according to Pericles, the Athenians, "unlike any other nation," regard the man who does not participate in the political life of the city "not as unambitious but as useless" (2.40). Pericles repeats his statist views in a later speech, opining that "national greatness is more for the advantage of private persons, than any individual well-being coupled with public humiliation."[2]

The express goal of Pericles' collectivism was national greatness, which he conceived of especially as power over other states. As we have already noted in chapter 2, it was Athens's power, and not its cultural or political superiority, on which Pericles relied for Athens's future reputation:

In short, I say that as a city we are an education for Hellas, and I doubt if the world can produce a man, who where he has only himself to depend upon, is equal to so many emergencies and graced by so happy a versatility as the Athenian. And that this is no mere boast thrown out for the occasion, but plain matter of fact, the power of the state acquired by these habits proves. For Athens alone of her contemporaries is found when tested to be greater than her reputation, and alone gives no occasion to her assailants to blush at the antagonist by whom they have been worsted, or to her subjects to question her title by merit to rule. Rather, the admiration of the present and succeeding ages will be ours, because we have not left our power without witness, but have shown it by mighty proofs; and because far from needing a Homer for our panegyrist, or others of his craft whose verses might charm for the moment only for the impression which they give to melt at the touch of fact, we have forced every sea and land to be the highway of our daring, and everywhere, whether for evil or for good, have left imperishable monuments behind us. (Thuc. 2.41; trans. Crawley, adapted)

Pericles returns to this theme at the end of his last speech in Thucydides:

Remember, too, that if your country has the greatest name in all the world, it is because she never bent before disaster, and because she has expended more life and effort in war than any other city, and has won for herself a power greater than any hitherto known, the memory of which will descend to the latest posterity; even if now, in obedience to the general law of decay, we should ever be forced to yield, still it will be remembered that we held rule over more Greeks than any other Greek polis, that we sustained the greatest wars against their united or separate powers, and inhabited a city unrivaled by any other in resources or magnitude. (Thuc. 2.64; trans. Crawley, adapted)

The raw militarism and jingoistic nationalism of these words have drawn little comment in most recent work on Athenian democracy. Very few authors have, like Paul Rahe, drawn attention to the dissonance between such belligerence and the modern conception of Athens as the politically progressive state that acted as the artistic and intellectual heart of ancient Greece.[3] Of course, Athens *was* (at least in retrospect) the cultural leader of fifth-century Hellas, but it is obvious from Thucydides and from other fifth-century Athenian literature and iconography that the Athenian demos's image of itself rested more on Athens's military power and empire than on the city's cultural hegemony. Thus Pericles encourages the Athenians to "realize the power of Athens, and feed your eyes upon her every day, even becoming her lovers *[erastai];* and then when all her greatness shall break upon you, you must reflect that it was by courage, sense of duty, and a keen feeling of honor in action that men were enabled to win all this" (2.43). Scholars question whether Pericles asks the Athenians to become the lovers "of *Athens*" or "of [Athens's] *power.*"[4] The Greek is ambiguous, but the question is moot. Athens and its power were one and the same for Pericles: the city's power was its glory in the present and the assurance of its reputation in the future.

As we have seen, this equation of "Athenian power = reputation in the future" seems to have been a central idea for Pericles, who pursued the goal of Athenian power and supremacy in Hellas throughout his career. This theme unites his policies of hostility toward Sparta and his radicalization of the democracy through empowering the demos.[5] Unwilling for Athens to remain an equal (much less an inferior) power to Sparta, Pericles saw that the common, propertyless citizen remained a (largely) untapped source of power in the Hellenic polis, and thus he determined to utilize this resource for Athens (as Themistocles had used the silver mines). Yet, it is clear that the statesman's actions in the demos's favor derived from no altruistic motives; for Pericles seems to have thought no more of spending the common citizens' lives as soldiers or trireme rowers than he did of reducing the relative political power of his own aristocratic class. Indeed, if we may believe Thucydides, Pericles boasted of Athens's great expenditure of lives. Both sacrifices—of citizens' lives and aristocratic privilege—were necessary to achieve Athenian greatness and thereby establish Athens's place in history.

Pericles prepared and then encouraged Athens to fight a war that would ultimately debilitate the Hellenic city-state system and kill thousands of Greeks. Again, if we believe that Thucydides' speeches attempt to reproduce Pericles' own views (at least broadly), Pericles himself understood the risks he and Athens were taking. But he considered those risks acceptable in view of the potential enhancement of Athens's future reputation. And as we have noted, Pericles' ability to convince the citizens to accept this proposition, the abstraction and inhumanity of his nationalism, his political integrity, and his willingness to risk his own life and his political career in the service of his ideals, make him one of the most charismatic—and dangerous—leaders in Western history.

Ironically, Pericles has come to represent ideals of Athenian democracy and humanism, and the phrase "Periclean Athens" immediately brings to mind literature and architecture, rather than war and imperialism. In fact, egalitarianism and humanism did not serve as the defining ideals of Periclean Athens or of Pericles himself. The building program sponsored by Pericles and funded to a significant degree by money extorted from other Greek states was nothing if not a vaunted testament to Athens's empowerment at the expense of both Greeks and barbarians.[6] And while fifth-century Athenian literature does occasionally seem to praise or encourage the Athenian practice of democracy,[7] this theme appears in only a very small part of Athenian drama. At other times, dramatists like Sophocles and Euripides seem to be questioning the values or practices of *demokratia* or humanism as much as reaffirming them.[8] In general, the themes that flow through Athenian literature are far more universal than praising or condemning the particular form Hellenic polis government could take. Certainly we may justifiably associate great literature and drama with Periclean Athens, but we can hardly give Pericles himself or democratic politics credit for their superlative quality.[9]

Moreover, Pericles got it wrong. Athens is remembered today *not* because it "spent more lives" or "ruled more Greeks than any other Greek state." Most people without a detailed knowledge of Greek history—and some with it—would (wrongly) associate those dubious accomplishments with Sparta.[10] Instead of the long passages on Athens's power and military successes in Pericles' speeches, it is the relatively few words about democracy that are quoted repeatedly by those wishing to characterize the Athenian regime or Pericles himself.[11]

But a few words about the open society or election based on merit in Pericles' speeches should not be allowed to obscure the overarching theme of his orations or his career. That theme was *Athenian power,* and that power relied (in part) on the active participation of the Athenian demos. And even if one believed that Pericles loved or sympathized with the poorer Athenian citizens (despite sending thousands of them to their deaths in wars to preserve and extend Athenian hegemony), this would say nothing about the thousands of foreigners, metics, and slaves exploited systematically by Periclean Athens. Pericles, after all, was not some kind of twentieth-century leader defending "democracy" or "the poor" against the attacks of those opposed to "freedom." He used *demokratia* as a force to build Athenian power, and that meant "spending more lives" than any other Greek state just as much as it necessitated allowing those without property to row warships, vote in the assembly, or serve on Athenian courts.

Under Pericles, the Athenian demos was offered a very straightforward exchange. If the common citizens would serve repeatedly in the military and vote for Pericles, his supporters, and their policies, they would receive in return not only payments for their public service, but also an increase in their political power, and the glory and wealth that attended their empire. When combined with Pericles' insistence that Athenians owed their first duties to the state, that these duties would compensate for their private failings, and that Athens ran a terrible risk if it gave up its empire, it is understandable why this message ultimately succeeded.

Perhaps most important for the modern world, Pericles felt free to adopt the position that "private failings" were less important than "public service" because *Athenian society as a whole already put restraints on private action*. Specific requirements for office-holding and citizenship addressed moral and social questions as much as political concerns.[12] As we saw in the previous chapter, Pericles himself recognized the "unwritten laws" of society that brought disgrace on those who violate them.[13] That disgrace—imposed (even if passively) by Athenians on fellow Athenians—provided Pericles with an environment in which he could tap the Athenians' sense of moral obligation even as he touted the benefits of empire. Such continuing societal norms demonstrate that the Athenians never enshrined freedom, choice, and diversity as demigods; instead, they remained constrained by ideals of duty to the gods, family, and polis. These social constraints represent the natural result of a healthy society in action, and they arguably provided both Pericles and the American Founders with the social foundations upon which their *political* systems could function successfully (at least for a time).[14] Pericles recognized this and relied on it—note his repeated references to duty in his speeches—although he admittedly introduced political forces into Athens that would begin to change this social fabric.[15]

Socrates seems to have known the dangers (and certainly he felt the effects) of these new forces, exemplified by the large courts of paid jurors created during Pericles' leadership in Athens.[16] It was a paid jury of five hundred citizens,[17] of course, that convicted Socrates and condemned him to death on the charges of introducing new gods, not believing in the traditional Athenian gods, and corrupting the youth.[18] Plato's account of Socrates' speech in his own defense against these charges contains—among other things—a refutation of Pericles' ideas about the relationship between state and citizen, public and private morality, the wisdom of the collective versus that of the individual, and other fundamental tenets of democratic thought.[19]

As we have seen, Pericles affirmed that Athenians (rightly in his view) regard any man who fails to take part in public affairs as useless.[20] Pericles also asserted that Athenians consider discussion in the assembly to be an indispensable precursor to any action, noting that Athenians both manage their private affairs and serve as good judges of public affairs. In short, at least as reported by Thucydides, Pericles held that all citizens had both the obligation and the ability to serve the state in a public capacity.

Such views are clearly antithetical to Socrates' in the *Apology*. Not only does Socrates make it clear on several occasions that he has consciously chosen *not* to participate in public affairs (23b), either in the assembly (31c–32a, 32e–33a) or in the law courts (17d, 32e), but he also asserts that his own kind of service to Athens has been far more valuable (see below) and that it is impossible and dangerous for an honest man to lead a political life in Athens:

> This is what has prevented me from taking part in public affairs, and I think it was quite right to prevent me. Be sure, gentlemen of the jury, that if I had long ago attempted to take part in politics, I should have died long ago, and benefited neither you nor myself. Do not be angry with me for speaking the truth; no man will survive who genuinely opposes you or any other crowd and prevents the occurrence of many unjust and illegal happenings in the city. A man who really fights for justice must lead a private, not a public, life if he is to survive even for a short time. (Pl. *Ap.* 31e–32a; trans. G. M. A. Grube)

One is struck not only by the contrast with Pericles' views in the Funeral Oration but also with the statesman's claims about his own honesty (2.60) and with Thucydides' evaluation of Pericles' character:

> Pericles indeed, by his rank, ability, and known integrity, was enabled to exercise an independent control over the multitude—in short, to lead them instead of being led by them; for as he never sought power by improper means, he was never compelled to flatter them, but on the contrary enjoyed so high an estimation that he could afford to anger them by contradiction. (Thuc. 2.65; trans. Crawley)

It seems unlikely that Socrates could have shared Thucydides' estimation of Pericles' integrity given the philosopher's views about an honest versus a public life and about the necessity for honest men to seek virtue instead of honors (see below). Given that Socrates asserted that it was impossible for the demos to tolerate a just politician, Pericles' continued political success in itself probably cast a shadow over his reputation in the philosopher's eyes.[21]

After explicitly questioning the idea that a successful politician could be an honest man, Socrates continues by citing an example of the problems inherent in living a public, or political, life. The example he chooses seems particularly pointed, since it concerns Socrates' service (having been chosen by lot) on the Council of 500 in 406, after the battle of Arginusae (32a–c). As we have seen, at that time the assembly wished to condemn the Athenian generals for failing to collect the dead and wounded after the battle. Socrates, sitting on the presiding committee *(prytaneis)*, opposed this action against the generals, which passed anyway and had as a notable upshot the execution of Pericles' son.[22] The historical irony of the demos taking its vengeance on Pericles' own son would not have been lost on the jurors at the trial. Socrates— if he indeed used this example—almost certainly realized and calculated the reference's potential impact on his audience. It was tantamount to proclaiming to the Athenians, "Look how you executed your own leaders, including Pericles' son (a rash act, which you certainly regretted later), while I was the only man who tried to stop you. Surely it is *you,* the demos, who are unwise and unjust. I, on the other hand, have simply tried to point this out. And now you wish to punish me as well!"[23]

Ironically, on a brutally ideological level, Pericles could perhaps have justified his son's conviction (if not his execution).[24] For service to the state, and in particular military service, was the supreme good to Pericles, necessary to maintain good standing in the community. Failure to perform such public duties, it follows, should bring with it public condemnation. Although Socrates himself (significantly) reminds the jury of his own military service at Potidaea, Amphipolis, and Delion (28e), he could not have accepted Pericles' view of personal merit based on public rather than private morality. For Socrates, the greatest good consisted of the daily discussion of virtue (38a). So far from arguing that a man's public service could compensate for private failings, Socrates maintains that a man "should look to this only in his actions, whether what he does is right or wrong, whether he is acting like a good or a bad man" (28b). In contrast, Pericles praises the Athenians' tolerance, even as he notes their respect for the law:

> The freedom which we enjoy in our government extends also to our ordinary life. There, far from exercising a jealous surveillance over each other, we do not feel called upon to be angry with our neighbor for doing what he likes, or even to indulge in those injurious looks which cannot fail to be offensive, although

they inflict no positive penalty. But all this ease in our private relations does not make us lawless as citizens. Against this fear is our chief safeguard, teaching us to obey the magistrates and the laws, particularly such as regard the protection of the injured, whether they are actually on the statute book, or belong to that code which, although unwritten, yet cannot be broken without acknowledged disgrace. (Thuc. 2.37; trans. Crawley)

Like Pericles, Socrates also maintains that the law should be obeyed (19a). But unlike Pericles, he also frequently refers to his own reproach of other citizens on moral grounds (29d–30a, 30e–31b): that is, Socrates explicitly contradicts Pericles' views about not questioning a neighbor's actions.

Moreover, Socrates makes it clear that *there is a higher authority even than the law.* The philosopher claims that he must obey the god first, and since he interprets his quest for a wiser man than himself as a response to Apollo's oracle, he asserts that he would continue to question those around him even if the jury were to forbid it (29c–e, 33c).[25] On this issue of divine authority, Socrates stands in sharp contrast to Pericles' statism. For the philosopher, the will of the community—the demos and its democracy—cannot be rated higher than the commands of the gods, a force conspicuously absent from Pericles' speeches in Thucydides.[26]

Pericles also makes little connection in his speeches between the Athenian government and the quest for justice *(dike)* or its definition, a quest that forms such an important part of Socrates' mission.[27] So little, in fact, is Pericles concerned with justice on a philosophical or practical level that he summarizes the Athenians' situation as rulers of an empire thus:

> For what you hold is, to speak somewhat plainly, a tyranny: to take it perhaps was unjust *[adikon]*, but to let it go is unsafe.[28] And men of these views, making converts of others, would quickly ruin a state; indeed the result would be the same if they could live independent by themselves; for the retiring and unambitious are never secure without vigorous protectors at their side; in short, such qualities are useless to an imperial city, though they may help a dependency to an unmolested servitude. (Thuc. 2.63; trans. Crawley)

Pericles' arguments are based on utility and security; the potential injustice *(adikon)* of the empire is openly admitted but then relegated to a position of secondary importance when it is compared with the dangers of acting in accordance with justice. On the other hand, Socrates repeatedly claims that to worry about one's own safety rather than to live justly is execrable (28b–d, etc.).[29]

One should also note that Socrates could not have endorsed Pericles' view that the Athenians (and common men in general) were capable judges in public matters, a view that served as a fundamental democratic principle.[30] In the famous passage in which he questions his accuser Meletus (24c ff.), Socrates makes it clear that, just as only the horse trainer improves horses while others corrupt them (because they lack horse-training skill), only a minority (the few) are able to improve humans, while the majority corrupt them. Thus, he concludes, it is impossible that Socrates alone harms the citizens while everyone else improves them (as Meletus had claimed). It follows, of course, that any majority—including the majority of jurors—is unlikely to choose rightly.

But this is not Socrates' only criticism of democratic principles, for although Pericles maintains that in Athens "advancement in public life falls to reputation for capacity" (2.37), Socrates asserts that "reputation for capacity" in no way guarantees wisdom. In fact, by questioning the politicians who were reputed to be wise, Socrates had found that *this class had the least wisdom of all* (21c–22a). At least, he said, craftsmen had some knowledge of their craft, and poets possessed inspiration (22c–e). The politicians, the very men advanced by their "reputation for capacity" according to Pericles, were "nearly the most deficient" in wisdom in Socrates' view. Since Socrates clearly does believe in the efficacy of special training or education in particular areas, surely for him the area in which these men most needed training was in human excellence or virtue *(arete)*. And if Socrates himself claimed that the teaching of excellence was problematic (e.g., 20a–c; cf. Plato's *Protagoras*), he nonetheless believed that one must continue to ask questions about it. Pericles, as we have noted, connected a man's virtue primarily with his service to the state.[31]

On the subjects of public wealth and power, Socrates and Pericles held significantly different views. While it is true that Pericles does not quite praise wealth for its own sake in the Funeral Oration, he does make it clear that the luxuries and elegant lifestyle in Athens (not to mention year-round games and sacrifices) made life for the Athenians sweet and helped "put aside cares" (2.38). Athenians employ wealth more for use than for show, he says (2.40), and succeeding ages will admire Athens for the great monuments of its power—for good or for ill—left behind everywhere (2.41). Socrates almost seems to answer Pericles' views on Athenian wealth and power directly when he informs the jury how he will continue to question those he meets, whether the Athenian demos approves of his actions or not. In particular, Socrates maintains that he will continue to ask his fellow citizens the following:

Good Sir, you are an Athenian, a citizen of the greatest city with the greatest reputation for both wisdom and power; are you not ashamed of your eagerness to possess as much wealth, reputation and honors as possible, while you do not care for nor give thought to wisdom or truth, or the best possible state of your soul? (Pl. *Ap.* 29d–e; trans. Grube)

Thus while Pericles argued that the state must be made powerful and that this would secure its future reputation and ultimately benefit individual citizens, Socrates maintained that the individual must first seek to improve his own soul, his own moral condition. *In Socrates' view this improvement of the individual would ultimately lead to a better state, although this was its by-product and not its express goal:* "Wealth does not bring about excellence, but excellence brings about wealth and all other public and private blessings for men" (30b).

Like Pericles, Socrates also expressed interest in the future reputation of Athens, although, again like the statesman, Socrates failed to predict what would secure the Athenians' place in history:

It is for the sake of a short time, gentlemen of the jury, that you will acquire the reputation and the guilt, in the eyes of those who want to denigrate the city, of having killed Socrates, a wise man, for they who want to revile you will say that I am wise even if I am not. If you had waited but a little while, this would have happened of its own accord. You see my age, that I am already advanced in years and close to death. . . .

Now I want to prophesy to those who convicted me, for I am at the point when men prophesy most, when they are about to die. I say, gentlemen, to those who voted to kill me, that vengeance will come upon you immediately after my death, a vengeance much harder to bear than that which you took in killing me. You did this in the belief that you would avoid giving an account of your life, but I maintain that quite the opposite will happen to you. There will be more people to test you, whom I now held back, but you did not notice it. They will be more difficult to deal with as they will be younger and you will resent them more. You are wrong to believe that by killing people you will prevent anyone from reproaching you for not living in the right way. To escape such tests is neither possible nor good, but it is best and easiest not to discredit others but to prepare oneself to be as good as possible. With this prophecy to you who convicted me, I part from you. (Pl. *Ap.* 38c, 39c–d; trans. Grube)

Socrates got it wrong. For, despite some eloquent defenses of the philosopher (beginning with that of Plato himself), *it has not been the execution of Socrates for which the Athenians or their democracy have been remembered or condemned in the modern world.* As we saw in the introduction, the execution of Socrates makes but a tiny ripple in the vast ocean of current historical material on Athenian democracy and politics. Like other Athenian injustices,

Socrates' trial and execution are usually treated as aberrations, acknowledged in passing as modern critics rush to praise democracy or condemn Athenian patriarchy, sexism, or some contravention of freedom, choice, or diversity. Pericles described a system geared to produce a citizen who placed the advantage of the state over the virtue of the individual—or rather, a state in which acting for the (perceived) good of the state *was* the highest virtue. Thus, through the social ostracism of the man who takes no part in public affairs (one such as Socrates), who is considered "useless" in Pericles' view, and through the prizes offered to those who do participate, the state ensures itself of a continued supply of servants. Pericles emphasizes this utilitarian role of citizens when he encourages parents of the deceased to have more children. These children, he asserts, will not only "help you to forget those whom you have lost, but will be to the state at once a reinforcement and a security" (2.44). Since for Pericles the greatest honors should be offered as rewards for state service, he ends his speech by reminding the mourners that the children of the Athenians killed in the war will be reared at the public expense, the polis thus granting a "most useful prize in this contest of valor. . . . And where the rewards for merit *[arete]* are greatest, there are found the best citizens" (2.46). Let us here recall that at the City Dionysia, Athens's war orphans were paraded before the citizens in their publicly provided military equipment; in this area, Pericles' ideals had been given a very concrete form.[32]

Ironically, Socrates also believed that public service—as he defined it, through improving the souls of individual citizens—should be rewarded, although he preferred remuneration for his services in a different coin. After the Athenians voted to convict him, Socrates first proclaimed that the punishment for his actions should be daily meals in the Prytaneum, a privilege granted by Athens to honored citizens, Olympic victors, or special guests of the city.[33] After nevertheless receiving the death penalty, Socrates ends his *Apology* by requesting a repayment from the Athenians who have condemned him:

> This much I ask from them: when my sons grow up, avenge yourselves by causing them the same kind of grief that I caused you, if you think they care for money or anything else more than they care for virtue, or if they think they are somebody when they are nobody. Reproach them as I reproach you, that they do not care for the right things and think they are worthy when they are not worthy of anything. If you do this, I shall have been justly treated by you, and my sons also. (Pl. *Ap.* 41e–42; trans. Grube)

Pericles promised the "useful prize" of public support for the children of Athens's war dead. Socrates makes no reference whatsoever to the economic condition of his sons (beyond hoping that they will not care *too much* for money), but rather asks that his fellow citizens vigilantly shepherd his fatherless children in virtue. Socrates' (or Plato's, if one wishes) touching reference to his sons at the end of his speech throws into high relief Pericles' own cold encouragement to the Athenians to produce more children. Indeed, there is barely anything so personal as Socrates's last request of the jurors in any recorded remark of Pericles, who lost his two eldest sons in the plague during the first years of the Peloponnesian War.[34] Like Pericles' willingness to sacrifice thousands of Athenians in the quest for increased Athenian power and glory, Socrates' words are a powerful reminder of the folly that equates political action in favor of "the people" with real concern for individual human beings.

SOCRATES AND PERICLES AS CITIZENS AND LEADERS

It is my hope that this brief discourse on the views expressed in Pericles' Funeral Oration and Plato's *Apology of Socrates* has not blurred this work's focus on the actual history of classical Athens. Ideologies aside, Pericles did encourage the Athenians to expand their empire and to radicalize their *demokratia,* and Socrates was executed on the vote of these same Athenians (his fellow citizens) in 399. While keeping our attention on Socrates and Pericles, I wish to close this essay by turning once more to the historical conditions in Athens during the classical period. For, although Socrates and Pericles appear to have been very unusual and perhaps even unique individuals, whose ideas and lives have resonated through the centuries with varying but undeniable force, they were both also very much men of their own time. In fact, both were ultimately products and reflections of the Athenian society that has been the subject of this book, and both represent the strengths of that society, even as they mark moments of its decline.

Perhaps most obviously, both Socrates and Pericles risked their own lives numerous times in service to their country. Pericles both proposed military actions in the assembly and then led them on the battlefield; his individual courage and real commitment to his policies cannot be questioned.[35] Socrates, despite personal views that must have made Athens's imperialism seem questionable if not completely unjust,[36] repeatedly served as a hoplite, famously saving the life of the young Alcibiades at Potidaea, and having the favor returned after the Athenian defeat at Delion. At the time of the latter battle (424), Socrates was a man of some forty-five years, hardly a youthful warrior, and a reminder of the onerous demands that Athenian society put on its middle-aged as well as its younger members.[37]

In the area of religion, Socrates is said to have been extremely pious, performing all the customary sacrifices even as his religious views, in the eyes of some, made him seem strange if not heretical. Let us recall here that ancient Greek piety largely depended on action rather than beliefs.[38] What Socrates said or believed about the gods was not nearly so important within Athenian society as his regular participation in public and private cult. Only Socrates' particular historical circumstances—his connection with controversial individuals like Alcibiades and Critias—made his unorthodox religious opinions a serious issue in Athens.[39] No one, not even his accusers, ever claimed that his actions were impious, and his last utterance reportedly concerned a sacrifice to the gods.[40]

We have every reason to believe that Pericles likewise performed all the religious duties of his political office as general and the religious actions that were expected of him as an Athenian citizen and father without demur. Had he not done so, we certainly would expect to hear about this in the historical record, which contains numerous unflattering details about Pericles' personal and public life and associates him closely with men of heterodox views like the philosopher Anaxagoras.[41] Pericles may have been thought by some to share Anaxagoras's strange opinions, but that apparently did not lead even to any rumor (much less an accusation) that he failed to perform his religious duties. Again, given the fact that so many other rumors circulating about Pericles made their way into the historical record, in this case we can put some faith in the argument from silence. We may also note that Pericles sponsored and served as a commissioner for the Athenian building program on the acropolis, a program that resulted in the rejuvenation of the sacral center of Athens and served religious as much as political or economic purposes. Again, as with Socrates, Pericles' actions, not his personal views about the gods, established his essential piety in most Athenian eyes.

Economically, both Socrates and Pericles seem to have subordinated personal gain to their own ideas about justice and public service. Despite Socrates' relative poverty, he apparently made no effort to collect fees for his teaching,[42] and Pericles (despite his wealth) reportedly lived on such a strict budget that it led to poor relations with his sons.[43] In short, the actions of both Socrates and Pericles seem to reflect a belief that money was not a thing to be pursued for its own sake. In this way, both demonstrate the fact that

Athenian society at large valued allowing other concerns beyond simple self-interest to influence economic decisions.[44]

We have treated the economic, religious, and military aspects of Pericles' and Socrates' lives, and found in each area that both reflect the prevailing social norms of fifth-century Athens.[45] Finally, I would point to a similarity between Socrates and Pericles that perhaps most clearly emphasizes the way in which modern American democracy differs from that of fifth-century Athens. Both Socrates and Pericles acted as leaders (of admittedly different kinds) in their society, and both proved themselves willing to run great risks, including the chance of losing their lives, in order to continue to express their sincerely held opinions.

Athenian history amply demonstrates that a statesman-general like Pericles could be ostracized or even executed by an unhappy demos. As we have seen, Pericles himself was fined and probably removed from office on at least one occasion. Despite this, Pericles "led the people instead of being led by them," in the words of Thucydides (2.65), repeatedly demonstrating his willingness to oppose the people's will and directly contradict the demos.[46] His determination to upbraid the people, to tell them when they were wrong, to assert his own wisdom and the wisdom of his policies in the face of public fines, exile, or execution, stands in stark contrast to the modern American politician's fear of merely failing in a reelection bid or in the opinion polls. Again, can anyone imagine a contemporary American politician, in the midst of an unpopular war that he had supported, standing before those who had lost relatives and friends in this war (and a resulting plague), and making the following statement?

> And yet if you are angry with me, it is with one who is, as I think, second to no man either in knowledge of the proper policy, or in the ability to expound it, and who is moreover not only a patriot but an honest one. (Pericles at Thuc. 2.60; trans. Crawley)[47]

Like Pericles, Socrates also regularly chastised the people, although he usually addressed them privately. Yet in his defense speech, Socrates (according to Plato) openly reproached the demos. The Athenians, he said, had no just cause to be angry with him, since he had been doing them a favor for many years (30d–e). Indeed, he warned the Athenians not to punish him, lest they lose a great advantage for the polis:

> Be sure that if you kill the sort of man I say I am, you will not harm me more than yourselves. . . . Indeed, gentlemen of the jury, I am far from making a de-

fense now on my own behalf, as might be thought, but on yours, to prevent you from wrongdoing by mistreating the god's gift to you by condemning me; for if you kill me you will not easily find another like me. I was attached to this city by the god—though it seems a ridiculous thing to say—as upon a great and noble horse which was somewhat sluggish because of its size and needed to be stirred up by a kind of gadfly. (Pl. *Ap.* 30c–e; trans. Grube)

I want to emphasize these images of Socrates and Pericles telling the Athenian citizens that *they* are morally and/or intellectually deficient precisely because the idea is so foreign to modern democratic politics or popular culture. When was the last time modern Americans heard a politician, journalistic commentator, or even a (sympathetic) character in a popular film openly claim that what the majority—what "the American people"—want or think is either morally wrong or intellectually bankrupt? But that is what real leaders must do, *especially* in a democracy. If modern leaders are not willing to risk even their own popularity or elected positions—much less risk their lives as did Socrates and Pericles—is there any reason to follow them?

Athenian history's most important positive lessons for modern America have little to do with *demokratia*. The nexus of social responsibilities and values binding the Athenian citizens to one another did not stem from democracy, but rather developed all over Hellas. Moreover, Athenian values associated with civic responsibilities and duties so thoroughly suffused the populace that the lives of individuals with ideological differences as vast as those that separated Socrates and Pericles still demonstrate the Athenians' dedication to the gods, their families, and their polis. Both Socrates and Pericles acknowledged and performed their duties in these areas, even if they interpreted them in very different ways. Both also risked their lives and the good opinion of their fellow citizens in order to lead the people in what they considered to be a better direction.

Still, these two great Athenians do represent very different ways of thinking about virtue, the polis, and the individual's relationship to the state. They therefore show that *a society that does not venerate diversity may nonetheless produce radically diverse ideas*. In a society that placed duties before rights and recognized the value of "unwritten laws" that were "shameful to break," Socrates and Pericles exercised a significant amount of "freedom," choosing to live their lives in very different ways and to espouse radically different views. Pericles' political actions, for all that they reflected an honest and patriotic desire for Athenian greatness, set forces in motion that would help corrupt the morale of the Athenian demos, weaken Athens militarily, and foster the most devastating war in Greek history. In asking himself and the Athenians how they could make Athens great in the eyes of history, Pericles ultimately planted seeds that would help destroy Athenian greatness. But we must also concede that as a by-product of his quest for Athenian power, Pericles sponsored buildings, literature, and political reforms that have not only inspired later generations but also all but obscured the theme of Athenian superiority that tied them together.

Like Pericles' actions, Socrates' own life and teachings have perhaps had a different effect than the philosopher intended. The discipline of philosophy that he arguably created would ultimately splinter into many schools and branches, with the question of justice and the condition of the soul sometimes far from philosophers' minds, while questions of politics per se became increasingly prominent even as they were distanced from the social world of the polis that so much concerned Plato and Aristotle. Finally, even the potential lesson of Socrates' execution at the hands of his fellow citizens in a free society has been obscured by the image of Athens as the great *democratic* city, to be admired more for its particular form of government and the poorer citizens' ability to vote than for the larger society that generated and (to some degree) controlled this regime.

For Socrates, the most important questions an Athenian citizen could ask were not about ways to make the city powerful or to improve Athens's government or the public's welfare. Instead, Socrates encouraged each citizen to ask how he could live a life of justice and excellence. It would be intriguing to know if Pericles ever discussed this idea with his younger contemporary, and even more fascinating to learn what either would have thought of modern democratic society. Both might have been surprised to learn that we have taken the Athenian political system, stripped away its historical and social context, and raised it from a simple form of government to the one remaining Form of virtue.

NOTES

In most cases I have provided references only to the most important ancient sources; however, I have also indicated useful secondary works (usually only those in English) that may be profitably consulted by readers wishing to pursue individual issues.

INTRODUCTION

1. Madison in *The Federalist Papers,* ed. I. Kramnick (New York, 1987), no. 55. Cf. also *Federalist* 6 (Hamilton), 63 (Madison); *The Works of John Adams, Second President of the United States: With a Life of the Author, Notes and Illustrations, by His Grandson Charles Francis Adams* (Boston, 1850–56), 4: 490–92 (from his *Defense of the Constitutions of the Government of the United States of America*); and see J. T. Roberts, *Athens on Trial: The Antidemocratic Tradition in Western Thought* (Princeton, N.J., 1994), pp. 179–93.

2. See esp. Meyer Reinhold, *Classica Americana: The Greek and Roman Heritage in the United States* (Detroit, 1984), pp. 97–99, 156–57, 214, and Roberts, *Athens on Trial,* pp. 179–93.

3. E.g., *Federalist* 10. See also Gordon S. Wood, *The Creation of the American Republic, 1776–1787* (Chapel Hill, N.C., 1969), p. 595, who notes that the term *democracy* was already increasing in popularity by the late 1780s.

4. On the Founders' idea of popular sovereignty expressed through representatives of the people, who simply grant their own power to these representatives, see esp. Wood, *Creation of the American Republic,* pp. 545–47, 593–606.

5. Most famously, Alexis de Tocqueville, *Democracy in America* (Paris, 1835–40). For the "democratization" of early America, cf. also Wood, *Creation of the American Republic,* pp. 595–615.

6. George Grote, *History of Greece* (London, 1846–56). See also I. Morris and K. A. Raaflaub, eds., *Democracy 2500? Questions and Challenges* (Dubuque, Iowa, 1998), pp. 3–4, who note that even in the early twentieth century, some classical

scholars held the view that Athens succeeded in spite of, and not because of, democracy. For the changing perception of Athens in the nineteenth century, see Roberts, *Athens on Trial,* pp. 208–55.

7. See M. I. Finley, *Democracy Ancient and Modern* (1973; rev. ed., New Brunswick, N.J., 1985), pp. 9–10.

8. *Federalist* 63 (emphasis in original); see also *Federalist* 10 (Madison), 71 (Hamilton), and Wood, *Creation of the American Republic,* pp. 513–18, 599.

9. See, e.g., the Earth Charter (www.earthcharter.org), which calls for support of democratic societies and democratic institutions, and which also demonstrates democracy's increasing appeal beyond the West.

10. Finley, *Democracy Ancient and Modern,* pp. 10–11.

11. Ibid., pp. 3–37, 76–141.

12. Josiah Ober and Charles Hedrick, eds., *Dêmokratia: A Conversation on Democracies, Ancient and Modern* (Princeton, N.J., 1996), p. 3.

13. See esp. ibid., pp. 3–6; Josiah Ober, *Mass and Elite in Democratic Athens: Rhetoric, Ideology, and the Power of the People* (Princeton, N.J., 1989), esp. pp. xiii–xiv (where the claims are more modest); J. P. Euben, John R. Wallach, and Josiah Ober, eds., *Athenian Political Thought and the Reconstruction of American Democracy* (Ithaca, N.Y., 1994), esp. pp. 1–20; Josiah Ober, *The Athenian Revolution: Essays on Ancient Greek Democracy and Political Theory* (Princeton, N.J., 1996); and id., *Political Dissent in Democratic Athens: Intellectual Critics of Popular Rule* (Princeton, N.J., 1998), esp. p. 373. See also n. 17 below. Cf. M. H. Hansen, *Was Athens a Democracy? Popular Rule, Liberty and Equality in Ancient and Modern Political Thought* (Copenhagen, 1989), where he argues that the ancient Greek democratic ideals of "liberty and equality" were similar to modern democratic notions, and Morris and Raaflaub, eds., *Democracy 2500?* esp. p. 1, on the currently popular view that history is reaching its *telos* or goal "in the form of western social democracy." For an astute evaluation of the effects of modern ideology on contemporary study of Athenian democracy, see P. J. Rhodes, *Athenian Democracy and Modern Ideology* (London, 2003). As for the "conservatives" who supposedly have usurped the classical legacy (see Euben, Wallach, and Ober, eds., pp. 11, 20), it is certainly true that some conservatives look to ancients like Plato and Aristotle for criticism of modern liberalism and associate modern "conservative" ideals with a "Western tradition" created in ancient Greece. However, the practices or supposed ideals of Athenian democracy per se represent only a small and arguably atypical fraction of "classical thought."

14. On this phenomenon, see Finley, *Democracy Ancient and Modern,* pp. 3–37, esp. 9–12, and cf. Robert A. Dahl, *Democracy and Its Critics* (New Haven, Conn., 1989), p. 2: "In our times, even dictators appear to believe that an indispensable ingredient for their legitimacy is a dash or two of the language of democracy." On the slippery meaning and connotations of the term *democracy,* see Dahl, pp. 1–5.

15. For a survey of this literature, see Roberts, *Athens on Trial,* pp. 256–314.

16. See, e.g., Euben, Wallach, and Ober, eds., *Athenian Political Thought,* pp.

1–26, esp. 14–17: "the appropriation of Athenian democracy and classical political theory could challenge the undemocratic aspects of our democratic institutions and discourse" (p. 17).

17. I do not wish to imply that modern scholars are advocating the importation of specific Athenian political practices or forms into modern American government. Their project is rather described as something like turning "to Athenian political thought and practices as a primary source for educating [American] democracy" (Euben, Wallach, and Ober, eds., *Athenian Political Thought*, p. 4). Nevertheless, the call for "normative political theory" (n. 12 above) suggests that their efforts are meant to produce tangible effects. As Euben, Wallach, and Ober put it:

> The challenge to respect difference posed by the politics of identity, the dissolution of the admittedly tepid unity rendered by the Cold War, and examples of democratic activism abroad provide an opportunity to pose, and have taken seriously, questions first raised by the Athenians: What is involved in being a citizen of a democratic polity? How does a democratic culture provide the experience of and education for democratic politics? If we take these questions as primary, our first concern about the process and substance of any decision should be whether it enhances or diminishes the capacity of democratic citizens to take their place in the deliberative forums of their society and share the responsibility of sovereignty.
>
> To make these questions and issues central to our public life would itself be an important step in democratizing it. (ibid., p. 14)

I take it that "democratizing" Americans' public life is therefore one of their goals. See also B. Manville and J. Ober, *A Company of Citizens* (Boston, 2003).

18. See the works listed in n. 13 above. For criticism of this approach (and of the present volume), see Rhodes, *Athenian Democracy and Modern Ideology*.

19. See, e.g., Euben, Wallach, and Ober, eds., *Athenian Political Thought*, p. 19.

20. See Victor Davis Hanson, *The Other Greeks: The Family Farm and the Agrarian Roots of Western Civilization* (New York, 1995); cf. R. W. Wallace, "Solonian Democracy," in Morris and Raaflaub, *Democracy 2500?* pp. 11–29, esp. pp. 12–15, on the emergence of "hoplite egalitarianism" (p. 13) in Sparta long before Athenian democracy. For the argument that the Athenians' concepts of liberty and equality were not so different from moderns', see Hansen, *Was Athens a Democracy?*

21. I write of government and society together because moderns attribute democratic values to both. We speak of democratic society *and* democratic government. But in Athens, as we shall see, *demokratia* was merely a form of government and not the defining characteristic of Athenian society.

22. Readers uninterested in the current debate among historians and classicists over appropriate ways to address questions about Athenian history and society may wish to pass over the remainder of this introduction and move immediately to chapter 1.

23. Ober, *Athenian Revolution*, pp. 133–34 (with n. 21 and pp. 3–12).

24. See Ober, *Mass and Elite in Democratic Athens,* and see also id., *Athenian Revolution.* For an attempt to apply the history of ideologies to archaic Greece, see Leslie Kurke, *Coins, Bodies, Games, and Gold: The Politics of Meaning in Archaic Greece* (Princeton, N.J., 1999).

25. See, e.g., Wallace, "Solonian Democracy," pp. 12–14, 23–24.

26. See Wood, *Creation of the American Republic,* p. 612, on the early emphasis on "public opinion" as the basis of American government.

27. For an example of this approach in American history, see Brendan McConville, *Those Daring Disturbers of the Public Peace: The Struggle for Property and Power in Early New Jersey* (Ithaca, N.Y., 1999).

28. Cf. now Ober, *Political Dissent in Democratic Athens,* and id., *Athenian Revolution,* esp. pp. 140–60, who, while admitting that he is "unconvinced" by democracy's ancient critics, suggests that the literature of dissent might well be numbered among the "sources of the democratic Athenian self" (*Political Dissent,* pp. 12, 372).

29. E.g., W. G. Forrest, *The Emergence of Greek Democracy, 800–400 B.C.* (New York, 1966), p. 16; A. H. M. Jones, *Athenian Democracy* (Oxford, 1957), pp. 41–43. Cf. David Stockton, *The Classical Athenian Democracy* (Oxford, 1990), pp. 165–87, who attempts to rehabilitate some ancient critics (by arguing that they are not as hostile to democracy as often thought) but still considers Plato a "totalitarian" (p. 176).

30. See S. Sara Monoson, *Plato's Democratic Entanglements: Athenian Politics and the Practice of Philosophy* (Princeton, N.J., 2000); Arlene W. Saxonhouse, *Athenian Democracy: Modern Mythmakers and Ancient Theorists* (Notre Dame, Ind., 1996); J. P. Euben, "Reading Democracy: 'Socratic' Dialogues and the Political Education of Democratic Citizens," in Ober and Hedrick, eds., *Dêmokratia,* pp. 327–59; for a nuanced and subtle statement of the view that Plato was not absolutely hostile to democracy, see David Roochnik, *Beautiful City: The Dialectical Character of Plato's "Republic"* (Ithaca, N.Y., 2003).

31. See, e.g., Leo Strauss, *The City and Man* (Chicago, 1964), id., *Liberalism Ancient and Modern* (New York, 1968), and Thomas L. Pangle, ed., *The Rebirth of Classical Political Rationalism: An Introduction to the Thought of Leo Strauss* (Chicago, 1989).

32. It is one of the virtues of Euben, Wallach, and Ober, eds., *Athenian Political Thought,* and of Ober in his other works (see n. 13 above), that they do not simply dismiss ancient political theory, but rather engage it (even if I cannot always agree with the results of the engagement).

33. Strauss himself emphasized the importance of a thinker's (and his audience's) historical context: see Pangle, *Rebirth of Classical Political Rationalism,* pp. xvii–xix. Of course, I can achieve no greater separation from my own historical context than could Plato.

34. Madison, *Federalist* 63 (p. 372). For a defense of the view that the ancient Greeks are not desperately foreign, see M. H. Hansen, *Polis and City-State: An Ancient Concept and Its Modern Equivalent* (Copenhagen, 1998), pp. 9–14.

35. See nn. 37 and 38 below and, e.g., J. B. Elshtain, *Democracy on Trial* (New York, 1995), pp. 92–96. Elshtain does go on to mention Socrates' execution (in a mock debate on democracy between Plato and Lincoln: p. 97).

36. Finley, *Democracy Ancient and Modern,* p. 33 (emphasis added).

37. Cf. I. F. Stone, *The Trial of Socrates* (New York, 1988), p. 197, who maintains that Pericles' speech celebrates "an open city and an open mind" and uses the address to characterize Athens, while the prosecution of Socrates is called a "paradox." Athens, "a city famous for free speech prosecuted a philosopher guilty of no other crime than exercising it." The paradox appears most profoundly in Stone's formulation, which, when attempting to characterize the Athenian regime, treats an actual event as inferior evidence to the reported words of a patriotic speech.

38. In Stockton's *Classical Athenian Democracy,* for example, Socrates is mentioned five times, with only one reference to his trial, and none to his execution. Perusal of other standard works reveals similar suppression or neglect of Socrates' death: Martin Ostwald's influential work *From Popular Sovereignty to the Sovereignty of the Law: Law, Society, and Politics in Fifth-Century Athens* (Berkeley, 1986), contains numerous references to Socrates' life and "prosecution," but almost none (cf. p. 277) to his execution; yet there are eighteen indexed references to Pericles' Funeral Oration. Euben, Wallach, and Ober's *Athenian Political Thought* has twelve headings in the index for Socrates, with nineteen loci (many several pages long), none of which treat the philosopher's execution (but cf. pp. 207, 224–25, where the trial—and the "political thought" it may have reflected—is mentioned). The list could be easily extended. Cf. J. P. Euben, "Reading Democracy," in Ober and Hedrick, eds., *Dêmokratia,* who writes of Socrates' "refusing to escape the death sentence," and of "a voice that reminds us of Socrates' death and anticipates the animus between philosophy and politics" (pp. 351, 343). This type of passive characterization, where words like "execution" are avoided and the onus for Socrates' death is put on his own "refusal to escape" or his failure to mount a reasonable defense, seemingly reflects modern democrats' need to provide an excuse for the Athenians' actions in indicting, trying, convicting, condemning, and executing Socrates. Of course the philosopher shared in the responsibility for his own demise, but that is no reason to obscure the Athenian people's direct and active role in his execution. See Alan Boegehold, "Resistance to Change in the Law at Athens," in Ober and Hedrick, eds., *Dêmokratia,* p. 210, and R. W. Wallace, "Law, Freedom, and the Concept of Citizens' Rights in Democratic Athens," ibid., p. 106, for less exculpatory characterizations of Socrates' fate.

39. On the trial and execution as aberrations, cf. M. H. Hansen, *The Athenian Democracy in the Age of Demosthenes* (Oxford, 1991), pp. 77–78.

40. Stone, *Trial of Socrates.* For useful scholarly treatments of the issue, cf. T. C. Brickhouse and N. D. Smith, *Socrates on Trial* (Princeton, N.J., 1989), and M. H. Hansen, *The Trial of Sokrates—from the Athenian Point of View* (Copenhagen, 1995). Hansen emphasizes that Socrates' associates included many individuals of oligarchic sympathies and that "the Athenians may have had reason to fear that Sokrates' crit-

icism of the democratic institutions might constitute a menace to the restored democracy, even though Sokrates himself seems to have been loyal to the democratic constitution" (p. 2).

41. Stone, *Trial of Socrates*, p. 97; see also n. 43 below.

42. Ibid., p. 156.

43. Stone's work contains a frontal assault on the "antidemocratic," "conservative," "totalitarian," semi-Christian, and monarchical views of Plato: ibid., pp. 9–19, 70, 114, 121, 125.

44. Stone (ibid., pp. 104–8) goes so far as to blame (in part) the Athenians' treatment of Melos on Socrates' apparent failure to oppose the measure in the assembly. For democracy's intolerance of antidemocratic views, see chapter 7; for the Athenians' destruction of Melos, see Thuc. 5.84–116.

45. For the darker side of the regime, see also Paul A. Rahe, *Republics Ancient and Modern* (Chapel Hill, N.C., 1992), pp. 191–218.

46. I would contrast this with the notes of one commentator on this volume. Whenever the text listed Athenian atrocities, the commentator invariably wrote, "Yes, but . . .", usually arguing that Athens's actions were not as bad as those of other ancient states. The Athenians' defense on such relativistic grounds has been made repeatedly; it is time to hear from the prosecution.

47. See, e.g., Aristophanes' *Knights*, Thuc. 8.97, and Plato's *Republic, Gorgias, Protagoras,* and *Apology.*

48. This or similar ideas may be found in the writings even of outspoken critics of democracy or some modern forms of liberalism. See, e.g., Tocqueville, *Democracy in America*, trans. Lawrence, pp. 12–13, and Strauss, *Liberalism Ancient and Modern*, p. 24.

49. For the reorganization of American society around the democratically generated principles of freedom, choice, and diversity, see chapter 7.

50. The quotations are taken from James Q. Wilson, former president of the American Political Science Association, *The History and Future of Democracy* (Malibu, Calif., n.d.), an address given at the Reagan Presidential Library on November 15, 1999, published as a pamphlet by the School of Public Policy, Pepperdine University, p. 4. See also Wilson's "Democracy for All?" American Enterprise Institute for Public Policy Research online, March 1, 2000. Wilson defends private property as one of the conditions that has made democracy possible. He also notes Aristotle's view that private property is a "good" in itself.

51. Cf., e.g., Elshtain, *Democracy on Trial.* Professor Elshtain perceptively characterizes American culture as in danger of losing civility, civic responsibility, and social structures like families and religious organizations. But she seems to lament this situation largely because these conditions and institutions are (she believes) necessary for democracy, which thus appears to be the good that society should be seeking. For example, she approvingly cites Tocqueville's conclusions that "[o]nly many small-scale civic bodies would enable citizens to cultivate democratic virtues and to

play an active role in the drama of democracy" (p. 10), and later writes that "[o]ne sign that democracy is on trial is the falling away from the firm, buoyant conviction of democrats that a rights-based democratic equality, guaranteed by the vote, will serve over time as the sure and secure basis of a democratic culture" (p. 22). While I would agree with much that she writes about contemporary society, surely our goals need to be something more than a "democratic culture" in which citizens can play an active role in "the drama of democracy." Families and churches can and should be defended as good things in and of themselves, irrespective of their putative relationship to any political system. But in fact, it is too often *their potential to foster democracy* that now serves as the typical justification for traditional institutions, and this clearly demonstrates the privileged position democracy occupies in contemporary thought.

52. See chapter 7, pp. 179–80, for the argument that "rights" rest on a foundation of moral obligations.

53. Admittedly, the Founders differed on the role of the new regime in fostering particular ideals or qualities: cf. Wood, *Creation of the American Republic;* Paul Eidelberg, *The Philosophy of the American Constitution: A Reinterpretation of the Intentions of the Founding Fathers* (New York, 1968); C. B. Thompson, *John Adams and the Spirit of Liberty* (Lawrence, Kans., 1998); and chapter 7.

54. Perhaps this may help us explain why the Athenians left almost nothing but criticism of the form of government they called *demokratia.* In an environment dominated by ideals of civic responsibility, democratic ideology and the ideal of individual freedoms were unable to dominate Athenian thought as they have pervaded modern American thinking.

55. Finley, *Democracy Ancient and Modern,* pp. 79–80; see also pp. 3–37, 95–98.

56. See esp. chapter 7.

57. The existence of slavery, undoubtedly an important factor, will be treated only tangentially, since this factor does not separate the Athenians from the other Hellenic peoples.

I. ATHENIAN SOCIETY AND GOVERNMENT

1. A few areas of Greece had a more rudimentary form of regime or settlement, sometimes based on tribes or federation and (often) extended territory. On these *ethne* ("nations"), see, e.g., Raphael Sealey, *A History of the Greek City-States, ca. 700–338 B.C.* (Berkeley, 1976), p. 19; A. M. Snodgrass, *Archaic Greece* (Berkeley, 1980), pp. 42–47. This view of the *ethnos,* however, has more recently been criticized; see Jeremy McInerney, *The Folds of Parnassos: Land and Ethnicity in Ancient Phokis* (Austin, Tex., 1999), esp. pp. 18–35; and cf. Edward E. Cohen, *The Athenian Nation* (Princeton, N.J., 2000), pp. 22–29. Cohen demonstrates the "chameleon-like nature" of the term *ethnos* (p. 25), and his treatment of Athens as an *ethnos* ("nation") as opposed to a polis proper illustrates the unusually large and diverse territory (and

population) of classical Athens. The differences between Athens and a "typical polis" therefore require careful attention. Nevertheless, Athens possessed a political super-structure and culture resembling those of other poleis, and our ancient sources typically treat it as an (admittedly unusual) polis. Hdt. 1.57–59, on which Cohen places significant stress, refers to the "Attic *ethnos*" (which Cohen translates as "Athenian nation") while discussing the ethnic (and linguistic) group that some Greeks believed had descended from the ancient inhabitants of Attica (e.g., Hdt. 1.56). That is, the term *ethnos* is here used specifically to differentiate Athens or Attica from the rest of Greece *ethnically:* the Athenians could thus be called an *ethnos* and Athens a polis with no contradiction. (See also chapter 2, n. 21, on the importance of context for determining the force of Greek terms in particular passages.)

2. On the rise of the polis, see Hanson, *Other Greeks,* esp. pp. 108–26, who connects the emergence of this particular form of state with the concurrent rise of the independent, middle-class citizen-farmer; A. M. Snodgrass, "The Rise of the Polis: The Archaeological Evidence," and K. A. Raaflaub, "Homer to Solon: The Rise of the Polis. The Written Sources," in M. H. Hansen, ed., *The Ancient Greek City-State* (Copenhagen, 1993), pp. 30–40, 41–105; and Lynette G. Mitchell and P. J. Rhodes, eds., *The Development of the Polis in Archaic Greece* (London, 1997). For a defense of the traditional translation of *polis* as "city-state," and comparisons between the ancient polis and the modern state, see Hansen, *Ancient Greek City-State,* pp. 7–18, and id., *Polis and City-State.*

3. The numbers are notoriously impossible to fix: cf. Rhodes, *CAH* VI², pp. 566–67; Hansen, *Athenian Democracy,* pp. 55, 90–94; and Cohen, *Athenian Nation,* pp. 12–15, who emphasizes Athens's unusually large territory and population and notes that Athens was comparable to a number of modern nations (including Barbados, Brunei, and Iceland) in one or both of these areas.

4. On early Sparta, see Paul Cartledge, *Sparta and Lakonia: A Regional History, 1300–362 B.C.,* 2d ed. (London, 2002); G. L. Huxley, *Early Sparta* (Cambridge, Mass., 1962); Sealey, *History,* pp. 66–86; and W. G. Forrest, *A History of Sparta, 950–192 B.C.* (New York, 1968), pp. 28–83.

5. See P. J. Rhodes, with D. M. Lewis, *The Decrees of the Greek States* (Oxford, 1997), esp. pp. 1, 502, and Sealey, *Athenian Republic,* pp. 91–98. Cf. Rhodes, *CAH* V², pp. 78, 91–95, and Nicholas F. Jones, *Public Organization in Ancient Greece: A Documentary Study* (Philadelphia, 1987).

6. Sparta retained two hereditary kings, with primarily religious and military duties, throughout the classical period (see Hdt. 6.52–59; Xen. *Constitution of the Spartans,* esp. 13, 15). However, the Spartans' ephors and the members of their council of elders (the *gerousia*) were elected (see also Arist. *Pol.* 1270b, II.9.19–1271a, II.9.28). At Athens, some important priesthoods were restricted to particular families, and it seems likely that most other poleis possessed some offices filled only by members of certain families. Property qualifications for the highest Athenian offices persisted throughout the classical period, but do not seem to have been enforced in the fourth

century (*Ath. Pol.* 7.4, 47.1, with P. J. Rhodes, *A Commentary on the Aristotelian Athenaion Politeia* [Oxford, 1981; rev. ed., 1997], pp. 145–46).

7. *Ath. Pol.* 8.1, 22.5.

8. See n. 6 above. For the council's role in Greek government and the concept of *probouleusis,* see also Rhodes, *Decrees,* pp. 475–501.

9. On the Areopagus and its controversial origins and early history, see R. W. Wallace, *The Areopagos Council* (Baltimore, 1989).

10. P. J. Rhodes, *The Athenian Boule* (Oxford, 1984), p. 7, believes the early councilmen may have been elected but maintains that "the introduction of the lot can hardly be later than the 450s."

11. On the Council of 500, see Rhodes, *Athenian Boule.* Years in the Athenian calendar (which ran from summer to summer) are conventionally expressed in the form 462/1. Expressions such as 462–461 denote the period covered by (in this case two) modern calendar years.

12. These ten tribes were primarily geographical, electoral, and military units created during the Cleisthenic reform ca. 507, and had nothing to do with descent.

13. On the qualifications for *bouleutai,* see Rhodes, *Athenian Boule,* esp. pp. 1–30.

14. On local property qualifications in America that persisted well after the Revolution, see Adams, *First American Constitutions,* pp. 196–217, 293–307, and Eidelberg, *Philosophy of the American Constitution,* pp. 261–63.

15. This traditional view of the Spartan *kleroi* ("lots" of land) has been challenged and, at best, perhaps only explains part of the Spartan system, which seems to have allowed more scope for private ownership and heritable land than was once thought: see Stephen Hodkinson, *Property and Wealth in Classical Sparta* (London, 2000), esp. pp. 65–94.

16. See Hanson, *Other Greeks,* pp. 201–19.

17. On the Athenians' willingness to overlook property qualifications in the fourth century, see n. 6 above.

18. See *Ath. Pol.* 7.

19. *Ath. Pol.* 26.2.

20. *Ath. Pol.* 8.1; on the office and Athena's treasury in general, see L. J. Samons II, *Empire of the Owl: Athenian Imperial Finance* (Stuttgart, 2000), pp. 30–50.

21. Some moderns therefore treat Solon as the real founder of Athenian democracy: see, e.g., Wallace, "Solonian Democracy." Aristotle (*Ath. Pol.* 9.1; *Pol.* 1274a, II.12.3) believed that it was Solon's supposed admission of all citizens to the juries that made his constitution "democratic," but the powerful popular courts he imagines probably did not develop so early: see also nn. 54–55, below.

22. On the *eupatridai,* cf. Rhodes, *Commentary,* pp. 74–76, 183–87; Andrewes, *CAH* III.3², pp. 367–68, 393; Sealey, *History,* pp. 116–19; H. T. Wade-Gery, *Essays in Greek History* (Oxford: Blackwell, 1958), pp. 86–115; Hansen, *Athenian Democracy,* pp. 27–28. For their control of cults, cf. Robert Parker, *Athenian Religion: A History* (Oxford, 1996), pp. 63–66.

23. For these subgroups, see J. D. Mikalson, *Athenian Popular Religion* (Chapel Hill, N.C., 1983), pp. 83–90.

24. On the phratries, see esp. S. D. Lambert, *The Phratries of Attica* (Ann Arbor, Mich., 1993); Rhodes, *Commentary,* pp. 68–71; Andrewes, *CAH* III.3², pp. 366–68; Parker, *Athenian Religion,* pp. 64, 108–9. For the *gene,* see Rhodes, ibid., Andrewes, *CAH* III.3², pp. 367–68, and Hansen, *Athenian Democracy,* p. 46, who maintains that the clan *(genos)* was "not necessarily an aristocratic kinship group." The precise nature of the clans and their possible role in the phratries have become very controversial subjects; see esp. Rhodes, *Commentary,* p. 768; Félix Bourriot, *Recherches sur la nature du génos* (Lille, 1976); Denis Roussel, *Tribu et cité* (Paris, 1976); and Nicholas F. Jones, *The Associations of Classical Athens* (New York, 1999), esp. pp. 195–220, 242–49.

25. On the Ionian tribes, cf. Rhodes, *Commentary,* pp. 67–68, 71; Snodgrass, *Archaic Greece,* pp. 25–28; Sealey, *History,* p. 23; Andrewes, *CAH* III.3², pp. 361, 366; and Parker, *Athenian Religion,* pp. 16–17. On Greek ethnic divisions in general, see Jonathan Hall, *Ethnic Identity in Greek Antiquity* (Cambridge, 1997). The origins of the tribes have also become quite controversial. Some scholars now tend to discount the old theory that saw the Greeks moving from a tribal to a polis-based society. But the question is irrelevant for our purposes, since the classical Greeks believed and acted as if their tribal and ethnic divisions were both ancient and meaningful. For the Athenians' later creation of ten tribes subdivided into demes, see p. 28 above.

26. For the tribes, see, e.g., Hdt. 6.111. For the possible military role of the phratries, see Hansen, *Athenian Democracy,* p. 46; Roussel, *Tribu et cité,* pp. 109–21; and A. Andrewes, "Phratries in Homer," *Hermes* 89 (1961): 129–40.

27. See, e.g., *IG* i³ 1147 = ML 33 = Fornara 78; cf. Thuc. 2.34, *SEG* XXXIV.45, with Lewis, *CAH* V², p. 113. Our evidence comes from the period after Cleisthenes instituted the new ten-tribe arrangement. But we may perhaps infer a connection between the original four tribes and the military from these tribes' division into *naukrariai* (*Ath. Pol.* 8.3), if these poorly understood organs were indeed related to the Athenian navy; see Rhodes, *Commentary,* pp. 151–52.

28. The demos as a whole also participated in the worship of Dionysus—especially during Athenian festivals such as the City Dionysia (at which comedies and tragedies were performed)—and other gods (such as those worshipped by initiates to the mysteries at Eleusis): see, e.g., Parker, *Athenian Religion,* pp. 89–101.

29. For the Panathenaea, see Parker, *Athenian Religion,* pp. 75–76, 89–92, and J. Neils, ed., *Worshipping Athena: Panathenaia and Parthenon* (Madison, Wis., 1996).

30. On the *dokimasia,* see *Ath. Pol.* 45.3, 55, 59.4, with Rhodes, *Commentary,* pp. 614–17; Hansen, *Athenian Democracy,* pp. 218–20; and chapter 2, pp. 47–48. In the fourth century, Athenian *rhetores* (political orators) may have faced a similar kind of *dokimasia,* including a provision against prostituting oneself: see Aeschin. 1.28–32, 81, 186, with Rhodes, *CAH* VI², pp. 574–76, and A. R. W. Harrison, *The Law of Athens* (Oxford, 1968–71), 2: 204–5.

31. *Ath. Pol.* 55.3; Rhodes, *Athenian Boule,* pp. 176–78.

32. Hansen, *Athenian Democracy,* p. 219.

33. See ibid., pp. 218–20.

34. Mikalson, *Athenian Popular Religion,* pp. 83–90.

35. Peisistratus first came to power in 561/0, but did not secure permanent control of Athens until probably the 540s: see *Ath. Pol.* 13.3–15.3, with Rhodes, *Commentary,* pp. 191–99.

36. Hdt. 1.59; Thuc. 6.54; *Ath. Pol.* 16.1–3, 7–8.

37. See esp. Hdt. 1.59–64; Arist. *Pol.* 1305a, V.5.9; and *Ath. Pol.* 13–17, with Rhodes, *Commentary,* esp. pp. 185–227, 255–56; and cf. C. W. Fornara and L. J. Samons II, *Athens from Cleisthenes to Pericles* (Berkeley, 1991), pp. 14–17, 151–57; Sealey, *History,* pp. 134–44; and A. Andrewes, *The Greek Tyrants* (London, 1956), pp. 100–115.

38. See chapter 4, pp. 101–2.

39. The dating of the so-called "Peisistratid" temple of Athena is controversial; see, e.g., J. Hurwit, *The Athenian Acropolis* (Cambridge, 1999), esp. pp. 116–22, who argues that the Peisistratids focused their attentions on the parts of the city below the acropolis, and that the temple of Athena constructed in the late sixth century belongs to the Cleisthenic rather than the tyrannic regime.

40. Cf. Andrewes, *Greek Tyrants,* pp. 100–115; id., *CAH* III.3², pp. 398–416; and Michael Stahl, *Aristokraten und Tyrannen im archaischen Athen: Untersuchungen zur Überlieferung, zur Sozialstruktur und zur Entstehung des Staates* (Stuttgart, 1987).

41. On the overthrow of the Peisistratid tyranny, which according to tradition was actually instigated by exiled Athenians, see Hdt. 5.55–57, 62–65; Thuc. 1.20, 6.53–59; *Ath. Pol.* 17–19. P. J. Rhodes suspects (and has suggested to me) that "Sparta's doctrinaire opposition to tyranny was invented after the expulsion of Hippias from Athens." Undoubtedly the fact that the Spartans overthrew more than one tyranny led to an exaggeration of the programmatic nature of their opposition to such regimes (see, e.g., Thuc. 1.18). But the land-loving Spartans' efforts to end tyrannies on distant islands (Samos and Naxos) demonstrate that their antipathy to (at least some) tyrants was real and capable of influencing Spartan policy. On the other hand, Sparta's alleged friendship with the Athenian tyrants (*Ath. Pol.* 19.4) is almost certainly a fabrication (cf. Rhodes, *Commentary,* p. 237), perhaps stemming from later (democratic?) authorities that saw oligarchy (Sparta) and tyranny (Peisistratids) as natural allies rather than as the enemies they actually were in the sixth century (a confusion common even today).

42. As noted, such timocratic regimes included assemblies of citizens in which votes were taken on major issues, and they can thus be said to reflect what moderns call "popular government." Retrospectively, the name *democracy* was (and is) sometimes applied to such regimes: see, e.g., E. W. Robinson, *The First Democracies: Early Popular Government outside Athens* (Stuttgart, 1997). But the specific qualities most often associated with *demokratia* in antiquity and the name itself apparently first developed in Athens after 507.

43. Hdt. 5.66, 69–73; *Ath. Pol.* 20–21. See L. J. Samons II, "Mass, Elite and Hoplite-Farmer in Greek History," *Arion* 5.3 (1998): 110–15, and Fornara and Samons, *Athens from Cleisthenes to Pericles*, pp. 37–58.

44. For deme membership and citizenship, see Hansen, *Athenian Democracy*, p. 46, citing Isoc. 8.88 and Dem. 57.46, and M. Ostwald, *CAH* IV², p. 312.

45. I leave aside the issue of an older Council of 400, perhaps created by Solon: *Ath. Pol.* 8.4, with Rhodes, *Commentary*, pp. 153–54.

46. *Ath. Pol.* 21.

47. For the tribes and the *trittyes* ("thirds") into which they were divided, see esp. John S. Traill, *The Political Organization of Attica: A Study of the Demes, Trittyes, and Phylai, and Their Representation in the Athenian Council* (Princeton, N.J., 1975); N. F. Jones, *Associations;* Ostwald, *CAH* IV², pp. 312–15, and Rhodes, *Commentary*, pp. 251–54. Cleisthenes associated each tribe with a semi-mythical or heroic "founder," and each tribe had its own religious officials and rites. See *Ath. Pol.* 21.6, with Parker, *Athenian Religion*, pp. 103–4, 117–21. For the tribes' potential relationship to the navy, see Dem. 14.22–23.

48. The precise nature of this change (or these changes) in the election of generals is controversial, but double and perhaps triple representation from single tribes in the mid fifth century shows that the Athenians had altered their earlier practice by at least the 440s. Cf. esp. L. G. Mitchell, *Klio* 82 (2000): 344–60; Rhodes, *Commentary*, pp. 677–78; Robert Develin, *Athenian Officials, 684–321 B.C.* (Cambridge, 1989), pp. 3–4; C. W. Fornara, *The Athenian Board of Generals* (Wiesbaden, 1971), esp. pp. 20–27; and M. H. Hansen, "The Athenian Board of Generals: When Was Tribal Representation Replaced by Election from All Athenians?" in *Studies in Ancient History and Numismatics Presented to Rudi Thomsen* (Aarhus, 1988), pp. 69–70.

49. The deme was also the most important religious organization within the community: see Parker, *Athenian Religion*, p. 102.

50. See *Ath. Pol.* 45.4, with Rhodes, *Athenian Boule*, pp. 52–81.

51. On the *graphe paranomon* in general, see Hansen, *Athenian Democracy*, pp. 205–12; cf. Sealey, *Athenian Republic*, pp. 32–52.

52. See esp. Ostwald, *From Popular Sovereignty to the Sovereignty of the Law;* cf. Sealey, *Athenian Republic.*

53. Cf. Rhodes, *CAH* VI², p. 572. Rhodes also provides a useful survey of changes in Athenian government in the fourth century: ibid., pp. 565–73.

54. M. H. Hansen has argued that the *heliaia* was not the assembly acting as a court but a separate court of sworn jurors, instituted by Solon: *Athenian Democracy*, pp. 30, 191, with references there; cf. Rhodes, *Commentary*, pp. 160–62, 771. In any case, the *heliaia* predated the reforms of Ephialtes.

55. For Ephialtes' reforms, see *Ath. Pol.* 25, with Rhodes, *CAH* V², pp. 67–75; Wallace, *Areopagos Council*, pp. 83–87; and Fornara and Samons, *Athens from Cleisthenes to Pericles*, pp. 58–72. For the system of dicasteries, see Hansen, *Athenian Democracy*, pp. 178–224.

56. *Ath. Pol.* 27; Arist. *Pol.* 1274a8–9, II.12.4. See Hansen, *Athenian Democracy,* pp. 188–89; and, for the date of the institution of jury pay, see Rhodes, *Commentary,* pp. 338–40, and Fornara and Samons, *Athens from Cleisthenes to Pericles,* pp. 67–75, both arguing against those who would place the payments' creation before 462/1. For wage rates, see chapter 3, n. 27.

57. For payment of the councilmen, see Thuc. 8.69.4, *Ath. Pol.* 62.2, with Rhodes, *Athenian Boule,* pp. 13–14; for the assembly, see *Ath. Pol.* 41.3; Austin, *CAH* VI², p. 544.

58. Exemplified in the forensic speeches of fourth-century orators like Demosthenes or Aeschines, who repeatedly treat the jurors as the same men who have voted for or against particular measures under discussion. Cf. Hansen, *Athenian Democracy in the Age of Demosthenes,* p. 179: "the courts had unlimited power to control the Assembly, the Council, the magistrates and the political leaders: political trials were the largest part of the business that came before them."

59. On the court of the *polemarchos,* see *Ath. Pol.* 58; *IG* i³ 10 = ML 31 = Fornara 68; Harrison, *Law,* 1: 193–96, 2: 9–11; and D. M. MacDowell, *The Law in Classical Athens* (Ithaca, N.Y., 1978), pp. 221–24. For the *thesmothetai* (six of Athens's nine archons), see esp. *Ath. Pol.* 59, and Harrison, *Law,* 2: 12–17.

60. For the Founders' ultimate separation of American government from American society, see Wood, *Creation of the American Republic,* pp. 587–615. For the virtual identification of "state" and society in classical Greece, see Rahe, *Republics Ancient and Modern,* pp. 30–31.

61. M. H. Hansen, ed., *The Ancient Greek City-State* (Copenhagen, 1993), Introduction: "The Polis as a Citizen-State," pp. 7–29, esp. 7–9.

62. Cf. Hansen, *Polis and City-State,* pp. 56–67.

63. Hdt. 5.74. For the unlikelihood of any real friendship between the Spartans and the Athenian tyrants, see n. 41 above.

64. Hdt. 5.78 (cf. 5.66); on this somewhat misleading passage, see chapter 4, p. 104.

65. See Hdt. 6.102–17. On the campaign of Marathon, see Hammond, *CAH* IV², pp. 506–16; C. Hignett, *Xerxes' Invasion of Greece* (Oxford, 1963), pp. 55–74; A. W. Gomme, *More Essays in Greek History and Literature* (Oxford, 1962), pp. 29–37; J. A. S. Evans, "Herodotus and the Battle of Marathon," *Historia* 42 (1993): 279–307; W. K. Pritchett, "Marathon," *University of California Publications in Classical Archaeology* 4, no. 2 (1960): 137–89; and J. F. Lazenby, *The Defence of Greece, 490–479 B.C.* (Warminster, U.K., 1993).

66. *Ath. Pol.* 22, with Hdt. 6.115, 121–25.

67. Hdt. 7.144; Thuc. 1.14.

68. The division among the Greeks on "the Persian question"—although sometimes glossed over in modern studies—remained significant throughout the fifth century and into the fourth. For example, Plato, *Laws* 692d–693a, notes that Greece was not united in its opposition to Persia, and that the Spartan-Athenian resolution to fight prevented the enslavement of Hellas.

69. For the campaigns of 480–479, see Hdt. bks. 7–9, and Hignett, *Xerxes' Invasion*. For a contemporary reaction, see Aeschylus's *Persians*.

70. Thuc. 1.94–95; Hdt. 8.3. On Athenian-Spartan relations in this period, see Fornara and Samons, *Athens from Cleisthenes to Pericles*, pp. 117–26.

71. Thuc. 1.96; on the foundation of the league and the institution of tribute payments, see Samons, *Empire of the Owl*, pp. 84–91. For the league's history down to 449 B.C., see esp. Rhodes, *CAH* V², pp. 36–61, and chapter 4, pp. 108–14.

72. Thuc. 1.98–99.

73. For the Eurymedon, see esp. Thuc. 1.100; Plut. *Cim.* 12–13.

74. Thuc. 1.100–101.

75. Thuc. 1.102; Plut. *Cim.* 17.

76. *Ath. Pol.* 25. For analysis, see Rhodes, *Commentary*, pp. 314–17; Wallace, *Areopagos Council*, pp. 83–87; and Fornara and Samons, *Athens from Cleisthenes to Pericles*, pp. 61–67.

77. Thuc. 1.104, 109.

78. On the transfer of the treasury from Delos, its date, and effects, see Samons, *Empire of the Owl*, pp. 92–163. On the building program, see esp. Wycherley, *CAH* V², pp. 215–22, and J. S. Boersma, *Athenian Building Policy from 561/0 to 405/4 B.C.* (Groningen, 1970).

79. Payment for public service like jury duty was apparently very unusual. There is little evidence of state pay in classical Greece outside of Athens: see Rhodes, *Commentary*, p. 338. On the citizenship law, see Cynthia Patterson, *Pericles' Citizenship Law of 451–50 B.C.* (Salem, N.H., 1981).

80. Thuc. 1.103, 105–8, 112.

81. On Cimon's campaign in Cyprus, see Thuc. 1.112; Diod. 12.3–4; Plut. *Cim.* 18–19.

82. On the debate over the Peace of Callias, see Samons, "Kimon, Kallias and Peace with Persia," *Historia* 47 (1998): 129–40; E. Badian, *From Plataea to Potidaea: Studies in the History and Historiography of the Pentecontaetia* (Baltimore, 1993), pp. 1–72; A. J. Holladay, "The Détente of Kallias?" *Historia* 35 (1986): 503–7; Russell Meiggs, *The Athenian Empire* (Oxford, 1972), pp. 129–51; and David Stockton, "The Peace of Callias," *Historia* 8 (1959): 61–79. See also chapter 4, n. 67.

83. See, e.g., the Athenians' regulations for Chalcis (*IG* i³ 40 = ML 52 = Fornara 103; cf. Fornara 99–100, 102). The dates of many imperialistic decrees conventionally placed in the early 440s based on their letter forms (especially the sigma) are controversial. H. B. Mattingly has argued that most of them belong in the 420s and thus reflect Cleon's policies rather than Pericles': see Mattingly, *The Athenian Empire Restored* (Ann Arbor, Mich., 1996), and cf. L. J. Samons II, ed., *Athenian Democracy and Imperialism* (Boston, 1998), pp. 120–34, where several of these inscriptions are translated and the controversy is discussed. Mattingly's general argument about letter forms seems to have been borne out by recent work (cf. Samons, *Empire of the Owl*, pp. 171–72, 188–89, and Fornara and Samons, *Athens from Cleisthenes to Pericles*, pp.

179–87), but at least some of the inscriptions he discusses (e.g., the regulations for Chalcis) probably still belong in the 440s. For the conventional view of this period, see Lewis, *CAH* V², pp. 121–46; for arguments supporting this view, see esp. Meiggs and Lewis, *Selection of Greek Historical Inscriptions,* esp. pp. 119–21; B. D. Meritt and H. T. Wade-Gery, "The Dating of Documents to the Mid-Fifth Century—I," *JHS* 82 (1962): 67–74; id., "The Dating of Documents to the Mid-Fifth Century—II," *JHS* 83 (1963): 100–117; Russell Meiggs, "The Dating of Fifth-Century Attic Inscriptions," *JHS* 86 (1966): 86–98.

84. On the use of this money, see Samons, *Empire of the Owl,* and Lisa Kallet, "Accounting for Culture in Fifth-Century Athens," in Deborah Boedeker and Kurt A. Raaflaub, eds., *Democracy, Empire, and the Arts in Fifth-Century Athens* (Cambridge, Mass., 1998), pp. 43–58.

85. Thuc. 1.115–17.

86. See Thuc. 1.31–45. Athens's interests in the West may perhaps be inferred from its treaties with Rhegium and Leontini, Greek city-states located in southern Italy and eastern Sicily, respectively. These treaties existed by 433/2 at the latest: see ML 63–64 (= Fornara 124–25), with commentary.

87. See Thuc. 1.56–67.

88. For the Peloponnesian War, see also chapter 5. On the first ten years of the war (431–421), see Thuc. 2–5.17, with Meiggs, *Athenian Empire,* pp. 306–23; Donald Kagan, *The Archidamian War* (Ithaca, N.Y., 1974); and Lewis, *CAH* V², pp. 370–432.

89. See Thuc. 5.18–116, with Meiggs, *Athenian Empire,* pp. 338–45, and Donald Kagan, *The Peace of Nicias and the Sicilian Expedition* (Ithaca, N.Y., 1981).

90. Thuc. 6.105, 7.18.

91. On the Sicilian expedition and the Decelean War, see Thuc. books 6–7, with Meiggs, *Athenian Empire,* pp. 345–74; Kagan, *The Peace of Nicias and the Sicilian Expedition;* and Andrewes, *CAH* V², pp. 446–63.

92. See Thuc. bk. 8, esp. 47–54, 64–70; *Ath. Pol.* 29–33. On the financial aspects of this revolution, see Samons, *Empire of the Owl,* pp. 254–75.

93. On the overthrow of the Four Hundred and the brief regime of the Five Thousand, see esp. Thuc. 8.80–98; *Ath. Pol.* 33–34; Donald Kagan, *The Fall of the Athenian Empire* (Ithaca, N.Y., 1987), pp. 187–246; and Andrewes, *CAH* V², pp. 474–85.

94. *Ath. Pol.* 34.1 and Andoc. 1.96–98, with Rhodes, *Commentary on the Aristotelian Athenaion Politeia,* pp. 414–15.

95. See Xen. *Hell.* 2.2.3, 10, 16–23, 3.5.8, 6.5.36, 46; Andoc. 1.142, 3.21; Isoc. 14.31; Justin 5.8.4–5; Plut. *Lys.* 14.

96. *Ath. Pol.* 34.2–35; Xen. *Hell.* 2.3–4. On the Thirty, cf. esp. Peter Krentz, *The Thirty at Athens* (Ithaca, N.Y., 1982), and Lewis, *CAH* VI², pp. 32–38.

97. Pl. *Ap.* 32c–e; Xen. *Hell.* 2.3.15–56; *Ath. Pol.* 34.2.

98. Xen. *Hell.* 2.4; *Ath. Pol.* 38–40.

99. See Pl. *Ap.;* Xen. *Ap.* and *Mem.* 1.1.2–21. Cf. T. C. Brickhouse and N. D. Smith, *Socrates on Trial* (Princeton, N.J., 1989), who underemphasize the political aspect of

Socrates' prosecution. (Hansen, *Trial of Sokrates*, argues that Socrates' prosecution may not have violated the amnesty of 403.) One cannot deny, however, that the existence of very real legal (and societal) norms where religion was concerned made it easier for Socrates' accusers to brand him as a dangerous figure, and that the use of such norms in this way therefore presents a troubling aspect of Athens's regime: cf. Rahe, *Republics*, pp. 195–96, who comments on the absence of formal protections for "civil liberties" in Athens: "No one—not even Socrates—ever dared to suggest that a man's religious beliefs and behavior were of no concern to the body politic, and no one argued that the city should concede full sexual freedom to all consenting adults" (p. 196).

100. Pl. *Seventh Letter* 325–26. For Xenophon's first adventure, see his *Anabasis*. Isocrates, another onetime follower of Socrates, became a great teacher of rhetoric: see esp. Pl. *Phaedrus* 278–79.

101. On the Corinthian War, see esp. C. D. Hamilton, *Sparta's Bitter Victories: Politics and Diplomacy in the Corinthian War* (Ithaca, N.Y., 1979), and Seager, *CAH* VI², pp. 97–119.

102. Xen. *Hell.* 3–5; Diod. 15.28.

103. For the inscription recording the league's charter, see *IG* ii² 43 = Harding 35. On the second league in general, see Jack Cargill, *The Second Athenian League: Empire or Free Alliance?* (Berkeley, 1981).

104. On Thebes's period of power, see esp. John Buckler, *The Theban Hegemony, 371–362 BC* (Cambridge, Mass., 1980). On Philip in Thebes, see Plut. *Pelop.* 26. On Epaminondas, see V. D. Hanson, *The Soul of Battle: From Ancient Times to the Present Day, How Three Great Liberators Vanquished Tyranny* (New York, 1999), pp. 17–120. On Sparta during this period, cf. C. D. Hamilton, *Agesilaus and the Failure of Spartan Hegemony* (Ithaca, N.Y., 1991), and Cartledge, *Agesilaos and the Crisis of Sparta*.

105. See Diod. 16.8 (Philip moves against Amphipolis, Pydna, and Potidaea and gains Crenides and the nearby mines); for Philip and Athens, see also chapter 6.

106. On Philip's early career, see esp. G. L. Cawkwell, *Philip of Macedon* (London, 1978), pp. 29–68, and N. G. L. Hammond, *Philip of Macedon* (Baltimore, 1994), pp. 18–44. On the Social War, see Diod. 16.7.3–4, 21–22. Isoc. *Philip* 2 records Athens's declaration of war against Philip in 357 after the king's aggressive acts in the northwest Aegean; on Amphipolis's failed attempt to secure Athenian aid against Philip in 357, see Tod, no. 150 (= Harding 63), with pp. 149–51 (with references).

107. On Chaeronea and its results, see Cawkwell, *Philip*, pp. 143–49, 166–76; Hammond, *Philip*, pp. 143–64. Philip is elected *hegemon/strategos autokrator:* Diod. 16.89.3; Harding 1B, 99A. See also Raphael Sealey, *Demosthenes and His Time: A Study in Defeat* (New York, 1993), pp. 194–201.

108. See, e.g., Aeschin. 3.132–34, who nonetheless proclaims that Thebes's destruction was not unjust due the city's misguided policy.

109. Despite an apparent appeal from Demosthenes or one of his associates that Athens join in the revolt: [Dem.] 17, *On the Treaty with Alexander,* with Cawkwell,

Philip, p. 170, who associates this speech with the events of 331/0. On Agis's revolt, see also E. Badian, "Agis III," *Hermes* 95 (1967): 170–92; G. L. Cawkwell, "The Crowning of Demosthenes," *CQ* 19 (1969): 163–80, esp. 170–80; and Sealey, *Demosthenes*, pp. 205–7.

110. On Athens in the period 336–322, see esp. Sealey, *Demosthenes*, pp. 202–19, (esp. pp. 215–19, on the Lamian War); for the period after 322, see Christian Habicht, *Athens from Alexander to Antony*, trans. D. L. Schneider (Cambridge, Mass., 1997), pp. 36–53.

2. DEMOCRACY AND DEMAGOGUES

1. Chapter epigraphs: José Ortega y Gasset, *History as a System*, trans. Helene Weyl (New York: Norton, 1961; original edition, 1941), p. 76, quoting Macaulay, *History of England from the Accession of James II*, vol. 1 (New York: Harper & Bros., 1850), p. 547. Macaulay's original text reads: "In every age the vilest specimens of human nature are to be found among demagogues." (One may appreciate Ortega's characterization of the intellectual degeneracy demagoguery represents while questioning his attribution of the "fall" of Greek and Roman civilization to demagogues.) Alexis de Tocqueville, *Democracy in America*, trans. G. Lawrence (1966), reprint, ed. J. P. Mayer (New York: Doubleday, 1969), p. 58.

2. I leave aside the admittedly relevant issue of the Athenian law courts, which operated on similar principles to the assembly, with citizens of all classes voting en masse (see chapter 1, pp. 29–31). A brief perusal of the legal oratory of the fourth century will not encourage anyone to overestimate the extent to which evidence and logic dictated the outcome of trials in Athenian courts. On Athenian courts in general, see M. H. Hansen, *Eisangelia: The Sovereignty of the People's Court in Athens in the Fourth Century B.C. and the Impeachment of Generals and Politicians* (Odense, Denmark, 1975), esp. pp. 58–65 (on impeachment *[eisangelia]* "as a political process"); id., *Athenian Democracy*, pp. 178–224; and MacDowell, *Law*, pp. 29–40.

3. Arist. *Pol.* 1294a, IV.9.4–5; 1273b, II.12.2; cf. 1273a, II.11.8–9.

4. On the courts, see Arist. *Pol.* 1273b, II.12.2–1274a, II.12.4; cf. *Ath. Pol.* 9.1; no (or low) property qualification: *Pol.* 1294b, IV.9.3–4; use of the lottery: *Rhet.* 1365b, I.8.4; the poorer classes ruling in their own interests: *Pol.* 1279b, III.7.5–1280a, III.8.8; 1290b, IV.4.6. Aristotle also associated democracy with the sovereignty of the demos (*Pol.* 1278b, III.6.2), although he believed that law (and not popular decrees) should ultimately be sovereign even in a democracy: *Pol.* 1292a, IV.4.25–31.

5. On the fifth-century generals as political leaders, see Hansen, *Athenian Democracy*, pp. 233–34, 269–70.

6. See Finley, *Democracy Ancient and Modern*, pp. 38–75. Some fourth-century critics of *demokratia* used the term *demagogos* in the pejorative modern sense of "demagogue": Xen. *Hell.* 2.3.27; Isoc. 8.129; Arist. *Pol.* 1274a, II.9.3, 1292a, IV.4.4, with Hansen, *Athenian Democracy*, p. 268.

7. The word *demagogos* may have emerged rather late in the fifth century, perhaps as a description of Cleon and others like him (as P. J. Rhodes has suggested to me) and thus may never have been applied to Pericles by his contemporaries (see Rhodes, *Commentary,* pp. 323–24). Nevertheless, it is clear that Pericles eventually came to represent (at least to many) the practices and policies associated with the term.

8. See Pseudo-Xenophon ("The Old Oligarch") *Constitution of the Athenians,* and, from the period just after Pericles' death, Aristophanes *Knights.*

9. Cf. Aristotle's view that *demokratia* implies the rule of the poor in their own interests (n. 4 above) and cf. Plato *Gorgias.*

10. See *Ath. Pol.* 27; Arist. *Pol.* 1274a, II.12.4.

11. Members of the Council of 500 were receiving pay by at least 411 (Thuc. 8.69–70; see also *Ath. Pol.* 62.2, with Rhodes, *Athenian Boule,* pp. 13–14), and at least some state officials were receiving stipends by 437/6 (Ar. *Ach.* 65–67; see also Ps.-Xen. 1.3, *IG* i³ 82.17–21). J. P. Sickinger has suggested to me that the council may well have received pay first, before magistrates and jurors. Given the importance of the council and the need for members to remain in Athens continually for part of the year, this would seem possible. The sources, however, imply that jurors were the first to receive payments.

12. Cf. Arist. *Pol.* 1317b, VI.2.6–7. On the Athenians' desire for public payments, see also chapter 3.

13. See chapter 3, pp. 91–94.

14. Obviously proposals for decreased taxation could lead to a similar advantage, but only in a state where a significant enough proportion of the electorate actually pays taxes. The percentage of the population making a net payment of taxes vs. the percentage receiving a net payment from public money is therefore a critical factor in democratic politics.

15. For the principle of serving one's fellow citizens in turn, see Arist. *Pol.* 1279a, III.6.9–10. On the Athenians' use of the lottery in general, see Hansen, *Athenian Democracy,* pp. 230–33, 235–37.

16. See also chapter 3.

17. See chapter 1, n. 14.

18. *Ath. Pol.* 7.4, with Rhodes, *Commentary,* pp. 145–46. Rough equivalency between *zeugitai* (or higher) status and regular eligibility for service as a hoplite is implied by Thuc. 6.43. We may perhaps justifiably infer that inquiries into a citizen's economic status—at the *zeugitai/thetes* level—effectively stopped around the time of the restoration of *demokratia* after the failed oligarchic revolutions in the fifth century's final years. Since the distinction between those above and below hoplite status figured so prominently in the oligarchic rhetoric supporting the revolutions (see chapter 3, pp. 91–94), popular political leaders after this probably avoided anything that smacked of this now invidious distinction.

19. There is some reason to think that the property qualifications for some of-

fices (like the treasurers of Athena's sacred wealth, officials who were supposed to come from the highest class, the *pentakosiomedimnoi*) remained technically in force even in the fourth century (*Ath. Pol.* 47.1). Since these offices came to be seen as something of a burden, the demos and its leaders perhaps saw no reason to insist on the formal admission of lower classes to such positions.

20. In this discussion of citizen duties I have left aside *leitourgiai,* "works done for the people," such as paying for a dramatic chorus or providing the upkeep of an Athenian warship, since only Athens's wealthier citizens were required to perform these duties: see Hansen, *Athenian Democracy,* pp. 110–15.

21. The description of this law in *Ath. Pol.* 26.4 usually has been interpreted as a requirement that citizens *(politai)* have citizen parents (called *astoi,* literally, "those from the *astu* [city]," in *Ath. Pol.*): see, e.g., Rhodes, *Commentary,* pp. 331–34, and MacDowell, *Law,* pp. 67–68, 87 (the latter also believes this measure made marriages to non-Athenians illegal, as we know they were by the mid fourth century: Dem. 59.16, with Rhodes, *CAH* VI², p. 566 n. 5). Cohen, *Athenian Nation,* pp. 48–63, challenges the orthodox view, arguing that the term *astoi* in *Ath. Pol.* means, essentially, "locals," as opposed to "citizens," and that the law therefore allowed the children of some resident non-Athenians (metics) to become citizens upon their enrollment in a deme. Cohen shows that in some contexts *astoi* can be opposed to *xenos:* i.e., local or "insider," as opposed to "foreigner" (pp. 50–53), but this does not prove that *astos* cannot also act as a synonym for *polites* ("citizen"). The ancient Greeks loved antithetical formulations: of another term, Cohen writes, "[a]s with many other ancient Greek terms, the clearest definition of *autokhthôn* arises from its interplay with its antithesis, *epêlys* or 'incomer,' 'immigrant' " (p. 93). In fact, the opposite would be closer to the truth (as a statement of principle): such antithetical formulations do not in fact provide a clear definition for Greek terms. Rather, they obscure the range of meanings/connotations possible for a term (like *astos*), since it is the antithesis itself (in such a context) that delimits the term. For example, compare the Greek *hiera* and *hosia; hosia* is often taken to mean "profane" through its contrast with *hiera* ("sacred"). In fact, *hosia* expresses a range of "sacredness" limited, in contexts where *hiera* occurs, by the presence of the other term. Cohen's own research suggests that the Athenians often conducted massive revisions of the citizen rolls and frequently denied significant numbers of "locals" citizenship at the deme level. Thus, even if he were right about *Ath. Pol.* 26.4, one might reasonably conclude that the Athenians' standards for citizenship were more capricious (if less ethnically flavored) than the orthodox view maintains. (For the view that metics were not *astoi,* see also D. Whitehead, *The Ideology of the Athenian Metic* [Cambridge, 1977], pp. 60–61.)

22. Some have thought this provision looked to the legitimacy of the candidate, that is, whether his parents were legally married. Rhodes disagrees (*Commentary,* pp. 499–500), but notes that this passage in *Ath. Pol.* does not prove that such a requirement of legitimacy did not exist.

23. *Ath. Pol.* 42.1, with 26.4, and Rhodes, *Commentary,* pp. 499, 501–2. Aristotle's

words here have led to a great deal of debate, centering on just who could be sold into slavery by the city. Some scholars argue that only the sons of slaves could be sold, but this view rests largely on the belief that the sale of others would have been particularly unjust. Rhodes (loc. cit.) shows that the ancient evidence casts doubt on this optimistic interpretation. In fact, ancient Greeks lived in a world where free individuals were frequently sold into slavery (especially after their capture in war). However we interpret Aristotle's words, the law shows that the Athenians considered an attempt to gain citizenship without the requisite qualifications by birth to be a heinous crime.

24. *Ath. Pol.* 42.2–5.

25. Cf. Rhodes, *Commentary,* pp. 494–95 (a late date—330s—for the formal institution, with "something of the kind" existing earlier); Hansen, *Athenian Democracy,* pp. 89, 108–9, who places the creation of the institution in the late fifth or early fourth century (370s at the latest); and Kurt A. Raaflaub, "Equalities and Inequalities in Athenian Democracy," in Ober and Hedrick, eds., *Dêmokratia,* pp. 157, with 172–73 n. 149, who supports an earlier creation (fifth century) and discusses the evidence.

26. Rhodes, *Commentary,* pp. 503, 778, thinks that the *thetes* did not participate; cf. Hansen, *Athenian Democracy,* pp. 108–9, who argues based on demographic figures that the *thetes* must have been included by at least 336/5.

27. Tod 204 = Harding 109A (trans. Harding, adapted). Cf. Lycurgus 1.77, Pollux 8.105–6 (= Harding 109B); Hansen, *Athenian Democracy,* p. 100. See Mikalson, *Athenian Popular Religion,* esp. pp. 31–38, on the importance Athenians attached to oaths.

28. On this aspect of Athenian society, see chapter 7.

29. See also chapter 7, n. 21. Noncitizen residents of Athens (metics) were also liable for military service and subject to certain taxes levied on Athenians and to special taxes levied only on metics: MacDowell, *Law,* pp. 75–78; Hansen, *Athenian Democracy,* pp. 116–20; and Whitehead, *The Ideology of the Athenian Metic.*

30. *Ath. Pol.* 55.3 (trans. Moore, adapted).

31. On the *dokimasia,* see MacDowell, *Law,* pp. 167–69, and chapter 1, n. 30.

32. Hansen, *Athenian Democracy,* pp. 218–20.

33. On ostracism, see chapter 1, p. 32.

34. On fifth-century *atimia* and partial *atimia,* which could be incurred merely for owing a debt to the state or evading military service, see Andoc. 1.73–80, discussed by A. L. Boegehold, "Andokides and the Decree of Patrokleides," *Historia* 39 (1990): 149–62. On the increased use of the legal system to punish failed military leaders in fourth-century Athens, see chapter 6, pp. 145–47.

35. Hansen, *Athenian Democracy,* p. 100; see also MacDowell, *Law,* p. 126. The death penalty seems to have been applied to those who violated their *atimia.* It is important to note that female prostitution (but not by citizen women) was legal in Athens (MacDowell, *Law,* p. 125). Cohen, *Athenian Nation,* pp. 155–91, argues that

citizen prostitution was legal, although it carried the disability of potentially debarring the practitioner from holding positions of political leadership. In my opinion, he perhaps overemphasizes the attested cases of prostitution, which may only show that the convention or statute against the act was sometimes violated. Nevertheless, Cohen's revisionist treatment of supposed political structures governing Athenian sexual relations merits careful attention.

36. MacDowell, *Law,* pp. 124–25, and Mikalson, *Athenian Popular Religion,* p. 87.

37. Hansen, *Athenian Democracy,* pp. 100–101, and Mikalson, *Athenian Popular Religion,* pp. 99–100 (on caring for parents).

38. MacDowell, *Law,* pp. 129–32, with Dem. 21.45–47; Arist. *Rhet.* 1374a, I.13.10, 1378b, II.2.5–6. Cohen, *Athenian Nation,* pp. 160–65, emphasizes that this provision apparently offered protection from *hybris* to *everyone*—citizen and noncitizen, adult and child, man and woman—and that Athenian citizens were therefore not free to act as a sexually predatory and dominant class (as they are sometimes depicted in modern scholarship): "at Athens, social structures and communal values (especially commitment to *philanthrôpia*) encouraged effective protection against sexual abuse of children, slaves, and women" (p. 165).

39. On the particular privileges of citizens, see Hansen, *Athenian Democracy,* pp. 97–99. On slaves, see also MacDowell, *Law,* pp. 79–83. The frequency with which slaves actually underwent torture and the precise role played by testimony gained through such means remain disputed issues: cf. M. Gagarin, "The Torture of Slaves in Athenian Law," *CP* 91 (1996): 1–18; D. C. Mirhady, "Torture and Rhetoric in Athens," *JHS* 116 (1996): 119–31; and G. Thür, "Reply to D. C. Mirhady: Torture and Rhetoric in Athens," *JHS* 116 (1996): 132–34.

40. On this difficult passage, see A. W. Gomme, et al., *A Historical Commentary on Thucydides* (Oxford, 1945–81), 2: 122–23, and Simon Hornblower, *A Commentary on Thucydides* (Oxford, 1991–96), 1: 305–6.

41. I do not wish to imply that this belief led to the creation of *demokratia,* only that it eventually came to serve as a justification for the regime. For justice given equally to human beings, see Plato *Protagoras,* esp. 322–24.

42. It might be argued that our historical sources from the fourth century or later periods betray an anti-Athenian bias and that our record of Athenian votes is therefore seriously distorted. But much of this material concerns decisions about foreign policy, which are difficult to misrepresent (i.e., the Athenians either voted to make a certain alliance or they did not). Moreover, the Athenians' own inscriptional records confirm many of these events and provide examples of similar actions.

43. Hdt. 5.73, with Fornara and Samons, *Athens from Cleisthenes to Pericles,* pp. 19–22.

44. The Greek alliance against Persia in 480 consisted of a small number of poleis, although it admittedly included a significant percentage of the larger states in southern Hellas (including Athens, Sparta, Corinth, Aegina, Megara, Chalcis and Eretria). For a list, see Fornara 59 = ML 27, with Meiggs and Lewis's commentary,

pp. 59–60. Important regions that ultimately remained outside the alliance or joined the Persians include Thessaly, Phocis (including Delphi), much of Boeotia (including Thebes), and Argos (on which see Hdt. 9.12).

45. On Naxos's attempt to leave the alliance (in the early 460s), see Thuc. 1.98–99. On the reversed alliances of 462/1, see Thuc. 1.102.

46. Or, perhaps, acceded to his request to return to Athens immediately.

47. On this nexus of events, see Thuc. 1.102; *Ath. Pol.* 25–26; Plut. *Cim.* 11, 16–17; Fornara and Samons, *Athens from Cleisthenes to Pericles*, pp. 58–61, 127–29; and Rhodes, *CAH* V², pp. 68–69. The order of events is controversial, but no serious doubt exists about Cimon's support of the expedition to assist Sparta and Ephialtes' use of the expedition or its result as an opportunity to push through his reform proposals, which ultimately resulted in Cimon's ostracism.

48. For the transfer in 454/3 and the building program, see Samons, *Empire of the Owl*, pp. 41–50, 92–163. Some scholars have attempted to paint the building program as a "league" matter, thus rightly paid for by the alliance's common funds. The Athenians may have made the same claim, but such propaganda cannot alter the fact that the program enhanced Athens and its demos, not the members of the league.

49. On this Thucydides (not the historian), see Plut. *Per.* 11–14, with Fornara and Samons, *Athens from Cleisthenes to Pericles*, pp. 29–34; cf. F. Frost, *Historia* 13 (1964): 385–99, and Wade-Gery, *Essays in Greek History*, pp. 239–70.

50. *Ath. Pol.* 27; Plut. *Per.* 9, 12, with Fornara and Samons, *Athens from Cleisthenes to Pericles*, pp. 67–74.

51. *Ath. Pol.* 26; Plut. *Per.* 37, with Patterson, *Pericles' Citizenship Law.*

52. On Athenian ideas of ethnic superiority, see L. J. Samons II, "Democracy, Empire and the Search for the Athenian Character," *Arion* 8.3 (2001): 147–48, and chapter 3, pp. 92–93; cf. Hall, *Ethnic Identity in Greek Antiquity.* For the related idea of Athenian autochthony, cf. Nicole Loraux, *Born of the Earth: Myth and Politics in Athens,* trans. Selina Stewart (Ithaca, N.Y., 2000).

53. See Plut. *Per.* 15–16, and Thuc. 2.65, with Fornara and Samons, *Athens from Cleisthenes to Pericles,* pp. 28–35.

54. Plutarch associates the initial decree against Samos with Pericles (*Per.* 25: see chapter 4, pp. 114–15). He also connected Pericles with the decree ordering a herald to be sent to Megara to complain of the Megarians' use of the sacred land at Eleusis. The alleged murder of this herald by the Megarians led to the famous decree barring them from the Athenian marketplace and harbors of the empire (Plut. *Per.* 30, with chapter 5, pp. 125–27). At Plut. *Per.* 10, Pericles proposes a decree to recall Cimon from ostracism.

55. E.g., *IG* i³ 34 = ML 46 = Fornara 98 (Cleinias's proposal on tribute collection, ca. 448/7 or ca. 425), *IG* i³ 40 = ML 52 = Fornara 103 (Diognetos's decree issuing regulations for Chalcis, ca. 446/5 or ca. 424/3, which omits the name of the secretary); after the year 421, the name of the eponymous archon was sometimes included in the prescript, although the practice was not regular until about 410: cf. Mattingly, *Athe-*

nian Empire Restored, pp. 325–27, Rhodes, *Athenian Boule,* pp. 226–27, and A. S. Henry, "Archon-Dating in Fifth-Century Attic Decrees: The 421 Rule," *Chiron* 9 (1979): 23–30.

56. On the controversy, see esp. Meiggs and Lewis, *Selection of Greek Historical Inscriptions* (e.g., pp. 114–17, 120–21); Mattingly, *Athenian Empire Restored;* Fornara and Samons, *Athens from Cleisthenes to Pericles,* pp. 182–87; and chapter 1, n. 83.

57. See the regulations for Erythrae, *IG* i³ 14 = ML 40 = Fornara 71 (460s or 450s).

58. Colophon (*IG* i³ 37 = ML 47 = Fornara 99: 440s or 420s), Brea (*IG* i³ 46 = ML 49 = Fornara 100; 440s, 430s, or 420s).

59. Oaths of loyalty: *IG* i³ 39, 40 = ML 102, 103; oath "to love" the demos: *IG* i³ 37 = ML 47 = Fornara 99.

60. See the Phaselis decree (*IG* i³ 10 = ML 31 = Fornara 68), with Thuc. 1.77, and Hornblower, *Commentary,* 1: 122–23.

61. E.g., *IG* i³ 71 = ML 69 = Fornara 136; see Samons, *Empire of the Owl,* pp. 17(–83.

62. Chapter 6 extends the analysis into the fourth century, demonstrating how the demos voted repeatedly to avoid serving in or funding the military operations necessary to ensure Athenian interests and security.

63. See Richard Brookhiser, *Founding Father: Rediscovering George Washington* (New York, 1996), esp. pp. 107–19, on Washington's personal traits, and pp. 55–69, on the Constitutional Convention.

64. For a notable exception, see Rahe, *Republics Ancient and Modern,* pp. 198ff.

65. The covers of textbooks on Western civilization and Greek history have often reproduced and strengthened this connection; see, for the acropolis: Stockton, *Classical Athenian Democracy.* It was therefore somewhat ironic (if not entirely unexpected) when the designers of this volume's cover chose a photograph of a modern reconstruction of the Parthenon—in Nashville, Tenn.—as an appropriate image for a book on ancient and modern democracy.

66. See, e.g., J. J. Pollitt, *Art and Experience in Classical Greece* (Cambridge, 1972), pp. 71–97 and especially, Manville and Ober, *A Company of Citizens,* pp. 3–5; cf. Russell Meiggs, "The Political Implications of the Parthenon," *Greece and Rome* 10 (1963), suppl., pp. 36–45, esp. pp. 43–45, where he connects the building with democracy (while noting its reliance on imperial funding), and, for a corrective, Kallet, "Accounting for Culture in Fifth-Century Athens," in Deborah Boedeker and Kurt A. Raaflaub, eds., *Democracy, Empire, and the Arts in Fifth-Century Athens* (Cambridge, Mass., 1998), pp. 48–52, 58.

67. This has been denied; but see Samons, *Empire of the Owl,* pp. 41–50 and n. 48 above.

68. See Parker, *Athenian Religion,* p. 91. On the Panathenaea in general, see Neils, ed., *Worshipping Athena;* on the name, cf. N. Robertson, "Athena's Shrines and Festivals," in Neils, p. 56: "Panathenaia presumably means 'Rites of all Athenians.'"

69. On Pandora's presence here, see Pollitt, *Art and Experience,* pp. 98–99.

70. D. M. Lewis, *CAH* V², p. 139. On the subject in general, cf. David Castri-

ota, *Myth, Ethos and Actuality: Official Art in Fifth-Century B.C. Athens* (Madison, Wis., 1992). For a more optimistic interpretation of the Parthenon and its sculpture, see Pollitt, *Art and Experience,* pp. 64–110.

71. Compare the Athenians' claim that such self-aggrandizement was only natural to men and gods (Thuc. 1.105, with chapter 5, pp. 133–34).

72. The Greek is ambiguous: see conclusion, p. 189.

73. On the Athenians' self-image, see Samons, "Democracy, Empire and the Search for the Athenian Character," and chapter 3, pp. 92–93.

74. On the Athenian funeral orations *(epitaphioi)* in general, see Nicole Loraux, *The Invention of Athens: The Funeral Oration in the Classical City,* trans. Alan Sheridan (Cambridge, Mass., 1986), who overemphasizes the importance of democracy in these speeches (p. 64), especially as relative to Athens's military virtues and history. See, e.g., Lysias 2, where democracy figures only in sections 18, 56, 61–66, and Plato's *Menexenus,* in which a funeral oration attributed to Pericles' consort Aspasia is "repeated" by Socrates. In that mock address, praise of Athens's *politeia* occupies only a small portion of the speech (238c–239a), and Athens's regime is called "an aristocracy with the approval of the multitude" (238c–d; trans. S. Collins and D. Stauffer). Athenian military victories, on the other hand, receive at least ten times as much space in the speech (239b–246a). Hyperides' funeral oration, delivered in 322, concentrates on protecting or gaining freedom *(eleutheria)* rather than praising Athens's particular regime (6.11, 16, 19, 34, 37). The *epitaphios* attributed to Demosthenes, and ostensibly delivered in 338, devotes only 2 of its 37 sections to Athens's form of government (60.25–26), and these sections praise *demokratia* for its ability to inspire shame *(aischune).* Interestingly, Cicero (*Orator* 151) relates that it was the funeral oration in the *Menexenus* that the Athenians arranged to be read publicly every year.

75. Long after Pericles' death, Athenians continued to identify the special qualities of Athens primarily in military rather than political terms. And while it is true that, by the fourth century, Athenian orators treated the democratic part of Athens's reputation and character as a standard subject or topos, Athens's power and glorious earlier military history continued to overshadow her political culture and specific constitution as defining characteristics: see, e.g., Isocrates *Panegyricus,* Plato *Menexenus,* Lysias 2.

76. For recent attempts to treat Pericles, see Donald Kagan, *Pericles of Athens and the Birth of Democracy* (New York, 1991); Fornara and Samons, *Athens from Cleisthenes to Pericles,* esp. pp. 23–36; Charlotte Schubert, *Perikles* (Darmstadt, 1994); and A. J. Podlecki, *Perikles and His Circle* (London, 1998).

77. See *Ath. Pol.* 1; Plut. *Solon* 12; and Diog. Laert. 1.110, with Fornara and Samons, *Athens from Cleisthenes to Pericles,* pp. 6–7.

78. See Samons, "Mass, Elite and Hoplite-Farmer in Greek History," 110–15, with the additional material in id., "Revolution or Compromise?" in E. W. Robinson, ed., *Ancient Greek Democracy: Readings and Sources* (Oxford, 2004), pp. 113–22, and Fornara and Samons, *Athens from Cleisthenes to Pericles,* pp. 13–23, 37–58.

79. Hdt. 5.70–73, with Fornara and Samons, *Athens from Cleisthenes to Pericles,* pp. 19–23, and Samons, "Mass, Elite and Hoplite-Farmer in Greek History," 110–15.

80. See Hdt. 6.115, 121–24; *Ath. Pol.* 22.

81. See Fornara and Samons, *Athens from Cleisthenes to Pericles,* pp. 24–36; Plut. *Per.* 4–6.

82. Fornara and Samons, *Athens from Cleisthenes to Pericles,* pp. 1–36.

83. Ibid., pp. 23–29. On Pericles' early career, cf. L. J. Samons II, "Aeschylus, the Alkmeonids, and the Reform of the Areopagos," *CJ* 94 (1998/99): 221–33, Podlecki, *Perikles and His Circle,* pp. 11–16, 35–54, and Kagan, *Pericles,* pp. 26–45, who notes that Pericles entered politics rather late (pp. 26–27), but attributes this to Pericles' calculation of the opportune moment to enter politics rather than to supposed popular suspicion of him. Later in his career, Pericles and his supporters were called by some the "New Peisistratids," and Pericles was said to resemble the tyrant Peisistratus, especially in his voice (Plut. *Per.* 7, 16). Pericles' enemies almost certainly used such devices to remind the Athenians of the connection between his family and the tyrants and their associates.

84. See chapter 4, pp. 110–11.

85. See *Ath. Pol.* 25–27; Plut. *Per.* 7–10. For the view that Pericles' role in Ephialtes' reforms has been exaggerated, see Fornara and Samons, *Athens from Cleisthenes to Pericles,* pp. 24–28, with the additional evidence in Samons, "Aeschylus, the Alkmeonids, and the Reform of the Areopagos."

86. Samons, "Aeschylus, the Alkmeonids, and the Reform of the Areopagos."

87. Thuc. 1. 104, 109–10. Plut. *Per.* 20 explicitly reports that Pericles opposed an expedition to Egypt, but the temporal context is unclear, and the report could simply reflect a logical inference by Plutarch or his source based on Pericles' later policy of avoiding conflict with Persia.

88. Plut. *Per.* 20–23 describes Pericles' interest in a mainland Greek empire, although the biographer cites this as an example of Periclean moderation, since he attempted to restrain the demos from foreign adventures beyond Greece.

89. See chapter 4, p. 113.

90. Plut. *Per.* 10 (cf. *Cim.* 17) reports a secret agreement between Pericles and Cimon by which Pericles would propose Cimon's recall from ostracism and the two would then divide their power into domestic (Pericles) and foreign (Cimon) spheres. Again, this may be no more than an inference from later events.

91. Pericles was a member of the board of generals in 454/3, and his later use of the allied money justifies the inference that he supported the transfer: see Samons, *Empire of the Owl,* pp. 92–106.

92. Citizenship law: *Ath. Pol.* 26.4, with pp. 34–35, 52 above; Patterson, *Pericles' Citizenship Law;* Rhodes, *CAH* V², pp. 76–77; and Plut. *Per.* 37, which reports that the Athenians convicted nearly five thousand individuals (a number considered implausible by Rhodes) of posing as citizens and sold them into slavery shortly after this law was passed. As we have already seen, the Athenians conceived of themselves as a

unique people in part because of their alleged autochthony (i.e., nonimmigrant status in their native land), and the idea of Athenian "purity" does appear in the sources: see Plato *Menex.* 245c–d. For the Athenians' belief in their superiority even to their Ionian relations, see Fornara and Samons, *Athens from Cleisthenes to Pericles*, pp. 106–10, and Samons, "Democracy, Empire and the Search for the Athenian Character," 147–48.

93. For the shallow nature of any Panhellenic feelings in Athens after the mid fifth century, see Samons, "Democracy, Empire and the Search for the Athenian Character," pp. 149–50.

94. For the resistance and revolts in the late 450s–mid 440s, see Meiggs, *Athenian Empire*, pp. 109–28, 152–74, with Rhodes, *CAH* V², pp. 54–61, and Lewis, *CAH* V², pp. 127–38.

95. Thuc. 1.112–15; Plut. *Per.* 22–23.

96. Plut. *Per.* 22–23; Ar. *Clouds* 858–59, with schol. (= Fornara 104).

97. Thuc. 1. 113, 115; Plut. *Per.* 24; Lewis, *CAH* V², pp. 133–38.

98. Parthenon work: *IG* i³ 436; Pericles as superintendent of acropolis building program and public payments from the work: Plut. *Per.* 12–14, 31.

99. Plut. *Per.* 12, 14; for the building program debate, analysis of Plutarch's report, and references to other literature, see Samons, *Empire of the Owl*, pp. 41–50.

100. Plut. *Per.* 15–16.

101. See n. 54 above.

102. Thuc. 1.115–17, Plut. *Per.* 24–28, with Fornara, "On the Chronology of the Samian War," *JHS* 99 (1979): 9–17, and Lewis, *CAH* V², pp. 143–45.

103. Plut. *Per.* 24, 28.

104. Plut. *Per.* 24, 31–32, with Fornara and Samons, *Athens from Cleisthenes to Pericles*, pp. 34–35, and chapter 4, pp. 114–15.

105. Schol. Ar. *Ach.* 67 = Fornara 111. Other explanations of the measure are, of course, possible. Jeffrey Henderson, "Attic Old Comedy, Frank Speech, and Democracy," in Boedeker and Raaflaub, eds., *Democracy, Empire, and the Arts in Fifth-Century Athens*, pp. 255–73, suggests that the measure was intended "to prevent the inflammation of partisan violence" during the Samian War (p. 262).

106. For fragments of the lost comedians ridiculing Pericles, see Plut. *Per.* 3–4, 13, 16, 24, 33.

107. One reason for Pericles' popularity in the assembly while serving as a regular object of the comic poets' abuse may have been that assembly meetings and the dramatic festivals at which comedies were performed attracted somewhat different audiences. We may speculate that the audience for Athenian comedies represented a truer cross-section of the Athenian populace, including many hoplite-farmers from outlying regions of Attica, who came to the city center only rarely. Meanwhile, the average assembly meeting probably had a higher percentage of urban poor and residents of Athens, both of whom were more likely to benefit directly from Periclean policies like jury pay and the building program than were the farmers.

108. Plut. *Per.* 28, with Arist. *Rhet.* 1365a, I.7.31–33; on the procedure of selecting the orator for the funeral ceremony, see Pl. *Menex.* 234a–236a.

109. Thuc. book 1, esp. 1.140–46; Plut. *Per.* 32–34. For this view of the war's outbreak, see chapter 5.

110. See Thuc. 2.60–65, with Hornblower, *Commentary,* 1: 341; Plut. *Per.* 35.

111. Thuc. 2.65 with 1.22. For this view of the speeches, see also conclusion, p. 187 with n. 1.

112. Many sources beyond Thucydides testify to Pericles' skills as an orator: see Plut. *Per.* 7, 8, 15; Plato, *Menex.* 235e, *Phaedrus* 269e–270a; schol. Ar. *Ach.* 530; and Fornara 74. As an example of the rhetorical strategies he employed, note the differences in the attitude expressed toward farmers and sailors between Pericles' first speech in Thucydides (1.140–44, made with relatively few farmers present) and the last two (2.35–46, 60–64, made after the farmers had been forced to move within the walls of the city).

113. Thuc. 2.42 (trans. Crawley); on this passage, see also conclusion, pp. 187–91.

114. Achilles had famously cursed his fellow Achaeans and withdrawn from the war with Troy after Agamemnon had diminished his honor or *time* (*Iliad* bk. 1). Such actions demonstrate a conception of human excellence based on an individual's performance of great deeds (Achilles was "the best of the Achaeans" because of his military prowess). This conception carried little or no ethical content beyond the duty to one's own honor, over which the group exercised no claim. (But compare Hector's part in the epic: his concerns for the city and its reaction to his actions may reflect the influence of early polis values.) Although Socrates would compare himself to Achilles (*Ap.* 28b–d), in fact he had a view of *arete* that contrasted starkly with that of the Achaean hero: "Are you not ashamed," Socrates claimed to ask the Athenians, "of your eagerness to possess as much wealth, reputation, and honors as possible, while you do not care for nor give thought to wisdom or truth, or the best possible state of your soul?" (*Ap.* 29d–e; trans. Grube). (Achilles, we may speculate, would have responded, "No, not in the least am I ashamed. But are you not ashamed of having gained no great honor and rewards for yourself by demonstrating your excellence on the field of battle?") While Socrates' ideas had perhaps been less than successful in implanting themselves in many Athenian hearts, the older Homeric ideals of *arete* and *time* were very much alive in fifth-century Greece, as the careers of Alcibiades, Lysander, Conon, and others demonstrate. (To some extent, the egalitarianism of the polis and the concept of citizenship stood in direct conflict with this aristocratic ideal. The tension these conflicting ideals created within classical city-states surely may be counted as one source of their tremendous vigor and volatility.)

115. For the more typical Greek emphasis on not falling short of one's ancestors, see chapter 6, p. 157.

116. Plutarch, *Per.* 15, expands on Thucydides' opinion, but draws a line between an early demagogic portion of Pericles' career (before the ostracism of Thucydides son of Melesias) and the later, statesmanlike period: see Fornara and Samons, *Athens from Cleisthenes to Pericles,* pp. 29–34.

117. Fortunately for Pericles, these promises came at a time when the Athenian empire and martial Athenian character made their fulfillment possible.

118. Obviously only those sons of hoplite-farmers who did not inherit sufficient property to maintain their position and those below this status would be likely to participate in Athenian colonies and cleruchies established in the empire. But we must conclude that this offered a major safety valve for social forces that, in other poleis, would have been likely to cause unrest. For Athens's surplus population in the Periclean period (perhaps as many as 60,000 citizens ca. 450), see Hansen, *Athenian Democracy*, pp. 52–54. For the regular hoplite-farmers of Athens benefiting economically from democracy and the empire, see esp. V. Hanson, in *Dêmokratia*, ed. Ober and Hedrick, pp. 289–312, esp. 298–303.

119. For Pericles' support of colonies and cleruchies (Athenian settlements within other states), see esp. Plut. *Per.* 11, 19–20; see also Podlecki, *Perikles and His Circle*, pp. 62–64, and Meiggs, *Athenian Empire*, pp. 260–62.

120. Pericles' lack of sociability: Plut. *Per.* 5, 7. For his words to the dead men's parents, see Thuc. 2.44–45 and conclusion, pp. 197–98; cf. Plato *Menex.* 247c–248d, containing a "funeral oration" that is significantly more personal in its words for the parents of the dead, and Arist. *Rhet.* 1365a, I.7.34, which attributes a compassionate phrase lamenting the loss of Athens's young men to a (perhaps different) funeral oration of Pericles.

121. See chapters 3 and 6.

122. Compare the complaints of Demosthenes and Tocqueville that serve as epigraphs to this chapter.

123. Compare Tocqueville's views on democracy's resistance to rule by superiors (*Democracy in America*, ed. Mayer [1969], pp. 197–99) and its tendency to attribute a politician's success to his vices rather than virtues or talents.

124. See Hansen, *Athenian Democracy*, pp. 268–71, with chapter 3, n. 93. In the fifth century, even Cleon served as a *strategos*. Yet his generalship apparently began late in his career (425), suggesting that the trend may already have begun by that time (as Kurt Raaflaub has suggested to me).

125. *Ath. Pol.* 68, with Rhodes, *Commentary*, p. 733.

126. Cf. Euben, Wallach, and Ober, eds., *Athenian Political Thought*, p. 14, quoted in introduction, n. 17.

127. On the appropriate goal or end of a state or "constitution," cf. Arist. *Pol.* 1280a–1281a, III.9.5–15 (state should exist to promote goodness and good actions), with Madison, *Federalist* 51 (government should seek justice by protecting the rights of individuals).

128. Nevertheless, it does seem that some individuals sincerely believe that the process itself is the important thing about democratic election. (Perhaps most do not really *believe* it; they simply have heard it said so many times that it has become a kind of slogan or mantra.)

129. For the others, see chapter 7.

130. Some of the framers and defenders of the American Constitution believed that they had overcome this problem, creating a document and a form of government that recognized and indeed relied on the acquisitive, self-interested, competing, and even vicious character of individuals within the society (see Wood, *Creation of the American Republic,* esp. pp. 587–92, 606–15). In my opinion, they could not look at modern America and conclude that their attempt had been a complete success. Popular government and society will tend to reflect one another, even if the Constitution treats the two forces as distinct entities: see ibid., esp. pp. 567–92, 596–600, on the Founders' ultimate rejection of John Adams's and the ancients' conception of government as a direct expression of, if not the same as, the society. For an attempt to bring Adams into the mainstream of revolutionary and early American (i.e., Federalist) thought, see Thompson, *John Adams and the Spirit of Liberty,* esp. pp. 258–66.

3. PUBLIC FINANCE: DEMOCRACY AND THE PEOPLE'S PURSE

1. Nevertheless, specific details (such as the nature and amounts of any payments or transfers made between various Athenian treasuries) remain controversial. For an attempt to treat the technical issues, see Samons, *Empire of the Owl.* For Athenian record-keeping in general, see J. P. Sickinger, *Public Records and Archives in Classical Athens* (Chapel Hill, N.C., 1999).

2. As previously noted, the other defining characteristics of Athens's democracy were popular control of the courts, payment for public service, the use of the lottery to fill important offices, and the influence of the demesmen (and not just the aristocratic families and the organizations they dominated) in the control of citizenship and the Council of 500. See chapter 1, p. 28 and chapter 2, pp. 42–44.

3. We cannot say precisely how the public came to control the mines. It is possible that the Peisistratid family that ruled Athens from ca. 546 to 511/10 had claimed the mines' revenues, and that when the tyranny was overthrown this "property" (like other property owned by the tyrants) became public. However, the few other Greek states that possessed mines also apparently treated them as public property (see n. 6 below), and thus Athenian practice may simply reflect an older Hellenic attitude toward mining revenues. On this subject, see Samons, *Empire of the Owl,* pp. 61 n. 155, 202–4.

4. See T. J. Figueira, *The Power of Money: Coinage and Politics in the Athenian Empire* (Philadelphia, 1998), pp. 533–34, and Samons, *Empire of the Owl,* p. 276.

5. See S. C. Humphreys, *Anthropology and the Greeks* (London, 1978), p. 145, and Samons, *Empire of the Owl,* pp. 60–62, with Hdt. 3.57.3, 6.46.3.

6. From very early times some land was apparently owned jointly by groups within the polis: see V. N. Andreyev, "Some Aspects of Agrarian Conditions in Attica from the Fifth to the Third Centuries B.C.," *Eirene* 12 (1974): 5–46. This may be one of the factors that led to the creation of other "common" property.

7. It is unclear when the trierarchy system was instituted at Athens. The Atheni-

ans may have had an earlier system of demanding funds or services from wealthy Athenians for the fleet, but even this system (the *naukrariai?*) probably relied on annual collections and expenditures rather than a surplus of moneys managed by the demos as a whole. Whatever the precise system employed, there is no real doubt that sixth-century Athens relied on its wealthier citizens to fund its major projects. On the trierarchy and the *naukrariai*, cf. Vincent Gabrielsen, *Financing the Athenian Fleet: Public Taxation and Social Relations* (Baltimore, 1994), esp. pp. 19–39, and Rhodes, *Commentary*, pp. 151–53, 679–82, 770–71.

8. These hoplites usually came from the ranks of the middling farmers that were ubiquitous in ancient Hellas. See Hanson, *Other Greeks*, pp. 221–89.

9. This wealth derived from sources such as dedications, tithes on booty, and *aparchai* (first-fruits) given to the gods. Expenditures of this wealth for temple building, upkeep, sacrifices, or other religious and civic affairs constituted a regular aspect of Greek religious practice. See Samons, *Empire of the Owl*, esp. pp. 30–54, 160–63.

10. We may assume this became standard practice, since no distributions of such money to individual citizens appears in our sources after 483/2, and since Herodotus explicitly states that the Athenians built more ships.

11. Fleet numbers: Hdt. 6.89, 132; 8.1, 44.

12. On the trireme, see J. S. Morrison, J. F. Coates, and N. B. Rankov, *The Athenian Trireme: The History and Reconstruction of an Ancient Greek Warship*, 2d ed. (Cambridge, 2000).

13. On the payment of sailors and hoplites, see Samons, *Empire of the Owl*, esp. pp. 34–35, 67–70, 305–6; Rhodes, *Commentary*, p. 306; and W. K. Pritchett, *The Greek State at War* (Berkeley, 1971–90), 1: 7–24.

14. See chapter 4, esp. pp. 107–9.

15. On the *hellenotamiai* and the early financial arrangements of the league, see Samons, *Empire of the Owl*, esp. pp. 70–82.

16. Thuc. 1.103, 105–8.

17. See Thuc. 1.109–10, 112.

18. For the controversy surrounding this so-called Peace of Callias, see chapter 4, n. 67.

19. See Samons, *Empire of the Owl*, pp. 35–38, 92–104. Some scholars hold that previously payments had been made to Delian Apollo; there is no evidence for this view other than the later payments to Athena.

20. See Boersma, *Athenian Building Policy*, pp. 59–61, 65–81.

21. Samons, *Empire of the Owl*, esp. pp. 41–50.

22. This subject is controversial; see, e.g., *IG* i³ 52 = ML 58 = Fornara 119, with Samons, *Empire of the Owl*, esp. chs. 1–3.

23. For this argument, see also Samons, *Empire of the Owl*, pp. 41–50. For the questionable authenticity of the passages from Plutarch, see esp. A. Andrewes, "The Opposition to Pericles," *JHS* 98 (1978): 1–8; cf. Lisa Kallet, "Did Tribute Fund the Parthenon?" *California Studies in Classical Antiquity* 20 (1989), 252–66.

24. E.g., Plato, *Rep.* 424c; cf. Fornara and Samons, *Athens from Cleisthenes to Pericles,* pp. 160–61, Rhodes, *Commentary,* pp. 341–42, and R. W. Wallace, "Damon of Oa: A Music Theorist Ostracized?" (forthcoming).

25. Cf. Rhodes, *Commentary,* p. 339; J. K. Davies, *Athenian Propertied Families, 600–300 B.C.* (Oxford, 1971), pp. 459–60.

26. Samons, *Empire of the Owl,* p. 36.

27. I do not wish to imply that there was a uniform or "standard" wage in Athens. For the changing rates of wages, see W. T. Loomis, *Wages, Welfare Costs and Inflation in Classical Athens* (Ann Arbor, 1998), and see n. 13 above.

28. Thuc. 2.13.3–5 with Samons, *Empire of the Owl,* ch. 3.

29. It is impossible to say how much the booty acquired from enemies in Athenian military actions contributed to Athens's wealth, although we know it amounted to something. See, e.g., Thuc. 2.13, with M. C. Miller, *Athens and Persia in the Fifth Century B.C.: A Study in Cultural Receptivity* (Cambridge, 1997), esp. pp. 38–40.

30. On this system, see Samons, *Empire of the Owl,* esp. pp. 160–63, 245–48.

31. See n. 13 above.

32. Thuc. 2.13.2. Thucydides himself argued (1.1–19) that stability and wealth made great operations like the Greek expedition to Troy or the Peloponnesian War possible; see Lisa Kallet, *Money, Expense, and Naval Power in Thucydides' History 1–5.24* (Berkeley, 1993), pp. 21–35.

33. Thus Pericles' first words in Thucydides' history announce the statesman's intransigent policy toward Sparta: "I am always of one opinion, Athenians: no concessions to the Peloponnesians [= Spartans]" (Thuc. 1.140.1). See chapter 5, pp. 127–31.

34. See, e.g., Thuc. 6.24, Ar. *Wasps,* esp. 684–85, Plut. *Per.* 12, Ps.-Xen. 1.3, 14–20; cf. Kurt A. Raaflaub, "Democracy, Power, and Imperialism in Fifth-Century Athens," in Euben, Wallach, and Ober, eds., *Athenian Political Thought,* pp. 103–46.

35. E.g., Thuc. 1.75–76, 5.105; cf. Plato *Rep.* 373d–374d, where war is treated as an evil but regular part of a state's existence.

36. Some might maintain that wars tend to generate wealth for the ruling class in all political systems. In Athens's case, the "ruling class" was arguably the entire free male population, especially the poorer citizens (who were in the majority). Wealthy Athenians probably bore a greater fiscal burden during Athenian wars, since they were often compelled to pay the property tax (after 428) and take on the expenses of a trierarchy (see chapter 6).

37. I leave aside here consideration of southern Italy and Sicily.

38. Hanson, *Other Greeks,* esp. pp. 221–323.

39. This remained true in the fourth century, when the Spartans briefly indulged imperial ambitions.

40. For the Boeotian confederation, see the *Hellenica Oxyrhynchia* 11.2–4 (translated with commentary by J. M. Moore, *Aristotle and Xenophon on Democracy and Oligarchy* [Berkeley, 1975], pp. 125–33), Thuc. 5.37–38 and 4.91 (with Gomme, *Com-*

mentary, 3: 560, and Hornblower, *Commentary,* 2: 288–89). For Thebes's brief period of "imperial" power, see Buckler, *Theban Hegemony.*

41. Cf. Kurt A. Raaflaub, "Power in the Hands of the People: Foundations of Athenian Democracy," in Morris and Raaflaub, eds., *Democracy 2500?* pp. 31–66, who emphasizes that Athens's development of democracy and integration of the *thetes* politically "came as a result of rapidly and fundamentally changing military, social, economic, and political conditions in the wake of the Persian Wars and Athens's rise to imperial power. These conditions were unique to Athens" (p. 61).

42. Thuc. 3.19.

43. For these matters, see Samons, *Empire of the Owl,* esp. pp. 208–11; for resentment of the *eisphora,* see also chapter 6.

44. Victor Davis Hanson, *Warfare and Agriculture in Classical Greece,* 2d ed. (Berkeley, 1998), has shown that such attacks on the farmland were unlikely to cause permanent or extensive damage to olive trees. But the psychological and symbolic effects of the Spartans' work should not be underestimated.

45. See Plut. *Cim.* 4, 15–16. For philo-Laconian attitudes among Athenian aristocrats, see also L. B. Carter, *The Quiet Athenian* (Oxford, 1986), pp. 44–49, 62–63, and 70–73.

46. Samons, *Empire of the Owl,* pp. 208–11. The Athenians retained a 1,000-talent reserve set aside for emergencies on the advice of Pericles in 431 (Thuc. 2.24), but may have had only a few hundred talents beyond this sum. For Athens's failed peace embassy to Sparta in 430 and the decision to send no more, see Thuc. 2. 59–65.

47. See Thuc. 4–5.24; on the peace itself, cf. Meiggs, *Athenian Empire,* pp. 340–43; Kagan, *Peace of Nicias;* and Lewis, *CAH* V², pp. 431–32.

48. Ar. *Knights* 1350–53 (Loeb ed., trans. Henderson).

49. Samons, *Empire of the Owl,* ch. 5, esp. pp. 244–48.

50. On the subject in general, see Laurence J. Kotlikoff and Scott Burns, *The Coming Generational Storm: What You Need to Know about America's Economic Future* (Cambridge, Mass.: 2004). It must be noted that even during years of annual budget surpluses the payment of hundreds of billions of dollars in service on the U.S. national debt *without any significant reduction of the principal* perpetuates this trend of borrowing from the next generation.

51. Thuc. 4.16–22. See also n. 46 above.

52. Thuc. 4.17, 21, where the idea is expressed without the noun *(pleonexia)* itself, for which cf. 3.82.6, 8. For Thucydides' treatment of the Athenian character in general, see Samons, "Democracy, Empire and the Search for the Athenian Character."

53. Cf. Thuc. 6.89–92, where Alcibiades tells the Spartans that the Athenians had intended first to conquer the western Greeks (and Carthage in North Africa) and then the rest of the Greek world. Alcibiades (or Thucydides) may well have been exaggerating, but the idea that some Athenians had such plans was obviously considered credible.

54. Thuc. 8.1, with Andrewes in Gomme et al., *Commentary,* 5: 6–7. For the *probouloi* and Athenian finance, see also Samons, *Empire of the Owl,* pp. 254–55.

55. On the financial machinations in this period, see Samons, *Empire of the Owl,* pp. 250–54.

56. Thuc. 7.27–28.

57. See Thuc. 8.29ff., with Andrewes, *CAH* V², pp. 464–71, and Kagan, *Fall of the Athenian Empire,* pp. 24–50.

58. His relations with his former Spartan hosts had soured; in fact, the Spartan king Agis had ordered Alcibiades' execution, since the Athenian had reportedly seduced the king's wife and fathered a child by her. The Spartans ultimately believed the child to be (in fact) the bastard son of Alcibiades, and he was denied the opportunity to accede to the throne: see Plut. *Alc.* 23, *Lys.* 22, and *Ages.* 3; Xen. *Hell.* 3.3.1–2, with Kagan, *Fall of the Athenian Empire,* p. 42.

59. Thuc. 8.47.

60. I leave aside the machinations that allowed an oligarchic movement in the Athenian fleet at Samos to spread to Athens, even after Alcibiades' promised Persian aid disappeared and the fleet reverted to democracy: see Thuc. 8.47–69 with Kagan, *Fall of the Athenian Empire,* pp. 106–86, and Andrewes, *CAH* V², pp. 471–74.

61. The assembly was admittedly extraordinary, in that it was held outside Athens's city walls in the village of Colonus, perhaps (in view of the Spartan occupation of Decelea) in order to reduce the number of non-hoplites who would feel safe enough to attend: see Thuc. 8.67–69, with *Ath. Pol.* 29–30, and cf. Rhodes, *Commentary,* pp. 362 ff.; Kagan, *Fall of the Athenian Empire,* p. 147; Andrewes in Gomme et al., *Commentary,* 5: 164 ff.; and id., *CAH* V², p. 475, who doubts that Colonus's short distance from Athens proper would have decreased attendance by those without armor or weapons.

62. As previously noted, there is little evidence of payment for public service in any polis other than Athens (Rhodes, *Commentary,* p. 338), although it is not entirely unattested (Rhodes, *CAH* V², pp. 94–95). For the property qualifications for full citizenship in other poleis, see Hanson, *Other Greeks,* pp. 201–14; Rhodes, *CAH* V², pp. 92–93; and *Hell. Ox.* 11.2.

63. See Samons, "Democracy, Empire and the Search for the Athenian Character." One should note that even the sailors in the Athenian fleet, a group made up primarily of those below hoplite status and usually thought to have been the most "democratic" in Athens, had accepted the idea of "reforming" the Athenian regime by establishing a more conservative constitution, admittedly in hopes of securing Persian money (Thuc. 8.48). The sailors' initial willingness to go along with the revolution provides eloquent testimony to the relatively low position "democracy" itself held in the Athenian self-image even as late as 411.

64. Admittedly, there is virtually no evidence for the fifth-century Athenians' "consciousness" of their aesthetic superiority: see Thuc. 1.10, 2.38, 40, and Boedeker and Raaflaub, eds., *Democracy, Empire, and the Arts in Fifth-Century Athens,* Introduction (pp. 1–13).

65. For some examples of the Athenians' self-image, see Thuc. 2.35–46; Lysias 2; Isocrates *Panegyricus;* Plato *Menexenus,* esp. 236d–249c; Plut. *Cim.* 7; Dem. 15.22; and chapter 2, nn. 52, 74. For Solon as one of the sages, see Hdt. 1.29–33; Plut. *Sol.* 3–6.

66. For Athenians' later emphasis on their particular constitution as a crucial defining element, see Dem. 8.41–43, 15.17–21, and Aeschin. 1.4–5 (which closely links democracy and the rule of law), 2.177.

67. Cf. Walter Eder, "Aristocrats and the Coming of Athenian Democracy," in Morris and Raaflaub, eds., *Democracy 2500?* pp. 105–40, who writes of the fourth-century Athenians' "growing and conscious support . . . for a democratic constitution that was based on law and self-control" (p. 115).

68. For this law, see Andocides 1.96–98, with MacDowell, *Law,* pp. 175–76. A similar law was passed in 336; see chapter 7, p. 172, with n. 39.

69. Although Demokratia became an Athenian goddess, democracy never functioned as an Athenian religion; see chapter 7.

70. On the regime of the Thirty, sometimes later called the Thirty Tyrants, see esp. Krentz, *The Thirty at Athens.*

71. Cf. ibid., pp. 126–27. Although Krentz believes most Athenians wanted a democracy, he comments: "The roots of Athenian democracy were perhaps shallower than is often thought" (p. 126). After the death of the Thirty's leader, Critias, in a battle against the Athenian democrats, the remaining three thousand full citizens voted to depose the Thirty, but replaced them with a board of Ten. Xenophon reports fears and distrust among the three thousand, but no general desire to restore a democratic regime (Xen. *Hell.* 2.4.19–24). Krentz comments: "One strongly suspects that the 3,000 were loyal oligarchs all along" (p. 127).

72. Xen. *Hell.* 2.4.1–41; Plut. *Lys.* 21; cf. *Ath. Pol.* 37–40.

73. See Samons, *Empire of the Owl,* pp. 281–93. The irony of the Nike coinage was apparently seen even in antiquity (Demetrios *Eloc.* 281).

74. For the failure of this amnesty to protect Socrates, see chapter 1, p. 38.

75. Hansen, *Athenian Democracy,* pp. 240–42, holds that magistrates in the fourth century were unpaid, but admits that his conclusion rests on the silence of the evidence. Cf. Arist. *Pol.* 1317b, VI.2.7, which implies that (theoretically) at least some magistrates were paid in democratic regimes.

76. *Ath. Pol.* 62.2; on pay for the assembly, see Hansen, *Athenian Democracy,* p. 150, who estimates the costs for this payment alone at around 45 talents per year.

77. See Rudi Thomsen, *Eisphora: A Study of Direct Taxation in Ancient Athens* (Copenhagen, 1964), pp. 194–249; Patrice Brun, *Eisphora-Syntaxis-Stratiotika;* Austin, *CAH* VI², pp. 546–61; and cf. A. H. M. Jones, *Athenian Democracy,* pp. 23–38, who maintains that the poorer property owners were most disadvantaged by the *eisphora,* which was not a progressive tax, and who offers a much more optimistic interpretation of Athenian domestic and foreign policy in the fourth century than that presented here.

78. See, e.g., Dem. 19.281–82 (where Demosthenes criticizes Aeschines' father's

failure to provide such support); on the subject in general, see Carter, *Quiet Athenian,* esp. pp. 103–30.

79. See Cargill, *Second Athenian League,* pp. 124–28, esp. p. 127 n. 34, with Meiggs, *Athenian Empire,* pp. 259–60; cf. Brun, *Eisphora-Syntaxis-Stratiotika,* with the review of S. Eddy, *AHR* 89 (1984): 1312–13. Cargill, *Second Athenian League,* esp. pp. 193–96, discounts the idea of increasing Athenian "imperialism" under the second league and places much of the blame for Athens's reputation and failures during the Social War on the "bumbling and vindictive leadership of [the Athenian general] Chares" (p. 194). But even Cargill admits that Chares' decision to rent his forces out to a Persian satrap was made "with the approval of the *demos*" (see Dem. 4.24; Aeschin. 2.71–77), a move that prompted the Persian king's intervention and forced the Athenians to make peace with their rebellious allies. (For the Social War, see also chapter 6.)

80. See esp. Rhodes, *Athenian Boule,* pp. 98–108, and Hansen, *Athenian Democracy,* pp. 260–64.

81. On Eubulus and the theoric fund, see esp. Sealey, *Demosthenes,* pp. 256–58; Thompson, *Eisphora,* p. 236; Rhodes, *Athenian Boule,* pp. 105–8; and chapter 6, pp. 157–59.

82. See, e.g., Dem. 1. 19–20, 8.21–26; Jones, *Athenian Democracy,* p. 30; and P. Millett, "Warfare, Economy, and Democracy in Classical Athens," in John Rich and Graham Shipley, eds., *War and Society in the Greek World* (London, 1993), pp. 191–94.

83. At least as early as 352/1: Demosthenes 4 *(First Philippic).* At 9.49–50, Dem. attributes Philip's success not to his heavy infantry but to his skirmishers, cavalry, archers, mercenaries, and siege machines.

84. For analysis of Athens's foreign policy in this period, see chapter 6.

85. See, e.g., Stockton, *Classical Athenian Democracy,* p. 164 (referring to 322). See also chapter 6.

86. Athens's allies certainly thought this, and at least sometimes requested citizen forces (as opposed to mercenaries): see Philochorus, *FGrHist* 328 F49–51 = Dion. Hal. *To Ammaeus* 1.9 = Harding 80, with Sealey, *History,* pp. 451–52. Jones, *Athenian Democracy,* pp. 30–31, emphasizes that Athenian citizens did (occasionally) serve in large numbers.

87. See chapter 6.

88. Rudi Thomsen, in his study of the Athenian property tax system, concludes that the "distinct fear of taxation shown by the wealthier Athenians, coupled with the parasitism of the lower classes centered on the theoric fund, led to a passive foreign policy in the period after the Social War. This policy enabled Philip II to obtain a predominant position in Greece, and so, in the long run, proved fatal to Athens' independence": *Eisphora,* p. 248.

89. See chapter 6. At the same time, they stopped undertaking the kind of massive and expensive building projects they had carried out in the fifth century. Given the choice between public payments and honoring the gods and themselves with new temples, the Athenians chose payments.

90. Pericles suggests as much in his Funeral Oration (Thuc. 2.40; cf. 2.63); see also Carter, *Quiet Athenian,* esp. pp. 27–51, 99–130.

91. On this phenomenon, see Carter, *Quiet Athenian,* pp. 99–130; Hansen, *Athenian Democracy,* pp. 216–18, quoting Dem. 4.47; id., *Eisangelia,* esp. pp. 58–65; and chapter 6, pp. 145–47.

92. See Plato's *Seventh Letter.*

93. Admittedly the word *career* is anachronistic, since these individuals were usually amateurs; that is, neither political rhetors nor *strategoi* could earn enough (legally) to support themselves. On the other hand, many wealthy American politicians also seek office and political "careers" for reasons other than remuneration, and thus the word is not completely inappropriate. For the trend separating rhetors from *strategoi,* see Arist. *Pol.* 1305a V.5.6–7; Plut. *Phoc.* 7; Rhodes, *CAH* V², p. 573; and Hansen, *Athenian Democracy,* pp. 268–71. On mercenaries and professional generals in the fourth century, see Pritchett, *Greek State at War,* 2: 59–116.

94. As we shall see in chapter 6, fourth-century Athenian generals were compelled to spend a certain percentage of their time acquiring funding from non-Athenian sources.

95. Phocion, supposedly a student of Plato's as a young man (Plut. *Phoc.* 4), was apparently one of the few leaders from the mid to late fourth century to serve as both general and rhetor. He was notoriously unsuccessful before the assembly, but the Athenians repeatedly elected him to the position of general (see esp. ibid., 7–9). Phocion was ultimately tried and executed by the Athenians in 318, during a period of restored democracy (ibid., 34–37).

96. E.g., Dem. 3.18–22, 32; 8.34.

4. FOREIGN POLICY I: DEMOCRACY IMPERIAL

1. By "Athenian nationalism" I mean nothing more than a belief in Athenian superiority, the desire to foster Athenian power and status (even at the expense of other Greeks), and a willingness to embrace such aspirations openly in the culture. I therefore do not seek to connect the term either with its use to describe emerging nation-states in modern Europe or with the Greek term *ethnos* ("nation"), on which, see chapter 1, n. 1.

2. See also Samons, "Democracy, Empire and the Search for the Athenian Character," pp. 145–47, where other similarities between Peisistratid and democratic Athenian foreign policy are noted. For the Peisistratids' attempts to patronize Delos and Ionian Greeks, a policy later adopted by democratic Athens, see Hdt. 1.64 and Thuc. 3.104.

3. For a useful introduction to the subject, see Andrewes, *Greek Tyrants.*

4. Hdt. 1.64; *Ath. Pol.* 15.2–4.

5. *Ath. Pol.* 15.2, with Rhodes, *Commentary,* pp. 207–8; and Hdt. 1.64.1.

6. I refer to the family of Cimon and Miltiades as "Cimonids" since their precise connection with the putative Athenian clan (*genos*) called the Philaids is disputed

(following Wade-Gery, *Essays in Greek History*, p. 164, with n. 3; cf. R. Thomas, *Oral Tradition and Written Record in Classical Athens* [Cambridge, 1989], p. 161, n. 12) and largely irrelevant to this study. Note that the Peisistratids' support of the Cimonids in the Chersonese is admitted by Herodotus at 6.39, even as he tries to explain it away. For the Peisistratids and Cimonids, see also Hdt. 4.137, 6.34–41; Plato *Hipparch.* 228b; Wade-Gery, *Essays in Greek History*, pp. 155–70, esp. 165–67 (whose conclusions I do not entirely share), and Rhodes, *Commentary*, p. 217. For the Peisistratids' connection with Sigeum (in the Hellespont region, where the Cimonids also established themselves), see Hdt. 5.65.3, 91.1, 94.1, and Thuc. 6.59.4. For earlier Athenian interests in Sigeum, see Hdt. 5.94.2–95, and Str. 599–600, 13.1.38–39, with Andrewes, *CAH* III. 3², pp. 373–74.

7. Hdt. 6.137–140; cf. 6.41, 104, with Rhodes, *Commentary*, p. 686, and Wade-Gery, *Essays in Greek History*, p. 163 (who dates the seizure of Lemnos and Imbros to ca. 499–498).

8. For the accusation ca. 493, see Hdt. 6.41, 104; Wade-Gery, *Essays in Greek History*, p. 165.

9. See Hdt. 6.132–36.

10. Thuc. 1.98; Plut. *Cim.* 8.

11. About the same time that they seized Scyros, the Athenians moved against Carystus, a city on the southern end of Euboea that also fell along a potential Athenian route to the Hellespont (Thuc. 1.98; Hdt. 9.105, with Hornblower, *Commentary*, 1:150–51, and Rhodes, *CAH* V², p. 42). On Athens and Lemnos, Imbros, and Scyros, see Rhodes, *Commentary*, pp. 686–87, and chapter 6, n. 71.

12. See Plut. *Cim.* 7–8; Thuc. 1.100–101.

13. The role of the Cimonid family in the sixth and fifth centuries points to one of the rarely appreciated facets of Athenian democratic history. The families that most dominated Athenian politics in the fifth century—the Cimonids, Alcmeonids, and Kerykes (Callias-Hipponicus) family—were precisely those families most closely connected with the Peisistratid tyrants in the sixth. Thucydides informs us that the tyrants were always careful to have "one of their own" in office (6.54.6), and the connections between the Peisistratids and these families are confirmed by the names of the first four eponymous archons after Peisistratus's death and the term of the (presumably) previously nominated Onetorides in 527/6: the tyrant's own son Hippias (526/5), the Alcmeonid Cleisthenes (525/4), the Cimonid Miltiades (524/3), and a certain Calliades (523/2), whom one is tempted to connect with the Kerykes (see P. J. Bicknell, *Studies in Greek Politics and Genealogy* [Wiesbaden, 1972], p. 71 n. 64, with Andoc. 1.127), although the name was common. (Hippias also married the daughter of an otherwise unknown Callias son of Hyperochides: Thuc. 6.55.1.) Calliades was followed by Hippias's son Peisistratus (522/1). For connections between the Kerykes and Alcmeonids, see also Bicknell, *Studies,* pp. 70–71; for the Cimonids and Alcmeonids, see ibid., pp. 89–95. The Alcmeonid Cleisthenes' revolution ca. 507 apparently was to a significant degree a reaction *against* aristocratic government headed by fam-

ilies that had *opposed* the tyrants, since early *demokratia* relied heavily on the old coalition supporting the Peisistratids. After Marathon reemphasized/exposed the Peisistratid/Alcmeonid/Persian connection (Hdt. 6.115, 121–24), and as the Athenian myth of the tyrannicides grew and oligarchic (i.e., antidemocratic) government became equated with "tyranny," families previously connected closely with the Peisistratids found it necessary to construct "defenses" designed to distance themselves from their sixth-century political heritage. The defenses of the Cimonidae/Philaidae (Hdt. 6.34–41, 103–4), Alcmeonidae (6.121–31), and Kerykes (6.121–22) clearly colored Herodotus's account of the period. Each family's defense apparently displayed a similar form: "We really weren't close to the tyrants (despite what you may have heard). Don't you know that we . . . [supply ostensibly antityrannical act here]." Herodotus was inclined to take these accounts, undoubtedly presented to him by members or associates of the greatest families in contemporary Athens, at face value, although even he expressed some concern about the Alcmeonids' *apologia* regarding the traitorous shield signal given to the Persians/Peisistratids after the battle of Marathon (6.115–116, 121–24). On the Cimonid defense, cf. Wade-Gery, *Essays in Greek History,* pp. 163–67, and Thomas, *Oral Tradition,* pp. 168–69, although neither explores the full implications of the evidence. In fact, the Cimonids needed a defense against charges of supporting tyranny *and* Persia just as much as (if not more than) the Alcmeonids.

14. Hdt. 4.137–38, 6.41, which also contains the Cimonid family's defense of their involvement (i.e., Miltiades' alleged unsuccessful proposal to sabotage the Persian Great King Darius's expedition).

15. As we have seen, post–Persian War tradition attempted to cleanse the Cimonid family's reputation, but Darius's gracious treatment of Cimon's half-brother Metiochus (Hdt. 6.41) demonstrates that the Persian king considered the family loyal allies and not traitors to his cause: see also Samons, *Empire of the Owl,* p. 332, n. 138.

16. Hdt. 5.73, with Fornara and Samons, *Athens from Cleisthenes to Pericles,* pp. 19–22. Cleisthenes' apparent fall from grace and later suspicions of Alcmeonid cooperation with the Persians may help explain why Cleisthenes himself—the founder of *demokratia*—makes so little impact on our sources.

17. Again, this interest in Euboea was foreshadowed by the Peisistratids, who used the city of Eretria as a base for their return to Attica in 546: Hdt. 1.61–62; *Ath. Pol.* 15.2.

18. Hdt. 5.78; cf. 5.66, 91.

19. It would not be until at least the mid fifth century that a less aggressive strand in Athenian foreign policy would (re?)emerge. Even then, opposition to Athenian expansion was weak and probably stemmed from some conservatives' recognition that the empire had become a tool for Pericles' radicalization of the democracy and that it threatened relations with Sparta, rather than from a belief that the Athenians were acting in an unjust fashion in attempting to rule other Greeks.

20. Hdt. 5.97 with 5.49–51.

21. Probably in 498: Hdt. 5.99–103.

22. For this Peisistratid relative (Hipparchus son of Charmus), see *Ath. Pol.* 22.4, with Rhodes, *Commentary,* pp. 271–72, who is agnostic on the possible political significance of his archonship in 496/5.

23. Hdt. 5.99–6.102.

24. Hdt. 6.102–6. The Spartans are sometimes portrayed as reluctant or unwilling defenders of Greece beyond the Peloponnese, who cynically used religious obligations as an excuse to remain at home (see J. B. Bury and Russell Meiggs, *A History of Greece to the Death of Alexander the Great,* 4th ed. [New York, 1975], pp. 158, 170, 172, 180). But this view relies on an anti-Spartan construction retrospectively placed on the actual events (cf. Hdt. 9.6–11), which consistently show the Spartans (and Athenians) leading the resistance to Persia. Moreover, the fifth-century Spartans were scrupulous about religious matters, allowing themselves to be pummeled with missiles at Plataea until they received the gods' sanction (through acceptable sacrifices) to attack the Persians (Hdt. 9.61–62; cf. 9.7, 6.106). For a similar case (involving a group of Hellenes from various states), see Xen. *Anab.* 6.4.12–5.3; cf. id., *Hell.* 3.1.17–19.

25. Hdt. 6.107–17; for the *Marathonomachai,* see Ar. *Ach.* 181, *Clouds* 986, and Pl. *Menex.* 240a–241c. See also Peter Krentz, "Fighting by the Rules: The Introduction of the Hoplite Agôn," *Hesperia* 71 (2002): 36.

26. See, e.g., Thuc. 1.18, 73; Ar. *Knights* 781–85; Isoc. *Paneg.* 86–87, 91; Lysias 2.23–24.

27. For this assault on Paros and Miltiades' involvement, see Hdt. 6.132–36, with Samons, *Empire of the Owl,* p. 86 n. 8.

28. *Ath. Pol.* 22, with Rhodes, *Commentary,* pp. 274–77.

29. Perhaps the loss of Miltiades, Callimachus, Xanthippus, Megacles (and others) in the 480s may help explain Themistocles' rise to prominence and the success of his proposal to devote the silver from the Laurium mines to building warships.

30. Hdt. 7.144 and *Ath. Pol.* 22.7, with Samons, *Empire of the Owl,* pp. 60–62 and chapter 3, pp. 73–75.

31. On the fleet, see, e.g., Hdt. 8.1–2 (Artemisium) and 8.82–86 (Salamis), with Hignett, *Xerxes' Invasion of Greece,* pp. 155–57.

32. Hdt. 9.1–85, with Hignett, *Xerxes' Invasion of Greece,* pp. 289–344.

33. Hdt. 9.90–106, 114, with Hignett, *Xerxes' Invasion of Greece,* pp. 247–61.

34. Hdt. 9.114, Thuc. 1.89.

35. Hdt. 8.3; cf. Thuc. 1.94–95, with Fornara and Samons, *Athens from Cleisthenes to Pericles,* pp. 84–85.

36. Thuc. 1.96, with Samons, *Empire of the Owl,* pp. 84–91. The term *proschema,* which I translate in this passage as "ostensible purpose," comes very close to "pretext." (For discussion of the word's meaning here, see Hornblower, *Commentary,* 1: 144.)

37. Ibid., and Rhodes, *CAH* V², pp. 34–38.

38. Thuc. 1.98–99; Hdt. 7.107; Plut. *Cim.* 7–8; with Meiggs, *Athenian Empire,* pp. 68–70; cf. Fornara and Samons, *Athens from Cleisthenes to Pericles,* pp. 76–87.

39. Hdt. 6.72, with Rhodes, *CAH* V², p. 35.

40. For other views on the formation of the Delian League, see N. D. Robertson, "The True Nature of the Delian League, 478–61 B.C." *AJAH* 5 (1980): 64–96, 110–33, and Samons, *Empire of the Owl,* pp. 84–87 (with references).

41. See n. 11 above.

42. For Naxos's (surprisingly low) tribute payments and speculation that the Naxians may have been forced to make payments to support the Athenian navy, see Samons, *Empire of the Owl,* pp. 103–4.

43. Thuc. 1.98, with Fornara and Samons, *Athens from Cleisthenes to Pericles,* pp. 79–85.

44. Thuc. 1.100–101.

45. See also Samons, *Empire of the Owl,* pp. 60–62, 202–4; for the mines of Siphnos (the only others known to have existed in the Aegean), see Hdt. 3.57. Siphnos was also a member of the Delian League; the island appears in the Athenian tribute quota lists from at least 450/49 (*IG* i³ 263, col. IV.20).

46. Thuc. 1.100, Plut. *Cim.* 12–13.

47. I do not doubt that at least a few Greeks contemplated such an attack on the Persian empire. The idea was, of course, later carried out not only by Alexander, but also by the Greek forces with Xenophon on the journey "up country" (see his *Anabasis)* in support of the Persian Cyrus against his brother, Artaxerxes, in 401.

48. See Thuc. 8.68; Lysias 2.55; Isoc. 4.106 (cf. id., 12.56); Dem. 9.23 and 13.26.

49. Thuc. 1.102, with Plut. *Cim.* 4, 14, 16–17.

50. Thuc. 1.112; Plut. *Cim.* 18–19. We have already noted (pp. 102–7) the Cimonid family's ambiguous relations with Persia. Cimon's feelings toward the Persians may have reflected a need to continue the rehabilitation of the family's reputation begun by his father at Marathon.

51. See Plut. *Cim.* 14, *Per.* 10; *Ath. Pol.* 27.1; cf. Fornara and Samons, *Athens from Cleisthenes to Pericles,* pp. 158–59, and Rhodes, *CAH* V², p. 73, who posits that Cimon may have been tried at his *euthynai* before the Areopagus Council. Pericles' restrained prosecution here may suggest that he did not yet wish to cross the popular Cimon: cf. Sealey, "The Entry of Pericles into History," *Hermes* 84 (1956): 237–38.

52. For the political reforms, see chapter 1, n. 55.

53. For the likely order of events, see chapter 2, n. 47.

54. Thuc. 1.102–115.1.

55. Ephialtes' murder: *Ath. Pol.* 25.4, Plut. *Per.* 10; plot to betray Athens: Thuc. 1.107; cf. Rhodes, *CAH* V², pp. 73–75.

56. Pericles and Aeschylus had a relationship stretching back to 473/2, when Pericles produced the playwright's *Persians* (see Podlecki, *Perikles,* pp. 11–16). Aeschylus's *Eumenides* may have suggested that the curse on Pericles' mother's family (the Alcmeonids) should be treated as a dead letter by the Athenians: Samons, *CJ* 94 (1998/99): 221–33.

57. Cf. Rhodes, *CAH* V², p. 75.

58. In fact, some sources later alleged that Cimon had appeared at Tanagra in central Greece ca. 458 and tried to join the Athenian phalanx, massed for battle against Sparta. This story most probably was invented to exemplify Cimon's unwillingness to take the Spartan side against his homeland, despite his friendly relations with Sparta and the fact that his fellow Athenians had ostracized him and rejected his foreign policy: see Plut. *Cim.* 17–18 and *Per.* 10 (both of which suggest the apologetic origins of the tale, as all of Cimon's friends are alleged to have died in the battle against Sparta), and cf. Meiggs, *Athenian Empire*, p. 423.

59. Thuc. 1.104, 109–10.

60. On the magnitude of this disaster, see esp. Isoc. 8.86, with Meiggs, *Athenian Empire*, pp. 105–6, and Rhodes, *CAH* V², pp. 52–53. Some have held that the 250 ships that Thucydides reports had been dispatched to Egypt cannot all have been destroyed, despite the fact that the historian does not relate that any had withdrawn before the disaster: see Hornblower, *Commentary*, 1: 176–77, and Gomme, *Commentary*, 1: 322. We certainly do not know what percentage of the more than 40,000 crewmen (not all, of course, Athenian) of the fleet failed to return home, but it can hardly have been fewer than several thousand and may have been many thousands more.

61. For Cimon's return, see Thuc. 1.112; Plut. *Cim.* 17–18.1; Theopompus, *FGrHist* 115 F88 = Fornara 76; and Rhodes, *CAH* V², p. 75; cf. Hornblower, *Commentary*, 1: 168; Meiggs, *Athenian Empire*, p. 111, who tentatively places the recall in 452; and Badian, *From Plataea to Potidaea*, pp. 18–19, who propounds the theory that Cimon was allowed to return early but could not exercise his political rights (i.e., *atimia* was imposed on him).

62. How much of this was explicit in the treaty is unknown: Thuc. 1.112 with 115.1; Diod. 11.86.1; Plut. *Cim.* 18, *Per.* 10; with Lewis, *CAH* V², p. 120.

63. Thuc. 1.112; Diod. 12.3–4; Aristodemos *FGrHist* 104 F13.1–2; Plut. *Cim.* 19 = Phanodemos *FGrHist* 325 F23.

64. *Ath. Pol.* 26.4.

65. See also chapter 2, pp. 59–60. On Cimon and Pericles' possible relations in the late 450s, see esp. Plut. *Cim.* 17 and *Per.* 10; for interpretation, see W. R. Connor, *The New Politicians of Fifth-Century Athens* (Princeton, N.J., 1971), pp. 58–64, and Bicknell, *Studies*, p. 94.

66. Pericles' first wife had either been married to Hipponicus son of Callias (Plut. *Per.* 24.8) or married Hipponicus after her divorce from Pericles. What this implies about relations between the two families is unclear (see Fornara and Samons, *Athens from Cleisthenes to Pericles*, p. 162). Callias the ambassador was also Cimon's brother-in-law. On these family relations, see Sealey, "The Entry of Pericles into History"; Bicknell, *Studies*, esp. pp. 71, 77–83, 93–94; Podlecki, *Perikles and His Circle*, p. 110; and n. 13 above.

67. The scholarship on the Peace of Callias is vast. The important evidence is collected and translated at Fornara 95. For the currently orthodox view, positing a treaty

between Athens and the Great King Artaxerxes in 449 (late 450/49), see Lewis, *CAH* V², pp. 121–27. For other recent treatments of the peace, see Samons, "Kimon, Kallias and Peace with Persia," arguing for one treaty arranged in 449, against Badian, *From Plataea to Potidaea,* pp. 1–72, who maintains that there were several treaties negotiated by Callias. Meiggs, *Athenian Empire,* pp. 129–51, supports the conventional view of a treaty ca. 450–449, against Stockton, "Peace of Callias," who argues against the authenticity of any such treaty. I continue to believe that Callias negotiated an arrangement with the Persians ca. 449 (cf. Hdt. 7.151), but lean increasingly toward the view that no *formal* treaty was signed by the Great King or ratified by the Athenian assembly, as I cannot see how either party would have gained from such an open and official/codified termination of hostilities. For the Persian king, such a treaty was tantamount to an admission of failure to expand the empire in the face of Greek opposition; for the Athenians, the agreement would have signaled the end of their ability to hold out the Persian threat as a justification for their continued collection of tribute from the allies. An informal arrangement would have been far more advantageous to both sides and would help explain why no source mentions the alleged peace until after the Spartans made their own even more ignominious arrangement with Persia in 387/6, and why the terms of the fifth-century "treaty" given in the sources seem so contradictory. For a similar view, see Holladay, "Détente of Kallias?"

68. On this period, see esp. Meiggs, *Athenian Empire,* pp. 152–74, Lewis, *CAH* V², pp. 121–33; and Rhodes, *CAH* V², pp. 54–61 (each relying in part on some questionable evidence: cf. Rhodes, p. 53 nn. 63, 65). For an example of Athenian legislation governing revolted allies, see the Athenian regulations for Chalcis (*IG* i³ 40 = Fornara 103, included in Samons, ed., *Athenian Democracy and Imperialism,* pp. 131–34). For the debate over the date of some of the documents conventionally attributed to this period, see chapter 1, n. 83.

69. For a translated selection of the relevant decrees, see Samons, ed., *Athenian Democracy and Imperialism,* pp. 120–34. Almost all of the most important decrees of the fifth century and many other relevant sources are collected and translated in Fornara; see esp. his numbers 68, 71, 92, 94–95, 97–100, and 102–3.

70. Thuc. 1.115.1; for discussions of the terms of this treaty, see Lewis, *CAH* V², pp. 136–37; Badian, *From Plataea to Potidaea,* pp. 137–45; G. E. M. de Ste. Croix, *The Origins of the Peloponnesian War* (London, 1972), pp. 293–94; and Hornblower, *Commentary,* 1: 227–28.

71. On the war, see Thuc. 1.115–17, with Lewis, *CAH* V², pp. 143–45, who speculates that the Athenians may have justified their intervention on the grounds that wars between the members of the league violated their oaths (p. 143; cf. Thuc. 6.76.3). Of course, such oaths could provide no justification for Athens's partisan support of Miletus and the Samian democrats. (Plut. *Per.* 25.1 reports that the Athenians' initial involvement in this conflict came when Athens ordered the Samians—who were winning the war—to end hostilities and submit to Athenian arbitration.)

72. Plut. *Per.* 24; cf. Ar. *Ach.* 513–39 (where Aspasia is given a minor role in the

outbreak of the Peloponnesian War); for Pericles and Aspasia, see Fornara and Samons, *Athens from Cleisthenes to Pericles,* pp. 163–65; Podlecki, *Perikles and His Circle,* pp. 109–17; and conclusion, n. 45.

73. Thuc. 1.117; Androtion *FGrHist* 324 F38 = Fornara 110; and Fornara, *Athenian Board of Generals,* pp. 48–50. Few scholars have identified this Thucydides with the historian, although the possibility cannot be excluded on strictly chronological grounds. The birthdate of the historian is only known to have been before 454, and it could have been significantly earlier: see C. W. Fornara, "Thucydides' Birth Date," in R. M. Rosen and J. Farrell, eds., *Nomodeiktes: Greek Studies in Honor of Martin Ostwald* (Ann Arbor, Mich., 1993), pp. 71–80. In any case, the name was popular among the extended relations of Cimon, and thus (along with Sophocles' presence) suggests the participation of political moderates or conservatives in the actions against Samos. (Of course, generals elected for a given year would have no alternative but to follow the demos's orders.)

74. See Thuc. 1.117, Plut. *Per.* 26–28. It is unclear whether *demokratia* was reimposed, but this seems most likely (Meiggs, *Athenian Empire,* pp. 193–94; cf. Lewis, *CAH* V², p. 144). For the Samian war indemnity and Athenian expenditures, see *IG* i³ 363 = ML 55 = Fornara 113, with Samons, *Empire of the Owl,* pp. 43–50.

75. For a possibly related story of Athenian (and Samian) branding of prisoners, see Plut. *Per.* 26. The historian Duris of Samos (whose work is no longer extant) went so far as to suggest that Pericles ordered the public crucifixion of Samian captives (Plut. *Per.* 28), but even Plutarch doubts the authenticity of this tale. For Athenian execution of revolutionaries in similar circumstances, see Thuc. 3.50 (Mytilene).

76. For Athenian intervention after strife perhaps deriving from a faction within a city allying with Persia, see the regulations for Erythrae, a city in Asia Minor (*IG* i³ 14 = Fornara 71; also in Samons, ed., *Athenian Democracy and Imperialism,* pp. 122–23), with Meiggs, *Athenian Empire,* pp. 112–15.

77. See Plut. *Per.* 28, with Lewis, *CAH* V², p. 146.

78. Damon and Pheidias may have been exiled in 438/7 or shortly thereafter; for the attacks on Pheidias, Damon, and Anaxagoras, see *Ath. Pol.* 27.4; Fornara 116, with Fornara and Samons, *Athens from Cleisthenes to Pericles,* pp. 30 with n. 68, 160–61; cf. Podlecki, *Perikles and His Circle,* pp. 103–9 (Pheidias perhaps tried ca. 433 and acquitted), pp. 17–34 (skeptical on Damon's ostracism and Anaxagoras's trial); Wade-Gery, *Essays in Greek History,* pp. 259–60 (Anaxagoras's trial ca. 433); Rhodes, *Commentary,* pp. 340–41 (Damon ostracized ca. 440s?); R. W. Wallace, "Private Lives and Public Enemies: Freedom of Thought in Classical Athens," in Alan L. Boegehold and Adele C. Scafuro, eds., *Athenian Identity and Civic Ideology* (Baltimore, 1994), pp. 127–55 (Damon ostracized in mid 440s; skeptical on Anaxagoras's trial); and id., "Damon of Oa: A Music Theorist Ostracized?" (forthcoming). For recent attempts to cast doubt on these accounts, see Stone, *Trial of Socrates,* pp. 231–47, and Kurt A. Raaflaub, "The Alleged Ostracism of Damon," in Geoffrey W. Bakewell and

James P. Sickinger, eds., *Gestures: Essays in Ancient History, Literature, and Philosophy Presented to Alan L. Boegehold* (Oxford, 2003), pp. 317–31.

5. FOREIGN POLICY II: THE PELOPONNESIAN WAR

1. For the war's effects, see, e.g., Austin, *CAH* VI², pp. 527–35. Hanson, *Other Greeks*, esp. pp. 357–90, argues that the problems of fourth-century Hellas and the "crisis of the Greek city-state" arose largely from the inherent "structural" factors, admittedly aggravated by Athens's imperialism and democratic radicalization. Hanson's analysis, though penetrating, in my view places too little emphasis on the Athenians' own choices and actions after ca. 478/7. I am uncomfortable with any historical analysis that treats a major event or series of events (like the decay of the city-state) as "inevitable" (p. 353). See also at no. 5, below.

2. See Aristophanes' *Ecclesiazusae* and (especially) *Plutus*.

3. On the reproduction of tragedies, see Pickard-Cambridge, *Dramatic Festivals of Athens*, pp. 86, 99–100.

4. For a defense of fourth-century Athenian politics and public spirit, cf. Cawkwell, "The Crowning of Demosthenes," 163–64. Cawkwell rightly warns against moderns' too readily accepting Demosthenes' characterizations of Athenian morale. But one need only examine the events at issue to comprehend the real decline in the public character of the Athenian people.

5. See Rhodes, *CAH* VI², pp. 565–91.

6. See Hansen, *Athenian Democracy in the Age of Demosthenes*, pp. 268–71, and chapter 3, n. 93.

7. See esp. de Ste. Croix, *Origins of the Peloponnesian War*, largely blaming the Spartans; Donald Kagan, *The Outbreak of the Peloponnesian War* (Ithaca, N.Y., 1969), largely blaming the Corinthians and Periclean miscalculations; and Badian, *From Plataea to Potidaea*, pp. 125–62, arguing that Thucydides attempts to hide Athenian aggression that led to the war. For a review of the literature, see E. A. Meyer, "*The Outbreak of the Peloponnesian War* after Twenty-five Years," in C. D. Hamilton and Peter Krentz, eds., *Polis and Polemos: Essays on Politics, War, and History in Ancient Greece, in Honor of Donald Kagan* (Claremont, Calif., 1997), pp. 23–54.

8. Cf. Polybius 3.31, and José Ortega y Gasset, *Man and Crisis* (1933), trans. Mildred Adams (New York, 1958), esp. pp. 16–19, 119–23.

9. Only at end of his statement of subject matter (the "great deeds" of Greeks and barbarians) and purpose (that these deeds might not be forgotten) does Herodotus add that he also wishes to explain "*why they fought with one another*" (Hdt. 1.1, Introduction).

10. For the factors of "fear, honor, and self-interest," see esp. Thuc. 1.75–76 and (e.g.) 1.9. For Thucydides' emphasis on wealth and naval power, see L. Kallet, *Money, Expense, and Naval Power.*

11. In the area of scholarly technique, we should note Thucydides' anticipation

of archaeological methods and his recognition of their important but limited value; his critical use of ancient sources (like Homer); his anthropological and sociological analysis of Hellenic and barbarian custom; his use of linguistic evidence to draw conclusions about history; his quantitative technique, which allows him to draw tentative conclusions from "averages"; and his insistence that the study of war must include more than the battles won and lost, and should give attention to politics, natural disasters like plagues, and the moral effects of these factors. All this (and more) emerges from the first twenty-three sections of Thucydides' first book.

12. Of course, not all later readers found this style of historical presentation entirely satisfying. See, e.g., Miss Catherine Morland's complaints in Jane Austen's *Northanger Abbey* (1818), ch. 14, ed. A. H. Ehrenpreis (London, 1972), p. 123.

13. In the last group, I think especially of historians like Duris of Samos (whose work survives only in fragments) and Livy, who emphasized the pleasure or supposed moral lessons derived from human tragedy or reversals of fortune in historical events. On this school of "tragic historians," see C. W. Fornara, *Nature of History in Ancient Greece and Rome* (Berkeley, 1983), pp. 120–37. Of course, there were no strict divisions between these camps, as (for example) Livy's use of Polybius demonstrates.

14. For discussion, see Humphreys, *Anthropology and the Greeks* (London, 1978), who emphasizes that "anthropologists and Classical scholars collaborated or at least regarded each other's work with sympathetic interest from about the middle of the nineteenth century up to the First World War, recoiled in mutual suspicion during the inter-war period, and have been slowly returning to a sympathetic attitude since the Second World War" (p. 17). See also Euben, Wallach, and Ober, *Athenian Political Thought*, pp. 9–10. For the use of literary theory, see, e.g., Ober, *Mass and Elite*, and Kurke, *Coins, Bodies, Games, and Gold*.

15. For a good example, see Josiah Ober, *The Athenian Revolution* (Princeton, N.J., 1996), and Kurke, *Coins, Bodies, Games, and Gold*.

16. The quotations are taken from Ober, *Athenian Revolution*, pp. 3, 47. See also his *Political Dissent in Democratic Athens*, e.g., pp. 368–69.

17. See Kagan, *Outbreak of the Peloponnesian War*, and de Ste. Croix, *Origins of the Peloponnesian War*. See also Donald Kagan, *On the Origins of War and the Preservation of Peace* (New York, 1995), pp. 15–79.

18. The best historical works perform multiple tasks, including recording and explaining the past, commenting on the present, and (very loosely speaking) predicting the future. See Ortega y Gasset, *Man and Crisis*, esp. pp. 16–19, 176–79.

19. For this and other problems in the professional fields of classics and ancient history, see Victor Davis Hanson and John Heath, *Who Killed Homer? The Demise of Classical Education and the Recovery of Greek Wisdom* (New York, 1998), and "Who Killed Homer?" *Arion* 5.2 (1997): 108–54.

20. I have no quarrel with the principle that the accumulation of knowledge for its own sake is a "good." But surely data are not the same as knowledge, and surely there are subjects that may be allowed to remain below the horizon of serious scholarly inquiry.

21. Cf. Morris and Raaflaub, *Democracy 2500?* pp. 1–9, who seem to call for historians to engage in the argument over "competing teleologies," and thus not "to retreat from responsibility, leaving others to impose their own ideologies on the past" (p. 8).

22. Literary critics might ask themselves the same questions put here to historians. Is there any justification for an entire book on an author like Valerius Maximus or Silius Italicus? Why should anyone read it? Is it useful or beautiful? One of Dr. Johnson's remarks on criticism seems just as relevant to historians: "There is no great merit in telling how many plays have ghosts in them, and how this Ghost is better than that. You must shew how terrour is impressed on the human heart" (James Boswell, *The Life of Samuel Johnson,* ed. and abridged by Frank Brady [New York: New American Library, 1968], p. 206). So far from such a goal, much modern literary criticism engages in codifying a supersubjective reader's particular "response" to "the text" or in replacing the now discredited "author's intent" with a discussion of the text's "function." For a cogent rejection of this approach, see D. M. MacDowell, *Aristophanes and Athens: An Introduction to the Plays* (Oxford, 1995), p. 2.

23. For other acts of Athenian aggression in the 430s, see Lewis, *CAH* V^2, pp. 145–46, citing Athens's foundation of Amphipolis in the northern Aegean in 437/6 and a possible military expedition to the Black Sea led by Pericles (Plut. *Per.* 20.1–2).

24. See in general, J. B. Salmon, *Wealthy Corinth: A History of the City to 338 BC* (Oxford, 1984).

25. For example, Thucydides (1.13) dates a great naval battle between Corinth and Corcyra to as much as 260 years before the end of the Peloponnesian (or perhaps Archidamian?) War, i.e., ca. 664 (or 681) B.C.

26. Thuc. 1.31–43.

27. For the machinations here, see Thuc. 1.44–45, and Plut. *Per.* 29. Of course, it is also possible (as P. J. Rhodes has suggested to me) that Lacedaemonius opposed the alliance with Corcyra and that he and other opponents of the alliance managed to have one of themselves appointed to the expedition in order to influence its result (cf. Nicias's role in the Sicilian expedition); see also Rhodes, "Who Ran Democratic Athens?" in Pernille Flensted-Jensen et al., eds., *Polis and Politics: Studies in Ancient Greek History* (Copenhagen, 2000), p. 473.

28. Thuc. 1.56–67. The Aeginetans asserted (1.67.2) that their *autonomia* had been guaranteed by the peace of 446/5; for discussion of the possible autonomy clause in this treaty and the meaning of *autonomia,* see Hornblower, *Commentary,* 1: 109–10; Badian, *From Plataea to Potidaea,* pp. 137–42; and Martin Ostwald, *Autonomia: Its Genesis and Early History* (Atlanta, Ga., 1982).

29. Thuc. 1.87–88, 118–19, 125–27, 139, 145–56. For Thucydides' emphasis on the delay between the vote for war and the actual invasion (1.125), see Gomme, *Commentary,* 1: 420–21 (Crawley's translation is misleading here).

30. Thuc. 1.139–40.

31. Thuc. 1.140.1. The view propounded here is admittedly heterodox. The Spar-

tans are sometimes blamed for the outbreak of the Peloponnesian War because they opened direct hostilities by invading Attica and because they had refused to accept arbitration, as they apparently should have under one of the terms of the treaty of 446/5 (Thuc. 1.78.4, 140: see esp. de Ste. Croix, *Origins of the Peloponnesian War*, e.g., pp. 55–56, 65, 290; and cf. also Hornblower, *Commentary*, 1:227–28, and Badian, *From Plataea to Potidaea*, pp. 142–44), and because the Spartans later even condemned themselves for their refusal (see Thuc. 7.18, with de Ste. Croix, locc. cit.). But this self-condemnation, fair enough if we (like the religiously scrupulous Spartans) wish to judge the ultimate morality of a foreign policy based on the letter of a treaty, ignores the realities of the situation in 432. Simply put, the Spartans had nothing with which to bargain in any arbitration. They were involved in no questionable alliance with an Athenian ally or colony (as Athens was with Corinth's colonies Potidaea and Corcyra); they were not besieging one of their own allies while it was being assisted by the Athenians (as Athens was besieging Potidaea, assisted by Corinth), and they had no special laws preventing Athenians from using the harbors of the Peloponnesian League (as the Athenians did against the Megarians), only their ancient rules against frequent or extended foreign visitations to Sparta. (Pericles apparently attempted to cite this last as roughly equivalent to Athens's legislation against Megara, but the equation was certainly specious: see Thuc. 1.144, with Gomme, *Commentary*, 1:462.) In short, every matter in contention stemmed from Athenian actions against Spartan allies, and thus the only possible results of any "arbitration" would have been Spartan acceptance (and thus legitimation) of some part of the Athenians' aggressive policies. Sparta's decision to refuse arbitration is thus more than comprehensible, while its willingness to concede most of Athens's gains informally and without arbitration shows the Spartans' real desire to avoid this war. The Spartans clearly were willing, in fact, to ignore the Corinthians' complaints if the Athenians would only give up the decree against Megara, but the Spartans could not be forced into any formal recognition of Athens's claims against Peloponnesian interests. In other words, the Spartans needed some concession from Athens to take back to their Peloponnesian allies, both as a demonstration that Sparta had not completely abandoned them to Athenian dominance and as an excuse to avoid war. "Throw us a bone," the Spartans almost seem to be saying to the Athenians.

32. See Thuc. 1.66–67.

33. For discussion of the literature, see Hornblower, *Commentary*, 1:64–66; on *aitiai* and *diaphorai*, see de Ste. Croix, *Origins of the Peloponnesian War*, pp. 52–58, 60–63, Fornara, *Nature of History*, pp. 79–81, and Fornara and Samons, *Athens from Cleisthenes to Pericles*, pp. 141–43.

34. De Ste. Croix, *Origins of the Peloponnesian War*, esp. pp. 52–58, clearly saw the Spartans' need for a pretext for the war—that is, a "cause" that they could cite before Athens, other Greeks, the gods, and even themselves. But he does not appreciate the great reluctance with which Sparta came to this conclusion or the fact that, even after they had reached this point, the Spartans continued to look for a way out

of their predicament. More important, de Ste. Croix does not adequately analyze Athens's inability to state Thucydides' "truest cause" of the war openly. Nothing the Athenians did between 435 and 432 would have been characterized openly by them as an attempt merely to increase their power and greatness (things that might justifiably have been seen as a reason for war by the Spartans). Both sides were forced to claim that the other had acted unreasonably, while both perfectly well understood each other's reasons.

35. For democracy's role in the war's length, see pp. 135–42.

36. Thuc. 1.44; for the fickle demos (or *ochlos, homilos;* "crowd," "mob"), see 8.1, with 2.65, 4.28, 6.63.

37. This, for Thucydides, was the mark of a true leader. See chapter 2, pp. 62–64.

38. For Aristophanes' lampoons of the war's causes, see *Acharnians* 513–39, with schol. on 532, and *Peace* 605–6, with schol. (= Fornara 116A, 123B).

39. Thuc. 5.26. In this passage Thucydides comments that the length of the war provided at least one case in which faith in prophecy was justified, because the oracles had continually foretold a war that would last "thrice nine years."

40. In his famous summary of Pericles' career (2.65), Thucydides implies that had the Athenians continued Pericles' strategy of avoiding any additional offensive operations during the war, the Spartans could have been defeated. Some modern scholars have expressed reservations about Pericles' strategy: see, e.g., Kagan, *Outbreak of the Peloponnesian War*, pp. 337–42; cf. D. W. Knight, "Thucydides and the War Strategy of Perikles," *Mnemosyne* 23 (1970): 150–61, and Ober, *Athenian Revolution*, pp. 72–85, who argues that Thucydides "provides his reader with evidence that will support interpretations to which he does not subscribe and which he cannot advocate" (73), and who attempts to reconstruct a putative Periclean strategy for the protection of rural Attica with cavalry—a strategy which Pericles supposedly devised to convince the Athenians to abandon their farms and move into the city during the Spartans' invasion. Strangely, in terms of Ober's theory, Pericles took three hundred cavalrymen with him on a naval raid in 430 when the Spartans were ravaging Attica (2.56.1); apparently, he must have forgotten or ignored his own strategy. Ober sees this as a problem for his theory but is undiscouraged. In any case, the simple fact that the Athenians/Pericles used cavalry to harass the Spartan invaders and thereby limit the damage they could do in Attica does not contradict Pericles' strategy (as expressed in Thucydides) of avoiding pitched battle with the Spartans (1.143; 2.13, 65). For a more optimistic view of Pericles' strategy, see de Ste. Croix, *Origins of the Peloponnesian War*, pp. 208–10.

41. Accusations of bribery were made: see Ar. *Acharnians* 6, with schol. (= Fornara 131B). On Cleon, see also Thuc. 2.65, 3.36–40, 4.21–22, 122, 5.2–16, and Ar. *Knights*, where Paphlagon is a thinly veiled Cleon. Hornblower, *Commentary*, 1: 340–41, 346–47, minimizes the supposed differences between Pericles and his successors, including Cleon, and discusses the scholarship.

42. Financial policy: Samons, *Empire of the Owl,* pp. 171–211, and Meiggs and Lewis, *Selection of Greek Historical Inscriptions,* pp. 184–201; executions: Thuc. 4.122 with 5.32 (Scione); cf. 3.36–50 (Mytilene); Spartan offers of peace refused: Thuc. 4.17–22.

43. Thuc. 8.97.

44. Thuc. 5.17–19.

45. Thuc. 5.27–75; for the battle of Mantinea, see esp. J. F. Lazenby, *The Spartan Army* (Warminster, 1985), pp. 125–34. For the period as a whole, see Kagan, *The Peace of Nicias and the Sicilian Expedition.*

46. Thuc. 5.84–116.

47. On Melos's support of Sparta, see Fornara 132, with W. T. Loomis, *The Spartan War Fund* (Stuttgart, 1992).

48. Thuc. 5.104–5 (trans. R. Crawley, adapted). In the Melian Dialogue, Thucydides presents us with the opposite side of the coin shown in the Mytilenian Debate (3.37–49). There we are allowed to see the debate occuring within Athens about the appropriate (that is, the most advantageous) treatment of revolted Athenian allies like Mytilene (or, we may assume, of recalcitrant states like Melos). In the Melian Dialogue, Thucydides presents us with Athenian foreign policy *as it would have appeared to those enduring it.* There is no debate within the Athenian camp; no dissenting opinions are expressed. Indeed, "the Athenians" are simply that, a completely unified group without dissenting voice and with no individual speaker named. Likewise "the Melians" are presented as a faceless mass (just as the Athenian policy treated them)—simply one more city for the Athenians to exploit in their own interests. From this perspective, the Melian Dialogue presents a picture of the historical situation perhaps as illustrative as a verbatim account of the speeches delivered. See also, Samons, "Democracy, Empire, and the Search," p. 135.

49. Xen. *Hell.* 2.2.3; Isoc. *Paneg.* 4.100, 109–10; cf. Roberts, *Athens on Trial,* p. 257. Melos became the most infamous example of Athenian brutality, but the Athenians carried out similar acts elsewhere: see Thucydides 1.114 (Histiaeans expelled from their lands/homes), 2.27 (Aeginetans expelled), 3.50 (1,000+ Mytilenians executed, their lands seized), 5.3 (enslavement of wives and children of Toroneans), 5.32 (execution of all males in Scione, enslavement of women and children). For similar actions by the Spartans, see Thuc. 3.68 (execution of Plataeans, enslavement of women), 5.83 (slaughter of all captured men of Hysiae). Tellingly, many Athenians themselves apparently thought little of the Melians' fate. It makes only a small impression on our sources outside Thucydides, and Aristophanes mentions Melos in passing without the faintest hint that the audience might be sensitive about their treatment of the island (*Birds* 186, with Andrewes and Gomme, *Commentary,* 4:187, 190–91).

50. Roberts, *Athens on Trial,* p. 30 (but cf. ibid., p. 289, for her recognition of modern scholarship's treatment of the Spartans as "other"). At least Roberts's characterization echoes that of real (fourth-century) Greek sources. Some scholars have

gone much further. Simon Hornblower, for example, refers to the "totalitarian monster" Sparta supposedly became (even as he notes the Spartans' anticipation of later Athenian "democratic" practices): "Creation and Development of Democratic Institutions in Ancient Greece," in John Dunn, ed., *Democracy: The Unfinished Journey 508 B.C. to A.D. 1993* (Oxford, 1992), p. 1. (The title of Dunn's work nicely encapsulates the teleological view of democracy that distorts so many recent treatments of the phenomenon.) From all we can tell, most classical Greeks would hardly have been ready to endorse the idea that the Spartans were either "other" or "monsters."

51. See, e.g., Plato *Laws* 666e (referring to Crete and Sparta), and Xenophon, *Constitution of the Spartans* 14. Scholars themselves often forget this fact, and treat sixth- or fifth-century Spartans as if they had already attempted to conquer or dominate central Greece, the Aegean islands, or Anatolia.

52. E.g., Thuc. 1.68–71, 118, 8.96. See also the Athenians' own estimation of the Spartans' foreign policy in the Melian Dialogue (Thuc. 5.105).

53. The source for events listed in Table 1 is Thuc. 1.98–117 except where indicated; see also Diodorus 11.38–12.37. The precise dates of many of these events are disputed. Question marks in the table indicate events of particularly problematic absolute or relative dates. For discussion and analysis of the evidence, see especially Rhodes, *CAH* V², pp. 34–61; Lewis, ibid., pp. 111–46; Meiggs, *Athenian Empire;* Badian, *From Plataea to Potidaea;* Fornara and Samons, *Athens from Cleisthenes to Pericles;* and Pritchett, *Thucydides' Pentekontaetia.* I have omitted the Athenians' installation of garrisons and their creation of colonies and cleruchies (attested in inscriptions and elsewhere) when we have no positive indication of military action. Nevertheless, some of these events certainly involved Athenian troops/naval forces and an implied threat of force if not its actual application. The fleet and (at least implied) force also were sometimes used in the collection of tribute, which Athens's allies/subjects paid on a yearly basis. Also omitted from the table are any (yearly?) secret Spartan missions into Messenia (known as the *krypteia*) to assassinate helots deemed dangerous. It should also be noted that Athenian military actions often resulted in the enslavement and sale of captives (e.g., Thuc. 6.62).

54. See Thuc. 6.6–26.

55. Thuc. 6.1–5 with 6.10–11.

56. Thuc. 6.15–24. For Alcibiades' speech, see also chapter 3, p. 89.

57. Thuc. 6.24, with chapter 3, p. 90.

58. Thuc. 7.84–87 (with omitted portions indicated); trans. Crawley, adapted.

59. See Samons, *Empire of the Owl,* pp. 254–55, and chapter 3, pp. 90–94.

60. Pl. *Ap.* 32a–c.

61. See Xen. *Hell.* 1.6.35, 7.1–35; Diod. 13.101–103.2, with A. Andrewes, "The Arginousai Trial," *Phoenix* 28 (1974): 112–22, who concludes, "We cannot acquit the Athenian people, only with [the historian] Grote remember the long strain they had undergone, but we might acquit Theramenes of premeditated crime" (122). (Theramenes had leveled the accusations that resulted in the generals' execution.) As

the son of Pericles' Milesian consort Aspasia, Pericles II was ineligible for citizenship under a law proposed by his father in 451/0 (see chapter 2, p. 60).

62. Xen. *Hell.* 1.7.12–15, 34–35, trans. Warner (adapted). Diodorus, 13.103.1–2, relates that Callixenus himself was indicted, tried, and convicted without being allowed to defend himself.

63. See chapter 6, pp. 145–47.

64. It is possible that Socrates himself actually served as the presiding member *(epistates)* of the ruling committee *(prytaneis)* in the assembly on this day, as Xen. *Mem.* 1.1.18, 4.4.2, explicitly reports. See also Pl. *Grg.* 473e–474a, with George Cawkwell's note in the Penguin edition of Xenophon, *A History of My Times [Hellenika]* (London, 1979), pp. 88–89.

65. For events in Athens during the last years of the war, see chapter 3, pp. 91–95.

66. Sparta's allies (Thebans) propose the destruction of Athens: Xen. *Hell.* 2.2.19, with 3.5.8 (where the Thebans try to place the blame for the proposal on one man, their representative at the allied council).

67. Socrates, of course, published nothing, and we rely on accounts by his followers (esp. Plato and Xenophon) for our knowledge of him.

68. We must not forget the fathers and grandfathers of fourth-century Athenians like Demosthenes: such men also would have been lost to us had the Spartans acceded to their allies' wishes.

69. For the Athenians' fear that Sparta would impose on them what they themselves had done to other poleis (Melos, Histiaea, Scione, Torone, Aegina), i.e., either execution, enslavement, or expulsion from their homes, see Xen. *Hell.* 2.2.3, 10, with n. 49, above.

6. NATIONAL DEFENSE: DEMOCRACY DEFEATED

1. On the mines in the fourth century, see Xen. *Vect.* 4 (where he puts forward a plan to increase their output); cf. H. Montgomery, "Silver, Coins and the Wealth of a City–State," *Opuscula Atheniensia* 15 (1984): 123–33, esp. 128–31; J. E. Jones, "The Laurion Silver Mines: A Review of Recent Researches and Results," *Greece and Rome* 29 (1982): 169–83; and C. E. Conophagos, *Le Laurium antique et la technique grecque de la production de l'argent* (Athens, 1980).

2. Sealey, *Demosthenes,* p. 119. A Cimon did serve on one of the embassies to Philip of Macedon in 346 (Aeschin. 2.21).

3. On this phenomenon, see Connor, *New Politicians of Fifth-Century Athens.*

4. Of course, Athenians were not Roman aristocrats, and they did not exhibit the thoroughgoing obsession with ancestry evident in the Roman Republic. Nevertheless, an Athenian's lineage and family relations clearly played a role in his ability to wield political power in the fifth century. The importance of one's parentage even in fourth-century Athenian politics becomes clear, for example, in the attacks leveled

by Demosthenes against Aeschines (e.g., Dem. 19.249, 281–82): on Aeschines' family background, see Edward M. Harris, *Aeschines and Athenian Politics* (New York, 1995), pp. 21–29. The accuracy of Demosthenes' attacks is irrelevant for us, since the orator expected his charges about Aeschines' family's low status to resonate with his audience. We must note, however, that these fourth-century attacks aimed more at the public service (especially through financial support) of one's ancestors than at any inherited nobility (again, cf. Roman attitudes). Hornblower, *Commentary*, 1: 387–88, notes that the Athenians apparently accepted the premise of "special qualities" attaching to particular families.

5. See chapter 3, n. 93.

6. For a list of the trials of Athenian commanders between 404 and 322, see W. K. Pritchett, *Greek State at War*, 2:4–33. The death penalty was handed down in about half the cases. Carter, *Quiet Athenian*, esp. pp. 99–130, argues for the existence of a group of professional generals (like Lamachus), who sought to stay out of politics. Such men certainly existed, but the history of Athens's condemnation of generals in the later fifth and fourth centuries shows that even these relatively apolitical generals were not in fact protected from the wrath of the demos: see n. 9 below.

7. See esp. Xenophon's *Anabasis;* Xenophon wrote an encomium of the Spartan king *(Agesilaus)*. For Xenophon's career and works, see Hornblower, *CAH* VI², pp. 1–8.

8. For Plato's decision to eschew political life, see his *Seventh Letter* 324–26, with Carter, *Quiet Athenian*, pp. 179–82. For Socrates' influence on Xenophon, see the latter's *Memorabilia*, esp. bk. 1, his *Apology of Socrates*, and *Anab.* 3.1.4–7. For this "retiring attitude" elsewhere, see also Eur. *Ion* 595–606, with Carter, *Quiet Athenian*, pp. 157–62.

9. See Hansen, *Athenian Democracy*, pp. 216–18; id., *Eisangelia*, pp. 58–65; for some examples, see Xen. *Hell.* 1.7.2 (Erasinides convicted of misuse of public funds and misconduct as general in 406), 1.7.3–35 (trial and conviction of the generals after Arginusae); and Sealey, *Demosthenes*, p. 89 (Callisthenes executed in 363/2 after making a truce with Perdikkas of Macedon); p. 66 (Timotheus recalled, deposed, and tried in 373 for allegedly wasting time [by trying to enlist crews!] instead of saving Corcyra; his treasurer was condemned and executed, Timotheus himself was acquitted but left Athens and offered his services to the Persians); p. 112 (Timotheus and Iphicrates tried ca. 354/3; Timotheus was convicted and fined 100 talents, but withdrew into exile).

10. Hansen, *Athenian Democracy*, pp. 216–17; as he points out, "many a general preferred to flee into exile and be condemned in his absence" (p. 217).

11. See also Dem. 4.47, where the orator suggests that the problem stemmed from the fact that not enough members of the juries had actually served on campaigns (where they could have been witnesses to the generals' actions).

12. Hansen, *Eisangelia*, p. 65; cf. J. T. Roberts, *Accountability in Athenian Government* (Madison, Wis., 1982), who attempts to provide some justification for Athenian practice in this area, and who minimizes the negative effects of Athenian practice on military leadership (pp. 177–78).

13. See n. 35 below.

14. See Sealey, *Demosthenes,* pp. 66–83, 94–95. Timotheus served under the Persians ca. 372–370; Iphicrates under King Kotys of Thrace (365–360/59). Chabrias and then Iphicrates served under Pharnabazos (the former satrap of Phrygia) in the attempted Persian reconquest of Egypt (ca. 380–373). Callistratus served under the Macedonian king while in exile (after having been condemned to death in 361) and was executed upon his return to Athens ca. 356. Of Callistratus, Sealey writes that he had "played a large part in bringing the Second League into being and later in accomplishing the Athenian rapprochement with Sparta. Both undertakings were inspired by a judicious realism, such as characterizes statesmanship of a high order" (p. 95).

15. Ibid., pp. 66, 83.

16. See n. 9 above.

17. On Pericles, see Thuc. 2.65.3; Diod. 12.45.4; Plut. *Per.* 35, with Hornblower, *Commentary,* 1: 331, 341. On Demosthenes, Thuc. 3.98.5, 3.114, with Gomme, *Commentary,* 2:408, 417, 429; cf. J. Roisman, *The General Demosthenes and His Use of Military Surprise* (Stuttgart, 1993), p. 27. See also Thuc. 4.65, on the Athenians' punishment of the generals commanding Athens's first expedition to Sicily (427–424): the *strategoi* were accused of accepting bribes in order to agree to a peace treaty with the Sicilians when it was believed that they could have subdued the island.

18. Phormio won brilliant and innovative naval victories for Athens at Naupactus in 429/8 (Thuc. 2.83–92). Despite this and his great reputation with Athens's allies (Thuc. 3.7), he disappears from the board of generals after this year. Androtion claimed (*FGrHist* 324 F8 = Fornara 130) that Phormio incurred the punishment of *atimia* (loss of citizen rights) when he failed to pay a large sum at his post-term audit *(euthynai),* and that he thus withdrew into private life (cf. Pausanias 1.23.10), only to be recalled and rehabilitated later: cf. Rhodes, *Thucydides: History,* III (Warminster, U.K., 1994), p. 180; Hornblower, *Commentary,* 1:387–88; Fornara, *Athenian Board of Generals,* p. 56; and Jacoby, *FGrHist* IIIb Suppl. I.125–37.

19. See Thuc. 7.48.

20. Diod. 13.106.6.

21. On the trial and execution of the generals after Arginusae, including Pericles II, see chapter 5, pp. 140–41.

22. The Athenians only charged their *strategoi* with violations of specific laws, not with failure per se. But there is no doubt that some generals faced prosecution or were convicted in large part due to their loss of a battle or a botched campaign: "A reasonable conclusion to draw from the available facts seems to be that any general who demonstrated incompetence in the field or suffered a major defeat was likely to be brought to trial" (Pritchett, *Greek State at War,* 2:20; see also Hansen, *Athenian Democracy,* p. 217, and Roberts, *Accountability in Athenian Government,* pp. 107–23; cf. Hansen, *Eisangelia,* pp. 64–65). The generals seem to have understood that failure would increase their chances of having charges of some kind brought against them

(Thuc. 3.98.5, 7.48). It is all the more remarkable that many were willing to serve (cf. Roberts, *Accountability,* p. 182).

23. See, e.g., Dem. 3.17, 9.30–31, and cf. Eugene N. Borza, *Before Alexander: Constructing Early Macedonia* (Claremont, Calif., 1999), pp. 27–43 (describing the continuing debate over the Macedonians' native language, which may or may not have been Greek), and id., "Greeks and Macedonians in the Age of Alexander: The Source Traditions," in R. W. Wallace and E. M. Harris, eds., *Transitions to Empire: Essays in Greco-Roman History, 360–146 B.C., in Honor of E. Badian* (Norman, Okla., 1996), pp. 122–39.

24. For the Argive origins of the Macedonian royal house, see Hdt. 5.22, 8.137–38, and Thuc. 2.99.

25. On the problematic subject of Macedonian government before the mid fourth century, see Eugene N. Borza, *In the Shadow of Olympus: The Emergence of Macedon* (Princeton, N.J., 1990), pp. 231–48; id., *Before Alexander,* pp. 44–48; and N. G. L. Hammond and G. T. Griffith, *A History of Macedonia* (Oxford, 1979), 2:150–65; Hammond, *The Macedonian State: Origins, Institutions, and History* (Oxford, 1989), pp. 16–99; and R. M. Errington, *A History of Macedonia,* trans. C. Errington (Berkeley, 1990), pp. 218–48.

26. Sealey, *Demosthenes,* pp. 95–96.

27. Plut. *Pelopidas* 26; on Epaminondas, see also Hanson, *Soul of Battle,* pp. 17–120.

28. On Philip's military advances, see esp. Hammond, *The Macedonian State,* pp. 100–136; Cawkwell, *Philip of Macedon,* pp. 150–65, and Hammond and Griffith, *A History of Macedonia,* 2:405–49. The development of the torsion catapult (or at least the introduction of its predecessor to the Balkans) probably occurred in Macedon in the late 350s or 340s: see E. W. Marsden, *Greek and Roman Artillery: Historical Development* (Oxford, 1969), pp. 59–60, Hammond and Griffith, *A History of Macedonia,* 2:445–49, and Hammond, *The Macedonian State,* p. 109.

29. On Philip's early career, see Cawkwell, *Philip of Macedon,* pp. 29–49, and Hammond, *Philip of Macedon,* pp. 8–44.

30. Sealey, *Demosthenes,* pp. 125, 160–63. Sealey usefully identifies conditions in Macedon and Greece that provided Philip scope for his talents and ambition.

31. Arther Ferrill, *The Origins of War: From the Stone Age to Alexander the Great* (Boulder, Colo., 1997), pp. 149–86, argues that Greek experiences with Persian armies had influenced Hellenic tacticians like Xenophon and Iphicrates, and that these influences (if not direct adaptation) may be seen in the army of Philip and Alexander.

32. These mines eventually produced over one thousand talents of annual revenue for Macedon: Diod. 16.8.6; Ellis, *CAH* VI², pp. 737, 766.

33. This peace essentially returned the Aegean to its pre–Persian War conditions, with Persia dominating the Greeks in Asia Minor. For the Corinthian War and the period before the peace, see esp. Xen. *Hell.* 3.5–5.1; R. Seager, *CAH* VI², pp. 97–119; Hamilton, *Sparta's Bitter Victories;* and Sealey, *History,* pp. 386–99.

34. For the second league's charter, see Harding 35 (= *IG* ii² 43); on the Athenians' guarantees to their allies, see Cargill, *Second Athenian League,* pp. 131–60, who also provides a thorough treatment of the league itself and attempts to show that "imperialism" in the second league has been overestimated (esp. pp. 161–96).

35. For the *syntaxeis,* see esp. Cargill, *Second Athenian League,* pp. 124–28; Brun, *Eisphora-Syntaxis-Stratiotika;* and Sealey, *Demosthenes,* pp. 64–65. They may never have amounted to more than 60 talents per year (Aeschin. 2.71, in 343/2); Demosthenes said they yielded 45 talents ca. 339/8 (18.234), but the league was much reduced in size by that time. For generals in need of funds, see, e.g., Isoc. 15.109 (Timotheus in 375); Xen. *Hell.* 6.2.37 (Iphicrates in 372/1), with Jones, *Athenian Democracy,* p. 30, and Millet, "Warfare, Economy, and Democracy," pp. 191–94. For the taxes *(eisphorai)* on the wealthy, see, e.g., Xen. *Hell.* 6.2.1; Thomsen, *Eisphora;* Brun, *Eisphora-Syntaxis-Stratiotika;* and M. M. Austin, *CAH* VI², pp. 546–51.

36. For Thebes's rise, see Buckler, *Theban Hegemony,* esp. pp. 15–69, and Seager, *CAH* VI², pp. 176–86.

37. On these machinations, see Xen. *Hell.* 6.4.1–7.1.14, and Diod. 15.63.1–2, with Buckler, *Theban Hegemony,* pp. 87–92.

38. Sealey, *Demosthenes,* pp. 76–82.

39. Ibid., p. 89. For Athenian cleruchs sent to Potidaea, see Harding 58.

40. On the battle, see Xen. *Hell.* 7.5, who ends his work with this event, and Buckler, *Theban Hegemony,* pp. 205–19. For the idea of a "common peace," which theoretically allowed all Greek states to participate and retain their autonomy, see T. T. B. Ryder, *Koine Eirene: General Peace and Local Independence in Ancient Greece* (Oxford, 1965).

41. This war has traditionally been seen as the result of increased Athenian "imperialism" in the second league, exemplified by the collection of *syntaxeis* and the Athenians' establishment of settlements in places like Samos and garrisons elsewhere. This view is questioned by Cargill, *Second League,* pp. 161–88, and Sealey, *Demosthenes,* esp. p. 107, who attributes the allies' revolt in part to the ambitions of the Carian dynast Mausolus.

42. Sealey, *Demosthenes,* pp. 110–11.

43. Ibid.; see also Ellis, *CAH* VI², pp. 737 ff., and Harding 70.

44. Ibid., pp. 109–12; cf. 155: Sealey notes that Philip may have promised (or intimated) that he would hand Amphipolis over to Athens after its capture.

45. For Athenian interest in these locations, see Dem. 1.8–9; 2.6–7; 4.4–5, 12; 6.17–18.

46. We may usefully compare Athenian reactions to perceived aggression or opposition in the fifth century.

47. See Dem. 14 (*On the Naval Boards,* delivered in 354), which does not mention Philip.

48. See Dem. 4 *(First Philippic),* probably delivered in 352/1. On Philip's actions

in Greece between 355 and 352 and the Third Sacred War, see John Buckler, *Philip II and the Sacred War* (Leiden, 1989), esp. pp. 30–99.

49. E.g., Dem. 4.50; 6.5–6, 24 (where he argues for *apistia*, "mistrust" or "doubt," where Philip is concerned).

50. See Dem. *First Olynthiac,* esp. 1.6, 19–20, 24; see also 2.12–13, 24, 30; 3.10–17, 19–20, 33–35. For the alliance of 349/8, see Harding 80.

51. For the law and Apollodoros's condemnation, see Dem. 3.10–11, and [Dem.] 59.3–8, with Sealey, *Demosthenes,* pp. 256–58; cf. Dem. 1.19–20, 14.24–28.

52. Sealey, *Demosthenes,* pp. 152–53, writes that Athens's policy "toward Olynthos in 349/8 may have been defensible or even statesmanlike," but admits the damage done to the Athenians' ability to inspire confidence in their allies. See also id., *History,* pp. 450–53, and Ellis, *CAH* VI², pp. 749–51.

53. For a somewhat similar idea, see Finley, *Democracy Ancient and Modern,* p. 93 (but cf. ibid., pp. 98–99).

54. Cf., e.g., the Athenians' reactions to the request for aid from their Sicilian ally Egesta in 416/5 (chapter 5, pp. 135–37).

55. P. J. Rhodes has suggested to me that this change in attitudes reflects the new policy of Eubulus and his supporters (cf. Isocrates, *On the Peace*), who, in reaction to the expensive and largely unsuccessful military actions of the preceding decades, sought to change Athens's policy after the Social War ended: on the policies of Eubulus and his opponents, see Rhodes, "On Labelling Fourth-Century Politicians," and id., *CAH* VI², pp. 576–79.

56. See n. 50 above and, e.g., Dem. 19.291, 15–16, 144, 307; Aeschin. 2.75–77.

57. For this attitude, its effects, and reactions, see Dem. 3.18–19; 6.28–32; 8.17–18, 31; 9.56, 67; 10.53–56.

58. Sealey, *Demosthenes,* p. 129.

59. Cf. Thuc. 7.14 (Nicias's letter to the Athenians).

60. E.g., Alcibiades before the Sicilian expedition (chapter 3, pp. 89–90 above). Pericles' realism apparently led him to consider the possibility of defeat frankly (Thuc. 2.64), but he nevertheless seems to have emphasized the potential for greater glory, power, and reputation.

61. Note that Pericles' war policy in 431 does not fit into this mold, since he was asking the Athenians to endure a costly war rather than to launch a profitable invasion (i.e., he was advocating a war to preserve rather than to extend Athens's power; cf. the situation in the 350s–340s). Pericles' success once again shows the tremendous political influence he wielded by 431.

62. Any attempt to reconstruct the events surrounding the Peace of Philocrates —as the treaty with Philip has come to be known—encounters virtually intractable problems of source analysis and chronology, in large part because we are so reliant on statements made by Aeschines and Demosthenes after the fact and in contexts where both men were motivated to shade or misrepresent the truth. I have tended to follow the reconstruction of Sealey, *Demosthenes,* pp. 137–57 (cf. id., *History*); for

alternative treatments, see Buckler, *Philip II,* pp. 114–42; Harris, *Aeschines,* pp. 50–101; and Ellis, *CAH* VI², pp. 739–59, who presents an interpretation of Philip's intentions in central and southern Greece that seems difficult to reconcile with the sources (cf. Buckler, *Philip II,* pp. 121–24, who discusses other literature).

63. At 19.95–96, 100–101, Demosthenes maintains that Aeschines is not to be blamed for the peace (treaty), but rather for the *kind* of peace. Harris, *Aeschines,* pp. 54–55, emphasizes the "widespread support for beginning peace negotiations with Philip at this time" (p. 55).

64. See Aeschin. 2, esp. 2.61–85, and Dem. 19, esp. 19.13–16.

65. Demosthenes claimed that he supported the attempt to open the treaty to other states and that Aeschines opposed Philocrates' proposal (while still favoring peace) on day one and then fervently supported Philocrates' peace at the second assembly: Dem. 19.13–16, 144; Aeschines himself, 2.63–68 (cf. 3.69–72), denied that he had changed his view. For analysis of the claims and counterclaims of each, see Harris, *Aeschines,* pp. 70–77.

66. Sealey, *Demosthenes,* pp. 153–56; id., *History,* pp. 458–59; Aeschin. 2.132–34.

67. Dem. 5.9–10; 19.19–24, 45, 48–51; cf. Aeschin. 2.119–20, 130–31, 136–37; cf. Harris, *Aeschines,* pp. 87–94, who argues that Aeschines sincerely believed Philip would act in a way favorable to Athens.

68. See n. 62 above.

69. Of course, the Phocians possessed a formidable force and remained a *potential* ally against Philip. The Athenians thus found themselves in a real quandary. Nevertheless, it cannot be argued that the Phocians' (or, eventually, the Macedonians') position in Thermopylae was unassailable, since the Thebans were able to retake the pass from the Macedonians sometime after 346 and since the Athenians had the naval forces necessary to operate on either side of this gateway to central Greece (and could thus outflank any force holding it).

70. Aeschin. 2.72; Dem. 4.34.

71. For the grain supply, see R. S. Stroud, *The Athenian Grain-Tax Law of 374/3* B.C. (Princeton, N.J., 1998), esp. pp. 31–32, on the importance of Lemnos, Imbros, and Scyros, which themselves produced significant amounts of grain. See also chapter 4, n. 11.

72. Contrast Sealey, *Demosthenes,* p. 155: "The war in the north was troublesome to the Athenians, but as long as they could hold the forts commanding Thermopylae, their security was not threatened."

73. Sealey, *Demosthenes,* pp. 151–52.

74. Dem. 19.291.

75. Cf. Aeschin. 2.75–77, with Dem. 19.15–16, 307. For analysis of the political programs and views of Demosthenes and Eubulus (and salutary warnings against applying modern terminology or models to Athenian politics), see Rhodes, "On Labelling Fourth-Century Politicians."

76. E.g., Dem. 14.41. For Pericles, see Thuc. 1.144.

77. Theopompus *FGrHist* 115 F166; Sealey, *Demosthenes,* p. 147.

78. Dem. 19.48–56, esp. 49, with Buckler, *Philip II,* pp. 137–38, who comments that the Athenians "abandoned an ally in its hour of peril to save their own skins" (p. 138).

79. Dem. 19.48–56, 310.

80. On the settlement ending the Third Sacred War, see esp. Diod. 16.59–60, and cf. Harris, *Aeschines,* pp. 95–101, and Buckler, *Philip II,* pp. 133–47, both of whom demonstrate the difficult nature of the evidence, and who offer interpretations sometimes different from my own. Ellis, *CAH* VI², pp. 755–59, maintains that Philip had intended to use this opportunity to humble his Theban allies (but cf. Buckler, *Philip II,* pp. 121–24).

81. Perhaps the fourth-century Athenians had forgotten what Thucydides alleges that their ancestors told the Melians about the dangers of hope (Thuc. 5.103, which opens this chapter).

82. See Dem. 5 *(On the Peace),* and Sealey, *Demosthenes,* p. 158.

83. See Sealey, *Demosthenes,* pp. 147–48, 159, who maintains that the Athenians could afford to lose Cersebleptes since Philip had promised not to encroach on Athenian territory in the Chersonese.

84. Buckler, *Philip II,* pp. 127–29, 132–33.

85. Cf. Buckler, *Philip II,* pp. 137–47, and Sealey, *Demosthenes,* pp. 158–59.

86. Dem. 19.112–13.

87. Calls for citizen service: Dem. 1.6, 24; 2.13, 31; 3.20, 33–35; 4.16, 19–21, 25; 13.4–7, 17.

88. Sealey, *Demosthenes,* p. 159.

89. Isoc. 5 *(Philippos), Epistles* 2 and 3; for Speusippos's letter to Philip *(Socratic Epistles* 30), the authenticity of which is disputed, see Sealey, *Demosthenes,* p. 167.

90. See Sealey, *Demosthenes,* pp. 175–79.

91. See Dem. 8.9, 20–26, 28, with Sealey, *Demosthenes,* p. 180.

92. See Dem. 8 *(On the Chersonese)* and the *Third Philippic* (esp. 9.19–20, 73).

93. See esp. Dem. 10.35–45, with Sealey, *Demosthenes,* pp. 182–85. Sealey suggests that Demosthenes exaggerated the likelihood that Persia would assist Athens.

94. Philochorus *FGrHist* 328 F56a = Harding 96a.

95. Sealey, *Demosthenes,* pp. 196–97; Ellis, *CAH* VI², pp. 779–81.

96. On the battle itself, see Diod. 16.85.2–86; Polyaenus *Strategems* 4.2.2. According to Sealey, *Demosthenes,* p. 198, "The two sides were almost evenly matched and the outcome of the battle could not be predicted." He nevertheless concludes from the result that the lesson learned in Athens was that "however many allies the Athenians might muster in Greece, it would be foolish to challenge the might of Macedon, as long as the Macedonians remained united."

97. For the results of Chaeronea and the honors voted for Philip, see [Demades] 9–10; Diod. 16.87ff., esp. 92.1–2; Plut. *Phoc.* 16; Harding 99, 1B (col. 3.9–12); Sealey, *Demosthenes,* pp. 198–201; Harris, *Aeschines,* pp. 133–36; and G. L. Cawkwell, "The

Crowning of Demosthenes," *CQ* 19 (1969): 180, who comments, "Macedon did not need to interfere [after Chaeronea]. Enough of the Greeks were cowed."

98. Diod. 16.88.1.

99. See, e.g., Sealey, *Demosthenes*, pp. 198, 219.

100. I thus disagree with Hanson, *Other Greeks*, p. 353, who also attributes Philip's success to problems within Greece, but sees these problems as "inherently structural and thus inevitable" (cf. Cawkwell, "The End of Greek Liberty," in Wallace and Harris, eds., *Transitions to Empire*, pp. 98–121, who suggests that the Greek defeat may have been inevitable due to the Greeks' apparent inability to unite against Philip). Hanson is nevertheless correct that a Greek victory at Chaeronea would not have "ensured . . . the continued autonomy of the city-state." But the Greeks' failure to withstand Philip meant that the admitted problems with the polis system would be confronted in a context of Macedonian (and then Roman) overlordship. One simply cannot know what Greece might have become outside of Macedonian dominance.

101. Plut. *Mor.* 818e–f; cf. Sealey, *Demosthenes*, pp. 206–7, who defends Athens's refusal to join in the revolts of Thebes or Sparta. Other scholars have taken a dimmer view of these actions; see esp. E. Badian, "Agis III," *Hermes* 95 (1967): 170–92, and Cawkwell, "Crowning of Demosthenes," who notes that Athens had "more ships in this period than ever before" (392 triremes and 18 quadriremes in 330/29: p. 179). Of Agis's revolt, Badian writes: "It is largely Athens that is to blame for the failure of the war, and within Athens Demosthenes—the only man who might have carried the people with him" (p. 183; see also Cawkwell, "Crowning of Demosthenes," p. 176, and cf. id., "The End of Greek Liberty"). Cawkwell argues that Demosthenes hoped for a Persian victory over Alexander and thus counseled restraint.

102. On the Lamian War, see Sealey, *Demosthenes*, pp. 215–19.

7. DEMOCRACY AND RELIGION

1. Chapter epigraphs: Finley, *Democracy Ancient and Modern*, pp. 29–30; George Washington's farewell address, September 19, 1796, in *George Washington: Writings*, ed. J. Rhodehamel (New York, 1997), p. 971; Leon Wieseltier, "The Incoherence," *New Republic*, October 29, 2001, p. 46.

2. See J. Henderson, ed. and trans., *Three Plays by Aristophanes* (New York, 1996), pp. 11–14, 20–29, who notes (for example) that young citizen women were almost completely off-limits in Athenian comedy, and that the comedies "respect [the Athenian] culture's strict separation of public and private [where women functioned primarily in the latter sphere]. To take his women out of the household in a plausible way Aristophanes associates them with the cults of the goddesses" (p. 26). For other conventions and standards observed by the comic poets, see Henderson, introduction to the Loeb *Aristophanes*, vol. 1 (Cambridge, Mass., 1998), pp. 17–19.

3. The ancient Greeks themselves were quite aware of the disparate conventions and laws *(nomoi)* governing different societies, but they nonetheless recognized cer-

tain acts as violations of their own prevailing code: see, e.g., Hdt. 3.38, with 1.61 (where the tyrant Peisistratus has relations with his wife "not in accordance with custom *[nomos]*").

4. For the festivals, see esp. A. Pickard-Cambridge, *The Dramatic Festivals of Athens,* 2d ed., rev. John Gould and D. M. Lewis (Oxford, 1988), and E. Csapo and W. J. Slater, *The Context of Ancient Drama* (Ann Arbor, Mich., 1995). For particular aspects, see John J. Winkler and Froma I. Zeitlin, eds., *Nothing to Do with Dionysos? Athenian Drama in Its Social Context* (Princeton, N.J., 1990).

5. See Winkler and Zeitlin, eds., *Nothing to Do with Dionysos?* pp. 3–11, and A. Pickard-Cambridge, *Dithyramb, Tragedy, and Comedy,* 2d ed. (Oxford, 1962), pp. 124–26.

6. For a stimulating treatment of the intertwined political/religious/civic aspects of the Dionysia, see S. Goldhill, "The Great Dionysia and Civic Ideology," in Winkler and Zeitlin, eds., *Nothing to Do with Dionysos?* pp. 97–129, an earlier version of which appeared in *JHS* 107 (1987), 58–76, excerpted in Samons, ed., *Athenian Democracy and Imperialism,* pp. 219–28. For Goldhill's overstatement of the role of democracy per se in the festival/tragedies, see conclusion, n. 9.

7. One reader has suggested to me that events similar in nature to the Athenians' festivals may still be encountered in certain ethnic/Catholic subcultures. The existence of such delimited subcultures in America helps illustrate that their religiosociopolitical practices are not part of official or "mainstream" culture, as they were in classical Athens.

8. On the ancient and medieval (pagan and Christian) conception of a society/political community as a group "united by concord regarding loved things held in common" (Augustine *City of God* 19.24, trans. Rahe) and the attempts in modern political philosophy to replace this conception, see Rahe, *Republics Ancient and Modern.*

9. Man's desire for and need of something like an integral society has been hypothesized (or observed) by many others. Compare, for example, the eighteenth-century "republican" views discussed by Wood, *Creation of the American Republic,* pp. 59–60, or those of the Anti-Federalists described by Herbert J. Storing, *What the Anti-Federalists Were For* (Chicago, 1981), pp. 19–20, or those of John Stuart Mill, discussed by Paul Rahe, *Republics Ancient and Modern,* pp. 22–26. On the individual's need for beliefs and convictions, cf. Ortega y Gasset, *Man and Crisis,* pp. 87–89, 95–101.

10. *American Heritage Dictionary* (New York, 1969), s.v. *society.*

11. On the development of diversity as an American value and principle (like freedom or equality), see Peter Wood, *Diversity: The Invention of a Concept* (San Francisco, 2003).

12. On the inherently aggressive and divisive aspects of human nature, see E. O. Wilson, *On Human Nature* (Cambridge, Mass., 1978), esp. p. 119: "Human beings are strongly predisposed to respond with unreasoning hatred to external threats and

to escalate their hostility sufficiently to overwhelm the source of the threat by a respectably wide margin of safety. Our brains do appear to be programmed to the following extent: we are inclined to partition other people into friends and aliens, in the same sense that birds are inclined to learn territorial songs and to navigate by the polar constellations. We tend to fear deeply the actions of strangers and to solve conflict by aggression." Ortega y Gasset, *History as a System,* pp. 165–233, denied that man has a nature: "*Man, in a word, has no nature; what he has is . . . history.* Expressed differently: what nature is to things, history, *res gestae,* is to man" (p. 217; emphasis in original). But his use of "history" here is very similar to my own view of "nature," since both act as the "stuff" upon which external stimuli and personal motivation act to produce individual actions and culture.

13. For the concept, see Paul Rahe, "The Primacy of Politics in Classical Greece," *AHR* 89 (1984): 265–93, and id., *Republics Ancient and Modern,* pp. 28–54. Although I disagree with his analysis of the extent to which public affairs and the competition for political glory and honor animated the common Greek citizen, Rahe's *Republics Ancient and Modern* provides an invaluable analysis of the relationship (indeed, virtual identity) between the "social" and "political" spheres in classical Greece. His book, therefore, differs from many modern works that tend to abstract the Greeks from their own society and history when discussing their supposed ideologies (see introduction).

14. Arist. *Pol.* 1253a, I.2.9–16; 1278b, III.6.3; cf. *Ethics* IX.9.3. As Cohen, *Athenian Nation,* p. 155, points out, Aristotle also called man an "economic" animal *(oikonomikon zoon)*: *Eudemian Ethics* 1242a, VII.10.5.

15. This idea appears in a less concrete form in parts of Plato's *Republic* (esp. bk. 4), where the structure and government of the polis are employed to describe the arrangement of man's soul. For a critique, see David Roochnik, *Beautiful City: The Dialectical Character of Plato's "Republic,"* pp. 10–30.

16. Arist. *Politics* 1252a, I.1.1: "Observation shows us, first, that every polis (or state) is a species of association, and, secondly, that all associations are instituted for the purpose of attaining some good—for all men do all their acts with a view to achieving something which is, in their view, good. We may therefore hold [on the basis of what we actually observe] that all associations aim at some good; and we may also hold that the particular association which is the most sovereign of all, and includes all the rest, will pursue this aim most, and will thus be directed to the most sovereign of all goods. This most sovereign and inclusive association is the polis, as it is called, or the political association" (trans. Barker). Cf. Rahe, *Republics Ancient and Modern,* pp. 30–36.

17. See chapter 1, pp. 24–26, chapter 2, pp. 45–49; for the family as anterior to the polis, see Arist. *Ethics* VIII.12.7.

18. Cf. Ar. *Ach.* 17–42 and *Eccl.* 183–88, 289–310; *Ath. Pol.* 41.3 and Arist. *Pol.* 1318b, VI.4.2–3, 1319a, VI.4.13–14, with Hanson, *Other Greeks,* pp. 212–13. For a somewhat different view, see Finley, *Politics in the Ancient World,* pp. 70–96. Finley's

argument that a very high percentage (by modern standards) of Athenians participated in government—through lotteried positions, etc.—is certainly correct, but will
not affect my conclusion about Athenian involvement and interest in what modern
Americans call "politics." It is, in fact, striking that the very high percentage of Athenians who fulfilled their civic duties by military service, jury duty, or holding lotteried offices for one year did not result in a higher degree of citizen participation in
public voting and elections.

19. On population and the Pnyx, see Hansen, *Athenian Democracy,* pp. 90–94,
130–32, and Rhodes, *Commentary,* pp. 491–92. For exceptions to the rule that "almost
all Assembly meetings were held on the Pnyx," see Hansen, ibid., p. 129.

20. See Thuc. 8.72 for the possibility that no assembly before 411 had reached
even 5,000 citizens. After the institution of payment for attendance at the *ekklesia,*
the Athenians had little difficulty in achieving the 6,000-person quorum then required. The red-painted rope used to herd Athenians into the assembly in the fifth
century (before assemblymen were paid: Ar. *Ach.* 17–22) was employed to prevent
crowding in the fourth: Hansen, *Athenian Democracy,* pp. 130–32.

21. Athenian men were liable for military service until age 59: see Hansen, *Athenian Democracy,* p. 100, and MacDowell, *Law,* pp. 159–60. In practice, active service
may have ended at age 50, and "Athens was quite exceptional in calling on men up
to the age of 49 for foreign service in the front line; Sparta stopped at 40, so did
Rome": Gomme, *Commentary,* 2: 35.

22. For group activities "to maintain the goodwill of the gods," see Mikalson,
Athenian Popular Religion, p. 89.

23. For tribes in the Athenian military and for their role in the Council of 500,
see chapter 1, pp. 24–28. Hansen, *Athenian Democracy,* pp. 137–38, discusses the possibility that the assembly was arranged by tribes and concludes that it was not; nevertheless, one tribe always provided the presiding committee (the *prytaneis*) and after
346/5, one tribe was required to sit together and maintain order in the assembly. In
Xen. *Hell.* 1.7.9–10, the assembly considers a motion to vote "by tribes" on the guilt
or innocence of the generals who served at Arginusae.

24. *Ath. Pol.* 21, with Parker, *Athenian Religion,* pp. 117–21.

25. See chapter 1, pp. 24–25.

26. For the gods associated with the Council of 500, see Mikalson, *Athenian Popular Religion,* pp. 13, 70 (citing Antiphon 6.45).

27. Mikalson, *Athenian Popular Religion,* p. 42 with n. 14.

28. Aeschin. 1.22–23; Mikalson, *Athenian Popular Religion,* p. 13.

29. For the "priority of the divine" in Athenian public life, see Mikalson, *Athenian Popular Religion,* pp. 13–17.

30. Cf. Finley, *Politics in the Ancient World,* pp. 93–95, who argues that Greek government became "generally secularized in reality though not in appearance" (p. 94).
This view rests on a failure to recognize the absence of a modern sacred/secular distinction in Greek society.

31. See Samons, *Empire of the Owl,* pp. 325–29.

32. Ibid., and Louise Bruit Zaidman and Pauline Schmitt Pantel, *Religion in the Greek City,* trans. Paul Cartledge (Cambridge, 1992), esp. pp. 92–101.

33. Mikalson, *Athenian Popular Religion,* p. 106.

34. Likewise, American society existed before the Revolutionary War and before the Constitution, although the war and the Constitution themselves then became factors influencing that society.

35. See chapter 2.

36. I am here discussing Athenian *attitudes.* Obviously democratic practices and government had a real impact on Athenian history in the fifth century, as we have seen. For the suggestion that the Athenians' attachment to and thought about democracy in the fifth century have been greatly overestimated in modern scholarship, see Samons, "Democracy, Empire and the Search for the Athenian Character."

37. In the case of the gods' protecting "freedom" *(eleutheria),* this freedom was almost certainly seen as a "negative" protection of the polis from foreign tyranny and not as an attribute of democracy. The cult of Zeus Eleutherios perhaps arose in the Periclean period, and may be a "specialization" of one function of Zeus Soter ("Savior"), probably representing Zeus as the liberator of the polis from outside oppression: see Kurt A. Raaflaub, *Die Entdeckung der Freiheit* (Munich, 1985), pp. 125–47; Mikalson, *Athenian Popular Religion,* p. 71; and Parker, *Athenian Religion,* pp. 157, 239 n. 76. The stele on which the Athenians inscribed the decree outlawing tyranny and the overthrow of democracy in 337/6 (*SEG* XII.87 = Harding 101) was decorated with a relief sculpture depicting Demokratia about to crown the (personified) demos of the Athenians.

38. Parker, *Athenian Religion,* pp. 228–37. On Dike as a personified force, cf. Connor, "Sacred and Secular," pp. 177–81, and Mikalson, *Athenian Popular Religion,* pp. 29–30 (discussing [Dem.] 25.10–11). Mikalson, pp. 110–18, also refutes the notion that "popular religious belief deteriorated significantly from, say, the mid-fifth to the mid-fourth century" (p. 112), a view that had rested in part on the Athenians' establishment of Fortune and Democracy as personified deities (on Fortune, cf. Mikalson, pp. 60–62).

39. On Eirene and the peace of 375, see Parker, *Athenian Religion,* p. 230: "The cult began and was for some time remembered as one of Glorious Peace, in a century in which Athens had to accept so many peaces that were bitter humiliations." He emphasizes that this was a "peace" stemming from victory in battle, not a goddess of pacifism. I infer the connection between the loss at Chaeronea and the cult of Demokratia from the "flurry of interest" in the goddess appearing in the 330s (ibid., p. 228), and the new Athenian law protecting the democracy against tyranny in 337/6 (Harding 101, with Hansen, *Athenian Democracy,* p. 295, and n.37 above).

40. Chapter 2, pp. 54–57, chapter 3, pp. 92–93; cf. Boedeker and Raaflaub, eds., *Democracy, Empire and the Arts in Fifth-Century Athens,* pp. 1–13.

41. Cf. Dem. 15.14–24 *(For the Liberty of the Rhodians),* which gets pretty close to

this idea; it certainly equates *demokratia* with *eleutheria*. (In this speech, probably delivered in 351, Demosthenes attempted—unsuccessfully—to persuade the Athenians to assist exiled democrats against Rhodian oligarchs.) For Demosthenes' attitude to democracy, see Rhodes, "On Labelling Fourth-Century Politicians."

42. For the views of democracy's critics, cf. Ober, *Political Dissent in Democratic Athens.*

43. Hanson, *Other Greeks.*

44. According to Elshtain, Tocqueville predicted that imperial aggrandizement would be "pleasing to the imagination of a democratic people": *Democracy on Trial,* p. 10, citing Alexis de Tocqueville, *Democracy in America,* trans. H. Reeve, rev. F. Bowen, ed. P. Bradley (New York: Knopf Books, 1945), 2:293, a reference I was unable to confirm.

45. This idea appears frequently in Demosthenes' speeches, in which the orator repeatedly exhorts the Athenians to be willing to serve themselves (chapter 6, nn. 48, 50). The orator's most modern idea appears in his proposal for a standing army of (conscripted?) citizens serving (for pay) for a limited and relatively short period of service (Dem. 4.19–23), a very similar kind of army to that fielded by the United States during the Vietnam War. It would seem likely that this kind of force reflects a lack of enthusiasm on the part of the citizenry for a war: that is, it amounts to the creation of a military force that can be used by a democratic regime even when the people are so opposed to a particular war that they are unwilling to serve themselves. (Demosthenes also suggests that this force adopt the tactics of continued harassment and piracy—"guerilla" tactics, if you will.)

46. Modern ideas of rights developed largely in monarchical environments and stemmed from a perceived need to protect citizens (or rather subjects) from a strong state, usually embodied in royal authority. (That is, such "rights" are the negative reflection of and are in large part generated by the desire to protect individuals from a government authority's "wrongs.") Neither a strong central government nor powerful monarchs existed in mainland Hellas during the classical period, and the tyrants had frequently been seen as the common people's champions rather than their oppressors. In this environment, and since they were also imbued with cultural norms that emphasized a citizen's duties to the polis, Athenian political theorists and statesmen lacked important stimuli for the development of a full-blown theory of rights.

47. See the *Republic* and the *Laws.*

48. See, e.g., the Ninth Circuit Court's decision in *Newdow v. U.S. Congress* (et al.), no. 00-16423, June 26, 2002 (amended February 28, 2003).

49. See the *Newdow* decision, ibid., pp. 9118–19 (p. 2804, amended), Discussion section D.1, which cites *Lee v. Weisman* (1992) to show that the Fourteenth Amendment has made the First Amendment's establishment clause "applicable with full force to the states and their school districts," and then goes on to discuss the legal "tests" that have been used "to analyze alleged violations of the Establishment Clause in the realm of public education."

50. Massachusetts had constitutional provisions for an established state church until 1833, while Maryland's constitution required a "declaration of a belief in the Christian religion" for all state officials into the 1850s. For religious requirements in early state constitutions, see Rahe, *Republics Ancient and Modern*, p. 749, and Eidelberg, *The Philosophy of the American Constitution*, pp. 264–71. For the efforts to remove church establishments in New England, see W. G. McLoughlin, *New England Dissent, 1630–1833* (Cambridge, Mass., 1971), esp. 1:591–693, on Massachusetts's religious establishment (through taxation to support local churches).

51. See Rahe, *Republics Ancient and Modern*, pp. 750–51.

52. On the loss of specific content in the meaning of the term *democracy*, see introduction, pp. 1–5 above; on "faith," cf. Elshtain, *Democracy on Trial*, esp. p. 22, who argues that faith in democracy is weakening. Even if she is right about democracy per se, the "values" generated by democracy (freedom, choice, and diversity) continue to enjoy exalted status (for diversity, see, e.g., Elshtain, p. 140 n. 5).

53. But for a similar view, see James Fitzjames Stephen, *Liberty, Equality, Fraternity* (1873), ed. R. J. White (Cambridge, 1967), which I unfortunately came upon late in the process of completing this volume. Stephen argues that the phrase "liberty, equality, fraternity" forms "the creed of a religion, less definite than any one of the forms of Christianity, which are in part its rivals, in part its antagonists, and in part its associates, but not on that account the less powerful" (p. 52).

54. Introduction, pp. 13–14.

55. "Freedom" would seem to be the deity worshipped through the religion of democracy, and "happiness" surely is the reward this god offers.

56. This fact, which at first glance might seem to lead us toward the "history of ideologies," by itself still has little explanatory power for particular actions: see introduction, pp. 7–9.

57. For the importance of such criticism, see Conclusion, pp. 200–201.

58. Ortega y Gasset predicted something like this, or rather, he saw it already in his contemporaries (*History as a System*, pp. 70–72).

59. By "unrestrained capitalism," I refer to economic activity unfettered by noneconomic societal restraints. Individuals react to such restraints, which are imposed by other individuals or groups, because they want to appear to be just or good as much as (or more than) they desire to accumulate wealth. The substances that represent the chemical manifestation of freedom include not only illegal drugs and alcohol, but also the pervasive mood-elevators prescribed for adults and children (and the increasing government role in providing these medications). In the area of religion, I would note the increased social acceptability of sects that approve the worship of freedom, as well as the freedom to worship in whatever way one pleases. The past decade has seen a marked increase in the popularity of the type of spiritualism that promises increased personal happiness through connection with supernatural forces that do not define one's duties to anything or anyone other than oneself, or otherwise restrain the practice of indulging in one's freedom. (See, e.g., the empha-

sis on "spiritual"—vs. "religious"—concerns in the Earth Charter: www.earth charter.org.)

60. One suspects that in such an environment, sexual acts that cannot produce children will eventually be most consecrated, since they have no biological purpose and thus (as pure expressions of the libido) can be seen as the greatest expressions of freedom.

61. Compare the words of the arch-democrat Pericles (at Thuc. 2.43.4), when he asks those attending the Athenian funeral oration to judge "happiness to be the fruit of freedom *[eleutheron]* and freedom of valor" and thus to "never decline the dangers of war" (trans. Crawley). For Pericles, freedom and happiness relied on the citizen's willingness to perform even dangerous duties.

62. How often does one hear the phrase "You can't legislate morality" from the same people who support laws to ensure rights?

63. Thus particular political regimes can endorse such a right and attempt to enforce it, endorse it without enforcing it, or neither endorse it nor enforce it.

64. Tocqueville noted that "mores are changing and the moral conception of rights is being obliterated with them" and advocated "linking the idea of rights to personal interest, which provides the only stable point in the human heart" (p. 239). One may certainly question whether the past century and a half have justified his confidence in "personal interest" and the implied ability of men to seek this rationally.

65. One rehabilitation counselor told the *Washington Post* (July 29, 1999) how female victims at Woodstock III were assaulted within the crowd: "They were pushed in against their will and really raped. . . . From my vantage point, it looked like initially there was a struggle, and after that there were other people holding them down. . . . No one I saw tried to go in and rescue them . . . it seemed like most of the crowd around was cheering them on. . . . It was so disturbing. You're thinking, if this girl was being raped, wouldn't all these people try to stop what was going on?"

66. Writing in the *New York Times* (on the web, Aug. 8, 1999), Neil Strauss noted (about the violence at Woodstock III) that "if a few bad eggs started it, then a lot of ambivalent eggs joined in. If they didn't physically take part, most everybody was complicit in the mayhem, simply by hanging around and enjoying the spectacle." But the "real generational damage . . . was not in the riots [during which there were few injuries]; . . . [but] in the reports of women raped in portable toilets, tents, and even in the audience." Although rapes had been reported at earlier rock festivals, "they certainly were never alleged to have taken place in plain view in a mosh pit." And the laissez-faire attitudes were not confined to young males watching women being outraged; a 47-year-old grandmother at the festival and apparently upset by the poor conditions and commercial exploitation at the event commented: "I didn't start a fire, but I have total sympathy for anyone who did" (Strauss, ibid., July 27, 1999).

67. See Elshtain, *Democracy on Trial,* p. 12, for a similar idea.

68. Admittedly, it is no longer as common to hear the argument that unhappy couples are creating a better world for their children by divorcing. Nonetheless, the U.S. tax code has long penalized marriage in various ways, and welfare benefits are often better for unmarried women with children than for those who are married. (One reader points out to me that the earned income tax credit also carries a stiff penalty for those who are married: http://www.ncpa.org/pub/ba/ba445/.) It is perhaps surprising that of the three "social ills" mentioned in the text, it is the abandonment of the family by one parent that still carries an official sociopolitical stigma, exhibited by legislation against "deadbeat dads." Why this choice (to abandon one's family) should be seen as less socially acceptable than abortion may not be immediately apparent. The fact that parental responsibility is interpreted in these laws in terms of an economic demonstration (child-support payments) may be one answer—that is, "deadbeat dads" are condemned not so much for their moral failings as for their failure to meet economic "responsibilities" (as if these were more important than the personal, human responsibility *to act as fathers* to their own children). Divorce and abortion, on the other hand, have the benefit of reflecting a "choice" (which "frees" women) without impinging on the economic health of society (it could be argued). Nevertheless, it is obvious that a society that supports a woman's "right" to have an abortion without any interference from the child's father cannot support laws that (nevertheless) require fathers to support their children financially. The two ideas are logically inconsistent, and the economic demands made on the father are ultimately incompatible with the idealization of freedom expressed through abortion. One might also ask just who receives the maximum freedom from current "no-fault" divorce laws and legalized abortion. A case could certainly be made that both essentially secure the male's freedom from responsibility at least as much as a woman's "right to choose." In the current American environment, why would a man committed to freedom and happiness (as moderns interpret the ideas) desire to incur the limitations imposed by marriage or child-rearing, especially when he can claim that having the child was entirely the woman's choice?

69. Antisocial in the sense that they are inconsistent with a real society.

70. Recent episodes of flag-burning and the debates over legislation or amendments to the Constitution to ban this act help demonstrate American society's weakened state, not because it is so unthinkable that someone would desire to burn the flag, but because it is somewhat pathetic that others feel the need to make the act illegal. A society in which such an act causes real insecurity and thus leads to legislation—because the people are incapable of suppressing egregiously antisocial action simply through the stigma that should attach to it (i.e., through extrapolitical means) —has already lost the values that a law against flag-burning seeks to retain.

71. For the Ninth Circuit Court's decision condemning the phrase "under God" in the Pledge of Allegiance, see n. 48 above. The phrase was added to the pledge in the mid twentieth century, but this act did no more than bring the pledge into line with religious expressions found on U.S. currency and the official state piety that had

served as part of American government since Jefferson wrote of rights endowed by a "creator."

72. Ironically, many activists, politicians, and common citizens still seem willing to assert moral principles in their concern for "the environment." Is it not telling that so many individuals and groups are willing to talk about a moral obligation to protect an inanimate object like "the earth" but are unwilling to support such an obligation in simple matters of duty and honor between human beings? I find it somewhat disturbing that a man who has abandoned his family for a younger woman and drives an S.U.V. is far more likely to receive a public reprimand for the latter.

73. "Diversity" in America is interpreted today almost exclusively through external criteria: gender, race, culture. Respect for a diversity that is more than skin deep seems hard to come by. What many academics today would consider a suitably diverse college classroom consists of men and women of various ethnic backgrounds all of whom express admiration for freedom, choice, and diversity.

74. Elshtain, *Democracy on Trial,* p. xvii (emphasis added).

75. Compare Abraham Lincoln's impassioned speech on the preservation of American political institutions before the Young Men's Lyceum of Springfield, Illinois (January 27, 1837), which calls for reverence for the laws in the face of civil disturbances, lawlessness, and a "mobocratic spirit" present in the United States, and for that reverence to become the "political religion of the nation." Lincoln does not name "democracy" as the expression of that religion. He only mentions the success of the "experiment" in testing "the capability of a people to govern themselves." The speech utilizes religious imagery: the "scenes of the Revolution" had been "pillars of the temple of liberty" but had now passed away. Even "bad laws," until they are repealed, "should be religiously observed." Passion must be replaced by reason, from which could be molded "general intelligence, sound morality, and, in particular, a reverence for the Constitution and the laws." For the speech, see J. G. Nicolay and J. Hay, eds., *Abraham Lincoln: Complete Works,* vol. 1 (New York: Century Co., 1894), pp. 9–15; for insightful analysis of it, see Rahe, *Republics Ancient and Modern,* pp. 773–79.

76. In his stimulating and revisionist work *The Athenian Nation,* Edward E. Cohen attempts to establish the presence (in Athens) of certain elements common to modern democratic societies, such as the ability of immigrants to gain citizenship (at least for their children), the empowerment of women (at least in the household), and the protection of all classes from outrages *(hybris)* by citizen adults. The diverse profile of Athens and the "ambivalence, ambiguity, and conflict" (here he is quoting David Cohen, *Law, Sexuality, and Society: The Enforcement of Morals in Classical Athens* [Cambridge, 1991], p. 21) in Athenian culture, Cohen argues, belie "'functionalist' doctrines that stress the 'social solidarity,' 'structural equilibrium,' or 'cultural uniformity' of societies" and show that "a striving for theoretical consistency necessarily obliterates the discontinuities, contradictions, and unintegrated deviations that are inherent in complex dynamic civilizations" (p. 191). To my mind, Cohen confuses the by-products of a society and of its values with the values them-

selves. The admittedly complex and dynamic character of classical Athens emerged from an environment of social cohesion and shared values. Complexity, dynamism, and diversity of opinion (for example) in a society thus do not imply the absence of cohesive values, especially if those values embrace the civic and *moral* responsibility of respect and duty toward others. This (perhaps) paradoxical fact—demonstrated also by American society before the late twentieth century—far from undercutting the need for "social solidarity" or moral structures, suggests that attempting to replace such structures with their by-products (freedom, choice, and diversity themselves) could have the kind of unintended consequences examined in this chapter.

77. For the "diversity movement's" effect on American religion, see Wood, *Diversity,* pp. 149–52, who notes that "the religion of diversity, though immensely tolerant of religious difference, still preserves an emotionally powerful sense of sin and guilt" (p. 150).

78. The virtue of this situation, of course, depends on the real virtues of the church itself.

79. Cf. Elshtain, *Democracy on Trial,* p. 6: the framers of the Constitution "counted on a social deposit of intergenerational trust, neighborliness, and civic responsibility." Of course, some Anti-Federalists lacked the Federalists' confidence that such civic traits would continue in the environment the new Constitution would create: cf. ibid., pp. 9–10; Storing, *What the Anti-Federalists Were For,* esp. pp. 19–23. For interesting critiques of the Founders' thought on virtue and excellence and the Constitution they created, see Rahe, *Republics Ancient and Modern,* esp. pp. 748–72, and Eidelberg, *Philosophy of the American Constitution,* esp. pp. 247–60.

80. See Rahe, *Republics Ancient and Modern,* pp. 748–64: "In 1789 and for a long time thereafter, even those Americans most fiercely opposed to anything that smacked of an establishment of religion and hostile to every vestige of a discrimination between the sects were prepared to promote religious belief; no one supposed that the federal government, much less the states, should be strictly neutral in the contest between agnosticism, atheism, and religious faith" (p. 757). See also p. 762, on Jefferson's willingness to use legislation in Virginia "to support the enforcement of traditional Judaeo-Christian morality within the society at large," including a measure (written by Jefferson and proposed by Madison) that "specified that a man who engages in polygamy, sodomy, or rape be castrated rather than executed."

81. E.g., Madison, *Federalist* 10, pp. 125–27.

CONCLUSION

1. For a defense of the view that Plato's *Apology* "captures at least the tone and substance of what Socrates actually said in the courtroom" (p. 9), see Brickhouse and Smith, *Socrates on Trial,* pp. 1–10. For the argument that Thucydides' version of the Funeral Oration presents a relatively contemporary account of Pericles' speech (but which may still contain Thucydidean ideas), see F. E. Adcock, *Thucydides and His*

History (Cambridge, 1963), pp. 27–38. For an overview of the scholarly debate about the "accuracy" of Thucydides' speeches, see K. J. Dover, *Thucydides* (Oxford, 1973), pp. 21–27, and Simon Hornblower, *Thucydides* (Baltimore, 1987), pp. 45–72. I assume that whenever Thucydides composed (or reproduced) the speech, he chose to do so partially because Pericles' address was sufficiently atypical of funeral orations and representative of Pericles' ideas to warrant inclusion. Even if the historian composed this part of his work after the war's end, enough Athenians who had heard the speech or reports of it will have been alive to make the wholesale invention of the oration's unusual ideas unlikely. This will be true no matter how much Thucydidean language is present in the speech. Pericles' arguments are, I take it, his own.

2. Thuc. 2.60 (all translations of Thucydides in this chapter are those of R. Crawley; all translations of Plato are those of G. M. A. Grube, sometimes adapted in both cases). Compare Nicias's view expressed before the Athenian assembly (Thuc. 6.9), a speech in which Nicias echoes Thucydides' description of Sicily (6.1–6), and which thus may be thought to express other opinions shared by the historian: "not that I think a man need be any the worse citizen for taking some thought for his person and estate; on the contrary, such a man would for his own sake desire the prosperity of his country more than others."

3. See Rahe, *Republics Ancient and Modern,* pp. 186–218.

4. See Hornblower, *Commentary,* 1:311, citing K. J. Dover's opinion that the reference is to Athens. Hornblower also discusses Ar. *Eq.* 732, where Paphlagon (= Cleon) proclaims, "I love you Demos, and I'm your lover *[erastes].*" The two passages together may reflect a kind of political language used by some Athenian leaders. It should be noted that the line makes the demos the passive recipient of Paphlagon's/Cleon's "affections." It also seems possible that Paphlagon's claim carries both the messages "I love you" and (roughly speaking) "You're screwed."

5. See chapter 2, pp. 54–65.

6. See Samons, *Empire of the Owl,* pp. 41–50, and chapter 2, pp. 54–55.

7. E.g., Eur. *Supp.* 399–494; cf. Aesch. *Eum.,* esp. 681 ff. (on the establishment of the Areopagus Council). For an attempt to use the scattered references to construct a fifth-century defense of democracy, see Kurt A. Raaflaub, "Contemporary Perceptions of Democracy in Fifth-Century Athens," *C&M* 40 (1989): 33–70, excerpted in Samons, *Athenian Democracy and Imperialism,* pp. 228–33.

8. See, e.g., Soph. *Ant.* 368–411 (esp. 400–411), and Eur. *Ion* 590 ff.

9. Recent work, especially by Simon Goldhill—"The Great Dionysia and Civic Ideology," *JHS* 107 (1987): 58–76 (= Winkler and Zeitlin, eds., *Nothing to Do with Dionysos?* pp. 97–129); and "Civic Ideology and the Problem of Difference: The Politics of Aeschylean Tragedy, Once Again," *JHS* 120 (2000): 34–56—has usefully emphasized the particular social and historical context of Athenian tragedy. Yet the association (and indeed identification) of this context with democracy per se seems to me much exaggerated. In essence, Goldhill assumes what first needs to be proved: he asks, e.g., "how . . . the festival of the Great Dionysia—its rituals and dramatic per-

formances—relate[s] to the dominant ideological structures of democracy?" ("Civic Ideology and the Problem of Difference," 34). But to assume the existence of such "dominant ideological structures" (of democracy) and then to search for their relation to the Dionysia obviously begs the question. In almost every case where Goldhill attaches the adjective *democratic* to the (Athenian) polis, words like *imperial* or simply *Athenian* would be far more appropriate. The ceremonies or "rituals" before the tragic competitions discussed by Goldhill ("Great Dionysia")—a libation by the generals, a tribute procession, the presentation of war orphans in military garb, and crowns presented to Athens's benefactors—are all "democratic" only in situation (i.e., they occurred within a democracy) and not in essence. All *could* have existed without *demokratia,* but none could have existed in the particular form it did without the empire and the Athenians' martial character. For criticism of Goldhill and others with similar views, see P. J. Rhodes, "Nothing to Do with Democracy: Athenian Drama and the *Polis," JHS* 123 (2003): 104–19, and cf. J. Griffin, "The Social Function of Attic Tragedy," *CQ* 48 (1998): 39–61. Griffin's positive case perhaps tends to overemphasize the aesthetic/emotional effect and intent of tragedy at the expense of its political/social content and context. But he usefully illustrates the weaknesses of scholarship that treats tragedy as (in essence) a product of collective and democratic social forces. Especially welcome is his emphasis on the typically underemphasized role played by the gods in tragedy.

10. For the shallowness of this view, see table 1 and chapter 5, pp. 134–35.

11. Ironically, Lincoln's brief address at Gettysburg (November 19, 1863), which is sometimes compared to Pericles' oration (see, e.g., Gary Wills, *Lincoln at Gettysburg: The Words That Remade America* [New York, 1992], esp. pp. 52–62), shares this myopia about the future. Lincoln predicted that "the world will little note, nor long remember what we say here, but it can never forget what they did here." How many modern Americans could relate the significance (much less the dates!) of the battle of Gettysburg compared with the number who know the phrases "Fourscore and seven years ago" and "government of the people, by the people, for the people"?

12. See chapter 2.

13. See Thuc. 2.37, with chapter 7, pp. 183–84.

14. Compare George Washington's farewell address from 1796 (which serves as an epigraph to chapter 7). On John Adams's recognition of the need of this social foundation for American government to succeed, cf. Thompson, *John Adams and the Spirit of Liberty,* p. 23, who emphasizes the supposed political utility of Adams's view. Neither Adams nor Jefferson was an entirely orthodox Christian, but both believed in the importance of religion and private morality, and both held that the nature of "true religion" consisted of the "moral precepts taught by Jesus": C. B. Sanford, *The Religious Life of Thomas Jefferson* (Charlottesville, Va., 1984), p. 4, quoting L. J. Hall, "The Religious Opinions of Thomas Jefferson," *Sewanee Review* 21 (1913): 163–76 (165); see also L. J. Cappon, ed., *The Adams-Jefferson Letters* (Chapel Hill, N.C., 1959), 2:509, 512; cf. E. S. Gaustad, *Sworn on the Altar of God: A Religious Biography*

of Thomas Jefferson (Grand Rapids, Mich., 1996), esp. pp. 210–11, on "Jefferson's belief in an intimate, indissoluble bond between religion and morality" (211).

15. Again, we can compare the Founders, who make some references to social restraints outside the Constitution, but who ultimately created a Constitution that itself did little to encourage those restraints. In fact, although they implicitly depended on the continuation of certain conditions they did not address, many Founders believed that their system could rely on the idea of competing (vicious) interests balancing each other out: for this idea, see Wood, *Creation of the American Republic*, pp. 587–92, 606–15; on the Founders' (i.e., the Federalists') ultimate rejection of religion as a guarantor of civic virtue, see esp. ibid., pp. 427–29. Of course, the Federalists (like Madison and Hamilton) constructed and then defended a Constitution of a particularly secular nature, which prevented religious "tests" for office (Art. VI, par. 3), and (eventually) legislation by Congress "respecting an establishment of religion" (First Amendment). Anti-Federalists noted (and lamented) that the U.S. Constitution gave "no public support for religious institutions" (*Federalist Papers*, ed. Krannick, p. 58). But this debate was epiphenomenal to the actual conditions of American society in the 1780s. That society was thoroughly religious, a fact reflected by many state constitutions well into the 1800s (see chapter 7, n. 50).

16. For the institution of the juries, see chapter 1, p. 30 above.

17. Brickhouse and Smith, *Socrates on Trial*, p. 26, note that the number of jurors at Socrates' trial cannot be determined with certainty. But the jury of five hundred was often used in similar cases, and this remains the most likely size of the panel that condemned Socrates.

18. For the formal charges, see Plato, *Ap.* 24b–c; Diog. Laert. 2.40; Xen. *Mem.* 1.1.1; and cf. Brickhouse and Smith, *Socrates on Trial*, pp. 30–37. Brickhouse and Smith emphasize the religious aspect of the accusations against Socrates, as against the political aspects (that is, his association with—especially—Critias and Alcibiades): esp. pp. 71–87, 194–97; see also their *Plato's Socrates*, pp. 166–75.

19. Socrates himself may not have heard Pericles' Funeral Oration, delivered in the winter of 431/0, since the philosopher served in the military force at Potidaea (Pl. *Ap.* 28e), the Athenian investment of which had already begun by this time. However, Socrates may have accompanied the supporting expedition in the summer of 430 led by Hagnon and Kleopompos (Thuc. 2.58), and thus it is not impossible that he attended the ceremony at which Pericles made his address. Thucydides himself is likely to have heard the speech, and in any event it would have been a relatively simple matter for either man to learn the basic thrust of what Pericles had said (cf. Thuc. 1.22). Moreover, the possibility exists that Plato (if not Socrates himself) had access to Thucydides' work, and thus to his record of the Funeral Oration, before the *Apology* was written. Whatever view of Thucydides' "publication" is adopted, his work must have been known by the second quarter of the fourth century, after which time Xenophon, Theopompos, and others continued his narrative from the point at which it now breaks off (in 411). More intriguing is the possibility of Xenophon's personal

involvement in the publication (Diog. Laert. 2.57), since Xenophon was himself a member of the Socratic circle. Other possible influences of Thucydides on this circle (besides the obvious effect on Xenophon) have long been recognized, at least where the Platonic *Menexenus* is concerned, a dialogue in which Aspasia is reported to have delivered a famous *epitaphios* of her own (Pl. *Menex.* 236d ff.). Reflections of her husband's well-known speech are ready to hand. There is, therefore, every reason to suppose that Plato (or whoever wrote the *Menexenus*) had access either to Thucydides' work or to other reports of Pericles' Funeral Oration, while the probability that Socrates had heard either the speech or a report of it should be considered high.

20. Cf. Thuc. 2.63: "Again, your country has a right to your services in sustaining the glories of her position. These are a common source of pride to you all, and you cannot decline the burdens of empire and still expect to share its honors" (trans. Crawley).

21. Socrates implies as much in Plato's *Gorgias*.

22. For this episode, see also chapter 5, pp. 140–41.

23. Socrates could have chosen any number of examples of the Athenians' conviction, condemnation, and/or execution of their own fellow citizens and leaders. Apart from nine *hellenotamiai* executed (but later found to be innocent) around mid-century (Antiphon 5.69–71), the convictions of the alleged Hermocopid conspirators in 415 (Thuc. 6.53, 60), and those of the oligarchic revolutionaries of 411 (Thuc. 8.68), the previously popular demagogue Cleophon had been indicted on apparently trumped-up charges and summarily executed in 405/4 (Lys. 13.12; Xen. *Hell.* 1.7.35). The most important difference (for Socrates' purposes) between these cases and the execution of the generals in 406 may have been Socrates' own involvement and the regret felt by the demos at the generals' deaths.

24. Especially considering his views about "protection of the injured" (Thuc. 2.37: see below), a group that might be thought to include the wounded and shipwrecked after Arginusae.

25. For Socrates' interpretation of the oracle, see Brickhouse and Smith, *Socrates on Trial*, pp. 87–100.

26. Gomme, *Commentary*, 2:113, notes that for Pericles, unlike Sophocles (*Oed. Rex* 863–70; *Ant.* 450–61), the "unwritten laws" were not divine. Pericles may have mentioned the gods in a funeral oration given during or after Athens's war with Samos: see Plut. *Per.* 8.

27. For Socrates on justice, see Plato's *Republic* (esp. bk. 1) and *Protagoras*. For the connection between *dike* and the gods, see chapter 7, n. 38.

28. Echoed in Thucydides by Cleon (3.37); see also 6.18, 85.

29. Socrates might have argued that by treating the allies unjustly, the Athenians were creating a force that would ultimately harm them: see his questioning of Meletus (Pl. *Ap.* 25c ff.). Elsewhere, Plato (or rather, Socrates or the "Athenian") seems to condemn states that "enslave" others: *Laws* 638b (Athens enslaves Keos); *Republic* 351a–b, 469b–c.

30. On this issue, see Plato's *Protagoras.*

31. For Pericles' connection of a man's *arete* with service to the state (and a woman's with being least spoken about among men), see Thuc. 2. 42–43, 45–46.

32. See chapter 7, pp. 165–66.

33. After describing how he has benefited the Athenians, Socrates continues: "Nothing is more suitable, gentlemen, than for such a man to be fed in the Prytaneum, much more suitable for him than for any one of you who has won a victory at Olympia with a pair or a team of horses. The Olympian victor makes you think yourself happy; I make you happy. Besides, he does not need food, but I do. So if I must make a just assessment of what I deserve, I assess it at this: free meals in the Prytaneum" (Pl. *Ap.* 36d–37a; trans. Grube). To appreciate fully the humor of this passage, one must understand that the condemned citizen was expected to propose a legitimate punishment for himself. The prosecutors then proposed another punishment, and the jurors chose between the two proposals. Socrates' prosecutors proposed execution, and the philosopher was probably expected to propose exile for himself. Eventually, at the urging of his associates (including Plato and Crito) and after this ironic speech and a claim that he could pay only 1 mina, Socrates agreed to propose a fine of 30 minae (38b). This is sometimes treated as a small sum, but 1 mina equaled 100 drachmas, and jurors received half a drachma per day for their service. Thirty minae was therefore a very large sum, and it was the amount Socrates' supporters urged him to propose and then pledged themselves as sureties for. Plato and the others certainly did not urge Socrates to propose a sum that would ensure his execution: see Brickhouse and Smith, *Socrates on Trial,* pp. 225–30. It was Socrates' speech before the proposal of 30 minae that turned even more jurors against the philosopher, not the amount of the proposed fine per se.

34. Cf. Plut. *Per.* 32, 36. I do not wish to imply that Socrates was a model father or husband. Stone, *Trial of Socrates,* pp. 192–93, attacks Socrates the husband and father based on Plato's report in the *Phaedo* of the philosopher's interaction with his family during his last hours. Stone's condemnation of Socrates/Plato for the dialogue's supposed lack of "compassion for the common man or the common woman" nicely demonstrates the way moderns confuse publicly proclaimed democratic political views (like those expressed by Pericles) with real humanity and the ability to inspire devoted friends (shown by Socrates). Pericles sent thousands of Athenians to their deaths and then (bizarrely) claimed on his deathbed: "No Athenian has put on mourning because of me" (Plut. *Per.* 38.4), apparently referring to the fact that he had not employed civil war or violence to achieve power (see P. A. Stadter, *A Commentary on Plutarch's Pericles* [Chapel Hill, N.C., 1989], pp. 345–46). Stone seems to want Plato to record or Socrates to have performed the kind of public display of private affection that pervades our own society, a display which would have been anomalous in Athens. For Socrates' personal qualities and the devotion they inspired in his followers, see Samons, "Socrates, Virtue and the Modern Professor," *Journal of Education* 182 (2000 [2001]), 19–27.

35. On Pericles' military service, see esp. Plut. *Per.* 18–28.

36. E.g., Pl. *Republic* 469b–c and n. 29 above.

37. On Socrates' military service, see also Pl. *Ap.* 28e, *Lach.* 181b, *Symp.* 220c–221c, and *Chrm.* 153b–c.

38. On Socrates' piety, see esp. Xen. *Mem.* 1.1.2–20, 4.8.11, and Plato, *Seventh Letter* 325. Plato was much concerned with piety, esp. in *Euthyphro* and *Laws*; Brickhouse and Smith, *Plato's Socrates*, pp. 64–69.

39. Against Brickhouse and Smith, *Socrates on Trial*, pp. 71–87, 194–97, and id., *Plato's Socrates*, pp. 166–75.

40. Pl. *Phd.* 118. If Socrates' last remark was intended to be ironic, it nonetheless reflects the action/opinion dichotomy. Brickhouse and Smith, *Socrates on Trial*, pp. 30–34, argue that Socrates' alleged impiety involved not his religious practices but rather atheism (cf. Xen. *Mem.* 1.1.2–5; Plut. *Mor.* 580b). In my opinion, they overemphasize the importance of belief (vs. practice) in the area of Athenian religion. The conglomeration of accusations made in the formal charges against Socrates suggests a broad-based attempt to enlist popular opinion against the philosopher rather than the manipulation of a particular law (against atheism or the like). See also chapter 1, n. 99.

41. These details mainly appear in Plutarch's life of Pericles, and some are undoubtedly later inventions. However, we happen to know that in the fifth century a certain Stesimbrotus of Thasos wrote a scandalous work on Pericles, Thucydides (son of Melesias, not the historian), and Themistocles. This work contained, at least, contemporary gossip, which was therefore available to Plutarch. The comic poets also provided Plutarch with ample contemporary material on Pericles.

42. Pl. *Ap.* 19d–e, with Brickhouse and Smith, *Socrates on Trial*, pp. 16–17.

43. See Plut. *Per.* 16, 36.

44. I do not wish to imply that the general human desire to improve oneself economically did not exist in ancient Greece. In Athens, some men were already practicing a kind of ancient capitalism: Nicias kept gangs of slaves that he rented out for work in the state silver mines (Plut. *Nicias* 4).

45. If we turn (somewhat whimsically) to their domestic situations, we find that neither man apparently lived a perfectly settled life. The details of Socrates' marriage(s?) are obscure, but his relationship with his wife Xanthippe was notorious for its volatility (e.g., Xen. *Symp.* 2.10; see also Brickhouse and Smith, *Socrates on Trial*, pp. 15–17). It is unclear, moreover, why Pericles came to divorce his first wife and then begin a new life with his foreign consort or spouse Aspasia (see Fornara and Samons, *Athens from Cleisthenes to Pericles*, pp. 162–65). Rumors of Pericles' philandering were apparently rife, including even accusations that he had seduced his son's wife (Plut. *Per.* 13, 36). Many, if not most, of these accusations probably stemmed from Aspasia's dubious status as a foreign woman from Ionia (an area with a troubled reputation) and Pericles' apparently brazen and open affection for her (Plut. *Per.* 24, 32). In any case, the new relationship certainly scan-

dalized Athens, and although Pericles is supposed to have loved Aspasia dearly, the Athenians' apparent hostility to his new consort probably made life at home difficult at times.

46. See chapter 2, pp. 54–68.

47. On this passage, see also chapter 2, pp. 65–66.

SELECT BIBLIOGRAPHY

This bibliography includes modern works referred to by short title and translations of ancient works quoted (sometimes in adapted form).

Adams, John. *The Works of John Adams, Second President of the United States: With a Life of the Author, Notes and Illustrations, by His Grandson Charles Francis Adams.* 10 vols. Boston: Little, Brown, 1850–56.

Adams, Willi Paul. *The First American Constitutions: Republican Ideology and the Making of the State Constitutions in the Revolutionary Era.* Translated by Rita Kimber and Robert Kimber. Chapel Hill: University of North Carolina Press for the Institute of Early American History and Culture, Williamsburg, Va., 1980.

Adcock, F. E. *Thucydides and His History.* Cambridge: Cambridge University Press, 1963.

Aeschines. *The Speeches of Aeschines.* Translated by Charles Darwin Adams. Loeb Classical Library. Cambridge, Mass.: Harvard University Press, 1919.

Andreades, A. *A History of Greek Public Finance.* Translated by C. N. Brown. Cambridge, Mass.: Harvard University Press, 1933.

Andrewes, A. *The Greek Tyrants.* London: Hutchinson, 1956.

———. "The Arginousai Trial." *Phoenix* 28 (1974): 112–22.

———. "The Opposition to Pericles." *Journal of Hellenic Studies* 98 (1978): 1–8.

———. "The Growth of the Athenian State." In John Boardman et al., eds., *The Cambridge Ancient History,* 2d ed., vol. 3, pt. 3, pp. 360–91. Cambridge: Cambridge University Press, 1982.

———. "The Tyranny of Pisistratus." In John Boardman et al., eds., *The Cambridge Ancient History,* 2d ed., vol. 3, pt. 3, pp. 392–416. Cambridge: Cambridge University Press, 1982.

———. "The Peace of Nicias and the Sicilian Expedition." In D. M. Lewis et al., eds., *The Cambridge Ancient History,* 2d ed., vol. 5, pp. 433–63. Cambridge: Cambridge University Press, 1992.

———. "The Spartan Resurgence." In D. M. Lewis et al., eds., *The Cambridge*

Ancient History, 2d ed., vol. 5, pp. 464–98. Cambridge: Cambridge University Press, 1992.

Andreyev, V. N. "Some Aspects of Agrarian Conditions in Attica from the Fifth to the Third Centuries B.C." *Eirene* 12 (1974): 5–46.

Aristophanes. *Three Plays by Aristophanes: Staging Women.* Edited and translated by Jeffrey Henderson. New York: Routledge, 1996.

———. [*Comedies.*] Edited and translated by Jeffrey Henderson. Loeb Classical Library. 4 vols. Cambridge, Mass.: Harvard University Press, 1998–2002.

Aristotle. *The "Art" of Rhetoric.* Translated by John Henry Freese. Loeb Classical Library. Cambridge, Mass.: Harvard University Press, 1926.

———. *The Constitution of Athens.* In J. M. Moore, ed. and trans., *Aristotle and Xenophon on Democracy and Oligarchy.* Berkeley: University of California Press, 1975.

———. *The Nicomachean Ethics.* Translated by H. Rackham. Loeb Classical Library. Cambridge, Mass.: Harvard University Press, 1934.

———. *The Politics of Aristotle.* Edited and translated by Ernest Barker. Reprint. New York: Oxford University Press, 1962.

Austen, Jane. *Northanger Abbey.* [1818.] Edited by A. H. Ehrenpreis. London: Penguin Books, 1972.

Badian, E. "Agis III." *Hermes* 95 (1967): 170–92.

———. *From Plataea to Potidaea: Studies in the History and Historiography of the Pentecontaetia.* Baltimore: Johns Hopkins University Press, 1993.

Bakewell, Geoffrey W., and James P. Sickinger, eds. *Gestures: Essays in Ancient History, Literature, and Philosophy Presented to Alan L. Boegehold.* Oxford: Oxbow Books, 2003.

Bicknell, P. J. *Studies in Greek Politics and Genealogy.* Historia Einzelschriften, 19. Wiesbaden: Franz Steiner, 1972.

Bloom, Alan. *The Closing of the American Mind.* New York: Simon & Schuster, 1987.

Boardman, John, and N. G. L. Hammond, eds. *The Cambridge Ancient History.* 2d ed. Vol. 3, pt. 3. Cambridge: Cambridge University Press, 1982.

Boedeker, Deborah, and Kurt A. Raaflaub, eds. *Democracy, Empire, and the Arts in Fifth-Century Athens.* Cambridge, Mass.: Harvard University Press, 1998.

Boegehold, Alan. "Andokides and the Decree of Patrokleides." *Historia* 39 (1990): 149–62.

———. "Resistance to Change in the Law at Athens." In Josiah Ober and Charles Hedrick, eds., *Dêmokratia,* pp. 203–14. Princeton: Princeton University Press, 1996.

Boegehold, Alan L., and Adele C. Scafuro, eds. *Athenian Identity and Civic Ideology.* Baltimore: Johns Hopkins University Press, 1994.

Boersma, J. S. *Athenian Building Policy from 561/0 to 405/4 B.C.* Groningen: Wolters-Noordhoff, 1970.

Borza, Eugene N. *In the Shadow of Olympus: The Emergence of Macedon.* Princeton, N.J.: Princeton University Press, 1990.

———. "Greeks and Macedonians in the Age of Alexander: The Source Traditions." In R. W. Wallace and E. M. Harris, eds., *Transitions to Empire: Essays in Greco-Roman History, 360–146 B.C., in Honor of E. Badian,* pp. 122–39. Norman, Okla.: University of Oklahoma Press, 1996.

———. *Before Alexander: Constructing Early Macedonia.* Claremont, Calif.: Regina Books, 1999.

Botsford, G. W., and Charles A. Robinson, Jr. *Botsford and Robinson's Hellenic History.* 5th ed. Rev. Donald Kagan. New York: Macmillan, 1969.

Bourriot, Félix. *Recherches sur la nature du génos: Étude d'histoire sociale athenienne, périodes archaïque et classique.* 2 vols. Lille: Université de Lille, 1976.

Brickhouse, Thomas C., and Nicholas D. Smith. *Socrates on Trial.* Princeton, N.J.: Princeton University Press, 1989.

———. *Plato's Socrates.* New York: Oxford University Press, 1994.

Brookhiser, Richard. *Founding Father: Rediscovering George Washington.* New York: Free Press, 1996.

Bruit Zaidman, Louise, and Pauline Schmitt Pantel. *Religion in the Ancient Greek City.* Translated by Paul Cartledge. Cambridge: Cambridge University Press, 1992.

Brun, Patrice. *Eisphora-Syntaxis-Stratiotika: Recherches sur les finances militaires d'Athènes au IVe siècle av. J.-C.* Paris: Les Belles Lettres, 1983.

Buckler, John. *The Theban Hegemony, 371–362 BC.* Cambridge, Mass.: Harvard University Press, 1980.

———. *Philip II and the Sacred War.* Leiden: E. J. Brill, 1989.

Burkert, Walter. *Greek Religion.* Translated by John Raffan. Cambridge, Mass.: Harvard University Press, 1985.

Bury, J. B., and Russell Meiggs. *A History of Greece to the Death of Alexander the Great.* 4th ed. New York: St. Martin's, 1975.

Camp, John McK. *The Athenian Agora: Excavations in the Heart of Classical Athens.* London: Thames & Hudson, 1986.

Cappon, L. J., ed. *The Adams-Jefferson Letters.* 2 vols. Chapel Hill: University of North Carolina Press, 1959.

Cargill, Jack. *The Second Athenian League: Empire or Free Alliance?* Berkeley: University of California Press, 1981.

Carter, L. B. *The Quiet Athenian.* Oxford: Oxford University Press, 1986.

Cartledge, Paul. *Agesilaos and the Crisis of Sparta.* Baltimore: Johns Hopkins University Press, 1987.

———. *The Greeks.* Oxford: Oxford University Press, 1993.

———. *Sparta and Lakonia: A Regional History, 1300–362 B.C.* 2d ed. London: Routledge, 2002.

Castriota, David. *Myth, Ethos and Actuality: Official Art in Fifth-Century- B.C. Athens.* Madison: University of Wisconsin Press, 1992.

Cawkwell, G. L. "The Crowning of Demosthenes." *Classical Quarterly* 19 (1969): 163–80.

———. *Philip of Macedon.* London: Faber & Faber, 1978.

———. "The End of Greek Liberty." In R. W. Wallace and E. M. Harris, eds., *Transitions to Empire: Essays in Greco-Roman History, 360–146 B.C., in Honor of E. Badian,* pp. 98–121. Norman: University of Oklahoma Press, 1996.

Cohen, David. *Law, Sexuality and Society: The Enforcement of Morals in Classical Athens.* Cambridge: Cambridge University Press, 1991.

Cohen, Edward E. *The Athenian Nation.* Princeton, N.J.: Princeton University Press, 2000.

Connor, W. R. *The New Politicians of Fifth-Century Athens.* Princeton, N.J.: Princeton University Press, 1971.

———. "'Sacred' and 'Secular' in Athenian Society." *Ancient Society* 19 (1988): 161–87.

Conophagos, C. E. *Le Laurium antique et la technique grecque de la production de l'argent.* Athens: Ekdotike Hellados, 1980.

Csapo, E., and W. J. Slater. *The Context of Ancient Drama.* Ann Arbor: University of Michigan Press, 1995.

Dahl, Robert A. *Democracy and Its Critics.* New Haven: Yale University Press, 1989.

Davies, J. K. *Athenian Propertied Families, 600–300 B.C.* Oxford: Oxford University Press, 1971.

Demosthenes. [*Orations.*] 7 vols. Vol. 1 translated by J. H. Vince; vol. 2 translated by C. A. Vince and J. H. Vince; vol. 3 translated by J. H. Vince; vols. 4–6 translated by A. T. Murray; vol. 7 translated by Norman W. DeWitt and Norman J. DeWitt. Loeb Classical Library. Cambridge, Mass.: Harvard University Press, 1930–49.

de Ste. Croix, G. E. M. *The Origins of the Peloponnesian War.* London: Duckworth, 1972.

Develin, Robert. *Athenian Officials, 684–321 B.C.* Cambridge: Cambridge University Press, 1989.

Dover, K. J. *Thucydides.* Greece and Rome: New Surveys in the Classics, no. 7. Oxford: Oxford University Press, 1973.

———. *Greek Homosexuality.* Cambridge, Mass.: Harvard University Press, 1978.

Dunn, John, ed. *Democracy: The Unfinished Journey, 508 BC to AD 1993.* Oxford: Oxford University Press 1992.

Eddy, S. Review of P. Brun, *Eisphora-Syntaxis-Stratiotika. American Historical Review* 89 (1984): 1312–13.

Eder, Walter, ed. *Die athenische Demokratie im 4. Jahrhundert v.Chr.: Vollendung oder Verfall einer Verfassungsform? Akten eines Symposiums 3.–7. August 1992, Bellagio.* Stuttgart: Franz Steiner, 1995.

———. "Aristocrats and the Coming of Athenian Democracy." In Ian Morris and Kurt A. Raaflaub, eds., *Democracy 2500? Questions and Challenges,* pp. 105–40. Archaeological Institute of America Colloquium Series. Dubuque, Iowa: Kendall/Hunt, 1998.

Eidelberg, Paul. *The Philosophy of the American Constitution: A Reinterpretation of the Intentions of the Founding Fathers.* New York: Free Press, 1968.

Elshtain, Jean Bethke. *Democracy on Trial.* New York: Basic Books, 1995.

Errington, R. M. *A History of Macedonia.* Trans. C. Errington. Berkeley: University of California Press, 1990.

Euben, J. P., John Wallach, and Josiah Ober, eds. *Athenian Political Thought and the Reconstruction of American Democracy.* Ithaca, N.Y.: Cornell University Press, 1994.

Evans, J. A. S. "Herodotus and the Battle of Marathon." *Historia* 42 (1993): 279–307.

Farrar, Cynthia. *The Origins of Democratic Thinking: The Invention of Politics in Classical Athens.* Cambridge: Cambridge University Press, 1988.

Ferrill, Arther. *The Origins of War: From the Stone Age to Alexander the Great.* Boulder, Colo.: Westview Press, 1997.

Figueira, T. J. *The Power of Money: Coinage and Politics in the Athenian Empire.* Philadelphia: University of Pennsylvania Press, 1998.

Finley, M. I. *Democracy Ancient and Modern.* [1973.] 2d ed. New Brunswick, N.J.: Rutgers University Press, 1985.

———. *Economy and Society in Ancient Greece.* Edited by Brent D. Shaw and Richard P. Saller. New York: Viking Press, 1982.

———. *Politics in the Ancient World.* Cambridge: Cambridge University Press, 1983.

Flower, M. A., and Mark Toher, eds. *Georgica: Greek Studies in Honour of George Cawkwell.* London: University of London, Institute of Classical Studies, 1991.

Fornara, C. W. *The Athenian Board of Generals from 501 to 404.* Historia Einzelschriften, 16. Wiesbaden: Franz Steiner, 1971.

———. "On the Chronology of the Samian War." *Journal of Hellenic Studies* 99 (1979): 9–17.

———, ed. and trans. *Archaic Times to the End of the Peloponnesian War.* Translated Documents of Greece and Rome, vol. 1. 2d ed. Cambridge: Cambridge University Press, 1983.

———. *The Nature of History in Ancient Greece and Rome.* Berkeley: University of California Press, 1983.

———. "Thucydides' Birth Date." In R. M. Rosen and J. Farrell, eds., *Nomo-*

deiktes: Greek Studies in Honor of Martin Ostwald, pp. 71–80. Ann Arbor: University of Michigan Press, 1993.

Fornara, C. W., and L. J. Samons II. *Athens from Cleisthenes to Pericles.* Berkeley: University of California Press, 1991.

Forrest, W. G. *The Emergence of Greek Democracy, 800–400 B.C.* New York : McGraw-Hill, 1966.

Frost, F. J. "Pericles, Thucydides Son of Melesias, and Athenian Politics before the War." *Historia* (1964): 385–99.

Gabrielsen, Vincent. *Financing the Athenian Fleet: Public Taxation and Social Relations.* Baltimore: Johns Hopkins University Press, 1994.

Gagarin, Michael. "The Torture of Slaves in Athenian Law." *Classical Philology* 91 (1996): 1–18.

Gaustad, E. S. *Sworn on the Altar of God: A Religious Biography of Thomas Jefferson.* Grand Rapids, Mich.: Eerdmans, 1996.

Goldhill, S. "The Great Dionysia and Civic Ideology." *Journal of Hellenic Studies* 107 (1987): 58–76 = John J. Winkler and Froma I. Zeitlin, eds., *Nothing to Do with Dionysos? Athenian Drama in Its Social Context* (Princeton, N.J.: Princeton University Press, 1990), pp. 97–129.

———. "Civic Ideology and the Problem of Difference: The Politics of Aeschylean Tragedy, Once Again." *Journal of Hellenic Studies* 120 (2000): 34–56.

Gomme, A. W. *More Essays in Greek History and Literature.* Oxford: Blackwell, 1962.

Gomme, A. W., A. Andrewes, and K. J. Dover. *A Historical Commentary on Thucydides.* 5 vols. Oxford: Oxford University Press, 1945–81.

Griffin, J. "The Social Function of Attic Tragedy." *Classical Quarterly* 48 (1998): 39–61.

Grote, George. *A History of Greece.* 12 vols. London: J. Murray, 1846–56.

Habicht, Christian. *Athens from Alexander to Antony.* Translated by D. L. Schneider. Cambridge, Mass.: Harvard University Press, 1997.

Hall, Jonathan M. *Ethnic Identity in Greek Antiquity.* Cambridge: Cambridge University Press, 1997.

Hall, L. J. "The Religious Opinions of Thomas Jefferson." *Sewanee Review* 21 (1913): 163–76.

Hamilton, Charles D. *Sparta's Bitter Victories: Politics and Diplomacy in the Corinthian War.* Ithaca, N.Y.: Cornell University Press, 1979.

———. *Agesilaus and the Failure of Spartan Hegemony.* Ithaca, N.Y.: Cornell University Press, 1991.

Hamilton, Charles D., and Peter Krentz, eds. *Polis and Polemos: Essays on Politics, War, and History in Ancient Greece, in Honor of Donald Kagan.* Claremont, Calif.: Regina Books, 1997.

Hammond, N. G. L. *The Macedonian State: Origins, Institutions, and History.* Oxford: Oxford University Press, 1989.

————. "The Expedition of Datis and Artaphernes." In D. M. Lewis et al., eds., *The Cambridge Ancient History,* 2d ed., vol. 6, pp. 491–517. Cambridge: Cambridge University Press, 1994.

————. *Philip of Macedon.* Baltimore: Johns Hopkins University Press, 1994.

Hammond, N. G. L., and G. T. Griffith. *A History of Macedonia.* Vol. 2. Oxford: Oxford University Press, 1979.

Hansen, Mogens Herman. *Eisangelia: The Sovereignty of the People's Court in Athens in the Fourth Century B.C. and the Impeachment of Generals and Politicians.* Odense University Classical Studies, vol. 6. Odense, Denmark: Odense Universitetsforlag, 1975.

————. *The Athenian Assembly in the Age of Demosthenes.* Oxford: Blackwell, 1987.

————. "The Athenian Board of Generals: When Was Tribal Representation Replaced by Election from All Athenians?" In *Studies in Ancient History and Numismatics Presented to Rudi Thomsen,* pp. 69–70. Aarhus, Denmark: Aarhus University Press, 1988.

————. *Was Athens a Democracy? Popular Rule, Liberty and Equality in Ancient and Modern Political Thought.* Historisk-filosofiske Meddelelser, 59. Copenhagen: Royal Danish Academy of Sciences and Letters, 1989.

————. *The Athenian Democracy in the Age of Demosthenes.* Translated by J. A. Crook. Oxford: Blackwell, 1991.

————, ed. *The Ancient Greek City-State: Symposium on the Occasion of the 250th Anniversary of the Royal Danish Academy of Sciences and Letters, July 1–4, 1992.* Copenhagen: Royal Danish Academy of Sciences and Letters, 1993.

————. *The Trial of Sokrates—from the Athenian Point of View.* Historisk-filosofiske Meddelelser, 71. Copenhagen: Munksgaard, 1995.

————. "The Ancient Athenian and the Modern Liberal View of Liberty as a Democratic Ideal." In Josiah Ober and Charles Hedrick, eds., *Dêmokratia,* pp. 91–104. Princeton, N.J.: Princeton University Press, 1996.

————. *Polis and City-State: An Ancient Concept and Its Modern Equivalent.* Copenhagen: Royal Danish Academy of Sciences and Letters, 1998.

Hansen, Mogens Herman, and Kurt A. Raaflaub, eds. *Studies in the Ancient Greek Polis.* Historia Einzelschriften, 95. Stuttgart: Franz Steiner, 1995.

Hanson, Victor Davis. *Warfare and Agriculture in Classical Greece.* Pisa: Giardini, 1983. [2d ed., Berkeley: University of California Press, 1998.]

————. *The Other Greeks: The Family Farm and the Agrarian Roots of Western Civilization.* New York: Free Press, 1995.

————. "Hoplites and Democrats: The Changing Ideology of Athenian Infantry." In Josiah Ober and Charles Hedrick, eds., *Dêmokratia,* pp. 289–312. Princeton, N.J.: Princeton University Press, 1996.

————. *The Soul of Battle: From Ancient Times to the Present Day, How Three Great Liberators Vanquished Tyranny.* New York: Free Press, 1999.

Hanson, Victor Davis, and John Heath. "Who Killed Homer?" *Arion* 5, no. 2 (1997): 108–54.

———. *Who Killed Homer? The Demise of Classical Education and the Recovery of Greek Wisdom*. New York: Free Press, 1998.

Harding, Phillip, ed. and trans. *From the End of the Peloponnesian War to the Battle of Ipsus*. Translated Documents of Greece and Rome, vol. 2. Cambridge: Cambridge University Press, 1985.

Harris, Edward M. *Aeschines and Athenian Politics*. New York: Oxford University Press, 1995.

Harrison, A. R. W. *The Law of Athens*. 2 vols. Oxford: Oxford University Press, 1968–71.

Henderson, Jeffrey. "Attic Old Comedy, Frank Speech, and Democracy." In Deborah Boedeker and Kurt A. Raaflaub, eds., *Democracy, Empire, and the Arts in Fifth-Century Athens*, pp. 255–73. Cambridge, Mass.: Harvard University Press, 1998.

Herodotus. *The Persian Wars*. Translated by G. Rawlinson. New York: McGraw-Hill, 1942.

Hignett, C. *Xerxes' Invasion of Greece*. Oxford: Oxford University Press, 1963.

Hodkinson, Stephen. *Property and Wealth in Classical Sparta*. London: Duckworth, 2000.

Holladay, A. J. "The Détente of Kallias?" *Historia* 35 (1986): 503–7.

Hooker, G. T. W., ed. *Parthenos and Parthenon*. Greece and Rome, Supplement to vol. 10. Oxford: Oxford University Press, 1963.

Hornblower, Simon. *Thucydides*. Baltimore: Johns Hopkins University Press, 1987.

———. "Creation and Development of Democratic Institutions in Ancient Greece." In John Dunn, ed., *Democracy: The Unfinished Journey, 508 B.C. to A.D. 1993*, pp. 1–16. Oxford: Oxford University Press 1992.

———. "Sources and Their Uses." In D. M. Lewis et al., eds., *The Cambridge Ancient History*, 2d ed., vol. 6, pp. 1–23. Cambridge: Cambridge University Press, 1994.

———. *A Commentary on Thucydides*. 2 vols. Oxford: Oxford University Press, 1991–96.

Humphreys, S. C. *Anthropology and the Greeks*. London: Routledge, 1978.

Hurwit, J. *The Athenian Acropolis*. Cambridge: Cambridge University Press, 1999.

Huxley, G. L. *Early Sparta*. Cambridge, Mass.: Harvard University Press, 1962.

Jones, A. H. M. *Athenian Democracy*. Oxford: Blackwell, 1957.

Jones, J. E. "The Laurion Silver Mines: A Review of Recent Researches and Results." *Greece and Rome* 29 (1982): 169–83.

Jones, Nicholas F. *Public Organization in Ancient Greece: A Documentary Study*. Philadelphia: American Philosophical Society, 1987.

———. *The Associations of Classical Athens: The Response to Democracy*. Oxford: Oxford University Press, 1999.

Kagan, Donald. *The Outbreak of the Peloponnesian War.* Ithaca, N.Y.: Cornell University Press, 1969.

———. *The Archidamian War.* Ithaca, N.Y.: Cornell University Press, 1974.

———. *The Peace of Nicias and the Sicilian Expedition.* Ithaca, N.Y.: Cornell University Press, 1981.

———. *The Fall of the Athenian Empire.* Ithaca, N.Y.: Cornell University Press, 1987.

———. *Pericles of Athens and the Birth of Democracy.* New York: Free Press, 1991.

———. *On the Origins of War and the Preservation of Peace.* New York: Doubleday, 1995.

Kallet, Lisa. "Did Tribute Fund the Parthenon?" *California Studies in Classical Antiquity* 20 (1989): 252–66.

———. *Money, Expense, and Naval Power in Thucydides' History 1–5.24.* Berkeley: University of California Press, 1993.

———. "Accounting for Culture in Fifth-Century Athens." In Deborah Boedeker and Kurt A. Raaflaub, eds., *Democracy, Empire, and the Arts in Fifth-Century Athens,* pp. 43–58. Cambridge, Mass.: Harvard University Press, 1998.

Ketcham, Ralph, ed. *The Anti-Federalist Papers; and, The Constitutional Convention Debates.* New York: New American Library, 1986.

Kotlikoff, Laurence J., and Scott Burns. *The Coming Generational Storm: What You Need to Know about America's Economic Future.* Cambridge, Mass.: MIT Press, 2004.

Krentz, Peter. *The Thirty at Athens.* Ithaca, N.Y.: Cornell University Press, 1982.

———. "The Ostracism of Thoukydides Son of Melesias." *Historia* 33 (1984): 499–504.

———. "Fighting by the Rules: The Invention of the Hoplite Agôn." *Hesperia* 71 (2002): 23–39.

Kurke, Leslie. *Coins, Bodies, Games, and Gold: The Politics of Meaning in Archaic Greece.* Princeton, N.J.: Princeton University Press, 1999.

Lambert, S. D. *The Phratries of Attica.* Ann Arbor: University of Michigan Press, 1993.

Lazenby, J. F. *The Spartan Army.* Chicago: Bolchazy-Carducci, 1985.

———. *The Defence of Greece, 490–479 B.C.* Warminster, U.K.: Aris & Phillips, 1993.

Lewis, D. M. "Public Property in the City." In Oswyn Murray and Simon Price, eds., *The Greek City from Homer to Alexander,* pp. 245–63. Oxford: Oxford University Press, 1990.

———. "The Archidamian War." In D. M. Lewis et al., eds., *The Cambridge Ancient History,* 2d ed., vol. 5, pp. 370–432. Cambridge: Cambridge University Press, 1992.

————. "Sparta as Victor." In D. M. Lewis et al., eds., *The Cambridge Ancient History*, 2d ed., vol. 6, pp. 24–44. Cambridge: Cambridge University Press, 1994.

Lincoln, Abraham. *Abraham Lincoln: Complete Works, Comprising His Speeches, Letters, State Papers, and Miscellaneous Writings*. Edited by J. G. Nicolay and J. Hay. 2 vols. New York: Century Co., 1894.

Loomis, W. T. *The Spartan War Fund*. Historia Einzelschriften, 74. Stuttgart: Franz Steiner, 1992.

————. *Wages, Welfare Costs and Inflation in Classical Athens*. Ann Arbor: University of Michigan Press, 1998.

Loraux, Nicole. *The Invention of Athens: The Funeral Oration in the Classical City*. Translated by Alan Sheridan. Cambridge, Mass.: Harvard University Press, 1986.

————. *Born of the Earth: Myth and Politics in Athens*. Translated by Selina Stewart. Ithaca, N.Y.: Cornell University Press, 2000.

MacDowell, Douglas M. *The Law in Classical Athens*. Ithaca, N.Y.: Cornell University Press, 1978.

————. *Aristophanes and Athens: An Introduction to the Plays*. Oxford: Oxford University Press, 1995.

Madison, James, Alexander Hamilton, and John Jay. *The Federalist Papers*. Edited by I. Kramnick. New York: Penguin Books, 1987.

Manville, P. B. *The Origins of Citizenship in Ancient Athens*. Princeton, N.J.: Princeton University Press, 1990.

Manville, Brook, and Josiah Ober. *A Company of Citizens: What the World's First Democracy Teaches Leaders about Creating Great Organizations*. Boston: Harvard Business School Press, 2003.

Marsden, E. W. *Greek and Roman Artillery: Historical Development*. Oxford: Oxford University Press, 1969.

Mattingly, H. B. *The Athenian Empire Restored*. Ann Arbor: University of Michigan Press, 1996.

McConville, Brendan. *These Daring Disturbers of the Public Peace: The Struggle for Property and Power in Early New Jersey*. Ithaca, N.Y.: Cornell University Press, 1999.

McInerney, Jeremy. *The Folds of Parnassos: Land and Ethnicity in Ancient Phokis*. Austin: University of Texas Press, 1999.

McLoughlin, W. C. *New England Dissent, 1630–1833*. 2 vols. Cambridge, Mass.: Harvard University Press, 1971.

Meier, C. *The Greek Discovery of Politics*. Translated by D. McLintock. Cambridge, Mass.: Harvard University Press, 1990.

Meiggs, Russell. "The Political Implications of the Parthenon." In G. T. W. Hooker, ed., *Parthenos and Parthenon*, pp. 36–45. Oxford: Oxford University Press, 1963.

————. "The Dating of Fifth-Century Attic Inscriptions." *Journal of Hellenic Studies* 86 (1966): 86–98.

————. *The Athenian Empire*. Oxford: Oxford University Press, 1972.

Meiggs, Russell, and David Lewis. *A Selection of Greek Historical Inscriptions to the End of the Fifth Century B.C.* [1969.] Rev. ed. Oxford: Oxford University Press, 1988.

Meritt, B. D., and H. T. Wade-Gery. "The Dating of Documents to the Mid-Fifth Century—I." *Journal of Hellenic Studies* 82 (1962): 67–74.

————. "The Dating of Documents to the Mid-Fifth Century—II." *Journal of Hellenic Studies* 83 (1963): 100–117.

Michell, H. *Sparta.* Cambridge: Cambridge University Press, 1952.

Mikalson, J. D. *Athenian Popular Religion.* Chapel Hill: University of North Carolina Press, 1983.

Miller, M. C. *Athens and Persia in the Fifth Century B.C.: A Study in Cultural Receptivity.* Cambridge: Cambridge University Press, 1997.

Millet, P. "Warfare, Economy, and Democracy in Classical Athens." In John Rich and Graham Shipley, eds., *War and Society in the Greek World,* pp. 177–96. London: Routledge, 1993.

Mirhady, D. C. "Torture and Rhetoric in Athens." *Journal of Hellenic Studies* 116 (1996): 119–31.

Mitchell, Lynette G. "A New Look at the Election of Generals in Athens." *Klio* 82 (2000): 344–60.

Mitchell, Lynette G., and P. J. Rhodes, eds. *The Development of the Polis in Archaic Greece.* London: Routledge, 1997.

Molho, Anthony, Kurt A. Raaflaub, and Julia Emlen, eds. *City-States in Classical Antiquity and Medieval Italy: Athens and Rome, Florence and Venice.* Ann Arbor: University of Michigan Press, 1991.

Monoson, S. Sara. *Plato's Democratic Entanglements: Athenian Politics and the Practice of Philosophy.* Princeton, N.J.: Princeton University Press, 2000.

Montgomery, H. "Silver, Coins and the Wealth of a City-State." *Opuscula Atheniensia* 15 (1984): 123–33.

Moore, J. M., ed. and trans. *Aristotle and Xenophon on Democracy and Oligarchy.* Berkeley: University of California Press, 1975.

Morris, Ian. "The Strong Principle of Equality and the Archaic Origin of Greek Democracy." In Josiah Ober and Charles Hedrick, eds., *Dêmokratia: A Conversation on Democracies, Ancient and Modern,* pp. 19–48. Princeton, N.J.: Princeton University Press, 1996.

Morris, Ian, and Kurt A. Raaflaub, eds. *Democracy 2500? Questions and Challenges.* Archaeological Institute of America Colloquium Series. Dubuque, Iowa: Kendall/Hunt, 1998.

Morrison, J. S., J. F. Coates, and N. B. Rankov. *The Athenian Trireme: The History and Reconstruction of an Ancient Greek Warship.* 2d ed. Cambridge: Cambridge University Press, 2000.

Neils, J., ed. *Worshipping Athena: Panathenaia and Parthenon.* Madison: University of Wisconsin Press, 1996.

Ober, Josiah. *Mass and Elite in Democratic Athens: Rhetoric, Ideology, and the Power of the People.* Princeton, N.J.: Princeton University Press, 1989.

———. *The Athenian Revolution: Essays on Ancient Greek Democracy and Political Theory.* Princeton, N.J.: Princeton University Press, 1996.

———. *Political Dissent in Democratic Athens: Intellectual Critics of Popular Rule.* Princeton, N.J.: Princeton University Press, 1998.

Ober, Josiah, and Charles Hedrick, eds. *Dêmokratia: A Conversation on Democracies, Ancient and Modern.* Princeton, N.J.: Princeton University Press, 1996.

Ortega y Gasset, José. *The Revolt of the Masses.* [Translator anonymous.] New York: Norton, 1932.

———. *Man and Crisis.* Translated by Mildred Adams. New York: Norton, 1958.

———. *History as a System, and Other Essays toward a Philosophy of History.* Translated by Helene Weyl. New York: Norton, 1961.

———. *An Interpretation of Universal History.* Translated by Mildred Adams. New York: Norton, 1973.

Ostwald, Martin. *Autonomia: Its Genesis and Early History.* Atlanta: Scholar's Press, 1982.

———. *From Popular Sovereignty to the Sovereignty of the Law: Law, Society, and Politics in Fifth-Century Athens.* Berkeley: University of California Press, 1986.

———. "The Reform of the Athenian State by Cleisthenes." In J. Boardman et al., eds., *The Cambridge Ancient History,* 2d ed., vol. 4, pp. 303–46. Cambridge: Cambridge University Press, 1988.

Page, D. L. *Sappho and Alcaeus.* Oxford: Oxford University Press, 1955.

Pangle, Thomas L., ed. *The Rebirth of Classical Political Rationalism: An Introduction to the Thought of Leo Strauss.* Chicago: University of Chicago Press, 1989.

Parker, Robert. *Athenian Religion: A History.* Oxford: Oxford University Press, 1996.

Patterson, Cynthia. *Pericles' Citizenship Law of 451–450 B.C.* Salem, N.H.: Ayer, 1981.

Patterson, Orlando. *Freedom.* New York: Basic Books, 1991.

Pickard-Cambridge, Sir Arthur. *Dithyramb, Tragedy, and Comedy.* 2d. ed. Rev. T. B. L. Webster. Oxford: Oxford University Press, 1962.

———. *The Dramatic Festivals of Athens.* 2d ed. Rev. John Gould and D. M. Lewis. Oxford: Oxford University Press, 1988.

Plato. *Phaedrus and Letters VII and VIII.* Translated with an introduction by Walter Hamilton. London: Penguin Books, 1973.

———. *The Republic.* Translated by G. M. A. Grube. Indianapolis: Hackett, 1974.

———. *Apology.* In G. M. A. Grube, trans., *The Trial and Death of Socrates: Euthyphro, Apology, Crito, Death Scene from Phaedo,* 2d ed. Indianapolis: Hackett, 1988.

———. *The Laws of Plato.* Translated by Thomas L. Pangle. [1980.] Reprint. Chicago: University of Chicago Press, 1988.

————. *Menexenus.* In S. Collins and D. Stauffer, trans., *Plato's Menexenus and Pericles' Funeral Oration: Empire and the Ends of Politics.* Newburyport, Mass.: Focus, 1999.

Plutarch. *The Rise and Fall of Athens: Nine Greek Lives: Theseus, Solon, Themistocles, Aristides, Cimon, Pericles, Nicias, Alcibiades, Lysander.* Translated with an introduction by Ian Scott-Kilvert. London: Penguin Books, 1960.

————. *The Age of Alexander: Nine Greek Lives: Agesilaus, Pelopidas, Dion, Timoleon, Demosthenes, Phocion, Alexander, Demetrius, Pyrrhus.* Translated by Ian Scott-Kilvert. Introduction by G. T. Griffith. London: Penguin Books, 1973.

Podlecki, Anthony J. *The Political Background of Aeschylean Tragedy.* Ann Arbor: University of Michigan Press, 1966.

————. *Perikles and His Circle.* London: Routledge, 1998.

Pollitt, J. J. *Art and Experience in Classical Greece.* Cambridge: Cambridge University Press, 1972.

Pritchett, W. K. "Marathon." *University of California Publications in Classical Archaeology* 4, no. 2 (1960): 137–75.

————. "Marathon Revisited." In *Studies in Ancient Greek Topography,* Part I, *University of California Publications in Classical Studies,* vol. 1 (1965): 83–93.

————. *The Greek State at War.* 5 vols. Berkeley: University of California Press, 1971–90.

————. *Thucydides' Pentekontaetia and Other Essays.* Amsterdam: Gieben, 1995.

Pseudo-Xenophon. [The "Old Oligarch".] *The Constitution of the Athenians.* In J. M. Moore, ed. and trans., *Aristotle and Xenophon on Democracy and Oligarchy.* Berkeley: University of California Press, 1975.

Raaflaub, Kurt A. "Democracy, Oligarchy and the Concept of the 'Free Citizen' in Late Fifth-Century Athens." *Political Theory* 11 (1983): 517–44.

————. *Die Entdeckung der Freiheit.* Vestigia, 37. Munich: Beck, 1985.

————. "Contemporary Perceptions of Democracy in Fifth-Century Athens." *Classica et Mediaevalia* 40 (1989): 33–70.

————. "Homer to Solon: The Rise of the *Polis.* The Written Sources." In M. H. Hansen, ed., *The Ancient Greek City-State,* pp. 41–105. Copenhagen: Royal Danish Academy of Sciences and Letters, 1993.

————. "Democracy, Power, and Imperialism in Fifth-Century Athens." In J. P. Euben, John Wallach, and Josiah Ober, eds., *Athenian Political Thought and the Reconstruction of American Democracy,* pp. 103–46. Ithaca, N.Y.: Cornell University Press, 1994.

————. "Equalities and Inequalities in Athenian Democracy." In Josiah Ober and Charles Hedrick, eds., *Dêmokratia,* pp. 139–74. Princeton: Princeton University Press, 1996.

————. "Citizens, Soldiers, and the Evolution of the Greek Polis." In Lynette

G. Mitchell and P. J. Rhodes, eds., *The Development of the Polis in Archaic Greece*, pp. 49–59. London: Routledge, 1997.

———. "Power in the Hands of the People: Foundations of Athenian Democracy." In Ian Morris and Kurt A. Raaflaub, eds., *Democracy 2500? Questions and Challenges*, pp. 31–66. Archaeological Institute of America Colloquium Series. Dubuque, Iowa: Kendall/Hunt, 1998.

———. "The Alleged Ostracism of Damon." In Geoffrey W. Bakewell and James P. Sickinger, eds., *Gestures: Essays in Ancient History, Literature, and Philosophy Presented to Alan L. Boegehold*, pp. 317–31. Oxford: Oxbow Books, 2003.

Rahe, Paul A. "The Primacy of Politics in Classical Greece." *American Historical Review* 89 (1984): 265–93.

———. *Republics Ancient and Modern: Classical Republicanism and the American Revolution*. Chapel Hill: University of North Carolina Press, 1992.

Reinhold, Meyer. *Classica Americana: The Greek and Roman Heritage in the United States*. Detroit: Wayne State University Press, 1984.

Rhodes, P. J. *The Athenian Boule*. Oxford: Oxford University Press, 1972. [Rev. ed. 1984.]

———. "On Labelling Fourth-Century Politicians." *Liverpool Classical Monthly* 3 (1978): 207–11.

———. *A Commentary on the Aristotelian Athenaion Politeia*. Oxford: Oxford University Press, 1981. [Rev. ed. 1997.]

———. "The Athenian Revolution." In D. M. Lewis et al., eds., *The Cambridge Ancient History*, 2d ed., vol. 5, pp. 62–95. Cambridge: Cambridge University Press, 1992.

———. "The Delian League to 449 B.C." In D. M. Lewis et al., eds., *The Cambridge Ancient History*, 2d ed., vol. 5, pp. 34–61. Cambridge: Cambridge University Press, 1992.

———. "Who Ran Democratic Athens?" In Pernille Flensted-Jensen, Thomas Heine Nielsen, and Lene Rubinstein, eds., *Polis and Politics: Studies in Ancient Greek History Presented to Mogens Herman Hansen on His Sixtieth Birthday, August 20, 2000*, pp. 465–77. Copenhagen: Museum Tusculanum Press, 2000.

———. *Ancient Democracy and Modern Ideology*. London: Duckworth, 2003.

———. "Nothing to Do with Democracy: Athenian Drama and the *Polis*." *Journal of Hellenic Studies* 123 (2003): 104–19.

Rhodes, P. J., with D. M. Lewis. *The Decrees of the Greek States*. Oxford: Oxford University Press, 1997.

Rich, John, and Graham Shipley, eds. *War and Society in the Greek World*. London: Routledge, 1993.

Roberts, J. T. *Accountability in Athenian Government*. Madison: University of Wisconsin Press, 1982.

————. *Athens on Trial: The Antidemocratic Tradition in Western Thought.* Princeton, N.J.: Princeton University Press, 1994.

Robertson, Noel D. "The True Nature of the Delian League, 478–461 B.C." *American Journal of Ancient History* 5 (1980): 64–96, 110–33.

————. "Athena's Shrines and Festivals." In J. Neils, ed., *Worshipping Athena: Panathenaia and Parthenon,* pp. 27–77. Madison: University of Wisconsin Press, 1996.

Robinson, E. W. *The First Democracies: Early Popular Government outside Athens.* Historia Einzelschriften, 107. Stuttgart: Franz Steiner, 1997.

————, ed. *Ancient Greek Democracy: Readings and Sources.* Oxford: Blackwell, 2004.

Roisman, J. *The General Demosthenes and His Use of Military Surprise.* Historia Einzelschriften, 78. Stuttgart: Franz Steiner, 1993.

Roochnik, David. *Beautiful City: The Dialectical Character of Plato's "Republic."* Ithaca, N.Y.: Cornell University Press, 2003.

Rosen, R. M., and J. Farrell, eds. *Nomodeiktes: Greek Studies in Honor of Martin Ostwald.* Ann Arbor: University of Michigan Press, 1993.

Roussel, Denis. *Tribu et cité.* Paris: Les Belles Lettres, 1976.

Ryder, T. T. B. *Koine Eirene: General Peace and Local Independence in Ancient Greece.* Oxford: Oxford University Press, 1965.

Salmon, J. B. *Wealthy Corinth: A History of the City to 338 BC.* Oxford: Oxford University Press, 1984.

Samons, L. J., II, ed. *Athenian Democracy and Imperialism.* Boston: Houghton Mifflin, 1998.

————. "Kimon, Kallias and Peace with Persia." *Historia* 47 (1998): 129–40.

————. "Mass, Elite and Hoplite-Farmer in Greek History." *Arion* 5, no. 3 (1998): 99–123.

————. "Aeschylus, the Alkmeonids, and the Reform of the Areopagos." *Classical Journal* 94 (1998–99): 221–33.

————. *Empire of the Owl: Athenian Imperial Finance.* Historia Einzelschriften, 142. Stuttgart: Franz Steiner, 2000.

————. "Democracy, Empire and the Search for the Athenian Character." *Arion* 8, no. 3 (2001): 128–57.

————. "Socrates, Virtue and the Modern Professor." *Journal of Education* 182 (2000 [2001]): 19–27.

————. "Revolution or Compromise?" In E. W. Robinson, ed., *Ancient Greek Democracy: Readings and Sources,* pp. 113–22. Oxford: Blackwell, 2004.

Sanford, C. B. *The Religious Life of Thomas Jefferson.* Charlottesville: University Press of Virginia, 1984.

Saxonhouse, Arlene W. *Athenian Democracy: Modern Mythmakers and Ancient Theorists.* Notre Dame, Ind.: Notre Dame University Press, 1996.

Schubert, Charlotte. *Perikles.* Erträge der Forschung, 285. Darmstadt: Wissenschaftliche Buchgesellschaft, 1994.

Sealey, Raphael. "The Entry of Pericles into History." *Hermes* 84 (1956): 234–47.

———. *A History of the Greek City-States, ca. 700–338 B.C.* Berkeley: University of California Press, 1976.

———. *The Athenian Republic: Democracy or the Rule of Law?* University Park, Pa.: Pennsylvania State University Press, 1987.

———. *Demosthenes and His Time: A Study in Defeat.* New York: Oxford University Press, 1993.

Sickinger, J. P. *Public Records and Archives in Classical Athens.* Chapel Hill: University of North Carolina Press, 1999.

Sinclair, R. K. *Democracy and Participation in Classical Athens.* Cambridge: Cambridge University Press, 1988.

Snodgrass, A. M. *Archaic Greece.* Berkeley: University of California Press, 1980.

———. "The Rise of the *Polis:* The Archaeological Evidence." In M. H. Hansen ed., *The Ancient Greek City-State,* pp. 30–40. Copenhagen: Royal Danish Academy of Sciences and Letters, 1993.

Stadter, P. A. *A Commentary on Plutarch's Pericles.* Chapel Hill: University of North Carolina Press, 1989.

Stahl, Michael. *Aristokraten und Tyrannen im archaischen Athen: Untersuchungen zur Überlieferung, zur Sozialstruktur und zur Entstehung des Staates.* Stuttgart: Franz Steiner, 1987.

Stephen, James Fitzjames. *Liberty, Equality, Fraternity.* Edited by R. J. White. Cambridge: Cambridge University Press, 1967.

Stockton, David. "The Peace of Callias." *Historia* 8 (1959): 61–79.

———. *The Classical Athenian Democracy.* Oxford: Oxford University Press, 1990.

Stone, I. F. *The Trial of Socrates.* Boston: Little, Brown, 1988.

Storing, Herbert J. *What the Anti-Federalists Were For.* Chicago: University of Chicago Press, 1981.

Strauss, B. *Athens after the Peloponnesian War: Class, Faction and Policy, 403–386 B.C.* Ithaca, N.Y.: Cornell University Press, 1987.

Strauss, Leo. *The City and Man.* Chicago: University of Chicago Press, 1964.

———. *Liberalism, Ancient and Modern.* New York: Basic Books, 1968.

Stroud, R. S. *The Athenian Grain-Tax Law of 374/3 B.C.* Hesperia Suppl. 29. Princeton, N.J.: American School of Classical Studies at Athens, 1998.

Thomas, Rosalind. *Oral Tradition and Written Record in Classical Athens.* Cambridge: Cambridge University Press, 1989.

Thompson, C. B. *John Adams and the Spirit of Liberty.* Lawrence: University of Kansas Press, 1998.

Thomsen, Rudi. *Eisphora: A Study of Direct Taxation in Ancient Athens.* Copenhagen: Gyldendal, 1964.

―――. *The Origin of Ostracism*. Copenhagen: Gyldendal, 1972.

Thucydides. *The History of the Peloponnesian War*. Translated by Richard Crawley. London: Longmans, Green, 1876. [In some cases I have also drawn upon the revisions of T. E. Wick, ed., *Thucydides: The Peloponnesian War* (New York: McGraw-Hill, 1982).]

Thür, G. "Reply to D. C. Mirhady, 'Torture and Rhetoric in Athens.'" *Journal of Hellenic Studies* 116 (1996): 132–34.

Tocqueville, Alexis de. *Democracy in America*. Translated by George Lawrence. [1966.] Reprint. Edited by J. P. Mayer. New York: Doubleday, 1969.

Tod, M. N. *Greek Historical Inscriptions*. 2 vols. in 1. Reprint. Chicago: Ayer, 1985.

Traill, John S. *The Political Organization of Attica: A Study of the Demes, Trittyes, and Phylai, and Their Representation in the Athenian Council*. Hesperia Suppl. 14. Princeton, N.J.: American School of Classical Studies at Athens, 1975.

Wade-Gery, H. T. *Essays in Greek History*. Oxford: Blackwell, 1958.

Wallace, R. W. *The Areopagos Council*. Baltimore: Johns Hopkins University Press, 1987.

―――. "Private Lives and Public Enemies: Freedom of Thought in Classical Athens." In Alan A. Boegehold and Adele C. Scafuro, eds., *Athenian Identity and Civic Ideology*, pp. 127–55. Baltimore: Johns Hopkins University Press, 1994.

―――. "Law, Freedom, and the Concept of Citizens' Rights in Democratic Athens." In Josiah Ober and Charles Hedrick, eds., *Dêmokratia: A Conversation on Democracies, Ancient and Modern*, pp. 105–19. Princeton, N.J.: Princeton University Press, 1996.

―――. "Solonian Democracy." In Ian Morris and Kurt A. Raaflaub, eds., *Democracy 2500? Questions and Challenges*, pp. 11–29. Archaeological Institute of America Colloquium Series. Dubuque, Iowa: Kendall/Hunt, 1998.

―――. "The Sophists in Athens." In Deborah Boedeker and Kurt A. Raaflaub, eds., *Democracy, Empire, and the Arts in Fifth-Century Athens*, pp. 203–22. Cambridge, Mass.: Harvard University Press, 1998.

Wallace, R. W., and E. M. Harris, eds. *Transitions to Empire: Essays in Greco-Roman History, 360–146 B.C., in Honor of E. Badian*. Norman: University of Oklahoma Press, 1996.

Washington, George. *Writings*. Edited by J. Rhodehamel. New York: Library of America, 1997.

Whitehead, D. *The Ideology of the Athenian Metic*. Cambridge: Cambridge University Press, 1977.

Wills, Gary. *Lincoln at Gettysburg: The Words That Remade America*. New York: Simon & Schuster, 1992.

Wilson, E. O. *On Human Nature*. Cambridge, Mass.: Harvard University Press, 1978.

Wilson, James Q. *The History and Future of Democracy*. Malibu, Calif.: School of Public Policy, Pepperdine University. [An address given at the Reagan Presidential Library on November 15, 1999, published in pamphlet form.]

Winkler, John J., and Froma I. Zeitlin, eds. *Nothing to Do with Dionysos? Athenian Drama in Its Social Context*. Princeton, N.J.: Princeton University Press, 1990.

Wood, Gordon S. *The Creation of the American Republic, 1776–1787*. Chapel Hill: University of North Carolina Press for the Institute of Early American History and Culture at Williamsburg, Va., 1969.

Wood, Peter. *Diversity: The Invention of a Concept*. San Francisco: Encounter Books, 2003.

Wycherley, R. E. "Rebuilding in Athens and Attica." In D. M. Lewis et al., eds., *The Cambridge Ancient History,* 2d ed., vol. 5, pp. 206–22. Cambridge: Cambridge University Press, 1992.

Xenophon. *Memorabilia and Oeconomicus, Symposium and Apology*. Translated by E. C. Marchant and O. J. Todd. Loeb Classical Library. Cambridge, Mass.: Harvard University Press, 1969.

———. *The Politeia [Constitution] of the Spartans*. In J. M. Moore, ed. and trans., *Aristotle and Xenophon on Democracy and Oligarchy*. Berkeley: University of California Press, 1975.

———. *A History of My Times [Hellenika]*. Edited by George Cawkwell. Translated by Rex Warner. London: Penguin Books, 1979.

INDEX

abortion, 182, 269n68
Acarnania, 137
Achilles, 229n114
acropolis, 20, 26, 34, 52, 54, 77, 82–83, 199,
    225n65
Adams, John, 231n130, 273n14
Aegina, 32, 73–74, 112, 125, 128, 136, 251n49,
    253n69
Aegospotami, 141
Aeschines, 67, 153, 155–58, 215n58, 254n4,
    258–59n62, 259nn63,65
Aeschylus, 59, 111, 118, 242n56
Agatha Tyche, 172. *See also* Fortune.
Agesilaus, 145
Agis III, 40, 161, 261n101
agora, 20, 77
aitiai, 127, 129–30
Alcibiades, 22, 27–38, 89–91, 98, 118, 131,
    135, 145, 198–99, 229n114, 234n53,
    235nn58,60, 258n60, 274n18
Alcmeonids, 27, 57–58, 107, 239–40n13,
    242n56
Alexander, 40, 110, 160–61, 242n47, 256n31,
    261n101
Amazons, 92
Ambracia, 137
Amendment: First, 175–76, 266n49,
    274n15; Fourteenth, 266n49. *See also*
    Bill of Rights; Constitution
amnesty, 38, 95
Amphiktyons, 157
Amphipolis, 86, 132, 137, 150–51, 156, 159,
    193, 248n23

Anaxagoras, 115, 199, 245n78
Andocides, 19, 142
anthropology, 121–22, 247n14
Anti-Federalists, 271n79, 274n15
Antiphon, 93–94
Apollo, 25, 47, 194, 232n19
arbitration, 249n31
Arcadians, 136
archaeology, 121
arche, 85. *See also* empire: Athenian
architecture, Athenian, 55, 92, 101, 190
archons, 22, 25–26, 45, 47–48, 95, 165;
    basileus, 22; eponymous, 22, 26, 106,
    224–25n55; *polemarchos*, 22, 30; *thes-
    mothetai*, 30
Areopagus Council, xvi, 22, 28, 30, 34, 52,
    242n51
arete. See excellence, human
Arginusae Islands, 140, 147, 193, 254n9,
    264n23
Argos, 34, 36, 38, 51–52, 73, 85, 111, 124, 128,
    133, 136, 148, 224n44
Aristeides, 22, 32, 41, 98–99, 101
aristocracy, 24, 26–28, 42, 58, 60, 64, 79,
    86, 115, 145, 189, 226n74, 253–54n4
Aristophanes, 8, 13, 86–87, 118, 130, 132,
    142, 168, 251n49, 261n2; *Knights*, 87
Aristophon, 157
Aristotle, 19, 42, 45, 70, 79, 168, 173,
    204n13
art, Athenian, 8, 55, 101, 118, 172, 189
Artaxerxes, 35, 59
Artemisium, 107

Aspasia, 61, 114, 140, 226n74, 253n61, 275n19, 278n45

assembly, xv, 1, 19–20, 50, 148, 213n42; Athenian *(ekklesia)*, xvi, 1, 15–16, 22–23, 28–30, 37, 42, 45, 49–53, 66, 73, 78, 86, 88–89, 91, 94–96, 104, 113–14, 129, 134–35, 140–41, 145–47, 149, 153–55, 157, 163, 168–70, 173, 185, 191–93, 198, 219n2, 228n107, 235n61, 253n64, 264nn20,23

Assinarus River, 138

astos, astoi, 221n21

astu, 20

Athena, 25, 55, 73–74, 77, 80–81, 83, 87–88, 93, 116; temple of, 25, 27, 55, 213n39; treasurers *(tamiai)* of, 44, 221n19; treasury of, 25, 77, 82, 87–88

Athena Nike, 37, 55, 95

atimia, 48, 243n61, 255n18

Attica, 20, 26, 32, 36, 38, 49, 73, 82, 92, 104, 106–7, 137, 150, 210n1, 250n40

autochthony, 92, 227–28n92

Babylonia, 105

basileus, 22

Battle Hymn of the Republic, 164

Bill of Rights, 175. *See also* Amendment; Constitution

Black Sea, expedition to, 137, 248n23

Boeotia, 20, 31, 60, 106, 112, 114, 136–37, 224n44; Boeotian confederation, 84

booty, 89, 105, 112, 232n9, 233n29

boule. See Council of 500

bouleutai, 23

Brasidas, 132

building program, 34, 52–55, 60–61, 64, 77–79, 116, 190, 199, 202, 224n48, 228n107, 237n89

Byzantium, 136

calendar, Athenian, 211n11

Callias: son of Hipponicus, 113, 243n66; Peace of, 35, 59, 77, 100, 113, 243–44n67

Callimachus, 106, 241n29

Callisthenes, 254n9

Callistratus, 255n14

Callixenus, 140–41, 253n62

candidates, xiv

capitalism, 178, 267n59, 277n44

Carter, Jimmy, 8

Carystus, 136, 239n11

catapult, 256n28

Cecryphalea, 136

Cersebleptes, 155, 158–59

Chabrias, 255n14

Chaeronea, 11, 40, 160, 172, 260n96, 261n100, 265n39

Chalcidian League, 152

Chalcidice, 36, 97

Chalcis, Chacidians, 31

character, 68–71, 117, 119, 182; Athenian, 17, 57, 134, 154, 171, 173, 188, 190, 273n9; of individual Athenians, 25, 67–68, 98

Chares, 237n79

Chersonese, 102–3, 136–37, 141, 150, 153–55, 158–59, 239n6

Chios, 110, 114, 149

choice, xiv, 16, 166–67, 179–85, 269n68

chora, 20

choregia, 59, 96

Christianity, 185, 262n8, 267nn50,53, 273n14

church, 166, 208–9n51

church and state, separation of, 175–76, 186

Churchill, Winston, 145

Cimon, xvi, 22, 32, 34–35, 51–52, 58–59, 67, 79–80, 86, 98–99, 101–2, 104, 108–13, 115, 125, 136, 144–45, 224n54, 227n90, 240n15, 242nn50,51, 243n58, 245n73

Cimonids, 102–4, 238–39n6, 239–40n13, 240n15, 242n50, 245n73

citizenship, xv, 16, 24, 45–49, 68–71; law of 451/0 restricting, 34–35, 46, 52, 60, 112, 221n21, 227n92, 253n61; qualifications for, xv, 16, 23–24, 26, 28, 42, 45–49, 177

citizen-state, 31

city-state. *See* polis

civil war, 111, 115, 117, 276n34

clans, 24, 26, 168

Cleisthenes, 27, 51, 57–58, 104, 239n13, 240n16

Cleomenes, 105

Cleon, xvi, 22, 66, 86, 88, 90, 99, 101, 131–32, 145, 178, 220n7, 230n124, 250n41, 272n4

Cleophon, 141, 275n23
cleruchies. *See* settlements, Athenian
Cohen, Edward E., 209–10n1, 221n21, 222–23n35, 223n38, 270–71n76
coinage, 73–74, 80
Cold War, 205n17
colonies, 53, 64, 134, 230n118, 252n53. *See also* settlements, Athenian
Colonus, 235n61
comedy, 118, 164–66, 228n107, 261n2, 277n41; restrictions on, 61
common peace, 150, 257n40
Congress, U.S., 176, 183
Conon, 146–47, 229n114
conservatives, xvi, 4, 182, 204n13, 240n19, 245n73
Constitution, U.S., xiv, 1–3, 23, 29, 45, 54, 175–76, 186, 231n130, 265n34, 269n70, 270n75, 271n79, 274n15. *See also* Amendment; Bill of Rights
Corcyra, 35–36, 124–25, 129, 134, 248nn25,27, 249n31, 254n9
Corinth, 20, 31, 34–36, 38, 59, 73, 77, 84, 111, 119, 124–29, 135–36, 149, 160, 246n7, 248n25, 249n31
Corinthian War, 38–39, 149
Coronea, 60, 137
Council of 500, xvi, 22–23, 25, 28–30, 37, 43–45, 47–49, 52, 77, 88, 93, 95, 97, 113, 140, 159, 168–69, 193, 220n11
courts: Athenian, 30, 48, 145, 154, 163, 191–92, 211n21, 215n58, 219n2; popular control of, 42
Crenides, 148
Crete, 57
Critias, 37–38, 199, 236n71, 274n18
critics, literary, 248n22
crucifixion, 115, 245n75
culture: American popular, 165, 179; Athenian, 6–7; Greek, 12–13
Cyprus, 35, 59, 110, 112–13, 136–37
Cyrus, 145, 242n47

Damon, 79–80, 115, 245n78
Darius, 102, 106, 240nn14,15
death penalty, 48, 50, 53, 65, 70, 115, 132, 134, 141–42, 145–46, 160–61, 191, 193, 196–97, 200, 222n35, 238n95, 245n75, 253n69, 254nn6,9, 255n14, 275n23, 276n33. *See also* Socrates, execution of
debt: national, 72, 87–88, 234n50; public, 72, 88, 95
Decelea, 36, 91, 235n61
decrees *(psephismata)*, 19, 29–31, 52–53, 113, 135, 219n4
deficits, annual budget, 72, 88
Delian League, 33–34, 51–52, 60, 76–77, 101, 108–10, 114, 149
Delion, 193, 198
Delos, 33–34, 52, 77–78, 108
Delphi, 157, 170, 224n44
demagogoi, 43, 145, 220n7
demagogues, 41–44, 65–66, 71, 219n1, 275n23
demes, 28, 46–47, 79, 168–69
democracy, *passim*; criticism of, 1, 4–5, 13; elitist theory of, 3–4; ideals of, 5; imposition of, 50, 53, 113–15, 137; practice of xiv–xv, 1, 3, 5, 9–10, 15, 17; radical, xvi, 83, 97, 131, 198, 240n19, 246n1; as religion, 14, 70, 164, 176–78, 182–86, 267n55, 270n75; representative, 1
democrats, xvi, 8, 94
Democrats, 177
demokratia, xv, 4–7, 16, 23, 26–28, 48, 50; as goddess, 93, 172, 185, 265nn37,38,39; law against overthrowing, 93, 265nn37,39
demos, 22–24: Athenian, 7, 10, 12, 13, 24, 26, 28, 31, 37, 43, 45, 52, 58, 64, 83, 88, 96, 105, 107, 113, 129–32, 134–35, 138, 141, 144–46, 152–54, 158–59, 166, 170, 189–90, 193–95, 200, 202, 254n6, 265n37, 272n4
Demosthenes (fifth-century general), 139, 146
Demosthenes (fourth-century orator), 19, 39–41, 67, 96–99, 118, 145, 151–61, 172, 178, 215n58, 253n68, 254n4, 258–59n62, 259nn63,65, 261n101, 266nn41,45
diaphorai, 127, 129–30
Dicaeopolis, 86
dicasts. *See* jurors
dikasteria. See juries
dike, 50, 194; as goddess, 172

Dionysia, City (Great), 165, 170, 197, 212n28, 272–73n9
Dionysus, 165, 170, 172, 212n28; theater of, 165, 169–70, 185
Diopeithes, 159
Dipaea, 136
disabled citizens, pension for, 49
diversity, xiv, 166–67, 177, 181–85, 201, 270n73, 271nn76,77. *See also* freedom, choice, and diversity
divorce, 182, 269n68
dokimasia, 25, 48
Dorians, 128
Doris, 136
Drakon, 29
drama, 118, 164–66, 190, 272–73n9; citizen judges of, 166
drugs, 178, 267n59
Duris of Samos, 245n75, 247n13
duty: for Athenians, 15–16, 25–26, 45–50, 62–63, 68, 70–71, 171–74, 178, 184–85, 189, 191, 198–99, 201, 264n18; for moderns, 70–71, 177, 180–81, 186, 270n72, 271n76

Earth Charter, 204n9, 268n59
Egesta, 11, 89, 135
Egypt, 34, 59, 105, 112, 136–37, 154, 227n87, 255n14
Eion, 136
Eirene, 172, 265n39
eisangelia, 146
eisphora. See taxes, on property
ekklesia. See assembly, Athenian
election, xv, 1, 3, 16, 22, 42–45, 67–71, 168, 190
Eleusis, 212n28
eleutheria, 5–7, 45, 172–73, 182, 226n74
Elshtain, Jean Bethke, 183–84
empire, Athenian, xvi, 12, 17, 38, 42, 59, 60–62, 64, 66, 76, 80–85, 87–88, 95, 98, 101–119, 127, 132, 135, 141, 149, 171, 174, 188–89, 191, 194, 198, 240n19, 273n9
Ennea Hodoi, 136
enslavement. *See* slavery
Epaminondas, 39, 148
ephebeia, 46–47
Ephialtes, xvi, 30, 34, 51–52, 59, 111, 136

Epidamnus, 35, 129
epitaphioi. See funeral orations
eponymous archon. *See* archons
Erasinides, 254n9
Erechtheion, 7, 27
Eretria, 106
ethne, 209–10n1, 238n1
Euboea, 31–32, 60, 104, 106, 137, 159, 239n11, 240n17
Eubulus, 67, 96, 98, 156, 258n55
Eukleia, 172
eunomia, 86, 171–73; as goddess, 172
eupatridai, 24
Euripides, 118, 190
Eurymedon River, 34, 50–51, 106, 109–10, 136
Euryptolemus, 140
euthynai, 242n51, 255n18
excellence, human, 14, 62, 139, 192–93, 195–98, 201–2, 229n114
execution. *See* death penalty
exile, 53, 57–58, 61, 107, 115, 141, 145–46, 255n14

faith, democratic, xiv, 14, 42, 70, 267n52
families, 16, 25–26, 144–45, 167–69, 171, 174, 177, 182–83, 185, 191, 201, 208–9n51, 253–54n4, 276n34; abandonment of, 182, 269n68, 270n72
farmers, 6, 23, 26, 28, 45, 61, 64, 75, 84, 86, 105, 154, 168, 173, 228n107, 229n112, 230n118. *See also* hoplites
Federalists, 271n79, 274n15
festivals, 164–65, 170–71, 185, 261n7
Finley, M. I., xvi, 3, 11, 182
Five Thousand, 37, 44, 94
Five Years' Truce, 112, 137
flag-burning, 269n70
fleet, Athenian, 33, 37, 73–77, 82, 91, 104, 107–8, 114–15, 141, 159, 231–32n7, 235n63, 252n53, 261n101
Fortune, 120–21, 265n38. *See also* Agatha Tyche
Founders, American, 1–2, 4, 14, 176, 186, 191, 231n130, 271n79, 274n15
Four Hundred, 37, 38, 44, 93–94
freedom, xiv, 93, 164, 167, 172, 175, 177–85, 190, 193, 201, 265n37, 267n59, 268nn60,61, 269n68; and equality, 5;

worship of, 14, 178–79, 183–86, 267nn55,59

freedom, choice, and diversity, xiv, 16, 191, 197, 267n52, 270n73, 271n76

French Revolution, 122

funerals, 25, 61; orations at, 226n74, 275n19

garrisons, installation of, 53, 61, 149, 160, 251n53, 257n41

gene. See clans

generals, 22, 28, 30–31, 42, 44, 67, 79, 85, 96, 98–99, 110, 114, 118, 138, 140–41, 144–47, 149, 155, 161, 165, 199, 200, 214n48, 238nn93,95, 245n73, 254n6; prosecution of, 145–47, 149, 254nn6,9, 255n17, 255–56n22, 274n23

gerousia, 210n6

God, 14, 164, 177, 183, 186, 270n71

gods, goddesses, 16, 25–26, 38, 50, 74–75, 87–88, 95–96, 100, 119, 133, 165, 168, 170–72, 174, 185, 191, 194, 199, 201, 212n28, 232n9, 237n89, 241n24, 249n34, 273n9, 275n26

government: American, passim; Athenian, passim; constitutional, 4, 16; representative, 4, 14–15; republican, 14

grain, 102, 259n71

graphe paranomon, 29

Gulf War, 8

Gylippus, 138–39

hagna, 170

Halieis, 136

Hamilton, Alexander, 274n15

Hanson, Victor Davis, xv, xvii

happiness, 179–80, 182, 267nn53,59, 268n61, 269n68

harbor, Athenian, 75

Hedrick, Charles, 4

heliaia, 30

Hellas, 6–7, 20

hellenotamiai, 34, 77, 88, 108, 275n23

Hellespont, 26, 33, 37, 76, 102–104, 107, 109, 149, 155–56, 159, 239nn6,11

helots, 20, 39, 50–51, 84, 111–12, 136, 150, 252n53

Hephaestus, temple of, 77

Hermocopids, conspiracy of, 275n23

Herodotus, 19, 31, 73–74, 104–5, 108, 110, 115, 120–22

hiera, 170, 221n21

Hipparchus, 27

hippeis, 23

Hippias, 27, 32, 106, 239–40n13

Hipponicus, 239–40n13, 243n66

Histiaea, 251n49, 253n69

history: ancient, 19, 118–24; Athenian, passim; beauty in, xvi, 120–23; practicality in, xvi, 9–10; utility in, 120–21

Homer, 56, 148, 188, 247n11

homoioi, 23

hope, 143

hoplites, 23, 32, 45–46, 51, 89–90, 91, 93–94, 96–97, 106, 133, 154, 168, 198, 220n18, 235n63; payment of, 75. See also farmers

hosia, 170, 221n21

hostages, 61

humanism, 53, 55, 190

hybris, 48, 270n76

Hysiae, 251n49

ideologies, history of, 7–9, 267n56

ideology, xvi, 7–9, 173, 182, 201, 272–73n9; democratic, 3, 5, 10

Illyria, 150

Imbros, 102, 109, 156, 259n71

imperialism: Athenian, 17, 57, 86, 101–116, 133–37, 144, 147, 154, 190, 198, 237n79, 246n1, 257nn34,41; Spartan, 134–37, 149

inscriptions, 19, 52–53, 72–73, 77, 216–17n83, 223n42

institutions, xvi, 7

Internal Revenue Service, 31

Internet, xiv

Ionia, 24, 32–34, 50–51, 92, 105, 108, 169, 278n45; revolt of, 32, 50, 105–6

Iphicrates, 118, 146, 254n9, 255n14, 256n31

Iraq, 70

isegoria, 32, 104

Isocrates, 19, 118, 142, 159, 218n100

isonomia, 5–7, 45

Ithome, 136

Jefferson, Thomas, 270n71, 271n80, 273–74n14

Jesus, 273n14

Johnson, Samuel, 248n22
journalists, 66, 201
Judaeo-Christian tradition, 181, 186, 271n80
judicial system: Athenian, 30; popular, xv
juries: Athenian, 17, 30, 34, 49, 53, 79, 97,
    163, 193–96, 200, 254n11, 263n18,
    274n17; hearing cases transferred to
    Athens, 53, 113
jurors, 25, 30, 69, 79, 145–46, 191–93, 195,
    198, 214n54, 215n58, 276n33; modern
    jurors/juries, 69, 70; payments for, 30,
    34–35, 37, 43–44, 49, 52, 60, 64, 77,
    79–80, 95, 97, 191, 228n107
justice, 14, 50. See also dike

Kennedy, Ted, 15
Kerykes, 239–40n13
King's Peace, 149
krypteia, 252n53

Lacedaemon, 20, 130. See also Sparta
Lacedaemonius, 86, 125, 248n27
Lamian War, 40, 161
Laurium, 32–33, 73–74, 83–84, 117, 241n29
law, rule of, xv, 29–30
laws, 29, 193–94, 275n26; Athenian revision
    of, 29, 38, 95. See also nomoi
league (against Persia), 12, 33, 100, 107, 111,
    223–24n44
legitimacy, 221n22
leitourgiai. See liturgies
Lemnos, 102, 109, 156, 259n71
Leotychides, 107–8
Lesbos, 114, 140
Leuctra, 39, 149
liberals, 182
liberty and equality, 4–6, 16, 45, 83, 171–73,
    267n53
Lincoln, Abraham, 54, 207n35, 270n75,
    273n11; Gettysburg address of, 273n11
literature, Athenian, 6–7, 9, 92, 101, 118,
    172, 189, 190, 202
liturgies, 75, 79, 221n20
Livy, 247n13
loans from Athena and other gods, 82,
    87–88, 95–96, 169–71
lottery, 22–23, 25, 28–29, 31, 37, 42, 44–45,
    48, 71, 93, 148, 163, 166, 264n18

Lygdamis, 101
Lysander, 94, 141, 229n114
Lysicles, 160

Macedon, 11, 17, 39–40, 50, 96–98, 110, 119,
    143, 147–62, 172–73, 254n9, 256n23,
    259n69, 260n96, 261n100
Madison, James, 1–2, 10, 186, 271n80,
    274n15
magistrates, 22, 25, 30–31, 43, 49, 95, 148,
    184, 194
Mantinea, 39, 133–34, 136, 150
Marathon, 32, 50, 58, 92, 102, 106–107, 157,
    160, 240n13, 242n50
Maryland, state church of, 267n50
Massachusetts, 15; state church of, 267n50
Mattingly, H. B., 216–17n83
Mausolus, 257n41
Medes, 32, 111
media, 2, 181, 185
medizing, 32, 34, 107, 111, 115
Megacles, 107, 241n29
Megara, 60, 125, 127, 136–37; Megarian De-
    cree, 125, 127, 132, 224n54, 249n31
Meletus, 195, 275n29
Melos, 36, 38, 100, 133–34, 142–43,
    251nn48,49, 253n69, 260n81; Melian
    Dialogue, 133–34, 251n48
mercenaries, 50, 68, 96–97, 114, 117, 146,
    148, 151, 154, 161, 173–74, 237n86
merismos, 96
Messenia, 20, 39, 136, 150, 252n53
Methone, 150–51
metics, 17, 20, 49, 190, 221n21, 222n29
middle class, 84, 86, 93, 98, 105, 154, 174
Mikalson, Jon, 171
Miletus, 35, 61, 114–15
militarism, Athenian v. Spartan, 134–37
military: Athenian, 17, 24–25, 28, 31, 40,
    42, 46–49, 59, 64, 68, 75, 77, 79, 82,
    84, 87, 91, 95–97, 100–116, 119, 135,
    144–46, 152–62, 169–70, 173–74, 185,
    187–88, 190, 193, 198–99, 222n29,
    226nn74,75, 252n53, 264n21, 266n45;
    pay for, 44, 146, 159. See also treasury,
    military.
Miltiades, 102, 106–107, 110, 145, 238–39n6,
    239–40n13, 240n14, 241n29

mimesis, 120–21
mines, 26, 32, 73–75, 80, 83–85, 91, 93, 95–98, 101–102, 104, 107, 110, 117, 128, 144, 147–49, 151, 189, 231n3, 241n29, 242n45, 256n32, 277n44
monarchs, 7
money, public, 73–75
morale, Athenian, 17, 63, 67–68, 72, 144, 154, 157, 161, 173–75, 185, 202, 246n4
morality, 4–5, 11, 13–16, 163, 165, 178, 180–85, 187, 191–94, 196, 268n62, 270nn72,75, 271n76, 273–74n14
Mytilene, 251nn48,49; Mytilenian Debate, 251n48

nationalism, 54–55, 62, 64, 68, 92, 100–101, 116, 131, 188–90, 238n1
nature, human, 120, 133, 166–67, 262–63n12
naukrariai, 212n27, 231–32n7
Naupactus, 136, 255n18
nautai. See rowers
nautikos ochlos, 174
navy, Athenian, 64, 95, 97, 174, 242n42, 251n53, 259n69. *See also* fleet, Athenian
Naxos, 84, 101, 109–110, 154
Newdow v. U.S. Congress, 266n49
newspapers, 69
Nicias, xvi, 31, 41, 87, 89, 101, 118, 132, 135, 138–39, 146–47, 154, 248n27, 272n2, 277n44; Peace of, 36, 87, 89, 132
Nixon, Richard, 183–84
nomoi, 29, 261–62n3
nomothesia, 29

oaths, 47, 50, 53, 113, 160, 163, 244n71
Ober, Josiah, 4, 7, 122
Odeion, 77
Oenoe, 136
Oenophyta, 136
"Old Oligarch," 19
oligarchy, 13, 28, 38, 40, 44, 93–94, 113, 132, 213n41, 236n71, 266n41; revolution of 411 (*See also* Four Hundred), 37, 91–93, 117–18, 140, 171–72, 235n60, 275n23; moderate oligarchy of 411/10, 92, 94, 132; revolution of 404–403, 38, 93–95, 117–18, 140–41, 171–72, 236n71

Olynthus, 152, 154, 156, 160
opinion, popular, 66; public, 7
oracles, 170
orators, 19, 43, 99, 118, 145, 152–54, 158, 212n30, 219n2, 238nn93,95
orphans, 49, 165–66, 197, 273n9
Ortega y Gasset, José, 42, 263n12
ostracism, 32, 34, 48, 52, 58–59, 61, 65, 79, 107, 111–12, 115, 163, 200, 229n116, 243n58
"owls," 73–74, 93

pagans, 262n8
Paionia, 150
Panathenaea, 25, 55
Pandora, 55
Panhellenism, 55, 60, 110, 159
parents, treatment of, 25, 47–48
Paros, 102, 107
Parthenon, 7, 27, 55, 57, 60, 77, 83, 100, 225n65
Pausanias (commander, died ca. 470), 33, 107
Pausanias (king, ca. 403), 38, 94
payments for public service, xv, 15, 17, 30, 35, 43–45, 49–50, 62, 77, 80, 87, 90–92, 94–95, 97, 99, 118, 147, 153–54, 157, 159, 161, 173, 235n62
peace, common, 150, 257n40
Peiraeus, 77, 157
Peisistratus, 26–27, 32, 57–59, 101–7, 227n83, 231n3, 239n6, 239–40n13, 262n3
Pelopidas, 148
Peloponnese, 20, 27, 33, 35, 59, 84, 89, 105, 111–12, 114, 128–29, 133–35, 138, 149, 159, 249n31
Peloponnesian League, 84, 124–25, 127, 249n31
Peloponnesian War, 11–12, 17, 36, 44, 61, 65, 79, 83, 85–95, 97, 110, 117–44, 146, 149, 151, 172–73, 198, 202, 233n32, 248n25, 249n31; "First" Peloponnesian War, 35, 59, 111–12, 136
pentakosiomedimnoi, 23–24, 221n19
people, "the American," xiv–xv, 2, 8, 15, 67, 176–78, 201. *See also* demos, Athenian

Pericles, xvi, 13, 16, 22, 30, 41–45, 50,
52–68, 77–80, 82–83, 85–86, 90, 93,
97–99, 101, 111–15, 118–19, 124, 127,
129–31, 136–37, 140, 144–46, 154, 157,
173, 178, 184, 187–202, 220n7, 224n54,
227nn83,90, 233n33, 234n46, 240n19,
242nn51,56, 246n7, 248n23,
250nn40,41, 258nn60,61, 268n61,
271–72n1, 276n34, 277n41,
277–78n45; Funeral Oration of
(431/0), 11, 55–57, 64, 93, 187–95, 198,
207nn37,38, 268n61, 271–72n1,
274–75n19; funeral orations of (after
Samian War), 61, 230n120, 275n26
Pericles II, 140, 193, 253n61
perioikoi, 20, 111
Persia, 27, 32–37, 39, 50–52, 55, 58–62, 73,
77, 78, 91–92, 100, 102, 105–12, 114–15,
129, 146, 149–50, 159–60, 240n13,
241n24, 244n67, 254n9, 255n14,
256n31
Persian Wars, 52, 84, 105–7, 110, 120,
234n41
Pheidias, 77, 115, 245n78
Philaids. *See* Cimonids
Philip II of Macedon, 39–40, 50, 96–97,
148–62, 237n88, 256n31, 258–59n62
Philippi, 148
Philocrates, 155–56, 159; Peace of, 40,
154–59, 258–59nn62,63
philosophy: ancient, 58, 118, 142; modern,
12, 16, 180, 202
Phocion, 238n95
Phocis, 151, 155–58, 224n44, 259n69
Phormio, 146, 255n18
phoros. See tribute
phratries, 24–26, 28, 169
phylai. See tribes
plague, 36, 61–63, 65, 198, 200, 247n11
Plataea, 32–33, 106–7, 241n24, 251n49
Plato, 7–13, 19, 37–38, 79, 98, 118, 142, 145,
164, 168, 173, 175, 191, 196–97, 204n13,
206n29, 207n35, 274–75n19, 275n29,
276nn33,34; *Apology* of, 187, 191–98,
271n1, 274n19; *Republic* of, 12
Pledge of Allegiance, 176, 183, 269–70n71
Pleistoanax, 60

pleonexia, 88
Plutarch, 19, 59, 78–79, 110–11, 277n41
Pnyx, 86, 169
polemarchos, 22, 30
police, 181–82
polis, 6, 16, 20, 24–26, 31, 43, 45, 117, 142,
148, 160, 168, 171, 175, 178, 201–2,
209–10n1, 229n114, 263n16; crisis of,
118, 246n1
politeia, 25, 30, 57, 93, 169
polites, 221n21
political science, 12, 14, 177
politicians, American, xv, 2–3, 5, 8, 65–67,
72, 176–78, 183, 200, 238n93, 270n72
politics, xiv, 5, 24, 168, 178, 187–88, 192,
201–2, 247n11, 263n13, 263–64n18;
primacy of, 168, 202
polls, 2, 200
Polybius, 121, 247n13
poor, 31, 42–43, 46, 49, 62, 64, 73, 85, 98,
104, 153, 174, 190, 202, 221n19,
228n107, 233n36, 235n61, 236n77
population of Athens, 20, 169, 230n118
Potidaea, 36, 83, 125, 137, 150–51, 156, 193,
198, 249n31, 274n19
power, Athenian, 93, 107, 188–91, 195, 198,
202, 250n34, 258nn60,61
powers, separation of, 30–31
prayer, 183; in schools, 175–76
presidency, 3, 184
priests, 24, 210n6, 214n47
probouloi, 90
"pro-choice," 182
professors, xvi
property: private, 14; qualifications for citizenship based on, 23, 28–29, 43,
45–46, 49, 73, 92, 173–74, 210–11n6,
220–21n19
prophasis, 127–28
Propylaea, 83
proschema, 241n36
prosopography, 7
prostitution, 48, 212n30, 222–23n35
proxenoi, 113
Prytaneum, 197, 276n33
prytany, 23, 30, 86, 140, 193, 253n64,
264n23

psephismata. See decrees
Pseudo-Xenophon (the "Old Oligarch"), 19
Puerto Rico Day, 181
Pydna, 150

Raaflaub, K. A., xvii, 230n124
Rahe, Paul, x–xvi, 188–89
Reagan, Ronald, 8
religion, 8–9, 24–26, 28, 46–48, 50, 58, 62, 75, 82, 106, 163–86, 199, 217–18n99, 241n24, 249n31, 265n38, 267n53, 267–68n59, 270n75, 271n80, 273–74n14, 274n15, 277n40
republic, 1–2, 5
Republicans, 177
resources, natural, 17
Revolution, American, 23, 45, 54, 265n34, 270n75
rhetors. *See* orators
Rhodes, P. J., xvii, 213n41, 220n7, 248n27, 258n55
rights, 3, 15–16, 45, 49, 168, 173–75, 177, 179–80, 183, 186, 201, 266n46, 268nn62,63,64, 269n68; to free speech, 45; human, 45; natural, 180; to own property, 45, 180
Rome, 1
Roosevelt, Franklin D., 145
rope, red-dyed, 86, 264n20
rowers, 75, 82, 90, 96, 138, 189, 191, 229n112, 235n63, 243n60; payment of, 75–76, 82

sacred v. secular, lack of distinction between in Athens, 170, 220n21, 264n30
Sacred War: Fourth, 160; Second, 137; Third, 151, 155, 157
sacrifice, 165, 168, 170–71, 199
sailors. *See* rowers
Salamis, 33, 50, 75, 79, 106–7
Samos, 35, 61, 84, 114–15, 137, 154, 224n54, 257n41
Sardis, 106
satyr plays, 166
scholars, xv, 4, 6, 8, 19, 31, 57, 118, 122–23, 128, 160, 168, 203–4n6, 205n17, 247n14, 251–52n50; scholarship, xvi, 5

Scione, 142, 251n49, 253n69
Scyros, 102, 109, 156, 259n71
Scythia, 102
Sealey, Raphael, 151, 156
Second Athenian League, 39, 96, 134–35, 143–44, 149–50, 155, 237n79, 255n14
secular realm, absence of Athenian, 170
self-image, Athenian, 57, 92–94, 107, 235n63
Serbia, 8, 70
settlements, Athenian, 32, 34, 53, 105, 159, 230n118, 252n53, 257n41
sex, 165, 178–79, 218n99, 223n38, 262n3, 268n60
shame, 183–85, 191, 194, 201, 226n74
Sicily, 135, 154, 255n17; Athenian invasion of, 11, 36, 89–90, 135–39, 146, 154, 174, 248n27, 258n60
Sickinger, James, xvii, 220n11
Sicyon, 27, 136–37
Sigeum, 102–4
silver, 32, 35, 73–75, 80, 83, 85, 91, 93, 95–98, 104, 107, 115, 117, 128, 144, 147, 151, 157, 189, 241n29, 277n44
Siphnos, 242n45
slavery, 6, 12, 20, 36, 38, 46, 49–50, 90, 132, 134, 138–39, 179–80, 190, 209n57, 222n23, 223nn38,39, 227n92, 251n49, 252n53, 253n69, 277n44
social programs, 177
Social Security, 177
Social Services, Department of, 31
Social War, 39, 150–51, 237nn79,88, 258n55
society: Athenian, *passim*; integral, 166–75, 178, 183, 186, 262n9; man's desire for, 166–67
sociology, xiii–xiv, 121
Socrates, 1, 13, 16, 38, 62, 98, 118, 140, 142, 145, 187–202, 207nn37,38, 207–8n40, 217–18n99, 229n114, 253nn64,67, 271–72n1, 274n17, 274–75n19, 275n29, 276n34, 277n40, 277–78n45; execution of, 6, 10–12, 38, 173, 191, 196–98, 202, 207nn35,38
Solon, 23–24, 26, 29, 93, 214nn45,54
Sophocles, 7, 22, 98, 101, 114, 118, 190, 245n73
sophrosyne, 86, 90

soul, 182, 196–97, 202, 229n114, 263n15
sovereignty: popular, 2, 7, 29; of the law,
    29–30
Sparta, xvi, 1, 6, 11, 20, 22–23, 27–28, 31–33,
    35–39, 50–52, 54, 56, 58–60, 62,
    64–65, 73, 75, 77, 82, 84–90, 94,
    100–102, 104–8, 110–12, 114, 119,
    124–25, 127–39, 141–43, 145, 149–50,
    160–61, 171–72, 189, 211n15, 213n41,
    233n33, 240n19, 241n24, 243n58,
    244n67, 248–49n31, 249–50n34,
    250n40, 251n49, 252nn50,51,53
speeches in history, 120
Speusippos, 159, 260n89
spiritualism, 178, 267–68n59
stasis. See civil war
statistics, xiii–xiv
stelai, 19, 80–81
Stenyclerus, 136
Stephen, James Fitzjames, 267n53
Stesimbrotus, 277n41
Stone, I. F., 12
strategoi. See generals
stratiotic fund. *See* treasury, military
Strauss, Leo, 9
Strymon River, 102
suppliants, Athenians as protectors of, 92
Sybota, 137
symposia, 164, 170
syngeneia, 105
syntaxeis, 96, 149, 154, 257nn35,41
Syracuse, 36, 89, 98, 135, 138–39

talent, Athenian, 80
tamiai (treasurers) of Athena, 24
Tanagra, 136, 243n58
taxation, 25, 31, 37, 45, 50, 69, 72, 87,
    89–90, 95–96, 98, 113, 147, 149, 174,
    178, 220n14, 222n29, 269n68; on agri-
    cultural produce, 26; on property (*eis-
    phora*), 36, 85, 95–97, 152–54, 157,
    233n36, 236n77, 237n88; U.S. tax
    code, 269n68
television, xiv, 69
temples, 75, 82–83, 89, 232n9
Thasos, 34, 102, 109–10, 154
theater, 15, 49; subsidy for attendance, 49,
    95, 97, 152

Thebes, 6, 20, 38–40, 60, 73, 84, 106, 143,
    148–50, 157–58, 160–61, 224n44,
    253n66, 260n80
Themistocles, 22, 32–33, 67, 73–75, 84, 99,
    107, 145, 157, 189, 241n29, 277n41
Theopompus, 274n19
theoric fund, 40, 96, 152–53, 157, 159, 237n88
theory: democratic, xv, 3–4, 15; literary, 121;
    political, 4
Theramenes, 37–38, 94, 252n61
Thermopylae, 33, 151, 155–56, 158, 259nn69,72
thesmothetai, 30
Thessaly, 34, 39, 51, 52, 108, 111, 136, 148,
    150–51, 158
thetes, 23, 45–46, 75, 220n18, 234n41
Thirty, the. *See* oligarchy, revolution of
    404–403
Thirty Years' Truce, 35, 60, 114, 125, 127,
    130, 137, 249n31
thought: democratic, 1, 5, 15, 192; political,
    122
Thrace, 26, 39, 97, 101–2, 146, 148, 150–52,
    155, 158
Thrasybulus, 38
Thucydides, 7–11, 13, 19, 22, 31, 34, 43, 51,
    54, 56, 62–63, 65–67, 80, 84, 88–90,
    93, 101, 108–10, 114, 118–21, 127–32,
    134–35, 137, 142, 144, 173, 187, 189, 192,
    194, 200, 239n13, 245n73, 246n7,
    246–47n11, 250nn34,40, 251n48,
    260n81, 271–72n1, 272n2, 274–75n19
Thucydides son of Melesias, 52, 61, 78–79,
    85, 115, 229n116, 277n41
timber, 101, 150–51
time, 62, 229n114
Timotheus, 118, 146, 150, 254n9
Tocqueville, Alexis de, 42
Tolmides, 136
Torone, 251n49, 253n69
torture, 48–49, 223n39
tragedy, 118, 164–66, 171, 272–73n9
treasury, military, 40, 96, 152–53, 157, 159
treaties, solemnization of, 170
tribes, 24–26, 168–69; Athenian, after
    Cleisthenes' reforms, 28, 169, 264n23
tribute, 34, 36–37, 53, 55, 60, 77, 80–84, 90,
    100, 108–9, 116, 131–32, 139, 149, 165,
    173, 252n53

trierarchy, 75–76, 86, 90, 96, 153, 231–32n7, 233n36

triereis. See triremes

triremes, 75–76, 87, 89, 97, 112, 157, 174, 261n101

Tyche. *See* Fortune, Agatha Tyche

tyranny, 26–27, 53, 58, 74, 94, 101–4, 113, 146, 163, 179–80, 182, 186, 194, 213n41, 265n37, 266n46; in Athens, 17, 26, 84, 101–7, 128, 144, 213n41, 227n83, 239–40n13

values, 166–67, 171, 175, 181, 183, 186, 190, 201, 270–71n76; American, 15–16; democratic, xv, 13, 15–16, 55, 62, 190, 205n21, 267n52; modern, 5

Vietnam War, 266n45

virtue. *See* excellence, human

voting, xv, 1, 3, 13–16, 42, 45, 49, 50–53, 64, 67–73, 88–89, 95, 98, 104–5, 113–16, 129, 137, 140–41, 147, 153, 160, 166, 176–77, 196, 198, 202, 209n51, 223n42

wages, average, 80, 233n27

Washington, George, 54, 180

wealthy, 31, 35, 42, 75, 85–86, 90, 94–96, 98, 117, 132, 144–45, 147, 149, 153–54, 174–75, 179, 221n20, 231–32n7, 233n36

welfare, 269n68

Western world, 3, 12

will, popular, xv, 1–3, 5, 7, 53, 70

women, 261n2, 270n76, 276n31

Woodstock III, 181, 268nn65,66

Xanthippe, 277n45

Xanthippus, 58, 107, 241n29

Xenophon, 9, 19, 38, 98, 118, 140, 142, 145, 164, 173, 242n47, 256n31, 274–75n19

xenos, 221n21

Xerxes, 33, 75, 160–61

zeugitai, 23–24, 45, 75, 220n18

Zeus, 25, 47, 170, 172, 265n37

zoon politikon, 168

Compositor:	Binghamton Valley Composition, LLC
Text:	11/13.5 Adobe Garamond
Display:	Adobe Garamond and Perpetua
Printer and binder:	Maple-Vail Manufacturing Group